United States Department of State

COUNTRY REPORTS ON TERRORISM 2010

United States Department of State

Office of the Coordinator for Counterterrorism

Released August 2011

Country Reports on Terrorism 2010 is submitted in compliance with Title 22 of the United States Code, Section 2656f (the "Act"), which requires the Department of State to provide Congress a full and complete annual report on terrorism for those countries and groups meeting the criteria of the Act.

COUNTRY REPORTS ON TERRORISM 2010
TABLE OF CONTENTS

Abu Nidal Organization (ANO)
Abu Sayyaf Group (ASG)
Al-Aqsa Martyrs Brigade (AAMB)
Al-Qa'ida (AQ)
Al-Qa'ida in the Arabian Peninsula (AQAP)
Al-Qa'ida in Iraq (AQI)
Al-Qa'ida in the Islamic Maghreb (AQIM)
Al-Shabaab (AS)
Ansar al-Islam
Asbat al-Ansar
Aum Shinrikyo (AUM)
Basque Fatherland and Liberty (ETA)
Communist Party of Philippines/New People's Army (CPP/NPA)
Continuity Irish Republican Army (CIRA)
Gama'a al-Islamiyya (IG)
Hamas
Harakat ul-Jihad-i-Islami (HUJI)
Harakat ul-Jihad-i-Islami/Bangladesh (HUJI-B)
Harakat ul-Mujahideen (HUM)
Hizballah
Islamic Jihad Union (IJU)
Islamic Movement of Uzbekistan (IMU)
Jaish-e-Mohammed (JEM)
Jemaah Islamiya (JI)
Jundallah
Kahane Chai
Kata'ib Hizballah (KH)
Kurdistan Workers' Party (PKK)
Lashkar e-Tayyiba (LT)
Lashkar i Jhangvi (LJ)
Liberation Tigers of Tamil Eelam (LTTE)
Libyan Islamic Fighting Group (LIFG)
Moroccan Islamic Combatant Group (GICM)
Mujahadin-e Khalq Organization (MEK)
National Liberation Army (ELN)
Palestine Liberation Front – Abu Abbas Faction (PLF)
Palestinian Islamic Jihad – Shaqaqi Faction (PIJ)
Popular Front for the Liberation of Palestine (PFLP)
Popular Front for the Liberation of Palestine-General Command (PFLP-GC)
Real IRA (RIRA)
Revolutionary Armed Forces of Colombia (FARC)
Revolutionary Organization 17 November (17N)

Revolutionary People's Liberation Party/Front (DHKP/C)
Revolutionary Struggle (RS)
Shining Path (SL)
Tehrik-e Taliban Pakistan
United Self-Defense Forces of Colombia (AUC)

8

CHAPTER 1.
STRATEGIC ASSESSMENT

Al-Qa'ida (AQ) remained the preeminent terrorist threat to the United States in 2010. Though the AQ core in Pakistan has become weaker, it retained the capability to conduct regional and transnational attacks. Cooperation between AQ and Afghanistan- and Pakistan-based militants was critical to the threat the group posed. In addition, the danger posed by Lashkar-e Tayyiba (LeT) and increased resource-sharing between AQ and its Pakistan-based allies and associates such as Tehrik-e Taliban Pakistan (TTP) and the Haqqani Network meant the aggregate threat in South Asia remained high.

In addition, the affiliates have grown stronger. While AQ senior leadership continued to call for strikes on the U.S. homeland and to arrange plots targeted at Europe, the diversity of these efforts demonstrated the fusion of interests and the sharing of capabilities among AQ groups with different geographical focuses. We saw TTP provide support to U.S. citizen Faisal Shahzad, who sought to carry out a car bombing in Times Square in May. Al-Qa'ida in the Arabian Peninsula (AQAP) continued to demonstrate its growing ambitions and a strong desire to carry out attacks outside of its region. The group followed up its December 25, 2009 attempt to destroy an airliner bound for Detroit with an October 2010 effort to blow up several U.S.-bound airplanes by shipping bombs that were intended to detonate while in the planes' cargo holds. Information about potential AQ plots in Europe prompted several European countries to raise their terror alerts toward the end of the year. On December 11, a car bomb device was detonated minutes before Sweden's first ever suicide bomber carried out an attack in a crowded pedestrian area in Stockholm.

Similarly, al-Shabaab in East Africa, some of whose senior leaders have declared adherence to the AQ brand of violent extremism, gained strength in 2010 and conducted its first major attack outside of Somalia in July when it claimed responsibility for twin suicide bombings that killed 76 people in Kampala, Uganda, during the World Cup. Al-Shabaab's widening scope of operations, safe haven in Somalia, and ability to attract Western militants, made it a continuing threat to U.S. interests in the region.

In addition to operations, AQ affiliates have taken on a greater share of the propaganda work. AQAP created AQ's first English-language magazine, Inspire. Although the magazine failed to arouse sustained interest from Western media, it proved a platform for dual U.S.-Yemeni citizen, Anwar al-Aulaqi, who emerged as an operational and ideological leader in AQAP.

In a troubling trend, English-speaking militants increasingly connected to each other through online venues like militant discussion forums and video-sharing platforms, which encouraged both violent behavior and individual action. Many participants in online communities have real-world relationships with extremists who bolster their radicalism and mobilize them toward violent action. Five Pakistani Americans contacted by a Taliban recruiter through YouTube encouraged one another to travel to Pakistan to train for warfare against the United States; they remained in Pakistani custody at year's end. Several Somali Americans decided to go overseas to fight with al-Shabaab – a decision that was likely shaped by a combination of online propaganda, face-to-face recruitment, and supportive real-world peer networks.

New York City: U.S. Secretary of State Hillary Clinton speaks during a UN Security Council meeting on terrorism September 27, 2010. AFP PHOTO/Don Emmert

Not all of AQ's formal affiliates and informal allies presented as grave a threat to U.S. interests in 2010. No group has made a bigger name for itself in the kidnapping for ransom business than al-Qa'ida in the Islamic Maghreb (AQIM), which relies on ransom payments to sustain and develop itself in the harsh Saharan environment. AQIM carried out several attacks and continued kidnapping foreigners for ransom but is not an existential threat to governments in the region. The U.S. government urged its allies to refuse to pay AQIM and other terrorist group's ransoms, which have become a primary means of financial support for terrorist organizations.

Al-Qa'ida in Iraq (AQI) continued to be politically marginalized as its constituency dwindled further. Though AQI remained capable of carrying out occasional sizable attacks, its violent tactics failed to ignite the sectarian violence the group sought. Instead, we saw two successful elections in Iraq and a decision by Sunni leaders in the country to participate in the political process.

The wave of non-violent democratic demonstrations that began to sweep the Arab world at the end of 2010 held promise but also some peril. Great numbers of citizens advanced peaceful public demands for change without reference to AQ's incendiary world view, upending the group's long-standing claims that change would only come through violence and underscoring anew the group's lack of influence over the central political issues in key Muslim-majority nations. But at the same time, the political turmoil distracted security officials and raised the possibility that terrorist groups would exploit the new openness and, in some cases, disarray, to carry out conspiracies, a possibility with significant and worrisome implications for states undergoing democratic transitions.

The apparent blow suffered by AQ had no significant effect on other terrorist groups with deep roots in the Middle East, as both Hamas and Hizballah continued to play destabilizing roles in the region. Hizballah's persistence as a well-armed terrorist group in Lebanon with an entrenched hold, if not veto, on the political process in Lebanon, as well as its robust relationships with Iran and Syria, and acquisition of increasingly sophisticated missiles and rockets threatened the interests of Lebanon and other U.S. partners in the region, especially Israel. Hizballah's aggressive stance and threatening statements about the Special Tribunal on Lebanon, which is investigating the 2005 murder of former Lebanese Prime Minister Rafiq Hariri, increased the danger of Lebanon moving even closer toward sectarian violence. Hamas retained its grip on Gaza, where it continued to stockpile weapons – supplied in large part by Iran – that posed a serious threat to regional stability.

CHAPTER 2.
COUNTRY REPORTS ON TERRORISM

AFRICA OVERVIEW

The Somalia-based U.S. designated Foreign Terrorist Organization al-Shabaab continued to conduct frequent attacks on government, military, and civilian targets inside Somalia while the group's leadership remained actively interested in attacking regional U.S. and Western interests. In July 2010, al-Shabaab claimed responsibility for carrying out twin suicide bombings in Kampala, Uganda that killed 76 people, underscoring the increased terrorist threat in East Africa due to al-Shabaab's demonstrated capacity to conduct bombings outside of Somalia. Foreign fighters, a small number of al-Qa'ida (AQ) operatives, and likeminded indigenous violent extremists continued to pose a threat to regional security throughout East Africa. Al-Shabaab's leadership continued its support of AQ, and in December, al-Shabaab entered into a tenuous merger with disparate factions of the now-defunct violent extremist group Hizbul Islam. While this infusion of clan militias may have slightly increased al-Shabaab's fighting numbers, the merger did not give the group a significant or new advantage in its on-going fight against the Somali government.

In the Trans-Sahara, al-Qa'ida in the Islamic Maghreb (AQIM) continued kidnap for ransom operations of Western Europeans and Africans. AQIM murdered a French citizen in response to Mauritanian attacks on AQIM cells in northwestern Mali and AQIM continued to hold five French, a Malagasy, and a Togolese citizen hostage, seized in Arlit, Niger. AQIM conducted small-scale ambushes and attacks on security forces in Algeria, Mali, Mauritania, and Niger. Regional efforts to contain and marginalize AQIM continued, as did capacity building efforts of military and law enforcement personnel. Inter-religious conflict in Nigeria continued throughout Northern Nigeria with hundreds of casualties while indigenous terrorism attacks increased with several bombings over the Christmas holiday season in Abuja and Maiduguri. The Nigerian extremist group, Boko Haram, claimed responsibility for some of these attacks but whether they carried out other attacks remained unclear.

Trans-Sahara Counterterrorism Partnership (TSCTP). Established in 2005, TSCTP is a U.S. funded and implemented multi-faceted, multi-year strategy designed to combat violent extremism and contain and marginalize terrorist organizations by strengthening individual country and regional counterterrorism capabilities, enhancing and institutionalizing cooperation among the region's security and intelligence organizations, promoting democratic governance, and discrediting terrorist ideology. The overall goals are to enhance the indigenous capacities of governments in the pan-Sahel (Mauritania, Mali, Chad, and Niger, as well as Nigeria, Senegal, and Burkina Faso); to confront the challenge posed by terrorist organizations in the trans-Sahara; and to facilitate cooperation between those countries and U.S. partners in the Maghreb (Morocco, Algeria, and Tunisia). TSCTP has been successful in slowly building capacity and cooperation despite political setbacks over the years caused by coup d'etats, ethnic rebellions, and extra-constitutional actions that have interrupted progress and work with select countries of the partnership. In 2010, select partner nations have been successful in disrupting extremist movement and operations in the trans-Sahara.

The Partnership for Regional East African Counterterrorism (PREACT). PREACT, formerly known as the East Africa Regional Strategic Initiative (EARSI), is the East Africa counterpart to the Trans-Sahara Counterterrorism Partnership (TSCTP). First established in 2009, PREACT is a U.S. funded and implemented multi-year, multi-faceted program designed to build the counterterrorism capacity and capability of member countries to thwart short-term terrorist threats and address longer-term vulnerabilities. It utilizes law enforcement, military, and development resources to achieve its strategic objectives, including reducing the operational capacity of terrorist networks, expanding border security, enhancing and institutionalizing cooperation among the region's security and intelligence organizations, improving democratic governance, and discrediting terrorist ideology. PREACT member countries include Burundi, Comoros, Djibouti, Ethiopia, Kenya, Rwanda, Seychelles, Somalia, Sudan, Tanzania, and Uganda.

BURKINA FASO

Overview: The Government of Burkina Faso remained a serious, stable ally, fully cognizant of the threats posed by regional extremism in the Sahel and elsewhere in West Africa. Burkina Faso's counterterrorism capabilities were limited owing to financial constraints, but it was consistently responsive to U.S. requests for cooperative operations. In an effort to improve its counterterrorism capabilities, senior Burkinabe officials requested U.S. assistance in the form of training and equipment and specifically identified regional intelligence sharing, border security, and airport security as three vulnerabilities to address. There was still no formal method for tracking movement into and out of the country at border checkpoints or at either of the country's two commercial airports in Ouagadougou and Bobo Dioulasso.

Although there were no terrorist incidents in Burkina Faso in 2010, al-Qa'ida in the Islamic Maghreb (AQIM) remained a threat, particularly in the Mali-Niger-Burkina Faso tri-border area where AQIM attempted to locate and kidnap Westerners.

Legislation and Law Enforcement: The President of Burkina Faso issued a decree in 2010 underscoring his support for the Suppression of Terrorism law passed in 2009 by the National Assembly. The law's passage and the President's decree demonstrated the country's political will to ensure that its territory is not used as a staging ground for violent extremists or transnational terrorist attacks.

Countering Terrorist Finance: Burkina Faso was a member of the Inter-Governmental Action Group against Money Laundering in West Africa, a Financial Action Task Force-style regional body. The Government of Burkina Faso provided UN lists of designated terrorists or terrorist entities to financial institutions. There were no known terrorist financing prosecutions in 2010.

Regional and International Cooperation: The Burkina Faso government participated in regional and international counterterrorism conferences and training exercises. It expressed its desire to collaborate with neighboring countries to counter violent extremism through a multilateral approach, such as participating in joint training exercises and regional partnerships. Burkina Faso cooperated with U.S. counterterrorism efforts and participated in the Trans-Sahara Counterterrorism Partnership (TSCTP). Its cooperation and partnership in the TSCTP were demonstrated in May when the government hosted U.S. Africa Command's (AFRICOM) annual regional counterterrorism exercise FLINTLOCK 10 and attended a related Joint Combined Exchange Training program in Mali. Burkina Faso's government also participated in numerous regional efforts to combat terrorism, including with the Economic Community of West African States, the AU, and other international organizations.

Countering Radicalization and Violent Extremism: The Government of Burkina Faso and the Embassy conducted several joint projects, including a medical outreach program in the far north of Burkina Faso, a predominantly Muslim and Touareg region. The government encouraged regular and ongoing inter-faith dialogues as a way to mitigate extremism.

Mogadishu, Somalia: Stains of blood cover a hallway inside the Hotel Mona in Mogadishu on August 24, 2010. Two extremist insurgents disguised as government soldiers went on a shooting rampage in the Mogadishu hotel, killing 30 people, before blowing themselves up. The brazen attack by al-Shabaab near the presidential palace marked a new escalation on the second day of clashes that had already left 29 civilians dead across the war-ravaged Somali capital. AFP PHOTO/Mustafa ABDI

BURUNDI

Overview: Since 2009, al-Shabaab has threatened repeatedly and publically to attack Burundi in retaliation for its participation in the African Union Mission in Somalia (AMISOM). Since the al-Shabaab terrorist attacks in Kampala, the Burundian security forces have shifted some of their focus from internal political issues and begun to build counterterrorism capacity. The lack of resources and training has meant that the focus has been primarily on the physical security of their more vulnerable sites. In addition to strengthening their physical security posture, the Burundians created an Anti-Terror Cell, chaired by the Minister of Public Security, which first convened in March but then remained dormant until the Kampala terrorist attacks. The cell consisted of investigators and intelligence and operations officers from the police, military, and intelligence services. At year's end, the Anti-Terror Cell did not have a plan or the capacity to develop the intelligence sources crucial to combating terrorism.

Legislation and Law Enforcement: Burundi has provisions in its penal code (Title IX, Chapter IV) defining all forms of terrorism. Sentences for acts of terrorism range from 10 to 20 years or life imprisonment if the act results in the death of a person. In 2010, this provision was not applied in a Burundian court of law, as no case had been tried by year's end. In August, Burundian authorities cooperated with Ugandan authorities in connection with a Ugandan national in Burundi who was believed to be associated with Ugandan terrorist suspects.

Regional and International Cooperation: Burundi and Uganda were the only two troop contributing nations participating in AMISOM, which, with support from the Transitional Federal Government's National Security Forces (NSF), was a critical partner in the fight against al-Shabaab in Somalia.

COMOROS

Overview: Comoran government security forces had limited resources and training in counterterrorism and maritime security, so the country remained vulnerable to terrorist transit. In April, a Comoran Coast Guard unit was created and received an ArchAngel patrol boat from the United States to help with maritime surveillance. Training to Comoran Coast Guard officials on its proper operation and maintenance was also provided.

Countering Terrorist Finance: Comoros has introduced a number of measures to establish an anti-money laundering/countering terrorist finance (AML/CTF) regime, including a 2009 law providing for the establishment of a financial intelligence unit, expanding the scope of preventative measures, and covering terrorism financing. However, the legal framework has many shortcomings and the government has not effectively implemented it. The Financial Action Task Force (FATF) mutual evaluation assessors found Comoros "largely compliant" (the FATF's second highest rating) for four of the FATF 40+9 recommendations, and it received ratings of partially compliant or noncompliant on the rest. An inadequate budget, dysfunctional ministries, and a nonfunctioning judiciary limit effectiveness of Comorian AML/CTF efforts, despite apparent high-level political support. Thus far, most institutions subject to the law have not yet put AML/CTF policies and procedures in place. Although the central bank has begun to monitor implementation of the AML/CTF preventive measures, limited resources hampered the government's ability to enforce the AML regulations, and local institutions and personnel lacked the training and capacity to enforce the law fully.

There have been no investigations or convictions for money laundering to date. The criminalization of terrorist financing does not comply with the 1999 UN Convention for the Suppression of the Financing of Terrorism. There were no provisions allowing the Comorian authorities to freeze the assets of terrorists and other persons designated by the UNSCRs 1267 and 1373.

As of December, Comoros was a member of the Eastern and Southern Africa Anti-Money Laundering Group (ESAAMLG), a FATF-style regional body. ESAAMLG became an Associate Member of the FATF in June.

Regional and International Cooperation: Comoros acted as Chair of the East African Standby Brigade (an AU body for peacekeeping and intervention missions) in 2010.

Countering Radicalization and Violent Extremism: President Sambi, democratically elected in 2006, with Comoran religious leaders, has publicly rejected religious extremism. President Sambi has also sought close partnership with the United States to develop Comoros economically and to create opportunities for the country's youth. To this end, he has requested that the Peace Corps return to Comoros as soon as possible.

DEMOCRATIC REPUBLIC OF THE CONGO

Overview: The Democratic Republic of the Congo (DRC) is a vast country bordered by nine neighbors; the government did not have complete control over significant swathes of its territories, especially in the east where various armed groups operate. The DRC is home to a large Lebanese expatriate community (several thousand), some of whom ran businesses linked to Hizballah fundraising.

Legislation and Law Enforcement: The Democratic Republic of Congo has no comprehensive counterterrorism legislation and has little capacity to enforce law and order in its vast territory.

Countering Terrorist Finance: The Democratic Republic of Congo has legislation criminalizing money laundering and terrorist financing, as well as a Financial Intelligence Unit. Many banks installed new computerized communications and accounting networks, which made it easier to trace formal financial transactions. Limited resources and a weak judicial system hampered the government's ability to enforce anti-money laundering (AML) regulations, however, and local institutions and personnel lacked the training and capacity to enforce the law and its attendant regulations fully. To date, the DRC has not completed any money laundering prosecutions or convictions.

Regional and International Cooperation: In 2010, the DRC ratified the International Convention for Suppression of Acts of Nuclear Terrorism in 2010. At year's end, the AU was working on establishing a joint brigade and operations center that would include the Central African Republic, Uganda, Sudan, and the DRC.

DJIBOUTI

Overview: Djibouti has been an active partner in countering terrorism. An increase in police and military training and new legislation improved Djibouti's ability to counter terrorism within its own borders and to aid in regional efforts to thwart terrorist activities.

Legislation and Law Enforcement: Due to its geographic location and porous borders, counterterrorism was a high priority for all Djiboutian law enforcement entities. The most visible of these efforts were ad hoc checkpoints within the capital city and a somewhat increased emphasis at border control points to screen for potential security threats. The government increased security at some key border checkpoints using biometrics and sought further counterterrorism training for its law enforcement and military personnel.

The Djibouti government proposed a law specifically defining terrorist acts and setting penalties at 15 years or life imprisonment for any act resulting in a loss of life. The proposed law also addresses arms and explosives trafficking, and criminal acts aboard an air or sea vessel. Djibouti has a clear legal framework for prosecuting terrorism-related crimes.

On June 23, a Djiboutian court convicted in absentia former prominent businessman Abdourahman "Charles" Boreh of inciting terrorist acts and criminal conspiracy in connection with a terrorist enterprise.

Djibouti continued to process travelers on entry and departure at its international airport and seaport with the Personal Identification Secure Comparison and Evaluation System (PISCES), and started building infrastructure for PISCES installation at Loyada land border.

Countering Terrorist Finance: The Central Bank of Djibouti has a Fraud Investigation Unit that investigates money laundering- and terrorist finance-related issues. In September, the government proposed a law to clearly define terrorist financing and establish preventative measures. The law addresses the freezing of assets or seizure of funds, cooperation with international entities and other states, and penalties.

Regional and International Cooperation: Djibouti hosts Camp Lemonnier, the only U.S. military base in Africa, which serves as headquarters to more than 3,000 U.S. troops, including those serving with the U.S. Africa Command's Combined Joint Task Force-Horn of Africa. The Government of Djibouti has committed to sending a small contingent of Djiboutian Armed Forces personnel to join the African Union Mission in Somalia. Djibouti hosted training for approximately 500 Somali police and an additional group of Transitional Federal Government security forces.

ERITREA

Overview: In May 2010, for the third consecutive year, the Department of State determined that Eritrea was not cooperating fully with U.S. antiterrorism efforts pursuant to section 40A of the Arms Export Control Act. In 2010, there was no counterterrorism dialogue between the United States and Eritrea. In 2010, the UN sanctioned the Government of Eritrea under Resolution 1907 in December 2009 demanding that the Eritrean government "cease arming, training, and equipping armed groups and their members including al-Shabaab, which aim to destabilize the region." There was no indication that the Government of Eritrea complied with the UN resolution in regards to ceasing the support of armed groups in Somalia.

Legislation and Law Enforcement: Security was strengthened on the Eritrean/Ethiopian border, but it appeared it was used only to deter citizens from fleeing Eritrea. (There was a shoot-to-kill order for Eritreans trying to flee their country.)

Regional and International Cooperation: The Eritrean government has linked broader cooperation on counterterrorism programs to the unresolved border dispute with Ethiopia.

ETHIOPIA

Overview: Over the last four years, East Africa violent extremist networks led by a limited number of al-Qa'ida personnel and other violent extremists linked to and supportive of al-Shabaab have increased in capability, numbers, and strength. The threat posed by these disparate and often times fluid decentralized networks, particularly the apparent increase of foreign fighters and other recruits, was a growing concern. The Government of Ethiopia has been historically concerned about the activities of terrorists in neighboring Somalia.

2010 Terrorist Incidents:

- On April 24, a bomb attack at a tea room in the northern town of Adi Aro near the Eritrean border killed five people and injured 20. Ethiopian officials blamed Eritrean mercenaries for the attack as an attempt to disrupt the May 23 national elections.

- On May 6, a group of people lobbed hand grenades at a group assembled for a political opposition party meeting in Adaba, Oromia. Two persons died and 26 were wounded. Ruling party and opposition party members blamed each other for the attack, and no group claimed responsibility for it.

- On May 20, three days before national elections, a bomb exploded on a bus near the Eritrean border wounding 13 people.

Legislation and Law Enforcement: Ethiopia's National Intelligence and Security Service (NISS), with broad authority for intelligence, border security, and VIP protection, was responsible for counterterrorism management. The Ethiopian Federal Police worked in conjunction with NISS. Ethiopia viewed instability in Somalia as a critical national security threat and maintained a defensive military presence along the Somali border to stem potential infiltration of extremists into Ethiopia.

Countering Terrorist Finance: In March, Ethiopia's central bank issued a customer due diligence directive for banks. In 2010, Ethiopia enacted anti-money laundering/counterterrorist financing (AML/CTF) legislation providing for the establishment of a financial intelligence unit, the Financial Intelligence Center (FIC). As of December, however, the FIC had not become operational nor did it issue specific AML/CTF directives. In August, Ethiopia applied for observer status in the Eastern and Southern African Anti-Money Laundering Group.

Regional and International Cooperation: Ethiopia was an active participant in AU counterterrorism efforts, participating in the AU's Center for Study and Research on Terrorism, and in meetings of the Committee of Intelligence and Security Services of Africa. Ethiopia acted as a member state of the Inter-Governmental Authority on Development (IGAD), and participated actively in IGAD's Capacity Building Program Against Terrorism to bolster the capacity of IGAD member states to mitigate, detect, and deter advances by terrorists.

Countering Radicalization and Violent Extremism: The Government of Ethiopia has established a vocational training program for former Ogaden National Liberation Front (ONLF) members from the ONLF faction that signed a peace agreement with the government in 2010.

KENYA

Overview: The Kenyan government demonstrated increased political will to secure its borders, apprehend suspected terrorists, and cooperate with regional allies and the international community to counter terrorism, despite facing perennial challenges that limited its growth in counterterrorism capabilities such as corruption, a lack of counterterrorism law, and severe resource constraints. Arms smuggling, reports of extremist recruiting within refugee camps and Kenyan cities, and increased allegations of terrorist plotting, enhanced recognition among government officials, the diplomatic community, and civil society that Kenya remained vulnerable to terrorist attacks. The government increased security along parts of the Kenya/Somalia border to stem the flow of armed militants who routinely crossed into Kenya to obtain supplies, funding, medical care, and recruits, but a lack of capacity and coordination among border officials undermined these efforts.

Legislation and Law Enforcement: Despite an increased concern over security and Kenya's strong counterterrorism partnership with regional and international allies, the lack of comprehensive counterterrorism legislation hindered Kenya's counterterrorism efforts. Existing laws did not permit police to detain terrorist suspects and prosecute them effectively. The government did not submit a revised version of counterterrorism legislation that was defeated in 2006 and no progress was made in 2010 by the Kenyan Parliament to pass counterterrorism legislation.

The Prevention of Organized Crime Law – unanimously adopted by Parliament in July – allows authorities to designate groups as criminal organizations, but does not explicitly criminalize terrorist activities. In October, the Kenyan government designated 33 groups as organized illegal gangs, including al-Shabaab. The broad definition of membership in an organized crime group probably will help Kenyan authorities detain, charge, and prosecute individuals associated with terrorist networks.

In September, Jomo Kenyatta International Airport (JKIA) successfully completed pilot testing for biometric upgrades to Kenya's Personal Identification Secure Comparison and Evaluation System (PISCES), which was used at nine Kenyan ports of entry to identify suspect travelers against a computerized Kenyan stop-list. JKIA's processing of travelers on entry and departure was the first to incorporate new PISCES biometric features; Kenyan officials at JKIA made productive use of their new capabilities.

Countering Terrorist Finance: On June 30, the Kenyan Anti-Money Laundering Act became effective. The act provides mechanisms for detecting and seizing proceeds of money laundering, including the establishment of a Financial Intelligence Unit (FIU). Kenya's FIU did not become operational in 2010, however. Kenya was a member of the Eastern and South African Anti Money Laundering Group, a Financial Action Task Force-style regional body.

Regional and International Cooperation: Kenyan law enforcement agencies worked closely with the international community to increase their counterterrorism abilities and secure porous land borders as well as address ongoing maritime security concerns. Kenyan authorities cooperated with Uganda in the investigation of the Kampala bombing.

MALI

Overview: The Government of Mali called for greater regional cooperation to counter al-Qa'ida in the Islamic Maghreb (AQIM) and participated in training programs to increase the capacity of its security and military forces. Although Malian leaders were generally sincere in their desire to counter terrorism, their ability to do so continued to be hindered by limited resources and the lack of an adequate state presence in the distant and vast northern regions of the country. During the year, AQIM continued to operate in parts of northern Mali, and held, released, and claimed to have killed hostages kidnapped for ransom. In addition, AQIM engaged in skirmishes with the Mauritanian military on Malian territory.

2010 Terrorist Incidents: In contrast to 2009, there were no terrorist incidents directed against Malian interests and no kidnappings of foreigners on Malian soil in 2010. AQIM continued to hold hostages on Malian territory throughout the year, including hostages kidnapped in Niger in 2010. On July 25, AQIM claimed to have executed French citizen Michael Germaneau, whom it was holding hostage in Mali in retaliation for French support of a Mauritanian July 22 raid on AQIM camps in Mali. There were conflicting reports, however, that Germaneau may have already died, due to natural causes exacerbated by his captivity, prior to the Mauritanian raid.

Six hostages abducted by AQIM or bandits associated with AQIM and held in Mali were released:

- On February 23, AQIM released French citizen Pierre Camatte who was taken hostage in Menaka, Mali in November 2009. The release occurred after Malian courts tried the four AQIM operatives taken into custody in April 2009 for misdemeanor arms possession and released them for time served.

- Three Spanish aid workers kidnapped in Mauritania in November 2009 were released in 2010, one on March 10 and the other two on August 22.

- On April 16, AQIM released two Italian citizens, Sergio Cicala and his wife Philomene Kaboure, who had been held hostage in Mali since their kidnapping in December 2009 in Mauritania.

Legislation and Law Enforcement: The Malian judiciary did not prosecute any terrorist cases except in connection with the release of Pierre Camatte.

Countering Terrorist Finance: In November, the Malian National Assembly adopted legislation to strengthen the authority of the National Financial Information Processing Unit, Mali's Financial Intelligence Unit. The National Assembly also reinforced the judicial controls available to Malian authorities to counter terrorist financing and money laundering offenses, as well as bring Malian code into conformity with regional standards and the International Convention on the Suppression of the Financing of Terrorism. The legislation had not been signed by the President of Mali at year's end, however. Mali is a member of the Inter Governmental Action Group against Money Laundering in West Africa, a Financial Action Task Force-style regional body.

Regional And International Cooperation: Mali ratified the Amendment to the Convention on the Physical Protection of Nuclear Material. Mali continued to press for greater regional cooperation to counter terrorism. Mali cooperated with U.S. counterterrorism efforts and is a Trans-Sahara Counterterrorism Partnership country. Along with Mauritania, Niger, and Algeria, Mali participated in the establishment of a Joint Command Center in Tamanrasset, Algeria, that once fully operational will allow the four countries to coordinate regional responses to AQIM activities.

MAURITANIA

Overview: The Government of Mauritania launched military operations against al-Qa'ida in the Islamic Maghreb (AQIM) camps in northern Mali in July and September and continued to strengthen its security forces' capacity and improve border security. It also continued arresting terrorism suspects, including those involved in targeting Westerners.

2010 Terrorist Incidents: After suffering from an unprecedented wave of kidnappings and terrorist attacks in 2009, Mauritania registered one suicide car bombing in 2010. On August 25, a car bomb drove through a checkpoint and exploded at the entrance of military barracks in Nema, 1200 kilometers east of Nouakchott. The driver died instantly and three soldiers were wounded. AQIM claimed responsibility for the attack in an August 31 Internet press release. This was the second suicide attack in Mauritania; the first attempt took place in August 2009 outside the French Embassy.

Legislation and Law Enforcement: In May, the largest terrorism trials in Mauritania's history took place. Fifty-six terrorist suspects received sentences ranging from fines and imprisonment to the death penalty in the case of the 2007 murders of four French nationals who were shot in the southern city of Aleg.

The Mauritanian government took steps to improve border security through plans to build 10 new border posts. The Ministry of the Interior was also establishing a program to produce secure national identity documents.

Countering Terrorist Finance: A new counterterrorism law enacted in July replaced the existing legislation and outlawed terrorist financing in all its forms. Mauritania has a Financial Intelligence Unit called "CANIF," under the Mauritanian Central Bank, which is in charge of investigating financial crimes, including terrorist financing. Mauritania is a member of the Middle East and North Africa Financial Action Task Force.

Regional and International Cooperation: Mauritania cooperated with U.S. counterterrorism efforts and is a Trans-Sahara Counterterrorism Partnership country. In March, Algeria, Burkina Faso, Chad, Libya, Mali, Niger, and Mauritania gathered in Algeria and issued a joint statement rejecting ransom payments. In September, Mauritania participated in a meeting gathering sub-regional chiefs of staff in Algeria to coordinate efforts to counter terrorism in the Sahel. On September 30, along with Mali, Niger, and Algeria, Mauritania participated in the establishment of a Joint Command Center in Tamanrasset, Algeria, that once fully operational will allow the four countries to coordinate regional responses to AQIM activities. On October 10, Mauritania participated in the Syrta meeting to coordinate counterterrorism efforts in the Sahel. Mauritania, which recalled its Ambassador to Bamako in February following Mali's release of four terrorist suspects, restarted cooperation with Mali in September, and had joint patrols in northern Mali in December.

Countering Radicalization and Violent Extremism: The Government of Mauritania adopted a series of measures to counter radicalization and violent extremism. The government conducted a census of mosques, opened a Quranic radio station, and featured television and radio programs emphasizing moderation in Islam. The government favored a conciliatory approach towards extremists willing to renounce violence. It sponsored a dialogue between moderate imams and imprisoned extremists in January leading to the repentance of 57 individuals, 52 of whom received Presidential pardons during the Muslim holidays of Eid-el Fitr and Eid-el Adha. A national dialogue on terrorism and extremism was held in October, and the Government of Mauritania organized conferences and roundtables regarding moderation in Islam and gathered key decision makers in the government, civil society, and among religious authorities to decide on a common strategy. At year's end, the Mauritanian government was planning reinsertion programs for repentant extremists.

NIGER

Overview: Al-Qa'ida in the Islamic Maghreb (AQIM) continued to exploit ungoverned space in Nigerien territory. It took advantage of porous borders and the huge expanse of Niger not under government control to conduct contraband smuggling and kidnappings. Niger was committed to fighting AQIM and worked with other regional partners and organizations to support its counterterrorism efforts, notably the General Staff Joint Operations Committee (CEMOC), which also included Algeria, Mali, and Mauritania.

2010 Terrorist Incidents: Niger continued to be a victim of AQIM attacks, including kidnappings and anti-government operations:

- In January, two local residents reported that two vehicles allegedly carrying AQIM-affiliated personnel were spotted in northwestern Niger looking for Westerners to kidnap. A Nigerien patrol sent to the area was attacked and the perpetrators fled towards the Mali-Niger border. Hunted by a Nigerien security force, 15 AQIM members were eventually killed, along with four Nigerien soldiers.

- On March 8, in what was believed to be a revenge attack for the January clash, AQIM attacked a Nigerien armed forces forward-operating post with a vehicle bomb, mortars, heavy machine guns, and small arms. Five Nigerien soldiers died in the attack.

- On April 22, a French humanitarian worker, Michel Germaneau, was kidnapped in northern Niger, taken across the border into Mali, and murdered three months later in apparent retaliation for French support of Mauritanian counterterrorism operations in northern Mali.

- On September 16, five French nationals, one Togolese, and one Malagasy, all sub-contracted employees of the French uranium mining firm Areva, were kidnapped in Arlit. Nigerien forces followed the tire tracks to the border with Mali. AQIM claimed responsibility for the kidnappings.

Countering Terrorist Finance: In January, Niger passed a law implementing the International Convention on the Suppression of the Financing of Terrorism. In July, Niger created the National Coordinating Committee on the Fight against Money Laundering and Terrorist Financing. Niger is a member of the Inter-Governmental Action Group against Money Laundering in West Africa, a Financial Action Task Force-style regional body.

Regional and International Cooperation: Niger cooperated with U.S. counterterrorism efforts and is a Trans-Sahara Counterterrorism Partnership country. Over the past year, Niger has entered into a partnership to establish and conduct operations with Mali, Algeria, and Mauritania out of the CEMOC center in Tamanrasset, Algeria. In September, after the kidnapping in Arlit, Niger agreed to permit French forces to conduct surveillance operations in Niamey.

NIGERIA

Overview: The Nigerian government took actions to improve coordination, communication, and cooperation among its various government agencies and internationally on counterterrorism matters. In the wake of the December 25, 2009, unsuccessful attempt by a Nigerian national to detonate an explosive aboard a U.S.-flagged air carrier over Detroit, Nigeria cooperated closely with the U.S. Department of Homeland Security, the U.S. Federal Aviation Administration, and the International Civil Aviation Organization to strengthen its safety and security systems at four major international airports. Other than ad hoc high-level security meetings after the October 1 car bombings in Abuja, the National Focal Point on Terrorism (an interagency task force formed in 2007 including the State Security Service, Nigerian Customs Service, the Ministries of Foreign Affairs and Immigration) did not actively operate in 2010.

Nigeria faced threats from Delta-based militants who claimed to be seeking better government services but who commonly resorted to violence, and from northern-Nigeria based militants known as Boko Haram who have attacked the Nigerian government with an aim to establish a government in the north functioning under a strict interpretation of Sharia law.

After the July 2009 confrontations between Boko Haram and Nigerian security forces, in which several hundred persons died, many Boko Haram members had reportedly dispersed to neighboring countries to regroup, recruit, and train. The Nigerian military deployed a brigade of troops to the Borno state in July 2010 in anticipation of a violent retaliation by members of Boko Haram on the one-year anniversary of the death of their leader Mohammed Yusuf, who was killed by the police, but no attacks occurred on that date.

2010 Terrorist Incidents: On September 7, 2010, Boko Haram members stormed a prison in Bauchi State, freeing over 700 prisoners including about 100 sect members, and killed seven guards and bystanders. For the rest of 2010, Boko Haram members in Borno and Bauchi states attacked police, military, state officials, and anyone perceived as assisting the Nigerian government in efforts to bring Boko Haram members to justice. Approximately 50 individuals were killed and scores were wounded. Police and military personnel have since arrested over 150 Boko Haram members. On October 21, Boko Haram placed posters at key road intersections in northern Nigeria warning the local public against assisting police in apprehending members of the sect. Each poster bore the signature of al-Qa'ida in the Islamic Maghreb (AQIM) and warned that "any Muslim that goes against the establishment of Sharia law will be attacked and killed." It has not been established whether AQIM and Boko Haram have operational links. In late December, violent extremists detonated explosives in Jos, Plateau State, killing at least 32 persons and wounding many others.

Legislation and Law Enforcement: Revised counterterrorism legislation has been stalled since 2008. After the October 1 bombings in Abuja, the executive branch announced plans to forward additional language to strengthen the bill, and leaders in both the Senate and the House publicly indicated that they would accelerate passage of the legislation. As of late December, however, the National Assembly had yet to conduct the final reading and approve the bill.

Corruption and lack of capacity hindered the ability of the National Police Force to respond to security and terrorist threats within Nigeria's borders. While senior police officers were well-educated and able to articulate the fundamentals of police organization theory and practices, most of the rank-and-file police personnel lacked skills, training, and equipment. Nigerian police conducted limited border security operations but lacked communications, surveillance, and vehicle support to detect and apprehend terrorists and criminals transiting the country's borders. The Nigerian Navy remained unable to patrol its coastal waters effectively, thereby making the Niger Delta region and offshore sites more vulnerable to attacks by criminals and extremists.

Countering Terrorist Finance: Nigeria has some laws that addressed terrorist financing, but they did not comply with international standards. Nigeria's laws for money laundering were more extensive. The Economic and Financial Crimes Commission Act covers the provision or collection of funds used to carry out terrorist acts, but does not cover provision or collection of funds used by terrorist organizations or individual terrorists. The Act does not reference terrorist financing as a predicate offense for money laundering.

Regional And International Cooperation: The Nigerian government participated in the Trans-Sahara Counterterrorism Partnership. Nigeria signed the Beijing Convention on the Suppression of Unlawful Acts Relating to International Civil Aviation and the Protocol to the Convention for the Suppression of Unlawful Seizure of Aircraft at the conclusion of an International Civil Aviation Organization diplomatic conference in September.

RWANDA

Overview: In 2010, a series of deadly grenade attacks targeted Rwandans in public areas of Kigali. No one has claimed responsibility. Armed rebel groups in eastern Democratic Republic of Congo (DRC), including the Democratic Forces for the Liberation of Rwanda (FDLR), continued to pose a threat to Rwanda. The Rwandan government, which restored official relations with the Government of the DRC in 2009, increased cooperation and information sharing to combat continuing mutual threats. The Rwandan government continued to train border control officials, police, army, and security forces to develop counterterrorism skills.

2010 Terrorist Incidents: In 2010, there were over 20 reports of grenade explosions throughout Rwanda, more than half of which were suspected cases of domestic terrorism. At least 11 grenades were thrown from motorcycles and exploded in public areas of Kigali where Rwandans typically congregate, killing six and injuring 47 people. Police arrested suspects and brought individuals in for questioning, but no suspects were brought to trial. The Government of Rwanda publicly accused two former high-ranking Rwandan military officials in South Africa of planning at least two of the attacks, using the attacks to create fear and destabilize Rwanda around the 2010 presidential elections.

Legislation and Law Enforcement: The security situation in the eastern DRC put pressure on Rwanda's western border area, and the Rwandan government continued to work to improve border control measures.

Countering Terrorist Finance: The Government of Rwanda enacted a comprehensive law, called the "Prevention and Suppression of Money Laundering and Financing of Terrorism Act," which established a legal anti-money laundering/counterterrorist financing framework. The government was in the process of implementing this law at year's end.

Regional and International Cooperation: The Rwandan government sought to strengthen regional cooperation and counter cross-border threats through increased information sharing with the DRC and with its neighbors in the East African Community.

SENEGAL

Legislation and Law Enforcement: Senegal does not have a terrorism-specific law but offenses are captured under other parts of the penal code. For example, Senegalese legislation criminalizes illegal possession of a firearm. Possession, bearing, transporting, importation, and marketing of weapons and ammunitions are subject to prior authorization from the Ministry of Interior.

Countering Terrorist Finance: Senegal has an anti-money laundering/countering terrorist finance legal framework in place via the West African Economic and Monetary Union Uniform Law. Senegal's Financial Intelligence Unit is called CENTIF, and is a member of the Egmont Group. CENTIF, law enforcement, and Ministry of Justice authorities worked to coordinate roles and responsibilities and to develop a deeper interagency understanding of terrorist financing. The Central Bank of West African States and CENTIF circulated the UN 1267 Sanctions Committee consolidated list to commercial financial institutions. Senegal is a member of the Inter Governmental Action Group against Money Laundering in West Africa, a Financial Action Task Force-style regional body.

Regional and International Cooperation: Senegal cooperated with U.S. counterterrorism efforts and is a Trans-Sahara Counterterrorism Partnership country. Senegal signed the Beijing Convention on the Suppression of Unlawful Acts Relating to International Civil Aviation and the Protocol to the Convention for the Suppression of Unlawful Seizure of Aircraft at the conclusion of an International Civil Aviation Organization diplomatic conference in September.

SOMALIA

Overview: Somalia's Transitional Federal Government (TFG) continued to have a fragile hold on power and exerted control over only a small portion of the capital of Mogadishu. This, together with Somalia's protracted state of violent instability, long unguarded coasts, and porous borders, made the country an appealing location for terrorists seeking a transit or launching point for operations there or elsewhere. The capability of the TFG and other Somali local and regional authorities to carry out counterterrorism activities or develop a counterterrorism agenda was extremely limited. Clan dynamics remained an influential factor in governance and security issues.

The terrorist and insurgent group al-Shabaab and other anti-TFG clan-based militias continued to exercise control over strategic locations in central Somalia. The TFG and peacekeepers of the African Union Mission in Somalia (AMISOM) remained confined to parts of Mogadishu such as the main seaport, airport, and neighborhoods near Villa Somalia. Al-Shabaab's continued destabilizing influence gave the group and allied violent extremists a safe haven to train and plan terrorist activities.

Several senior al-Shabaab leaders have publicly proclaimed loyalty to al-Qa'ida (AQ). In some terrorist training camps, AQ-affiliated foreign fighters led the training and indoctrination of the recruits. Al-Shabaab conducted suicide attacks, remote-controlled roadside bombings, kidnappings, and assassinations of government officials, journalists, humanitarian workers, and civil society leaders throughout Somalia. Al-Shabaab also threatened UN and other foreign aid agencies and their staff, resulting in the withdrawal of significant humanitarian operations, including that of the World Food Program (WFP) from southern Somalia in January 2010.

Al-Shabaab's influence in Somaliland and Puntland, though on a much smaller scale than in southern Somalia, remained a concern to local and regional authorities.

2010 Terrorist Incidents:

Puntland: An estimated 50 government officials, security officers, and leading elders were killed in terrorist-related attacks in Puntland. A clan militia led by Siad Atom, connected to al-Shabaab, in the mountainous Sanag region, was believed to be behind these attacks. From July to November, Puntland forces launched military operations against Atom and his allied clan fighters. Puntland's president announced the end of the operation in November although the ability of Atom to continue future attacks remained viable and strong.

Somaliland: Attacks and government responses included the following:

- On June 10, Somaliland police clashed with a heavily armed unidentified group with likely links to terrorists in Burao's eastern neighborhood. A police officer was killed, and Eastern Burao's police commander and Togdheer's regional police commander were reportedly wounded in the clashes. Police arrested five people and impounded three sacks of explosive powder and weapons. On November 15, a Berbera court sentenced one of the arrestees, Ahmed Ibrahim Farah, to death by hanging after he pled guilty to terrorism charges. The court delivered death sentences to three other accomplices, two men and a woman, who were tried in absentia. The court also sentenced three women to serve a one-year jail term each for their role in the terrorist raid while two other women were set free due to lack of evidence.

- On January 28, a remote control explosion targeting Farah Askar Hussein, Governor of the Sool region, killed one of his staff and wounded Hussein and his driver. The explosion occurred at the front gate of his Las Anod residence during the visit of eight Somaliland ministers. Somaliland police have not made any arrests related to this incident.

Mogadishu/South and Central region: During 2010, al-Shabaab carried out multiple attacks, including a number in Mogadishu against the TFG and African Union Mission in Somalia. Among the most deadly were a series of attacks in March, which killed at least 60 people and wounded 160 more; and a string of attacks in late August, which killed at least 87 people and wounded 148. Also in August, al-Shabaab suicide bombers entered the Muna Hotel in Mogadishu and killed 31 people, including six members of parliament and four other government officials, when they detonated their explosives on the roof of the hotel. Attacks and government responses included the following:

- On May 1, twin explosions inside a packed mosque in the Bakara market of Mogadishu killed 45 worshippers and left an estimated 100 others injured, including top al-Shabaab militants. A similar mosque attack on May 2 in Kismayu killed two and injured 13 people after congregational prayers.

- Qn August 24, two al-Shabaab gunmen disguised in TFG military uniforms made a forced entry into Hotel Muna in Mogadishu's Hamarweyne district and killed 31 of the guests, including members of parliament and other government officials. The two attackers, according to TFG official sources, went on a shooting spree while inside the hotel before one of them blew himself up with a suicide vest.

- On September 9, AMISOM peacekeepers disrupted an al-Shabaab attack on the Mogadishu airport. After attackers detonated twin suicide truck bombs near the airport, AMISOM reportedly shot five more bomb-strapped al-Shabaab militia members as they tried to sneak into the airport during the resulting mayhem. Four civilians and three peacekeepers were killed in the attack.

- On November 10, al-Shabaab militia beheaded four people in Galgaduud for their suspected association with Ahlu Sunna Wal Jama'a (ASWJ), a moderate Islamic organization that often-times fights against al-Shabaab and has links, albeit weak, with the TFG.

Legislation and Law Enforcement: Somalia's Transitional Federal Government in Mogadishu, under siege by insurgents, called on regional governments to help stem the flow of terrorist financing, requesting local governments trace, freeze, and seize al-Shabaab financing. On May 3, the TFG passed a counterterrorism law, and in July, Puntland followed with similar legislation establishing special courts to try terrorism suspects. Somaliland has not passed any such laws, though its court system has been able to hand out death sentences to al-Shabaab and other extremists for crimes committed.

Countering Terrorist Finance: Somalia was a terrorist financing center. Existing anti-money laundering and counterterrorist finance laws were unenforceable, given the security threat to the government and its lack of capacity. The financial system in Somalia operated almost completely outside of government oversight either on the black market or via international money transfer entities known as hawalas. Financial entities in Somalia self-imposed international standards, to the extent they exist, in order to do business elsewhere in the world.

Al-Shabaab derived most of its funding internally, particularly from control over the key port of Kismaayo and taxation of goods and legitimate commerce. Some of the external financing entered Somalia as cash, but most likely arrived through hawalas. Al-Shabaab also financed its operations through extortion of private citizens and local businesses, revenue from air and seaports under their control, and to an unknown extent by diversion of humanitarian and development assistance. The TFG, Puntland, and Somaliland regional administrations were unable to control transit across their borders, and goods flowed into and out of Somalia without government knowledge. In areas controlled by al-Shabaab, the group "taxed" goods' movements.

The TFG did not have an independent system or mechanism for freezing terrorist assets. No government entities were charged with, or capable of tracking, seizing, or freezing illegal assets. In theory, the Treasury Ministry would be responsible for investigating financial crimes, but it lacked the capacity, including financial, technical, and human resources. U.S. Embassy personnel in Kenya were aware of the interdiction of one suspected terrorist financier carrying cash illegally into Somalia. Interdictions of these sorts by TFG officials result in an arrest, and then indefinite detentions or releases given Somalia's inadequate judicial system.

There was no mechanism for distributing information from the TFG to financial institutions, and the TFG enforced no suspicious transactions or large currency transactions reporting requirements on banks or other financial institutions. However, many institutions operating in Somalia maintained international offices and therefore adhered to minimum international standards, including freezes on terrorist entities' finances.

The government did not distribute to financial institutions the names of suspected terrorists and terrorist organizations listed on the UN 1267 Sanctions Committee's consolidated list associated with Usama bin Ladin, members of AQ, or the Taliban.

Somalia did not have any mechanisms in place to share information related to terrorist financing with the United States.

Regional and International Cooperation: Some Western and regional nations worked to assist the TFG/National Security Forces through training and support.

Countering Radicalization and Violent Extremism: The TFG's Ministry of Information began issuing news releases, which helped make it a credible source of information for both Somali citizens and the Somali media. This in turn has bolstered the credibility of their reports of al-Shabaab atrocities. The Ministry's most effective outreach tool was its multi-media public broadcasting platform, Radio Mogadishu, which broadcast over FM radio, streamed live on the Internet, and maintained a webpage and Facebook presence. The station has made considerable strides in objective reporting about both the extremists and the government and thereby gained audience share.

Radio Mogadishu also launched a religious affairs call-in show that examined, from an Islamic perspective, al-Shabaab's claims to religious legitimacy. The show aired three times a week and received callers and text messages from all over Mogadishu (including al-Shabaab controlled areas) and Facebook messages from around the world. The messaging was overwhelming critical of al-Shabaab.

SOUTH AFRICA

Overview: In preparation for the 2010 World Cup, there was close cooperation between South African and U.S. law enforcement and intelligence agencies. South Africa took measures to address border security vulnerability and document fraud, which had hindered the government's ability to pursue counterterrorism initiatives. Under the leadership of Minister Dlamini-Zuma, the Department of Home Affairs continued implementation of its turnaround strategy to end corruption and accelerate documentation of all bona fide South African citizens and residents.

Legislation and Law Enforcement: The South African Revenue Service (SARS) has a Customs and Border Protection (CBP) Container Security Initiative team located in Durban. SARS is a member of the World Customs Organization and worked closely with the U.S. Department of Homeland Security Customs and Border Protection to develop the SARS Customs Border Control Unit, which was modeled after the CBP Antiterrorism Contraband Enforcement Team.

Countering Terrorist Finance: South Africa was a member of both the Financial Action Task Force (FATF) and the Eastern and Southern Africa Anti-Money Laundering Group. South Africa cooperated with the United States in exchanging terrorist financing information. South Africa's Financial Intelligence Center (FIC) is a member of the Egmont Group. Amendments to the FIC basic legislation came into effect on December 1, granting the FIC authority to impose administrative sanctions such as monetary penalties. In November, South Africa hosted a joint experts meeting of FATF and the Egmont Group.

TANZANIA

Overview: Elements of the terrorist network responsible for the 1998 U.S. Embassy bombing remained active in the region making Tanzania vulnerable to international terrorism. The Government of Tanzania continued to be an active and helpful partner in bringing Ahmed Khalfan Ghailani, one of the key perpetrators of the bombings, to justice in the United States. Following the Kampala bombings on July 11, Tanzania worked closely with authorities in Uganda and Kenya to investigate the attacks.

2010 Terrorist Incidents: On the evening of May 16, a 15-year-old boy ran past a guard in front of the U.S. Embassy, lit a bottle containing kerosene and threw it under one of two water trucks parked outside the Embassy walls. The bottle broke, but did not ignite. Embassy security guards captured the boy before he could throw a second bottle. There was no breach of the Embassy compound, no injuries, or property damage. A Tanzanian police officer arrived immediately after the incident and arrested the perpetrator. The boy had a note on him threatening possible future attacks. He told police he was motivated to attack the United States Embassy by violent extremist ideology.

Legislation and Law Enforcement: Following the Kampala bombings, Tanzania stepped up its efforts to counter terrorism, increased its collaboration, both regionally and internationally, and adopted a more proactive approach. The National Counterterrorism Center continued its participation in several multi-year programs to strengthen Tanzania's law enforcement and military capacity, improve aviation and border security, and combat money laundering and terrorist financing. The Ministry of Home Affairs worked jointly with the U.S. Embassy to strengthen maritime security, particularly in Africa's Great Lakes. A National Maritime Training Academy was under construction on the shores of Lake Victoria and two new boats began patrolling these waters during the year. Immigration authorities collaborated with the International Organization for Migration to improve security along the northern and southern borders. This included introducing electronic screening systems, improving regional coordination, and establishing a Border Information Center in Mwanza to help address issues arising from the adoption of the East African Community's (EAC) Common Market Protocol, which allows for the free movement of citizens within the EAC.

In advance of the trial of terrorism suspect Ahmed Ghailani, accused and convicted for his involvement in the 1998 U. S. Embassy bombing, Tanzanian officials helped U. S. law enforcement agents prepare for the trial, including assisting with witness preparation.

In the case involving the 15-year-old Tanzanian involved in the May 16 U.S. Embassy incident, the police responded quickly, arresting the perpetrator. However, the subsequent investigation and prosecution has proceeded slowly. The suspect, a minor, was released into the custody of his guardians.

Tanzania continued to process travelers on entry and departure at three international airports, two seaports, and one land border with the Personal Identification Secure Comparison and Evaluation System (PISCES).

Countering Terrorist Finance: Tanzania's Financial Intelligence Unit (FIU) established its Anti-Money Laundering Act. However, with only three technical staff, the FIU had limited resources to investigate potential money laundering or terrorist financing activities. Tanzania's laws do not allow the assets of suspected terrorists to be frozen unless the individual has been convicted for criminal acts. The Prevention of Terrorism Act, however, gives the Attorney General the authority to submit an application to the court for an order of forfeiture of assets owned or controlled by a terrorist group. Tanzania was a member of the Eastern and Southern African Anti-Money Laundering Group, a Financial Action Task Force-style regional body.

Regional and International Cooperation: Regional counterterrorism cooperation intensified following the Kampala bombings. Tanzanian authorities worked closely with their Ugandan and Kenyan counterparts to investigate the incidents and limit the ability of such dangerous elements to operate in the region.

UGANDA

Overview: The Somali-based al-Shabaab posed the most significant terrorist threat to Uganda. Al-Qa'ida (AQ)-linked terrorists moving between the Horn of Africa, North Africa, and Europe used Uganda as a transit point. While in transit, AQ members were believed to have illegally procured government documents and engaged in recruitment activities. In response to the July 11 bombings and continued threat levels, the Government of Uganda increased efforts to track, capture, and hold individuals with suspected links to terrorist organizations. Uganda's Joint Anti-Terrorism Taskforce, which is composed of military, police, and intelligence entities, led Uganda's counterterrorism response.

In addition to investigating and charging terrorist bombing suspects, Uganda continued to pursue the Lord's Resistance Army in coordination with the Democratic Republic of Congo, Sudan, and the Central African Republic.

2010 Terrorist Incidents: On July 11, two al-Shabaab suicide bombers attacked an Ethiopian restaurant and a Rugby Club in Kampala where Ugandans and others gathered to watch the World Cup finals, killing 76 people and wounding many more. Accomplices to the suicide bombers detonated a separate explosive device, in addition to the bomb detonated by the suicide bomber, at the Rugby Club. A fourth bomb placed at a nightclub failed to explode.

Legislation and Law Enforcement: Following the Kampala bombings, U.S. law enforcement worked closely with Uganda to gather evidence and investigate the terrorist attacks. This collaboration improved the coordination and levels of information sharing between Uganda's own security services and strengthened police capacity to investigate terrorist incidents. An archaic criminal records system that relies on fingerprint cards to connect individuals with past crimes continued to hinder Ugandan police. Uganda continued to need a modern criminal records management system to conduct effective counterterrorism cooperation.

Uganda continued to process travelers on entry and departure at two international airports and four land borders with the Personal Identification Secure Comparison and Evaluation System.

Countering Terrorist Finance: Uganda's comprehensive draft anti-money laundering legislation has long been pending before Parliament. As a result, current efforts to combat money laundering are piecemeal and based on older legislation. The Anti-Terrorist Act made terrorist financing illegal, and there was no evidence that the Ugandan government used it to prosecute effectively financiers of terrorism. In addition, the list of terrorist organizations covered by the bill was static, and only included four terrorist organizations (al-Qa'ida and three domestic organizations). There was no suspicious transaction-reporting requirement for terrorist financing. The Inspectorate General of Government has the power to investigate cases brought to it by the public, but in practice has not investigated money laundering and terrorist financing cases. The Criminal Investigations Department (CID) of the Uganda Police Force was responsible for investigating financial crimes. However, until Parliament approves the anti-money laundering legislation, the understaffed and undertrained CID maintains only limited authority to investigate and prosecute money-laundering violations. According to Ugandan government officials, criminals often had access to technology that was more sophisticated than what was available to police investigators. Internal corruption within the CID also hampered police investigative capacity.

Regional and International Cooperation: Uganda signed the Beijing Convention on the Suppression of Unlawful Acts Relating to International Civil Aviation and the Protocol to the Convention for the Suppression of Unlawful Seizure of Aircraft at the conclusion of an International Civil Aviation Organization diplomatic conference in September. The Ugandan government is a strong advocate for cross-border solutions to persistent security concerns in the Great Lakes Region and East Africa. Burundi and Uganda were the only two troop contributing nations participating in AU Mission in Somalia.

Countering Radicalization and Violent Extremism: Because regions lacking rule of law are often incubators of extremism, Ugandan law enforcement is working with the United States to improve levels of collaboration and trust between the police force and the public in northern Uganda.

EAST ASIA AND PACIFIC OVERVIEW

Throughout 2010, key countries in East Asia and the Pacific achieved significant counterterrorism successes through multilateral cooperation, capacity building, popular support, and political will. In February, Indonesian authorities, alerted by local residents, raided a terrorist training camp in Aceh and arrested over 120 suspected terrorists, who had come together from a variety of Indonesian extremist organizations. Indonesian prosecutors secured convictions for 11 terrorists connected with the fatal 2009 Jakarta hotel bombings and several detainees from the Aceh camp. The number of "reformed" convicts arrested at the Aceh camp highlighted the need for more effective counter radicalization and prison reform programs. Law enforcement agencies in Malaysia and Singapore were effective in identifying and detaining terrorist suspects, and cooperated with each other and with the international community on counterterrorism. In September, Malaysia extradited Jemaah Islamiya terrorist, Mas Selamat Kastari, to Singapore, from where he had escaped incarceration in 2008.

Philippine security forces continued to combat terrorists principally in the southern Philippines. On February 21, prominent Abu Sayyaf Group (ASG) sub-commander Albader Parad and five other ASG militants in Jolo were killed. ASG attacks included an April 13 bombing in Isabela City, Basilan, which killed nine outside a cathedral.

The United States continued to partner with countries in the region through diplomacy, bilateral security cooperation, multilateral organizations, and capacity building to support counterterrorism efforts. In May, the United States and the People's Republic of China held bilateral counterterrorism consultations in Beijing. In November, the United States hosted bilateral counterterrorism consultations with the Republic of Korea. In December, the annual Trilateral Strategic Dialogue Counterterrorism Consultations with the United States, Australia, and Japan took place in Melbourne, Australia.

AUSTRALIA

Overview: On February 23, the Government of Australia released the Counterterrorism White Paper outlining Australia's counterterrorism strategy. The strategy has four key elements: Analysis, Protection, Response, and Resilience. Additional funding was announced for a counter-radicalization program. The National Terrorism Public Alert System level remained at medium, indicating that a terrorist attack could occur.

Legislation and Law Enforcement: In October 2009, five Sydney men, arrested as part of a series of raids in 2005, were found guilty of plotting terrorist attacks. On February 15, they were sentenced to jail terms ranging from 23 to 28 years. The Australian Attorney-General noted that the trial extended over nearly one year and involved approximately 300 witnesses, 3,000 exhibits, and 30 days of surveillance evidence.

In February, the government announced the creation of the Counterterrorism Control Center (composed of the Australia Security Intelligence Organization (ASIO), Australian Secret Intelligence Service, the Australian Federal Police and Defense Signals Directorate) to coordinate counterterrorism activities; it was officially opened on October 21.

In March, parliament passed the Independent National Security Legislation Monitor Bill 2010 that appoints an Independent Monitor to help ensure counterterrorism laws strike an appropriate balance between protecting the community and human rights.

Between July 2009 and June 2010, ASIO identified "several Australians" seeking contact with extremist religious figures overseas, and issued eight adverse security assessments against Australian passport holders, which "reflected an increase in the number of Australians identified as seeking to travel overseas for terrorism-related activities." ASIO reported that a number of Australians made contact with extremist figures in Yemen and "Australians resident in Yemen have also participated in terrorism-related activity." During this period, ASIO issued 14 adverse assessments against visa applicants on counterterrorism grounds.

In November, parliament passed the National Security Legislation Amendment Bill, which includes new powers for police to enter premises without a warrant in emergency circumstances; establishing a seven day limit on the amount of time a terrorism suspect can be held, without charges; expanding counterterrorism laws to apply to those who incite violence on the basis of race, religion, ethnic origin, and political opinion; extending the expiration period of regulations proscribing a terrorist organization from two to three years; amending the National Security Information (Criminal and Civil Proceedings) Act 2004 so that national security and counterterrorism court proceedings may be expedited; and creating parliamentary oversight of the Australian Federal Police and Australian Crime Commission.

On December 23, three Melbourne men were found guilty of conspiring to plan a terrorist act at Sydney's Holsworthy Army Base in 2009. The Attorney-General said the prosecution was the result of a complex joint investigation involving state and federal police cooperation with the intelligence community.

Australia listed 19 groups as terrorist organizations. Al-Qa'ida in the Arabian Peninsula was listed for the first time and al-Qa'ida, Jemaah Islamiya, al-Qa'ida in the Islamic Maghreb, Abu Sayyaf Group, al-Qa'ida in Iraq, and Jamiat ul-Ansar were re-listed in 2010.

The Australian Communications and Media Authority was investigating Hizballah's al-Manar television station's program content to determine its compliance with regulatory obligations relating to terrorist-related content, as well as racial vilification and hate speech.

Countering Terrorist Finance: Australia's laws make it a criminal offense to hold assets that are owned or controlled by terrorist organizations or individuals sanctioned under UNSCR 1267. The Australian Transaction Reports and Analysis Center (AUSTRAC) acts as Australia's money-laundering and counterterrorist financing regulator. AUSTRAC continued to fund capacity building technical assistance programs in Southeast Asia, South Asia, the Pacific, and Africa.

To better coordinate and exchange financial information, the government launched the Criminal Intelligence Fusion Center within the Australian Crime Commission in July 2010. The center co-located expert investigators and analysts from AUSTRAC and other government agencies. On November 11, the government released proposals to strengthen regulation of businesses providing international cash transfer services.

Regional and International Cooperation: Australian multilateral engagement continued in a wide range of forums. Australia has counterterrorism memoranda of understanding with Indonesia, the Philippines, Malaysia, Cambodia, Thailand, Brunei, Fiji, Papua New Guinea, East Timor, India, Pakistan, Afghanistan, Turkey, Bangladesh, and the United Arab Emirates. Australia continued to provide legal drafting assistance to regional states seeking to adopt international conventions and protocols against terrorism, and to bring their law codes into conformity with these conventions. Australia was instrumental in the International Civil Aviation Organization's efforts to update the Montreal and Hague Conventions, resulting in the successful conclusion of two new counterterrorism instruments in Beijing.

Australia and the United States exchanged information using APEC's Regional Movement Alert System. Australia has biometric data-sharing arrangements with the United Kingdom, Canada, the United States, and New Zealand.

From March to August 2010, Australia's largest ever national counterterrorism exercise, Mercury 10, was held across Australia. The "deployment phase" was conducted in late August. It was the first to include another country, with the involvement of New Zealand. In November, Australia and Malaysia established a bilateral counterterrorism working group. In December, Australia hosted the Ninth Annual Trilateral Security Dialogue Counterterrorism consultations with the United States and Japan.

Countering Radicalization and Violent Extremism: The government funded projects encouraging tolerance of religious diversity. In November, the government announced approximately US$ 9.7 million to fund a youth mentoring program as part of a program to address radicalization.

CAMBODIA

Overview: Cambodia's political leadership has demonstrated a strong commitment to taking legal action against terrorists and, since the passage in 2007 of separate laws on terrorism and terrorist financing, the Government of Cambodia has remained committed to strengthening its counterterrorism capability through training and international cooperation.

Legislation and Law Enforcement: In September, the Cambodian National Counterterrorism Committee (NCTC) took delivery of an Emergency Communication Vehicle system, which strengthens response capabilities by enabling communications in the event of failed power and telecommunications systems. Cambodia continued to process travelers on entry and departure at two international airports and three land border sites with the U.S.-provided Personal Identification Secure Comparison and Evaluation System (PISCES).

Regional and International Cooperation: In June, Cambodia became the fourth ASEAN member state to ratify the ASEAN Convention on Counterterrorism. In July, Cambodia hosted a large-scale multinational peacekeeping exercise as part of the U.S.-UN 2010 Global Peace Operations Initiative. In September, the NCTC hosted the Pacific Area Sector Working Group with representatives from the partner nations of ASEAN. The workshop provided a forum for increasing cooperation on counterterrorism, disaster management, and information sharing in a multilateral, interagency environment.

In July, Cambodian authorities arrested two Thai nationals and returned them to Thailand, where they faced criminal charges for their alleged role in detonating a grenade outside the headquarters office of a political party. Cambodian officials pointed to the arrests and repatriation, which took place despite then-fractious ties between Cambodia and Thailand, as an indicator of Cambodia's commitment to cross-border cooperation on terrorism.

Countering Terrorist Finance: While the Cambodian government made some progress in strengthening its counterterrorist finance regime, it is subject to prima facie review by the Financial Action Task Force's International Cooperation Review Group for apparent deficiencies in its anti-money laundering and counterterrorist finance regime. The Financial Intelligence Unit, which operates within the framework of the National Bank of Cambodia, conducted on-site examinations of banks and financial institutions to gauge their implementation of measures designed to counter terrorist financing and money laundering.

CHINA

Overview: China held counterterrorism military exercises with Thailand in October, participated in regional counterterrorism exercises with Shanghai Cooperation Organization (SCO) member states in September, and provided equipment to Pakistan for counterterrorism training in May. China's domestic counterterrorism efforts remained primarily focused against the East Turkistan Islamic Party (ETIP), also known as the East Turkistan Islamic Movement (ETIM). In January 2010, ETIP released videos in Uighur, a Turkic language indigenous to China's western Xinjiang Uighur Autonomous Region (XUAR), to claim credit for alleged actions in revenge for the "July 5 incident" of 2009, when racially-motivated riots in the XUAR capital led to the reported deaths of both Uighurs and Han Chinese, and to call on Muslims in Xinjiang to carry out a "jihad" against China.

China does not always distinguish between legitimate political dissent and the advocacy of violence to overthrow the government, and has used counterterrorism as a pretext to suppress Uighurs, a predominantly Muslim ethnic group that makes up a large percentage of the population within the XUAR.

2010 Terrorist Incidents: On August 19, three people drove an explosive-laden vehicle into a crowd in the city of Aksu, XUAR, killing three civilians and three police officers, and wounding 15 other civilians and police officers. The Chinese government attributed this incident to "separatists, extremists, and terrorists."

Legislation and Law Enforcement: The U. S. Federal Bureau of Investigation (FBI) Legal Attaché's Office in Beijing held several meetings and briefings with the Chinese Ministry of Public Security (MPS) Terrorism Department on a number of terrorist-related issues. The Legal Attaché's Office has presented specific investigations that potentially could be worked jointly between the FBI and MPS; to date, the MPS has not responded to these requests.

China participated in the Megaports program. Through provision of training and donation of radiation detection equipment, the U.S. Department of Energy improved China's capacity to detect and interdict smuggled nuclear and radiological materials in preparation for the 2010 Shanghai World Expo and the 2010 Asia Games.

Countering Terrorist Finance: China has yet to develop a regime to freeze terrorist assets that meets international standards or that adequately implements UNSCRs 1267 and 1373. This was identified by China's central bank as a future priority in China's "2008-2012 National Anti-Money Laundering/Counterterrorist Financing (AML/CTF) Strategy" paper. There remained a need for better implementation and enhanced coordination between financial regulators and law enforcement authorities. U.S. agencies continued to seek expanded cooperation with Chinese counterparts on terrorist and other illicit finance matters and to strengthen both policy- and operational-level cooperation in this critical area.

Terrorist financing is a criminal offense in China. In 2010, China demonstrated progress in addressing certain deficiencies in AML/CTF. China increased the number of money-laundering investigations, prosecutions, and convictions. The central bank issued a new regulation clarifying the suspicious transaction reporting obligations of Chinese banks, as well as penalties for lack of compli-

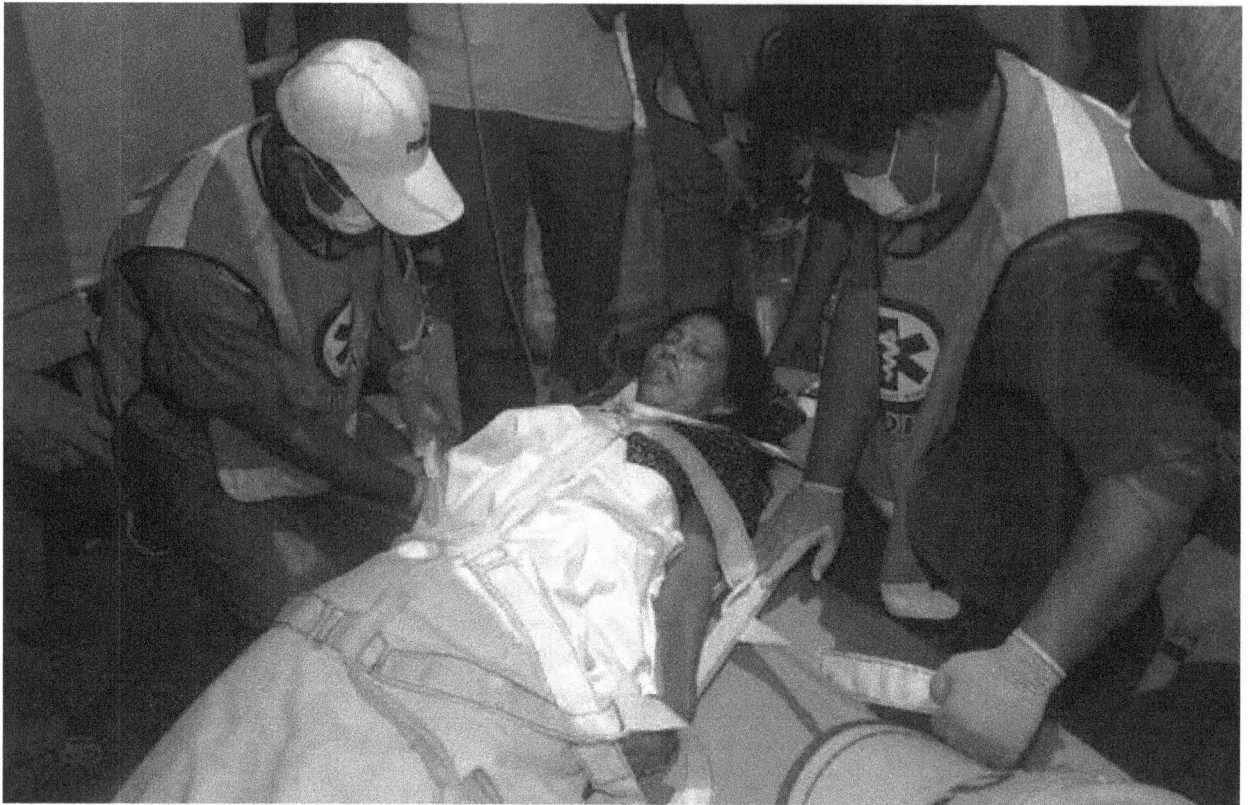

Zamboanga City, Philippines: Members of the Abu Sayyaf extremist group and other gunmen raided the town of Maluso on Basilan island before dawn, killing a government employee and 10 civilians, said regional health chief Dr. Kadil Jojo Sinolinding. Seventeen people were also wounded in the attack with nine in critical condition, four of whom were children. Above, medical personnel prepare to carry one of the 17 wounded out of a ferry boat used to transport the wounded to a hospital in Zamboanga City on February 27, 2010. AFP PHOTO/ THERENCE KOH

ance. In April, the U.S. Treasury Department and China's central bank established an AML/CTF working group under the auspices of the U.S.-China Strategic and Economic Dialogue to provide an important channel for addressing both policy and operational cooperation. China is an active, full member of the Financial Action Task Force (FATF), the Asia-Pacific Group (APG), and the Eurasian Group, but has not joined the Egmont Group.

Regional and International Cooperation: In November, Chinese Foreign Minister Yang Jiechi, with his Russian and Indian counterparts, emphasized the need for full international cooperation in counterterrorism efforts, particularly within the framework of the UN, to prevent terrorist attacks and to prosecute terrorists and their supporters. In September, China hosted a diplomatic conference under the auspices of the International Civil Aviation Organization that resulted in two new legal instruments related to civil aviation security. China signed both instruments at the conclusion of the diplomatic conference. China also ratified the International Convention for Suppression of Acts of Nuclear Terrorism.

In response to an October 2009 proposal by the United States, Chinese President Hu Jintao endorsed the joint development of a Nuclear Security Center of Excellence at the April 2010 Nuclear Security Summit. The center's functions will include training to bolster bilateral efforts to prevent terrorists, terrorist organizations, and proliferating states from accessing nuclear and radiological materials. In 2010, we had regular bilateral counterterrorism consultations with the Chinese, including at the Second Annual Strategic and Economic Dialogue, but cooperation remained limited.

<u>HONG KONG</u>

Hong Kong law enforcement agencies provided full support to and cooperation with their foreign counterparts in tracing financial transactions suspected of links to terrorist activities. They participated in U.S. government-sponsored training, including terrorism investigations and complex financial investigations. Hong Kong continued its effective partnership on the Container Security Initiative. The year-old Hong Kong Police Counterterrorist Readiness Unit continued to develop capability in its mission areas of deterrence, assisting police districts with counterterrorist strategy implementation, and providing support to Hong Kong's existing specialist units.

Terrorist financing is a criminal offense in Hong Kong. Hong Kong's financial regulatory authorities directed banks and other financial institutions to continuously search for terrorist financing networks and accounts using designations lists made by the U.S. under relevant authorities, as well as the UN 1267 Sanctions Committee's consolidated lists. All entities and persons are legally required to file suspicious transactions reports (STRs) irrespective of transaction amounts involved. However, Hong Kong does not have reporting requirements for cross-border currency movements.

Hong Kong is an active member of the FATF and the (APG, a FATF-style regional body. Responding to the latest FATF and APG mutual evaluation, Hong Kong authorities in October presented draft legislation that would increase supervision of money changers and remittance agents; create statutory requirements for customer due diligence and record-keeping in the banking, securities, and insurance sectors; and establish civil penalties for violations.

<u>MACAU</u>

Macau's law enforcement and customs agencies participated in U.S. government-sponsored training, including bulk cash smuggling detection and investigations, terrorism investigations, and complex financial investigations. Macau's Police Tactical Intervention Unit is responsible for protecting important installations and dignitaries, and for conducting high-risk missions, including the deactivation of improvised explosive devices.

Terrorist financing is a criminal offense in Macau. Macau's financial regulatory authorities directed banks and other financial institutions to continuously search for terrorist financing networks and accounts using designations lists made by the U.S. under relevant authorities, as well as the UN 1267 Sanctions Committee's consolidated lists. All entities and persons are legally required to file suspicious transactions reports (STRs) irrespective of transaction amounts involved. However, Macau does not have reporting requirements for cross-border currency movements.

Macau is an active member of the APG, a FATF-style regional body. Through its Financial Intelligence Office (FIO), Macau is also an active member of the Egmont Group of Financial Intelligence Units.

INDONESIA

Overview: In 2010, the Indonesian government continued to build counterterrorism capacities, successfully prosecuted a number of terrorists, and strengthened legislative efforts to counter terrorist financing. A new National Counterterrorism Agency (BNPT) was formally established on July 16 and President Yudhoyono swore in retired Police Inspector General Ansyaad Mbai as its head on September 7.

In February 2010, Indonesian police discovered a large paramilitary terrorist training camp in Aceh. Officials identified at least eight terrorist factions involved in the terrorist training camp. The factions included militants who trained in Mindanao in the southern Philippines, graduates of terrorist training camps in Afghanistan and Pakistan, students, government workers, and released terrorist convicts who had undergone de-radicalization programs while in the Indonesian corrections system. Police believed the Aceh-based terrorist group intended to target Indonesian government officials, including President Susilo Bambang Yudhoyono.

The success of police actions following the breakup of the Aceh training camp, however, continued to demonstrate increased police capacities, including successful operations carried out with a minimum loss of life to both terrorists and civilians, though some terrorists were killed during police raids. Police captured over 120 terrorists associated with the Aceh training camp, including Abdullah Sunata, a leader of the radical group Kompak, known for its involvement in ethnic conflicts in Poso and Ambon, and Abu Tholut, a bomb maker believed to have funded the Aceh terrorist training camp. In addition, the death of a third well-known terrorist, Dulmatin, an electronics expert and bomb maker who received al-Qa'ida training in Afghanistan and was wanted in connection to the 2002 Bali bombing, brought to an end an intensive international manhunt across Southeast Asia.

The number of corrections recidivists involved in the Aceh training camp concerned the Indonesians. At least 18 recidivists were either killed or captured in police actions connected to the camp. The Government of Indonesia recognized that the high rate of recidivism was one of a number of concerns related to the Indonesian prison system that needed to be addressed. Prison sector issues also included rehabilitative capacity, security procedures, organizational structure, and training. Evidence that terrorists within and outside of the corrections system (including Dulmatin) were in contact with each other and were able to further develop terrorist networks while incarcerated further highlighted the need for broad prison reform.

2010 Terrorist Incidents: On the heels of successful police actions, militants conducted retribution strikes against police stations. On March 12, terrorists associated with the Aceh training camp attacked a police outstation in Aceh. On September 22, after a series of police actions in North Sumatera, 12 heavily-armed men on six motorcycles killed three police officers in a heavy-arms attack on a sub-district police station.

Indonesian law enforcement authorities believe terrorists conducted a series of bank robberies to finance terrorist activities. The most brazen bank robbery took place midday August 18 when 16 heavily armed robbers robbed a bank in the Medan central commercial district. The robbers killed a police officer and wounded two bank security guards.

Legislation and Law Enforcement: While Indonesia's Terrorism and Transnational Crime Task Force has a successful track record in prosecuting terrorism cases, the 2010 arrests linked to terrorist camps in Aceh revealed a limitation in Indonesia's ability to counter terrorism; nothing in Indonesian law directly criminalizes participation in terrorist training camps. The Ministry of Law and Human Rights formed an inter-agency working group to draft amendments to Indonesia's 2003 Terrorism law to address deficiencies in the current law. In addition, draft legislation to address the use of intelligence information in terrorism cases was also in progress.

One major development in terms of pending legislation was the formal establishment of the BNPT. On July 16, Presidential Decree Number 46/2010 formally established the BNPT as a free-standing agency. The new agency replaced the Anti-Terrorism Coordinating Desk, which was housed in the Coordinating Ministry for Political, Legal, and Security Affairs. On September 7, President Yudhoyono swore in retired Police Inspector General Ansyaad Mbai as the head of the BNPT. Mbai reported directly to the President and attended relevant cabinet sessions. However, the Coordinating Ministry for Political, Legal, and Security Affairs retained oversight over the BNPT, similar to its oversight over other ministries or agencies, including the Foreign Ministry, National Intelligence Agency (BIN), and the Indonesian National Police. The BNPT's organizational structure contained a secretariat responsible for administration and program coordination, three deputies responsible for prevention, protection, and de-radicalization efforts; operations and capabilities; and international cooperation.

In addition, the Indonesian National Police's (INP) counterterrorism unit, Special Detachment 88, was separated from the INP's Criminal Investigation Unit and placed under the BNPT deputy responsible for operations and capabilities, but remained under the direct command of the national police chief. In a move to consolidate their efforts, provincial Detachment 88 units were abolished and replaced with 10 regional units.

Prosecutions: In 2010, the Attorney General's Office Task Force on Terrorism and Transnational Crime (SATGAS) secured convictions of 11 terrorists connected with the 2009 bombings of the J.W. Marriott and Ritz-Carlton hotels in Jakarta. A twelfth defendant, Saudi national Al Khalil Ali, was charged with financing the July 17, 2009 twin Jakarta hotel bombings under Indonesia's fledgling terrorist finance law. Ali was acquitted of the terrorism charge on June 28, 2010, but found guilty of immigration violations and sentenced to 18 months imprisonment.

SATGAS prosecutors have developed extensive experience prosecuting terrorism cases, which are brought under a specialized terrorism law with different procedures than ordinary criminal cases. SATGAS prosecutors have developed long-term, close professional relationships with the specialized police unit, Detachment 88, which investigates Indonesia's terrorism cases. This has led to a new criminal model in Indonesia – police and prosecutors working together on cases from the onset instead of prosecutorial engagement beginning after a police investigation has concluded. At the end of 2010, SATGAS was currently prosecuting more than 70 defendants associated with the Aceh training camp.

Border Security: Since 2006, a photo and 10 fingerprints have been taken for all passport applicants. This information was sent back to a central site for biometric checking which ostensibly must be completed before a passport can be issued. However, duplicative passports with false identities were easily obtainable. This systemic weakness was highlighted when police discovered that Muhammad Jibriel Abdur Rahman, aka Muhammad Ricky Ardhan, who was sentenced in 2010 to five years in jail for his role in the July 17, 2009 Jakarta bombings, was found to possess one. In addition, when terrorist Dulmatin was killed in March 2010 press reports state he had an Indonesian passport issued by the East Jakarta Immigration Office in the name of Yahya Ibrahim. The Government of Indonesia has noted the weaknesses in official documentation controls and has been working to address the issue.

Countering Terrorist Finance: Indonesia demonstrated concrete progress in improving its Anti-Money Laundering/Countering Financing of Terrorism (AML/CTF) regime. In February, the government committed to work with the Financial Action Task Force and the Asia/Pacific Group (APG) to address remaining AML/CTF deficiencies.

On October 22, President Yudhoyono signed Law No. 8 of 2010 on the Prevention and Eradication of the Crime of Money Laundering, which will help Indonesia counter terrorist finance and transnational crime. The legislation permits rapid freezing and seizure of assets and bank accounts, which will make it easier for Indonesia to comply with UNSCRs 1267 and 1373 and bolster the ability of police and prosecutors to pursue individuals who provide critical financial support to terrorists.

This law expanded the number of agencies permitted to conduct money laundering investigations; increased the ability of the independent Financial Intelligence Unit (PPATK) to examine suspicious financial transactions; expanded institutions authorized to obtain results of PPATK analysis or examination of transactions; created a streamlined mechanism to seize and freeze criminal assets; expanded the entities which must file reports with PPATK; and increased some criminal penalties for money laundering offenses. The law designated non-financial businesses, in addition to Indonesian banks and providers of financial services, which were required to report suspicious transactions to PPATK. Throughout the remainder of 2010, the PPATK led a government team preparing regulations and guidelines to implement the new law. The government was in the process of developing a comprehensive bill on countering terrorist financing at year's end.

In addition, the Central Bank issued new regulations, effective December 1, which apply to all rural banks and require more extensive provisions for due diligence for high-risk customers and politically exposed persons, and checks against the Central Bank's Terrorist List, based on data published by the UN.

Regional and International Cooperation: Indonesia signed the Beijing Convention on the Suppression of Unlawful Acts Relating to International Civil Aviation and the Beijing Protocol to the Convention for the Suppression of Unlawful Seizure of Aircraft at the conclusion of an International Civil Aviation Organization diplomatic conference in September.

Countering Radicalization and Violent Extremism: While Indonesia's new BNPT has stated its intent to incorporate counter-radicalization into its overall counterterrorism strategy, civil society organizations continued to take the lead in developing and implementing counter-radicalization programs at the local level. For example, the Association for Victims of Terrorism Bombings in Indonesia, which includes family members of victims of terrorism in Indonesia, worked to counter violent extremism through public outreach events held at schools and for communities in Indonesia.

The corrections system lacked formal rehabilitation and reintegration programs for all prisoners, including terrorists. As with counter-radicalization, the BNPT stated it intended to play a more significant role in de-radicalization efforts moving forward.

DEMOCRATIC PEOPLE'S REPUBLIC OF KOREA (NORTH KOREA)[1]

Overview: The Democratic People's Republic of Korea (DPRK) is not known to have sponsored any terrorist acts since the bombing of a Korean Airlines flight in 1987. On October 11, 2008, the United States rescinded the designation of the DPRK as a state sponsor of terrorism in accordance with criteria set forth in U.S. law, including a certification that the government of the DPRK had not provided any support for international terrorism during the preceding six-month period and the provision by the DPRK of assurances that it will not support acts of international terrorism in the future.

Four Japanese Red Army members who participated in a jet hijacking in 1970 continued to live in the DPRK. The Japanese government continued to seek a full accounting of the fate of 12 Japanese nationals believed to have been abducted by DPRK state entities in the 1970s and 1980s. The DPRK has not yet fulfilled its commitment to reopen its investigations into the abductions.[2] There also continues to be evidence of North Korean involvement in weapons proliferation, in violation of UN Security Council Resolutions 1718 and 1874.

---

1 *This section was inadvertently omitted in the original publication.*
2 *This information was inadvertently omitted in the original publication. It has been in previous editions of this report.*

Legislation and Law Enforcement: In May, the United States re-certified North Korea as "not cooperating fully" with U.S. counterterrorism efforts under Section 40A of the Arms Export and Control Act, as amended. In making the annual determination on "not fully cooperating," we undertake review of a country's overall level of cooperation in our efforts to fight terrorism, taking into account our counterterrorism objectives with that country and a realistic assessment of its capabilities.

Countering Terrorist Finance: The DPRK became a signatory to the Convention for the Suppression of Financing of Terrorism and a party to the Convention Against the Taking of Hostages in November 2001. However, there was no indication the DPRK has taken steps to counter money laundering and terrorist financing threats.

Regional and International Cooperation: The DPRK did not actively participate bilaterally or multilaterally in counterterrorism efforts in 2010.

JAPAN

Overview: Japan continued to take active measures to prevent the spread of terrorism through stringent border security enforcement, counterterrorism capacity building assistance, and legislation aimed at stemming the flow of terrorist financing. In coordination with the U.S. Department of Homeland Security-Customs and Border Protection (CBP), several Japanese agencies have strengthened immigration procedures as well as port and shipping security.

Legislation and Law Enforcement: Japan's Ministry of Foreign Affairs, Japan's Immigration Bureau, the National Police Agency (NPA), and the Ministry of Land, Infrastructure, Transport and Tourism coordinated with the CBP's Immigration Advisory Program on preventing terrorists and other high-risk travelers from boarding commercial aircraft bound for the United States.

Under the Container Security Initiative (CSI), Japanese Customs authorities worked with CBP Officers at four Japanese seaports to review ship manifests and to screen suspicious containers bound for the United States. Under a reciprocal bilateral agreement, Japanese Customs also deploys officers to work with CBP at the Port of Long Beach, California to screen U.S. export shipments bound for Japan.

The NPA and the Public Security Intelligence Agency continued to monitor the activities of Aum Shinrikyo, renamed Aleph, and splinter group Hikari no Wa, or "Circle of Light."

Countering Terrorist Finance: Japan continued to assist counterterrorism capacity building in neighboring countries through dialogue, seminars, workshops, and training. The Japanese Coast Guard, for example, provided capacity building services and training seminars to authorities from states that border the Straits of Malacca. In March, Japan decided to extend Counterterrorism and Security Enhancement grant aid to Uzbekistan. In June, Japan extended similar grant aid to Indonesia.

In March, the Japanese hosted an Aviation Security Ministerial Conference, attended by U.S. Homeland Security Secretary Napolitano, for top officials from the Asia/Pacific region and the International Civil Aviation Organization to discuss ways to bolster global aviation security. Also in March, the Japan-Singapore Joint APEC Seminar on Securing Maritime Trade through Counterterrorism Efforts was held in Tokyo. In June, Japanese officials took part in the Fourth Japan-Republic of Korea (South Korea) Counterterrorism Consultations. The same month, Japan co-chaired the Fifth Japan-ASEAN Counterterrorism Dialogue in Bali, Indonesia. In December, Japan participated in the sixth annual U.S.-Japan-Australia Trilateral Strategic Dialogue Counterterrorism Consultations in Melbourne, Australia.

Regional and International Cooperation: The Diet (Japanese Parliament) amended Customs Act secondary legislation, which addressed in part a Financial Action Task Force recommendation pertaining to cross-border currency declaration and disclosure.

MALAYSIA

Overview: As a result of a combination of effective law enforcement efforts and close counter-terrorism cooperation with the United States and the international community, Malaysia has not suffered a serious incident of terrorism in recent years. Malaysia has been used as a transit and planning site for terrorists, however. Royal Malaysian Police (RMP) cooperated closely with the international community on counterterrorism efforts, and RMP officers received training in a range of counterterrorism skills. The effectiveness of the police in identifying terrorist networks was limited by their continued reliance on the Internal Security Act to detain suspects on the basis of intelligence rather than on information gained through investigations. Moreover, in spite of new measures to tighten immigration requirements for some foreign citizens, the country remained vulnerable to potential terrorist activity as a result of weak border controls and gaps in maritime security in the areas bordering Thailand in Northern Malaysia and the Philippines and Indonesia in Eastern Malaysia. Persons with terrorist affiliations were able to take advantage of these weak controls to travel within Malaysia and to transit to third countries.

2010 Terrorist Incidents: In January, Malaysian police detained 10 persons reportedly involved in a plot to carry out terrorist attacks against Hindu and Buddhist religious shrines in Kuala Lumpur. In February, two Malaysians citizens were kidnapped in Sabah state, by members of the Abu Sayyaf Group terrorist organization, and taken to the Philippines to be held for ransom. The two men were subsequently rescued by Philippine armed forces in late December.

Legislation and Law Enforcement: During 2010, the Royal Malaysian Police Special Task Force-Operations/Counter-Terrorism detained 15 suspected terrorists under the Internal Security Act. Most of those detained were foreigners with connections to Jemaah Islamiya or to Jamaah Anshorut Tauhid, and were later deported to their home countries. At the end of the year, three terrorist suspects remained in detention. The recruiting activities within Malaysian universities of a number of these suspects led the Malaysian Government to more closely scrutinize foreign students and to begin publicizing its counterterrorism successes.

In general, immigration authorities' vetting of arriving travelers was perfunctory, although the Ministry of Home Affairs announced the implementation of a new biometrics system for arriving travelers beginning in December 2010. Malaysian authorities detained terrorist suspects when the authorities became aware of the suspects' presence in the country. Malaysian authorities also actively cooperated with other countries to deport suspect foreigners to their home countries.

Countering Terrorist Finance: Malaysia's central bank (Bank Negara Malaysia) has signed memoranda of understanding on the sharing of financial intelligence with the Financial Intelligence Unit of many countries in the region. Malaysia is an active member of the Asia/Pacific Group on Money Laundering, and its subsidiary Donors and Provider Group for Technical Assistance, and has worked with the World Bank, International Monetary Fund, Asian Development Bank, the UN Counterterrorism Committee Executive Directorate, and the UN Office on Drugs and Crime.

Malaysia acted on UNSCRs 1267 and 1373 requests to freeze terrorist assets. While Malaysia improved the legislative framework to criminalize terrorist financing, there have been no investigations, prosecutions, or convictions related to terrorist financing under this new scheme. The Govern ment of Malaysia continued to use the Internal Security Act as a preventive measure instead of investigating cases.

Regional and International Cooperation: The Malaysian government engaged on issues related to counterterrorism and transnational crime with its neighbors, both bilaterally and in international fora such as the ASEAN and APEC. The Ministry of Foreign Affairs operated the Southeast Asian Regional Center for Counterterrorism, which has served to facilitate the training of Malaysians officials involved in counterterrorism efforts, but has done less to identify forward-looking or regional counterterrorism priorities. The Ministry of Home Affairs announced plans to establish a Counterterrorism Training Center, focused on improving the skills of law enforcement officers, on Langkawi Island.

In September, Malaysian authorities extradited known terrorist Mas Selamat Kastari to Singapore, from where he had been imprisoned and had escaped in 2008. The RMP has a good working relationship with both regional and international law enforcement agencies.

Countering Radicalization and Violent Extremism: Malaysia took the view that "extremists," at least those who have not yet committed a crime, are misguided individuals who can best be treated by rehabilitation rather than by punishment. School curricula and instruction encouraged tolerance and Malaysian authorities were quick to take action when they detected efforts to undermine social harmony. The Malaysian government monitored radical Internet web sites, but generally did not attempt to disrupt these sites, believing it can better follow radical activity by allowing such sites to operate. The government did not have a comprehensive strategic communication approach to counter-radicalization, but during the year, the RMP began to publicize the detentions of terrorist suspects, which has resulted in greater public awareness of the dangers posed by extremists and has led to an increase in public tips to the police regarding activities of extremists, according to RMP contacts.

The RMP operated a de-radicalization program for terrorist suspects in Malaysia's Kamunting Prison. The police employed clerics, family members, and former radicals to convince terrorist suspects to renounce violence. On release from detention, these persons continued to face restrictions on their activities, including curfews and limits on their travel and contacts, until they have demonstrated that they no longer have affiliations with violent extremists.

While the government touts the deradicalization program as highly successful, there were no available figures on the rates of recidivism of those who have completed it.

NEW ZEALAND

Overview: New Zealand continued working cooperatively with the United States and other countries on bilateral, regional, and global levels to fight terrorism, including nuclear terrorism. New Zealand particularly took an active leadership role in the Asia-Pacific region in multilateral counterterrorism organizations. New Zealand focused a great deal of effort on helping build the capacity of small pacific island countries in all areas of counterterrorism and actively contributed to international efforts to counter the radicalization of Islam and violent extremism.

Countering Terrorist Finance: New Zealand is not a major regional or offshore financial center and was a low threat environment for terrorist finance. Under the Financial Transaction Reporting Act 1996, financial institutions were required to report transactions suspected of being linked to money-laundering to the New Zealand Police Financial Intelligence Unit (FIU). In 2010, the FIU received approximately 3,040 Suspicious Transaction Reports.

In February 2010, New Zealand announced its first designations of non-UN listed terrorist entities; 14 non-UN listed entities were designated. All designated terrorist entities are subject to criminal sanctions under New Zealand law and those prosecutions based on non-UN lists are subject to court challenge.

New Zealand provided funding for the Asia-Pacific Group on Money Laundering's 2010 technical assistance and training program with Pacific Island countries.

Regional and International Cooperation: New Zealand actively worked in the Asia-Pacific region on counterterrorism issues and demonstrated a strong commitment to building the counterterrorism capabilities of the small island states of the Pacific region, in particular, legislative and operational capacity building projects.

On November 16-18, New Zealand and the United States co-hosted the Trans-Pacific Symposium on Dismantling Transnational Illicit Networks in Christchurch. Over one hundred officials from 23 Pacific Rim economies and several international organizations participated. The event brought together law enforcement, customs, and other agencies from around the Pacific basin to discuss how to best counter transnational illicit activity, including terrorist-related threats. The event concluded with the Co-Chairs' Summary of Outcomes document in which participants agreed to increase cooperation in the region.

On March 29-30, New Zealand hosted the Second ASEAN Regional Forum (ARF) inter-session meeting on maritime security in Auckland. New Zealand, Indonesia, and Japan jointly chaired the meeting, which included 150 delegates representing the 26 member nations of the ARF with the exception of North Korea.

New Zealand continued its active contribution to the Global Initiative to Combat Nuclear Terrorism (GICNT) with a particular focus on supporting GICNT activities in the Asia-Pacific region and working with GICNT partners to develop a "model GICNT tabletop exercise".

Countering Radicalization and Violent Extremism: The Government of New Zealand continued its funding of counter-radicalization work in Southeast Asia out of the Ministry of Foreign Affairs' Asia Security Fund. Most of New Zealand's funding went to cross-cultural and interfaith projects focused on youth, media, and education. The government also contributed to the development of 'Know Your Neighbors,' a regional education resource aimed at high school students in Southeast Asia and Australasia that sought to build greater understanding and respect of different cultures and religions, thereby helping to bridge some of the divides between societies around the region.

PHILIPPINES

Overview: The ability of terrorist groups, such as Abu Sayyaf Group (ASG), Jemaah Islamiya (JI), and the New People's Army, to conduct terrorist activities inside the Philippines continued to decline. The Philippine government, with U.S. support, has kept constant pressure on terrorist groups, even as their security services were stretched thin by other demands, such as carrying out humanitarian assistance and disaster relief and providing security for the national election in May. The election of President Benigno Simeon "Noynoy" Aquino III did not result in major changes to counterterrorism policy, and his new administration has continued strong counterterrorism cooperation with the United States.

2010 Terrorist Incidents: Capturing the true picture of terrorist incidents in the Philippines is difficult – kidnappings, grenade attacks, and other acts of violence often seem indiscriminate and most remain unsolved. In addition, during the periods before the nationwide elections in May and the village elections in October, there was an upsurge in violence by terrorist groups against political candidates and the general populace to influence the elections. Notable 2010 terrorist incidents included:

- On February 27, an attack in Basilan killed 13 civilians and a paramilitary member, and injured 13 more civilians; allegedly perpetrated by ASG in revenge for the February 21 killing of six ASG militants, including commander, Albader Parad.

- On April 13, ASG members led by Puruji Indama conducted a multiple improvised explosive device (IED) attack in Isabela City, Basilan. The armed assailants wore Philippine National Police (PNP) uniforms, detonated an IED outside a church, shot at fleeing civilians, and ambushed responding Armed Forces of the Philippines (AFP) marines and police officers. Five civilians, three marines, and one police officer were killed in the attack. The assailants had planned a more significant attack, but a second vehicle carrying explosives exploded in an unpopulated area before the attack, killing three ASG members including Indama's brother. A third IED planted in front of a judge's house failed to explode and was later disabled by police. Two ASG members were killed during the fighting that ensued and two more were captured.

- On August 4, a bomb blast at Zamboanga airport injured 24 people, including Sulu provincial governor Sakur Tan and a U.S. citizen, and killed two people, including the bomber. PNP believed that Tan's political rivals targeted him, likely with some assistance from ASG.

Legislation and Law Enforcement: Philippines law enforcement personnel continued vigorous efforts to arrest terrorists and eliminate safe havens and closely coordinated efforts with U.S. law enforcement officers. The Philippine Department of Justice filed a petition with the Regional Trial Court in Basilan for the proscription of the ASG as a terrorist group and 202 identified associates as terrorists. The petition was pending at year's end.

JI associate Zulkipli bin Abdul Hir, aka Marwan, and ASG commander Isnilon Hapilon appeared on the FBI's Most Wanted Terrorist list at numbers 29 and 17, respectively, and were believed to be in the Philippines along with other wanted ASG members. The Philippine National Bureau of Investigation (NBI), PNP, and AFP were each cognizant of the high-profile terrorist fugitives in the Philippines and provided reasonable and consistent attempts to locate and apprehend them.

Significant law enforcement actions and the Philippine judiciary response included:

- On May 21, a Regional Trial Court issued 26 arrest warrants for individuals allegedly involved in the construction or deployment of a large IED at Kagay, Jolo on September 29, 2009, which resulted in the deaths of two U.S. servicemen and one Philippine Marine. The FBI provided investigative assistance.

- On December 17, Madhatta Haipe was sentenced in U.S. District Court, Washington, D.C., to 23 years incarceration for his role in a 1995 hostage taking incident in Mindanao involving U.S. and Philippine citizens. He was apprehended by the NBI in May 2009, pursuant to a provisional arrest warrant and extradited to the United States on August 27, 2009 by the NBI and FBI. This investigation was conducted by the FBI with direct participation by the PNP and NBI.

Countering Terrorist Finance: Legislation amending the anti-money laundering law to criminalize terrorist finance as a stand-alone offense was pending in the Philippine Congress at year's end. The Philippines is a member of the Asia Pacific Group on Money Laundering, a Financial Action Task Force (FATF)-style regional body. The Philippines is likewise a member of the Egmont Group of financial intelligence units (FIUs). The Philippines' FIU must obtain a court order to freeze assets, including those of terrorists and terrorist organizations placed on the UN 1267 Sanctions Committee's consolidated list and the lists of foreign governments. This requirement was inconsistent with the international standard, which calls for the preventative freezing of terrorist assets "without delay" from the time of designation.

Regional and International Cooperation: In 2010, the Philippines ratified the 2007 ASEAN Convention on Counterterrorism. The Philippines hosted the Third U.S.-ASEAN Senior Official's Dialogue on Transnational Crime in October.

Countering Radicalization and Violent Extremism: In 2010, the Philippine government launched a counter-radicalization program called Payapa at Masaganang Pamayanan or PAMANA (Resilient Communities in Conflict Affected Communities). This was President Aquino's flagship program on peace-building, reconstruction, and development in more than 5,000 conflict-affected areas in the country. Activities included addressing the needs of internally displaced people, reintegrating former combatants, and development programs. Additionally, the AFP developed and adopted a Civil Relations Doctrine that is the first of its kind. The AFP conducted operations to counter violent extremism, including through radio programs, public service announcements, a "junior hero program," and publication of a comic book with anti-extremist themes. The PNP also sought to expand its Community Relations Group to address at-risk groups prone to radicalization.

SINGAPORE

Overview: Singapore continued its strong bilateral and multilateral counterterrorism intelligence and law enforcement cooperation. As of December, Singapore held in detention 15 persons with links to terrorist groups. Detainees included members of Jemaah Islamiya (JI) who had plotted to carry out attacks in Singapore in the past and members of the Moro Islamic Liberation Front (MILF). Singapore released 48 persons on Restriction Orders (RO) and two on Suspension Direction (SD); detainees released on ROs and SDs were monitored by the Singapore authorities and required to report to authorities on a regular basis. Among those subjected to religious rehabilitation, there are no reported cases of recidivism to date.

Legislative and Law Enforcement: Singapore used its Internal Security Act (ISA) to arrest and detain suspected terrorists without trial. The ISA authorizes the minister for home affairs, with the consent of the president, to order detention without filing charges if it is determined that a person poses a threat to national security. The initial detention may be for up to two years, and the minister for home affairs may renew the detention for an unlimited number of additional periods of up to two years at a time with the president's consent.

In August, Singapore passed the Hostage Taking Act 2010, which gives effect to the International Convention against the Taking of Hostages.

Singapore's law enforcement actions included:

- In January, Singapore detained JI and MILF member Mohammed Azmi Ali for terrorist activities and placed him in detention under Singapore's Internal Security Act (ISA). Azmi had originally fled Singapore in 2001 following the government's crackdown on JI.

- In February, Singapore released self-radicalized detainee Abdul Basheer Abdul Kader under SD. The government had originally detained Basheer in April 2007 after he had made plans to go to Afghanistan to engage in militant activities.

- In July, Singapore placed Muhammad Anwar Jailani and Muhammad Thahir Shaik Dawood directly on to RO. Both Jailani and Thahir had links to Anwar al-Aulaqi. According to press reports, Thahir had gone to Yemen to seek out al-Aulaqi to engage in militant activities outside of Singapore. He also enrolled in an educational institution run by an associate of Usama bin Ladin.

- Also in July, Singapore announced the detention of soldier Muhammad Fadil Abdul Hamid under Singapore's Internal Security Act. The government announced that Fadil had become self-radicalized and had made contact with al-Qa`ida in the Arabian Peninsula operative Anwar al-Aulaqi, who encouraged him to go to Afghanistan to engage in militant activities. Authorities arrested Fadil before he could depart Singapore.

Countering Terrorist Finance: Singapore cooperated with the United States to identify and freeze terrorist assets. The opening of Singapore's two casinos in 2010 increased concerns about the potential for illicit flows to pass through Singapore. Singapore has implemented legal and regulatory changes involving cash transactions at casinos to better align itself with the international standards for anti-money laundering/counterterrorist financing regimes.

Regional and International Cooperation: In June, the Republic of Singapore Navy participated in the annual Southeast Asia Cooperation Against Terrorism exercise. In November, the Singapore Armed Forces participated in Cooperation 2010, a nine-day joint counterterrorism training exercise with a personnel contingent from China's People's Liberation Army.

Countering Radicalization and Violent Extremism: Singapore maintained a de-radicalization program that focused on countering detainees' extremist ideology. Detainees are required to undergo a program of religious counseling with a group of volunteer religious counselors. Singapore enlists the support of religious teachers and scholars to study JI's ideology to develop teachings to counter the group within Singapore's Muslim community and provide counseling to detainees. Religious counseling for detainees continued after release from detention. Among those individuals released from detention, there were no reported cases of recidivism.

THAILAND

Overview: While officials have long expressed concern that transnational terrorist groups could establish links with southern Thailand-based separatist groups, there have been no indications that transnational terrorist groups were directly involved in the violence in the south, and there was no evidence of direct operational links between southern Thai insurgent groups and regional terrorist networks.

The ethno-nationalist separatist insurgency in Thailand's southernmost provinces of Pattani, Narathiwat, Yala, and portions of Songkhla continued in 2010. A two-month political protest organized by the United Front for Democracy Against Dictatorship (UDD) in Bangkok between March and May 2010 paralyzed the capital, descended into violence, and resulted in 92 deaths. The Government of Thailand has since filed charges under the terrorist-based provisions of the criminal code against a number of the UDD core leaders and fugitive former Prime Minister Thaksin Shinawatra for allegedly having engaged in or abetted acts of domestic terrorism. The circumstances surrounding the violence and the deaths were under investigation at year's end by both the Thai government's Department of Special Investigation (DSI) and an independent fact-finding commission.

Legislation and Law Enforcement: The porous nature of Thailand's southern border with Malaysia remained an issue of concern. At the same time, cross-border law enforcement cooperation based on long association between Thai and Malaysian police officers was good.

On November 16, the Thai government extradited international arms trafficker Viktor Bout to the United States. Bout was indicted in New York for conspiring to kill U.S. nationals and officers, to acquire and use anti-aircraft missiles, and to provide material support to the Revolutionary Armed Forces of Colombia, a designated Foreign Terrorist Organization.

On November 30, Thai police arrested three persons with alleged links through a document forgery ring with links to terrorist groups. The arrests were part of a joint Thai-Spanish operation in which Spanish police also arrested seven other persons in connection with the same document forgery ring.

Thai police, security officials, and court system personnel participated in a series of U.S. training programs sponsored through the Antiterrorism Assistance Program, the Force Protection Detachment (the criminal justice sector capacity building programs for police, prosecutors, and judiciary mounted by the Transnational Crime Affairs Section), and the International Law Enforcement Academy in Bangkok. The Thai National Security Council and its Thai Immigration Bureau reconfirmed its commitment to the U.S.-provided Personal Identification Secure Comparison and Evaluation System (PISCES) program.

Countering Terrorist Finance: The Thai government expressed high-level political commitment to addressing deficiencies that the Financial Action Task Force (FATF) had identified in Thailand's anti-money laundering/counterterrorist finance (AML/CTF) regime, and reported taking multiple steps to address FATF recommendations. Ministry of Finance regulations governing cross border cash carrying were in line with the FATF Special Recommendation on Terrorist Financing. On December 7, the Thai cabinet approved the Ministry of Justice's proposed AML/CTF National Strategy Plan (2011-2015), and as part of the government's actions under this plan, the Anti-Money Laundering Office and a Thai government working group drafted a proposed Counterterrorism Financing Act which, in part, would criminalize the collection or provision of funds for the purpose of supporting terrorist acts or organizations. The Justice Minister has committed to FATF that this legislation will be passed by October 2011. Thailand is a member of the Egmont Group of financial intelligence units.

To comply with international standards and to develop further an effective regime to freeze terrorist funds and assets of designated entities under UNSCRs 1267 and 1373, the Thai government established the Anti-Money Laundering Board in November. The Thai government drafted multiple amendments to its anti-money laundering act, including one to increase the number of predicate offenses and to decrease the minimum cash transaction reporting threshold for electronic-payments. The amendments were submitted to the Council of State where they remained under review at year's end.

Regional and International Cooperation: Thailand participated actively in international counterterrorism efforts through the Asia Pacific Economic Cooperation, ASEAN, the ASEAN Regional Forum, and other multilateral fora.

EUROPE OVERVIEW

European countries remained a focus of terrorist plots in 2010, a year marked by several attempted attacks by violent extremists in Denmark, the first suicide bombing in Scandinavia, and bombings on the Moscow metro and in the Russian North Caucasus. Non-religious violent extremist groups also remained active; anarchists in Greece repeatedly targeted government offices, foreign missions, and symbols of the state in both Greece and other European capitals. Long-active radical nationalist groups like the Kurdistan Workers Party (known as the PKK) in Turkey, and dissident Republican groups in Northern Ireland continued their campaigns of violence. Concerns about potential terrorist activities prompted countries ranging from the UK to Germany to raise their terrorism threat alert levels at various times during the year.

For the most part, however, the year was marked by counterterrorism successes. European countries from Spain to Sweden attempted to strengthen counterterrorism legislation by criminalizing training in terrorist camps and terrorist recruitment. The Government of Spain, with cooperation from the Government of France, had continued success against ETA. Turkey shared draft legislation with the Financial Action Task Force designed to address identified shortcomings in its counter-terrorism-finance laws, and also worked with Iraq and the United States on joint steps against the PKK. Successful prosecutions of terrorist suspects took a toll on facilitation networks across the continent. In Belgium, for example, seven defendants in an ongoing terrorism case, including Malika El-Aroud (the so-called "Internet jihadist") were convicted in May, the first convictions under the country's 2005 terrorism law.

The continuing effectiveness of European security services, close cooperation between and among European countries, and the sheer technical capabilities available to most partner countries enabled authorities to prevent any major terrorist plot from coming to fruition in 2010.

ALBANIA

Overview: The Government of Albania worked on amendments to the terrorism statutes on the Criminal Code, maintained asset freezes against two individuals and thirteen foundations and companies on the UN Security Council's list of identified financers of terrorism, and established a law on the civil forfeiture of assets acquired through criminal activity. The Albania Border Police consistently improved security at border crossing points.

Legislation and Law Enforcement: The Government of Albania sought to revise terrorism statutes of the Criminal Code and established a law on the civil forfeiture of assets acquired through criminal activity. The draft, pending approval by Parliament since November 2010, contains statutes covering acts with terrorist purposes, financing of terrorism, and money laundering. The amendments are based on Financial Action Task Force (FATF) and Committee of Experts on the Evaluation of Anti-Money Laundering Measures and the Financing of Terrorism (MONEYVAL) recommendations, as well as several UN conventions ratified by Albania.

On December 10, local imam Artan Kristo, who in 2002 worked with the al-Qa'ida-linked charity al Haramain Foundation, was found guilty by a court in Durres and sentenced to five years in prison for "publicly inciting and propagating terrorist acts" in the AlbSelafi.net online forum. Kristo, also known as Muhamed Abdullah, appealed the decision and remained in detention.

On December 22, 2009, the First Instance Court for Serious Crimes found Hamzeh Abu Rayyan guilty of hiding funds used to finance terrorism. Rayyan was sentenced to four years of imprisonment and ordered to pay a fine of US $6000. Rayyan appealed to the Supreme Court and on March 24, 2010, the Chief Justice suspended execution of the sentence pending a hearing of the case.

The Albania Border Police (ABP) consistently improved security at border crossing points and the vast areas between the formal crossings, and implemented roving patrols in the mountains along the border resulting in arrests and narcotics seizures.

Countering Terrorist Finance: Albania maintained asset freezes against two individuals and 13 foundations and companies listed under UNSCR 1267. There were no new cases of asset seizure or confiscation for 2010. In total, by the end of Fiscal Year 2010, the government was administering seized assets having a value of US$ 6,848,893, and had confiscated assets valued at US$ 851,998.

The government of Albania has continued to try and improve its Anti-Money Laundering/Counter-terrorist Financing (AML/CTF) Regime. In 2010, the Albanian government proposed amendments to the AML/CTF legislation in order to address deficiencies that had been previously identified by MONEYVAL, the FATF style regional body to which Albania belongs. Albania recently underwent its fourth round of mutual evaluation in April 2011. The report stated that Albania has made "significant progress" in its AML/CTF regime since its last mutual evaluation in 2006, but noted that further progress was required to ensure that its terrorist financing law fully meets international standards, that the FIU has complete operational independence, and that more cases are developed, investigated, and prosecuted.

Regional and International Cooperation: Albania continued to cooperate with regional and multilateral organizations focused on countering terrorism.

ARMENIA

Overview: Armenia took a number of positive steps in the fight against international terrorism, which included improvements to its border security, significant changes to export control laws, and participation by Armenian experts in internationally sponsored anti-terrorism training courses.

Legislation and Law Enforcement: In recent years, Armenia has achieved measured progress in improving its border security. This progress has included the installation of radiation portal alarms at all ports of entry including its main airport, the addition of sensors for increased monitoring of Armenia's border with Georgia, and significant legislative changes in its export control laws. The Armenian Border Guard Service used the automated Border Management Information System (BMIS) at all points of entry, including a BMIS criminal and terrorist watch list updated by the Armenian National Security Service (NSS). In November, the heads of the Armenian NSS, Ministry of Defense, and State Revenue Committee (Customs) established a new Border and Customs Enforcement Operations Task Force to oversee and further enhance border security operations. In November, President Sargsian approved a National Integrated Border Management Strategy.

Countering Terrorist Finance: Armenia ratified the International Convention for Suppression of Acts of Nuclear Terrorism in 2010. Armenia participated in bilateral and multilateral assistance, security, and training initiatives targeted at strengthening its ability to counter terrorism, terrorist financing, and the smuggling of illicit and hazardous materials. Armenia's activity in these initiatives in 2010 included the EU's South Caucasus Integrated Border Management project, which will provide funds to make major upgrades to several of Armenia's border crossing points, thus facilitating enhanced integrated border security operations.

Armenia continued to make progress in counterterrorism cooperation with NATO. Armenia submitted a new Individual Partnership Action Plan that noted Armenia's desire to continue cooperation with NATO on counterterrorism issues, and it participated in the Partnership Action Plan on Terrorism. This participation included sharing intelligence and analysis with NATO, enhancing national counterterrorism training capabilities, and improving border security. NATO and Armenia also cooperated on the establishment of a "situation center" in Yerevan, which assisted in crisis management and counterterrorism coordination.

In December, the OSCE hosted in Yerevan a national expert workshop on countering terrorist use of the Internet and comprehensively enhancing cyber-security.

Regional and International Cooperation: In January, the Council of Europe's Committee of Experts on the Evaluation of Anti-Money Laundering Measures and the Financing of Terrorism (MONEYVAL) published an evaluation report on Armenia. In the report, MONEYVAL noted that the criminal provisions relating to terrorism financing are broadly in line with international standards but further amendments were necessary. The report added that the continuing development of human and technical resources with regard to terrorism financing remained an ongoing challenge.

AUSTRIA

Overview: Austria passed new legislation to outlaw participation in terrorist training camps abroad, signed a bilateral agreement with the United States on Preventing and Combating Serious Crime (PCSC), and concluded a bilateral agreement, also with the United States, on the sharing of forfeited assets from criminal activities. Austria's Parliament adopted a government-sponsored amendment package effective in July that brought its anti-money laundering/countering terrorist financing (AML/CTF) regime more in line with the Financial Action Task Force's (FATF) standards.

According to Austria's counterterrorism agency, the Bureau for the Protection of the Constitution and Counterterrorism (BVT), homegrown violent extremism and terrorism within transnational networks constituted the greatest threat to Austria. Counterterrorism experts noted a growing number of radicalized individuals among second- and third-generation Muslim immigrants and among converts to Islam.

Legislation and Law Enforcement: The BVT served as the key counterterrorism agency within the Ministry of the Interior. An internal review by the National Audit Court called on the Ministry to increase the BVT's human resources for the fight against terrorism, to train more analysts for the protection of critical infrastructure, and to draft strategies for intercultural dialogue and countering violent extremism.

Key counterterrorism legal initiatives included new legislation criminalizing participation in terrorist training camps abroad, signing of a bilateral Austrian-U.S. agreement on PCSC, and a bilateral agreement on sharing confiscated assets from criminal activities.

In February, a Vienna appellate court rejected the request for early release from prison of a 22-year-old Muslim extremist and her husband convicted in 2009 for making terrorist threats against Austria on the Internet. In September, an Austrian court sentenced the 2009 killer of a Sikh guru visiting Austria to life imprisonment. This murder triggered violent riots in India in 2009. In December, an alleged terrorist from Chechnya living in Neunkirchen, Lower Austria, was arrested at Vienna's Schwechat Airport upon his return from Saudi Arabia. The subject of a European arrest warrant issued by Belgian authorities, the man was allegedly part of a terrorist organization suspected of terrorist activity. Extradition proceedings were pending at the end of the year.

Countering Terrorist Finance: Austria closely followed EU policies to fight terrorist financing. Austria has become a more active member of the FATF. In reaction to FATF criticism of Austria in 2009, Austria's Parliament adopted a government-sponsored amendment package, effective July 2010, which brought Austria's AML/CTF regime more in line with FATF standards. The new legislation extends the scope of money laundering offenses to self-laundering, and broadens the conditions for disclosure of information on bank accounts and bank operations during criminal proceedings. It also facilitates processing of mutual legal assistance requests, introduces stricter identification for savings deposits and stronger due diligence obligations for banks, and authorizes Austria's Financial Market Authority to issue regulations mandating additional measures where there are heightened risks, particularly in connection with states where higher money laundering or terrorist financing risks exist. The revised legal framework also provides for more transparency for trusts and foundations and extends the power and responsibility of Austria's Financial Intelligence Unit.

Austria's new Sanctions Act, effective July 1, 2010, facilitates asset seizure, forfeiture, and other counterterrorism measures; and asset freezes pursuant to UN and EU sanctions are based on the Sanctions Law rather than on the Foreign Exchange Act. The new law significantly expands and improves implementation of financial sanctions on terrorists (including measures set forth in directly applicable EU Regulations), expands the range of assets seized, provides for banning travel, bans the rendering of services to designated entities, and establishes administrative and criminal penalties for violations. The Austrian government used the new law, effective July 26, to implement enhanced EU sanctions on Iranian entities.

Regional and International Cooperation: Austria has security partnerships with several countries in the region and the Ministry of the Interior has dispatched counterterrorism liaison officers to a number of Austria's embassies in Southeastern Europe. Austria participated in various regional security platforms, including the Central European Initiative and the Salzburg Forum. It was a founding member of the Pruem Treaty, an agreement among various European states to exchange information regarding DNA, fingerprints, and vehicle registration data of concerned persons and to cooperate against terrorism. Austria chaired the al-Qa'ida/Taliban 1267 Sanctions Committee during its two-year tenure as a non-permanent member of the UNSC in 2009-2010. Austria ratified the two 2005 Protocols on Suppression of Unlawful Acts against the Safety of Maritime Navigation and Fixed Platforms.

In October, Austria, Turkey, and Bosnia-Herzegovina co-sponsored a workshop on national coordination and regional cooperation in counterterrorism matters in Sarajevo. More than 15 countries and regional security organizations attended the UN-organized event. In December, Austrian Interior Minister Maria Fekter signed a cooperation protocol with Russia's Interior Ministry codifying deportation and repatriation procedures for illegal immigrants and Russian/Austrian criminals involved in terrorism, money laundering, and human and drug trafficking.

Countering Radicalization and Violent Extremism: A main component of Austrian efforts to counter violent extremism is to support integration in a holistic way. The Austrian government committed to a National Action Plan for Integration. Most initiatives to promote integration were publicly subsidized and took place at the local and regional level. A national integration award promoted on national TV mobilized many schools and businesses to submit creative project proposals.

AZERBAIJAN

Overview: Azerbaijan actively opposed terrorist organizations seeking to move people, money, and material through the Caucasus. The country stepped up efforts and has had some success in reducing the presence of terrorist facilitators and hampering their activities.

Legislation and Law Enforcement: Law enforcement bodies continued to pursue terrorist groups and facilitators operating in Azerbaijan. In October 2009, a Baku court sentenced two Lebanese nationals, Ali Muhammad Karaki and Ali Hussein Najmeddin, to prison terms of 15 years each, and sentenced four Azerbaijani accomplices to terms of two to 14 years. The court found that the group was planning attacks on the Israeli Embassy. The investigation revealed that Karaki and Hussein were linked to Hizballah and others in Iran. According to press reports, Karaki and Najmeddin were released in a prisoner exchange with Iran and deported in August 2010, along with 12 Iranian nationals.

Countering Terrorist Finance: The Azerbaijani government continued to implement its law on anti-money laundering and counterterrorist financing (AML/CTF) and established a Financial Investigative Unit (FIU). In October, the Central Bank prepared an action plan to bring Azerbaijan's AML/FIU into conformity with the standards of the UN, the Financial Action Task Force (FATF), and other international organizations and conventions. In addition, the Azerbaijan government submitted its plan to the Council of Europe's Committee of Experts on the Evaluation of Anti-Money Laundering Measures and the Financing of Terrorism (MONEYVAL), the FATF-style regional body. MONEYVAL reviewed Azerbaijan's proposals in December and agreed to withdraw its advisory on non-compliance for Azerbaijan, and removed Azerbaijan from the FATF Watch List. The United States worked with the FIU to improve the legal AML/CTF framework, establish information systems, build capacity for AML/CTF stakeholders, and develop a strategy plan for the FIU. Azerbaijan continued to identify possible terrorism-related funding by distributing lists of suspected terrorist groups and individuals to local banks.

Regional and International Cooperation: In September, Azerbaijan and Russia signed a border demarcation agreement regarding Azerbaijan's 390-kilometer border with Russia. On November 18, Azerbaijan signed a security cooperation agreement with Caspian Sea littoral states to coordinate law enforcement efforts aimed at smuggling, narcotics trafficking, organized crime, and terrorism.

BELGIUM

Overview: Belgium's government remained vigilant in its counterterrorism efforts. The Ministers of Interior and Justice oversee a capable but understaffed federal police corps, state security service, threat analysis unit, and federal prosecutor's office. Belgian courts set a high standard for prosecutors to prove a suspect is a terrorist. Terrorism investigations were often long, requiring several months to more than a year before a case can be built that leads to arrests.

Legislation and Law Enforcement: Belgium instituted enhancements to airline passenger screening in December 2009. Air cargo screening enhancements were adopted in summer 2010. A law that allows Belgium's security services to use new investigative techniques against suspects in terrorism and national security cases came into effect in September 2010.

Seven defendants in an ongoing terrorism case, including Malika El-Aroud (the so-called "Internet jihadist") were convicted in May under Belgium's 2005 terrorism law. This was the first successful prosecution under the law. Nine suspected terrorists were detained on November 23 and were held in custody through the end of the year. Seven of the nine, plus an additional suspect detained later, were arrested in Antwerp; they were accused of membership in the Caucasus Emirate, a terrorist organization that seeks to create an emirate in the northern Caucasus. Two suspects were detained in Brussels for financing and recruiting in Iraq and Afghanistan.

The Belgian government continued to work with the U.S. government on the extradition to the United States of convicted terrorist Nizar Trabelsi, who had not yet exhausted his appeal options on the extradition request.

Countering Terrorist Finance: Belgium led the effort in late 2009 to find a solution that would allow EU countries to continue to freeze terrorist assets under UNSCR 1267 after European court cases ruled there must be a workable means for a person to contest his or her listing and be delisted, if appropriate. Belgium also hosted meetings to respond to the European Court's 2010 ruling that UNSCR 1904 did not go far enough in allowing those listed to contest a listing. Belgium is a member of the Financial Action Task Force.

Regional and International Cooperation: Belgium chaired the EU's counterterrorism working group during Belgium's Rotating Presidency of the European Council from July 1 to December 31. Belgium voted in favor of UNSCR 1904.

Countering Radicalization and Violent Extremism: Belgium's Ministry of Interior began developing its own Countering Violent Extremism (CVE) strategy in 2010. The Belgian Federal Police distributed a Community Policing Preventing Radicalism and Terrorism guide to assist local police to recognize the signs of radicalization. The Belgian police worked on this guide for several years with seven other EU member states.

Belgium held two CVE seminars in September and October during its rotating EU presidency. Participants, including representatives of the U.S. Department of Homeland Security, the State Department, and the National Counterterrorism Center, discussed approaches governments can take to recognize and counteract violent extremism.

BOSNIA AND HERZEGOVINA

Overview: Bosnia and Herzegovina made progress increasing its counterterrorism capacity in 2010 and improved its interagency communication and cooperation between the various state and entity-level law enforcement agencies. Joint operations were conducted against suspected terrorist groups, the State Court prosecuted perpetrators of acts of terrorism, and Bosnia revamped its Counterterrorism Task Force to better counter potential terrorist threats.

2010 Terrorist Incidents: On June 27, a bomb was detonated at a police headquarters in the central Bosnian town of Bugojno resulting in the death of one police officer and injuries to six other officers. The State Prosecutor indicted six suspects on terrorism charges for their roles in the attack. The suspects reportedly belonged to a local violent extremist movement.

Legislation and Law Enforcement: In order to harmonize Bosnia and Herzegovina's criminal code with UN and EU standards related to countering terrorism, the parliament adopted new legislation in January to criminalize terrorist recruitment, terrorist training, and the incitement of terrorist attacks.

The trial against Rijad Rustempasic and three other defendants on terrorism and weapons trafficking charges commenced in February. In early February, in an extensively coordinated effort involving several different law enforcement institutions and police forces, approximately 600 police and law enforcement officers conducted a raid on the village of Gornja Maoca, where authorities suspected the local religious extremist movement of involvement in criminal activity. A significant amount of evidence was seized during the raid and the suspects remained under investigation by law enforcement authorities at year's end.

In December, the State Prosecutor's Office and State Investigative and Protective Agency (SIPA) began discussions on forming an operational Joint Task Force based on the FBI model to deal with counterterrorism. The Ministry of Security will fund the Joint Task Force and it will operate out of SIPA. The Ministry of Security recently adopted a strategy to prevent and counter terrorism covering the period of 2010-2013.

Countering Terrorist Finance: In August, the Directors of the Federation and Republika Srpska Tax Administrations and SIPA agreed to form an operations team to evaluate financial information of persons and groups of interest to counter terrorist financing. This initiative will assist the Joint Task Force's focus on the financing of terrorism-related activity.

Regional and International Cooperation: Bosnia and Herzegovina's law enforcement agencies regularly interact with their U.S. and European counterparts on counterterrorism investigations. Bosnia ratified the Amendment to the Convention on the Physical Protection of Nuclear Material.

Countering Radicalization and Violent Extremism: In December in Sarajevo, the Ministry of Security co-sponsored the OSCE's workshop on Suppressing Terrorist Financing and Countering Violent Extremism and Radicalization that Leads to Terrorism. The OSCE sponsored-event brought together representatives from the NGO-sector, banking industry, and representatives from 15 countries and regional organizations.

CYPRUS

Overview: The Government of Cyprus was responsive to efforts to block and freeze terrorist assets, implemented Financial Action Task Force (FATF) recommendations, and conformed to EU counterterrorism directives. Cyprus continued to allow blanket overflight and landing rights to U.S. military aircraft supporting operations in Iraq and Afghanistan, and provided regular, routine protection for transiting personnel. Since 1974, the northern part of Cyprus has been administered by Turkish Cypriots and proclaimed itself the "Turkish Republic of Northern Cyprus (TRNC)" in 1983. The United States does not recognize the TRNC, nor does any country other than Turkey. The largely porous, lightly patrolled "green line" separating the two sides is routinely exploited for trafficking people, narcotics, and other illicit goods.

Members of the Kurdistan Workers' Party (PKK) engaged in fundraising in Cyprus and transited Cyprus en route to third countries. Cypriot authorities believed there was little risk the group would conduct operations in Cyprus and maintained that the Cypriot government was fulfilling all responsibilities with respect to the EU designation of the PKK as a terrorist organization.

Legislation and Law Enforcement: In November, the Republic of Cyprus Parliament passed a law to bring Cyprus into conformity with European Council terrorism guidelines. The law specified what constituted a terrorist group and formally accepted the list of terrorist organizations compiled by the European Council. The law identified terrorist offenses and corresponding criminal penalties. In October, the Government of Cyprus designated a Counterterrorism Coordinator. In June, an amendment was made to the Constitution with the intent of enabling police to obtain information – provided the Attorney General secured a court order – from telephone and other communications of persons suspected of serious crimes and in the interest of national security.

Countering Terrorist Finance: The United States and Cyprus cooperated closely on anti-money laundering and counterterrorist financing (AML/CTF) issues. The Cypriot Anti-Money Laundering Authority implemented new UNSCR 1267 listings immediately and informally tracked suspect names listed under U.S. Executive Order 13224. The Cypriot government maintained a "Prevention and Suppression of Money laundering Activities Law" that contained provisions on tracing and confiscating assets. In June, Cyprus amended its legislation to enhance its asset freezing and confiscation regime. All financial entities must have a national AML/CTF coordinator who will be responsible for the group's domestic and foreign offices, and banks must have a separate compliance department and apply risk management procedures.

In 2008, the FATF listed the Turkish Cypriot-administered area as a jurisdiction susceptible to money laundering. In February 2009, FATF found "significant progress" had been made. However, implementation of Turkish Cypriot measures to counter AML lagged in 2010.

Regional and International Cooperation: The de facto division of the island has precluded counterterrorism cooperation between the two communities' law enforcement authorities, and between Cyprus and Turkey. In the Turkish Cypriot-administered area, issues of status and recognition inevitably restricted the ability of authorities to cooperate on counterterrorism with international organizations and countries other than Turkey. Turkish Cypriots cannot sign treaties, UN conventions, or other international agreements, and lacked the legal and institutional framework necessary to counter money laundering and terrorist financing effectively. Within these limitations, however, Turkish Cypriots cooperated in pursuing specific counterterrorism objectives.

Cyprus signed the Beijing Convention on the Suppression of Unlawful Acts Relating to International Civil Aviation and the Protocol to the Convention for the Suppression of Unlawful Seizure of Aircraft at the conclusion of an ICAO diplomatic conference in September.

DENMARK

Overview: Denmark has developed both short-term and long-term counterterrorism strategies. In the short term, terrorist networks and groups were constantly monitored through intelligence, police, and military efforts. In the long term, Denmark focused on factors that counter radicalization and recruitment to terrorism, including integration, anti-discrimination, active citizenship, democratization, protection of human rights, conflict prevention, and focused development assistance.

Since the re-printing of the cartoons of the Prophet Mohammed in February 2008 by newspapers across Europe, Denmark and Danish interests have been considered high-priority terrorist targets among violent extremists. There were new indications that terrorist groups abroad conspired to send terrorists to Denmark to carry out terrorist attacks. Statements from al-Qa'ida members and related groups underlined their continued focus on Denmark.

2010 Terrorist Incidents: There were at least three attempted terrorist attacks in 2010. In January, an individual sought to attack Danish cartoonist Kurt Westergaard in his residence. The perpetrator was arrested before he could harm Westergaard and was charged with attempt to commit a terrorist act. In September, an individual prematurely detonated a bomb at the Hotel Joergensen in Copenhagen, injuring himself. The bomb was possibly meant for Jyllands-Posten, the newspaper that originally commissioned and published the cartoons. In December, police in Copenhagen and Stockholm arrested five individuals for conspiring to commit acts of terrorism. The target was also thought to be Jyllands-Posten.

Legislation and Law Enforcement: Two Danish agencies were most involved in countering terrorist threats in Denmark: the Danish Security and Intelligence Service (PET) and the Danish Defense Intelligence Service (FE). PET and FE maintained a close and collaborative relationship. This relationship was deepened through the establishment of the Center for Terror Analysis (CTA). CTA provided strategic and tactical support in the form of systemically prepared assessments of terrorist threats against Denmark.

In March, the Copenhagen City Court ruled in a case involving terrorist financing, sentencing an individual to six-months in prison for attempting to provide financial support to terrorist groups such as the Revolutionary Armed Forces of Columbia and the Popular Front for the Liberation of Palestine.

Countering Terrorist Finance: In January, PET published a pamphlet in conjunction with the Professional Association for Fundraising Organization entitled "Your Contributions Can Be Misused," as part of its work in preventing terrorist financing. Based on recommendations identified in the Financial Action Task Force Mutual Evaluation of June 2006, Denmark has made significant advances with respect to Anti-Money Laundering and Combating the Financing of Terrorism (AML/CTF). Because of its close cooperation with Greenland and the Faroe Islands, over which it has sovereignty, Denmark has sufficiently implemented the Financial Action Task Force recommendations in order to be considered for removal from the regular follow-up process, with a view to only submitting biennial updates. However, Denmark needs further development in areas such as incorporating Greenland and the Faroe Islands in legislation with respect to AML/CTF.

Regional and International Cooperation: The Danish government continued to cooperate with international organizations, particularly within the UN framework and through the EU.

Countering Radicalization and Violent Extremism: In order to understand the dynamics behind terrorism and become more effective in countering it, the Danish Institute for International Studies (DIIS) has conducted research on the different aspects of radicalization and the link with terrorism. As part of its 2010 budget, the Danish government allocated approximately US$ 1.8 million to DIIS for its continued research on terrorism.

The Danish government also supported the establishment of the Center for Studies in Islamism and Radicalization (CIR) based in the Political Science Department at Aarhus University. CIR research has focused on three major topics: radicalization, recruitment, and the international consequences of political Islam. Because of efforts of Danish and foreign researchers, CIR published four major research reports during 2010 on radicalization and recruitment in Denmark, Italy, and England.

Development assistance was an important part of the overall Danish effort against international terrorism and radicalization. In April, the Danish government established a new US$ 25+ million inter-ministerial stabilization fund to promote the coordination of civil and military efforts. There was also a strong civil society component to the Danish strategy. Groups such as the International Humanitarian Service (IHB) contributed by sending civilians to conflict and crisis areas to encourage peace and stability. The IHB is a collection of civilians who are trained to participate in international development projects that are coordinated through the Danish Ministry of Foreign Affairs.

FRANCE

Overview: Several public announcements by al-Qa'ida (AQ) and other groups reiterated that French interests remained key targets. In September, concerns about the threat of al-Qa'ida in the Islamic Maghreb (AQIM) prompted the Government of France to raise the color-coded alert system to the second highest security posture. Several false alerts occurred in the latter part of 2010 resulting in evacuations of the Eiffel Tower (on two occasions), two Paris train stations, an airport in Martinique, and the Notre Dame de Lourdes shrine. The French have responded by becoming more involved in the Sahel and the Maghreb, working closely with the United States to build the capacity of African nations to counter terrorist groups in Africa before they can attack in France itself. French authorities made multiple arrests throughout the year and claimed to have prevented two planned attacks in 2010. France has shown both a robust capability to track and prevent internal threats as well as a readiness to engage in regional dialogue, training, and capacity building to minimize the risk of terrorist events.

2010 Terrorist Incidents: Traditionally, local Corsican separatists, Basque Fatherland and Liberty (ETA) members, and ultra-left anarchist factions have been responsible for the majority of attacks and arrests classified as terrorism in France. In 2010, there were no attacks related to the ultra left or violent extremists on French soil; there were however more than 80 persons arrested in cases related to terrorism.

Corsica: While there were a larger number of attacks by Corsican separatists in 2010 than in 2009, there were fewer fatal attacks by Corsican separatists in 2010.

ETA: Arrests and weapons seizures in 2010, combined with the cumulative effect of years of joint French-Spanish counterterrorism operations, effectively decapitated ETA's leadership and neutralized its capacity to sustain a prolonged operational campaign.

Kidnapping: Kidnapping for ransom has become a major concern for the French government. In 2010, 10 French citizens were taken hostage by AQ affiliates. AQIM claimed responsibility for eight hostages, five were taken on September 16 in Niger and three were taken on September 22 in Nigeria. The Taliban claimed responsibility for two hostages taken in Kabul on November 3. In addition, one French intelligence officer who was kidnapped in 2009 in Somalia remained in captivity. French hostage Michel Germaneau was killed in July by AQIM.

Legislation and Law Enforcement: In the first half of the year, 62 suspected ETA members were arrested in France. In February, police arrested the group's top leader in France in a joint Spanish-French pre-dawn raid. In March, the shooting of a French police officer near Paris during a bungled getaway was ETA's last fatal attack and believed to be the first murder of a French police officer by that organization. In April 2009, the French government formed a joint security committee with Spain to fight terrorism and drug trafficking. The group, which is an expansion of existing police cooperation targeted at ETA, created a joint general staff headquarters on security to lead the fight on terrorism. Less than 18 months later on September 5, ETA called for a halt to all armed attacks and is actively seeking talks with the Spanish government.

The following high profile arrests took place in 2010:

- On February 28, French police arrested Ibon Gogeaskoetxea Arronategui, suspected military chief of ETA.

- On October 3, a French citizen suspected of being an AQ operative was arrested in Naples, Italy for possession of bomb making materials.

- On October 5, 12 individuals were arrested in the South of France and accused of running a foreign fighter pipeline to Afghanistan.

- On November 26, a 27-year-old French citizen was arrested and prosecuted under suspicion of having been involved in a terrorist cell. He is accused of participating in terrorist activities in the Afghan/Pakistan border region.

Countering Terrorist Finance: The French government has a comprehensive anti-money laundering/ counterterrorist financing (AML/CTF) regime and is an active partner in international efforts to control money laundering and terrorist financing, including its prominent role as a founding member of the Financial Action Task Force. France actively participated in UN 1267 and 1373 Committee sessions. France maintains the ability to designate individuals or entities under French domestic authorities in addition to those designated by EU regulations.

Regional and International Cooperation: France was actively engaged with the UNSC Counterterrorism Committee, the G8's Counterterrorism Action Group, the UNSCR 1267 Sanctions Committee (for the Taliban and AQ), and the European Council's Antiterrorism Strategy action plan. The French government undertook counterterrorism operations with other countries including the UK, Belgium, Germany, Italy, and Spain.

Countering Radicalization and Violent Extremism: France continued implementing programs to address radicalization and extremism using social and economic incentives to reduce the susceptibility of at-risk populations. Of particular note, the French government went to great efforts to train police personnel to be aware of the signs of radicalization. In 2010, the French government began to consider ways to address radicalization through after school programs for at-risk youth, greater access to higher education, and increased economic mobility. In addition, the French government offered imams a professional training program run by mainstream Muslim leaders.

GEORGIA

Overview: The Georgian government continued to improve border security and monitor terrorist finance. It also took steps to implement the requirements of several UNSCRs on counterterrorism and worked with the United States and several EU countries on counterterrorism issues. The Georgian government investigated and arrested several suspects involved in terrorism-related activities, including individuals involved in smuggling nuclear and radioactive substances. Its lack of control of Abkhazia and South Ossetia limited its ability to counter terrorism in these regions and to secure its border with Russia.

2010 Terrorist Incidents:

- On September 22, an improvised explosive device (IED) detonated about 100 meters from the U.S. Embassy buildings. Police destroyed another IED that was located in the same area. No one was injured.

- On October 7, an IED was discovered on a railway bridge near Chaladidi village in Western Georgia's Samegrelo-Zemo Svaneti region. The IED failed to detonate, and no one was injured.

- On October 22, two IEDs exploded near a train station in Tbilisi. No one was injured.

- On November 28, one IED exploded in front of the Labor Party office in Tbilisi, killing one woman. On the same day, another device exploded in front of a building, which housed a grocery store and apartments, in the Mukhiani district in Tbilisi.

Open source reporting indicated that several possibly terrorism-related incidents occurred in the separatist territory of Abkhazia. Information on incidents in the separatist regions of Abkhazia and South Ossetia is limited and in many cases has not been corroborated because the Georgian government does not have control over these territories. Foreign embassies and international missions have limited access to these areas.

Legislation and Law Enforcement: In early 2010, President Saakashvili tasked the National Security Council with preparing a decree to establish the Permanent National Interagency Antiterrorist Commission. The purpose of this commission is to implement the requirements of UNSCR 1267 and subsequent resolutions, UNSCR 373, and Georgian policies on countering terrorism. The commission will also be responsible for coordination between appropriate agencies and making recommendations aimed at improving Georgia's counterterrorism efforts.

The U.S. and Georgian governments worked together to improve border security. The U.S. government funded programs that focused on the identification, investigation, and detention of criminals at the Georgian border; the detection of nuclear or radioactive material; the targeting and inspection of high-risk conveyances, cargo, and travelers; detecting contraband; and surveillance techniques. In addition, the U.S. Coast Guard provided training to Georgian officials in maritime law enforcement and the use of the Incident Command System.

In early December, Georgian police arrested six suspects believed to be responsible for a series of explosions in Tbilisi. In addition, the Georgian government accused two individuals living in Abkhazia and a Russian military officer of being involved in the attacks and requested the Russian government's help in detaining and interrogating those individuals.

In November, two Armenian nationals were sentenced to 13 and 14 years for smuggling 18 grams of highly enriched uranium (HEU) into Georgia. The defendants were arrested with the 18 grams of HEU in Tbilisi in March. The defendants attempted to sell the substance to undercover agents of Georgia's Ministry of Internal Affairs.

Countering Terrorist Finance: Georgia is a member of the Committee of Experts on the Evaluation of Anti-Money Laundering Measures and the Financing of Terrorism (MONEYVAL). It has developed laws and infrastructure needed to counter money laundering and terrorist financing but did not meet standards in investigating and prosecuting money laundering cases and fell short in enforcing anti-money laundering and terrorist financing reporting requirements.

Regional and International Cooperation: Georgia ratified the International Convention for Suppression of Acts of Nuclear Terrorism and continued its counterterrorism cooperation with regional and multilateral organizations. Georgia signed bilateral agreements with Estonia, France, Italy, and Austria in 2009-2010. These agreements covered a broad range of issues, including counterterrorism. Georgia was working on similar agreements with the Czech Republic, Bulgaria, Germany, Lithuania, and Malta at year's end.

GERMANY

Overview: German security officials indicated that the threat from violent extremism remained high and that terrorist groups continued to target Germany. In November, Interior Minister de Maizière warned about an increased likelihood of a terrorist attack in Germany and ordered heightened security measures at airports, railway stations, and other public sites. As of late 2010, more than 1,000 individuals were monitored by security authorities, 129 of whom were considered dangerous. Authorities estimated that roughly 220 individuals, both German nationals and permanent residents, have undergone paramilitary training since the early 1990s at terrorist training camps, primarily located in the border regions of Afghanistan and Pakistan. Approximately 110 of these individuals have returned to Germany and 10 of them were in custody at year's end. Germany investigated, arrested, and prosecuted numerous terrorism suspects and disrupted terrorist-related groups within its borders with connections to religious extremist, Kurdish nationalist, and Marxist-Leninist terrorist organizations. Authorities conducted approximately 390 active investigations against 405 terrorist suspects, the largest number conducted to date. Of these investigations, 129 were Afghanistan-related. Throughout the year, a number of terrorist organizations, including the German Taliban Mujahedin and the Islamic Movement of Uzbekistan, released videos featuring German speakers.

2010 Terrorist Incidents: On November 2, a package bomb postmarked from Greece and addressed to Chancellor Merkel was detected at the Chancellery and destroyed. One of the two Greeks subsequently arrested in Athens allegedly belonged to the group "Conspiracy of Fire Nuclei."

Legislation and Law Enforcement: In reaction to the October 28 parcel bomb plot from Yemen, an interagency task force on air cargo security on December 8 recommended procedural changes. The federal police were given increased authority at airports and they implemented more frequent spot checks of cargo companies.

German courts began trials or reached verdicts in a number of notable counterterrorism cases, including:

- On March 4, four violent extremists belonging to the Islamic Jihad Union (IJU) cell arrested in Sauerland were found guilty of planning to attack U.S. diplomats, soldiers, and civilians. They received five to 12 year sentences.

- On July 19, a court sentenced Turkish citizen Oemer Ozdemir to six years and German citizen Sermet Ilgen to two years and six months for supporting/belonging to al-Qa'ida (AQ).

- On October 20, the Federal Prosecutor's office charged seven Germans and one Turkish citizen with supporting AQ, al-Qa'ida in Iraq (AQI), Ansar al-Islam, and the Global Islamic Media Front's German section.

In 2010, German law enforcement authorities arrested a number of individuals suspected of involvement in terrorism. Prominent new actions and arrests included:

- Eric Breininger, a German citizen, was reportedly killed in Waziristan in late April. Breininger, an IJU member, appeared in extremist videos and is suspected of having ties with the IJU Sauerland cell.

- On July 4, authorities arrested Syrian national Hussam S. on suspicion of recruiting for AQ, AQI, al-Qa'ida in the Islamic Maghreb, and the IJU. Hussam S. was suspected of about 100 counts of posting criminal propaganda material online.

- On July 12, Interior Minister de Maizière banned the Frankfurt-based Hamas-affiliated International Humanitarian Relief Organization.

Countering Terrorist Finance: Germany is a member of the Financial Action Task Force, and its Financial Intelligence Unit is a member of the Egmont Group. Of the 9,046 suspicious transaction reports filed in 2009 (2010 figures were not available at year's end), 98 were filed for suspected terrorist financing, and an additional 415 were examined for possible links to terrorist financing. Germany remained a strong advocate of the UNSCR 1267 al-Qa'ida/Taliban sanctions regime.

Regional and International Cooperation: Germany ratified the Amendment to the Convention on the Physical Protection of Nuclear Material. Germany continued to participate in multilateral counterterrorism initiatives, including the G8 Roma-Lyon and Counterterrorism Action Group.

Countering Radicalization and Violent Extremism: On July 19, the German Federal Office for the Protection of the Constitution launched an opt-out program for violent extremists called HATIF, which is the Arabic term for telephone and also the abbreviation in German for "Heraus Aus Terrorismus und Islamistischem Fanatismus", or "leaving terrorism and Islamist fanaticism." The Interior Ministry also continued a project first launched in 2001 to stop radicalization among young right-wing offenders. The program was expanded in 2007 to include young militants and ran in eight states. The recidivism rate of participants was very low. In 2010, the Interior Ministry also continued a project in three states to counter radicalization of young delinquents influenced by violent extremist ideology.

GREECE

Overview: Large cities in Greece continued to face a significant challenge from domestic terrorism. Throughout the year in Athens and Thessaloniki, anarchists attacked banks, police stations, the homes and offices of politicians, and other "imperialist-capitalist" targets with weapons such as improvised explosive devices and Molotov cocktails. Police arrested suspected members of Revolutionary Struggle, but attacks by other terrorist groups continued, resulting in six deaths. Of the six, two were killed by bombings, one in a targeted killing, and three in an arson attack on a bank.

2010 Terrorist Incidents: Athens and Thessaloniki together experienced hundreds of security incidents, including incendiary and explosive strikes, as well as attacks involving small arms, grenades, and other infantry-style weaponry. Extremists struck businesses, Greek law enforcement, journalists, embassies, and for the first time, targets outside of Greece. Some of the more significant attacks included:

- Conspiracy of Fire Nuclei claimed responsibility for a continuing series of attacks in March, May, November, and December that targeted political groups, foreign embassies, leaders of foreign governments, and symbols of the Greek state.

- A bomb left outside the Athens office of a corporate management company killed a fifteen-year-old Afghan immigrant boy on March 28 and blinded his younger sister, when he apparently when he triggered the bomb by accident. The perpetrators remained unknown.

- A parcel bomb, addressed to Minister of Citizen Protection Michalis Chrysochoidis, killed Chrysochoidis's aide, police Lieutenant Colonel Yorgos Vassilakis, on June 24 at Ministry of Citizen Protection headquarters. An anonymous group claimed responsibility.

- Sect of Revolutionaries claimed responsibility for the July 19 assassination of blogger and radio station executive Sokratis Giolias outside his residence in Athens – the group's first operation after 13 months of inactivity – and threatened further attacks against police, government employees, journalists, and others as part of a stated desire to turn Greece into a "war zone."

Legislation and Law Enforcement: The following arrests/court actions occurred in 2010:

- In April, police arrested six suspected members of the domestic terrorist organization Revolutionary Struggle (RS), after following the trail of physical evidence obtained at the scene of a deadly shootout between police and suspects in suburban Athens on March 9. In addition to the arrests, police discovered sites associated with the group, which contained extensive evidence, including bombs, ammunition, attack plans, and the rocket launcher RS is believed to have used in an attack on the U.S. Embassy in 2007.

- On July 26, the Supreme Court rejected final appeals by six convicted members of the Revolutionary Organization 17 November (17N), which was responsible for deaths of 23 people between 1975 and 2002. The Court sent the cases of two less prominent 17N convicts back to a lower court for review.

- On November 1, police arrested two suspected members of Conspiracy of Fire Nuclei in Athens soon after they had dropped off parcel improvised explosive devices (IEDs) at a courier service office. The two suspects were carrying two unsent parcel IEDs in a backpack when they were detained by Greek authorities.

Greek authorities participated in the Container Security Initiative and cooperated with U.S. officials on information sharing, as well as the training of Greek security and customs officials, and judicial personnel. Greece continued to work with the EU border agency FRONTEX to strengthen border security.

Countering Terrorist Finance: Since a critical 2007 Financial Action Task Force (FATF) report, Greek authorities have made substantial progress in meeting shortcomings identified by FATF, including passing a new anti-money laundering/counterterrorist finance law that addressed most of the FATF recommendations. Most recently, Greece ratified the UN Convention against Transnational Organized Crime and amended its law to criminalize and broadly define terrorist finance offenses. The government drafted legislation introducing suspected terrorists' designation and listing, assets freezing, and de-listing procedures in accordance with UNSCRs 1267 and 1373. Given the absence of specific legislation governing the freezing of terrorist assets, Greece used an administrative procedure to freeze assets of suspected terrorists designated domestically or upon request of foreign authorities. Though Greek authorities worked to improve the effectiveness of the Greek Financial Intelligence Unit, additional work remained to meet international standards.

Regional and International Cooperation: Greece participated in regional information exchange and seminars through such bodies as the OSCE, the Southeast European Cooperative Initiative regional Center for Combating Trans-Border Crime, and the Organization of Black Sea Economic Cooperation. Greece is a member of the UN Counterterrorism Committee.

Countering Radicalization and Violent Extremism: Municipal governments in Athens established immigrant councils to foster dialogue on issues such as discrimination, social benefits for immigrants, legalization, employment, and security. Police officials met with representatives of the different immigrant communities to discuss ways to address discrimination and incidents of police abuse.

IRELAND

Overview: In 2010, violent actions by members of the Real Irish Republican Army and the Continuity Irish Republican Army terrorist groups committed in neighboring Northern Ireland *(see UK country report for further information on Northern Ireland)* were traced back to support provided by persons living in the Republic of Ireland. The immediate targets of violence were the law enforcement and security structures of neighboring Northern Ireland and the ongoing peace process. Relations between the U.S. government and Irish law enforcement officials were increasingly positive.

Countering Terrorist Finance: Ireland is a member of the Financial Action Task Force (FATF). The Criminal Justice (Money Laundering and Terrorist Financing) Bill of 2010 enacted the EU's third money laundering directive into Irish law, which gave effect to several FATF recommendations. The act consolidated Ireland's existing anti-money laundering and counterterrorist finance laws and increased the obligations on a wide range of individuals and organizations to disclose information related to suspected money laundering and terrorist financing.

Regional and International Cooperation: Ireland actively participated in the counterterrorism efforts of the EU, the OSCE, and the UN.

Countering Radicalization and Violent Extremism: The Government of Ireland continued significant efforts to mitigate conditions conducive to the radicalization of minority groups. These measures included social benefits, language training, and an ombudsman's office to advocate on behalf of immigrants.

ITALY

Overview: Italy continued aggressively to investigate and prosecute terrorism suspects, dismantle terrorist-related cells within its borders, and maintained high-level professional cooperation with its international partners in all areas. Terrorist activity by anarchists and other violent extremists remained a threat.

2010 Terrorist Incidents: On December 23, letter bombs exploded in the Swiss and Chilean embassies in Rome, wounding two. On December 27, police defused a parcel bomb that was delivered to the Greek embassy. A group called the Informal Anarchist Federation claimed responsibility. On December 29, two small explosive devices caused minor damage to the Northern League party office in the town of Gemonio, province of Varese, near the residence of Northern League party leader and Minister for Federalism Umberto Bossi.

Legislation and Law Enforcement: The Italian Civil Aviation Authority (ENAC) began a pilot program testing the use of body scanning devices at four airports. After initial results raised concerns about privacy and accuracy, ENAC began collaborating with the U.S. Transportation Security Administration to identify software that will address the concerns.

The Italian government continued to make use of reinforced counterterrorism legislation enacted in 2005, which facilitated detention of suspects, mandated arrest for crimes involving terrorism, and expedited procedures for expelling persons suspected of terrorist activities.

Italy participated in the Container Security Initiative. On March 29, the U.S. Ambassador to Italy and Italian Customs Agency Director signed a Memorandum of Understanding launching the Megaports Initiative to deploy nuclear material scanners in Italian ports.

Law enforcement actions in 2010 included:

- On February 25 and 27, 12 Turkish nationals and an Italian were arrested in Venice and Modena. They were accused of training individuals to fight for the Kurdistan Workers' Party.

- On July 6, a Monza court acquitted two Moroccans, Abdelkader Ghafir and Rahid Ilhami, arrested in December 2008 and charged with international terrorism. They had been accused of allegedly supporting al-Qa'ida and planning violent attacks in Italy. Rahid Ilhami was sentenced to 19 months in jail for abetting illegal immigration.

- On July 8, a Milan court sentenced 15 Tunisians, Algerians, and Moroccans to prison terms between six months and eight and a half years for international terrorism. Their Milan-based cell recruited followers, maintained contacts with foreign extremists, and planned to send suicide bombers to Iraq and Afghanistan. Ten other persons were acquitted.

- On July 9, Mohammed Game, who attempted a suicide attack against an Italian army barracks in Milan in October 2009, was sentenced to 14 years in prison and fined 100,000 euros (US$ 142,000). His accomplice, Mahmoud Abdelaziz Kol, received a four-year sentence, while another accomplice, Mohamaed Imbaeya Israfel, awaited trial.

- On October 2, police arrested Ryad Hannouni in Naples after tips from French police. Hannouni was reported to have traveled from near the Pakistan-Afghanistan border and to have carried bomb-making materials on his person when arrested. On November 29, he was transferred to France on a European arrest warrant.

Countering Terrorist Finance: Italy worked closely with the United States on anti-money laundering and information sharing, and cooperated with other foreign governments as an active member of the Financial Action Task Force and the Egmont Group. Italy also participated in the UNSCR 1267 process, both as a sponsoring and co-sponsoring nation.

Regional and International Cooperation: Italy supported counterterrorism efforts through the G8 Lyons-Roma Group (including capacity building through the Counterterrorism Action Group), OSCE, NATO, the UN, and the EU. Italy contributed personnel to various regional training centers, such as the South East Asia Regional Centre on Counterterrorism in Malaysia, the Joint Centre on Law Enforcement Cooperation in Indonesia, and the African Union's Anti-Terrorism Centre in Algeria.

Countering Radicalization and Violent Extremism: The Ministry of Justice Penitentiary Police started a non-governmental organization-administered counter-radicalization program placing moderate imams in the three prisons where Muslims convicted of terrorism are incarcerated.

KOSOVO

Overview: The Government of Kosovo cooperated with the United States on terrorism-related issues and made progress in passing legislation to fight terrorism, including the Kosovo Security Strategy, the Law on Trade of Strategic Goods, and the Law on the Prevention of Money Laundering and Terrorist Financing. The government's capacity to enforce security-related legislation remained a concern, however. The Kosovo Police Counter Terrorist Unit (CTU) was still developing its capacity to conduct effective counterterrorism operations, and needed to develop effective cooperation and coordination between departments within the Kosovo Police.

Legislation and Law Enforcement: Kosovo made progress in adopting counterterrorism legislation. The Kosovo Security Strategy was approved by the Kosovo Assembly on

September 23. It outlines the responsibilities of the Kosovo Police (KP), Kosovo Customs (KC), the Kosovo Border Patrol (KBP), and the Kosovo Intelligence Agency (AKI), to coordinate their counterterrorism efforts and "ensure that Kosovo will not become a host to individuals or groups that intend to incite violent extremism and train or equip potential terrorists."

The KP's CTU was primarily responsible for Kosovo's counterterrorism efforts. Its capacity to conduct effective operations remained under-developed. The CTU increased to 27 officers, and it continued to train and develop the capacities of its officers. Training took place in conjunction with U.S. funded programs, the OSCE, and European partners – especially Turkey – in areas including surveillance, interrogation, investigation, and counterterrorism intelligence and analysis. The CTU's operational efforts were hampered by a lack of inter-departmental coordination and cooperation.

Kosovo continued to process travelers on entry and departure at one international airport and at 11 land border sites with the Personal Identification Secure Comparison and Evaluation System.

Athens, Greece: Police investigators search for evidence at the site of a bombing near a courier company's offices on November 1, 2010 in the Athens suburb of Pangrati. Four people were arrested. AFP PHOTO/LOUISA GOULIAMAKI

Countering Terrorist Finance: On September 30, with U.S. government technical assistance, Kosovo adopted a comprehensive anti-money laundering law, the Law on the Prevention of Money Laundering and Terrorist Financing (LPMLTF). The law imposed international and Financial Action Task Force-compliant reporting obligations, including reporting suspicious and structured transactions. The LPMLTF also established an independent Financial Intelligence Unit, which must report any transaction above 10,000 Euros, suspicious transactions, and structured transactions.

Regional and International Cooperation: Within the constraints posed by its financial situation, the Government of Kosovo has expanded its efforts to cooperate with international partners to address the flow of individuals illegally transiting Kosovo and to identify and screen potential threats both domestically and from abroad. The KBP leadership holds regular monthly meetings with their counterparts from Albania, Macedonia, and Montenegro, and the KP is pursuing a border operations initiative, which includes cross border cooperation and communication, the sharing of intelligence, and joint operations with the border police of the three countries. The KP also supported regional law enforcement relationships and worked with the governments of Bulgaria and Turkey on border related issues.

During the year, the Kosovo government cooperated closely with the United States in an attempt to extradite a Kosovo national to face criminal prosecution on terrorism-related charges in the United States. The Office of the State Prosecutor and the Special Prosecution Office of the Republic of Kosovo presented the United States' request for the fugitive's extradition, but a panel of the Kosovo Supreme Court, composed of two EU Rule of Law Mission Supreme Court judges and one Kosovo Supreme Court Judge, denied the extradition request.

THE NETHERLANDS

Overview: The Netherlands continued to show its commitment to counterterrorism cooperation in the areas of border and transportation security and terrorist financing. In its December 2010 quarterly terrorism threat analysis, the Dutch National Counterterrorism Coordinator (NCTb) maintained the national threat level at limited, meaning chances of an attack in the Netherlands or against Dutch interests were relatively small but could not be ruled out entirely. According to the report, there were few incidents in the Netherlands resulting from violent radicalization, although the conditions for radicalization remained present, particularly among the Somali community. However, the NCTb concluded that resistance against politically or ideologically motivated violence among the Dutch population remained high.

On May 31, the International Center for Counterterrorism, which received three years of seed money from the Foreign Ministry, was officially opened in The Hague.

Legislation and Law Enforcement: In 2009, the Dutch Justice Ministry and the U.S. Department of Homeland Security established the Fast Low Risk Universal Crossing (FLUX) system at some 20 U.S. airports enabling registered travelers that have submitted to a security assessment to go straight through U.S. immigration controls using iris scanners. U.S. citizens registered in the FLUX system enjoy this expedited travel at the Netherlands' Schiphol airport. In January 2010, the Netherlands began deploying full body scanners on flights from Schiphol airport to the United States, and by year's end the number of scanners in use expanded to a total of 75. These scanners were operated as an EU pilot program pending EU-legislation for the routine use of this technology.

In the appeal case against seven members of the Hofstad terrorist group, the appeals court in Amsterdam ruled on December 17 that the seven had indeed formed a criminal organization with terrorist intent. The court imposed prison sentences of between 15 months and 13 years against the seven defendants. The highest sentence was for Jason Walters, a dual U.S.-Dutch national, for having thrown a hand grenade at police officers in November 2004. Most members, except for Walters and his accomplice, have already served their sentences.

In addition to the arrest of six Tamils in late April, the National Crime Squad in June arrested four Tamils on suspicion of illegal activities in the Netherlands, including raising funds to support the struggle of the Liberation Tigers of Tamil Eelam movement. The investigation was ongoing at year's end.

At the request of Belgian justice authorities, the National Crime Squad in November arrested three Moroccan-Dutch nationals in Amsterdam suspected of engaging in international terrorism. The three reportedly had advanced plans to travel to Chechnya to join the Chechen terrorist group Caucasus Emirate. At year's end, the three were in custody pending a decision to extradite them to Belgium.

Following information supplied by the General Intelligence and Security Service (AIVD), the National Crime Squad on December 24 arrested 12 Somalis in Rotterdam on suspicion of being involved in terrorist activities. All 12 were subsequently released though three remained under investigation.

Countering Terrorist Finance: Dutch officials remained committed to active cooperation with the United States in designating known terrorist organizations and freezing their assets. The Dutch also supported the continued exchange of information on financial transactions. The Dutch government worked to emphasize the importance of balancing security and the effectiveness of the financial system. In July 2009, the Netherlands assumed Presidency of the Financial Action Task Force (FATF) for a one-year period. Together with the United Arab Emirates, the Netherlands organized the Middle East and North African FATF (MENA FATF) meeting in February 2010.

Regional and International Cooperation: The Netherlands played an active role in UN and EU counterterrorism discussions. During a summit of foreign ministers from the G8 and Middle East states in London in January, it was agreed that the Netherlands would take the lead in helping Yemen develop its judicial and legal system. The Netherlands has long been involved in development assistance programs in Yemen. The Dutch served as co-chair of the Friends of Yemen Justice and Rule of Law working group.

In November, the NCTb and INTERPOL organized a global exercise aimed at the prevention of biological terrorism (BIOSHIELD Global 2010), in which more than 80 representatives from 28 countries (including the United States) and international organizations participated.

The Netherlands currently has counterterrorism capacity building projects in Pakistan, Yemen, Morocco, and Algeria. The Netherlands also contributed to the counterterrorism work of the UN Office on Drugs and Crime. The Netherlands ratified the International Convention for Suppression of Acts of Nuclear Terrorism in 2010.

Countering Radicalization and Violent Extremism: The Justice Ministry's "Netherlands against Terrorism" campaign continued with a particular focus on preventing radicalization and polarization. The campaign has a local approach, in which police officers, social workers, and teachers are trained to recognize signs of radicalization and how to engage key figures/leaders in Muslim communities. A March study by the AIVD concluded that too much emphasis is placed on the effect of an "ideological counter message" in the battle against radicalization in the Netherlands. AIVD researchers noted that the conscious dissemination of "moderate Islam" or use of liberal imams hardly had any effect on the ideals of potential militants, but having a job, partner, and children are a much better remedy. The Netherlands played a leading role in countering terrorism on the Internet.

NORWAY

Overview: The Norwegian government continued to build its counterterrorism capacity and issued an action plan to counter extremist ideology. Authorities arrested and charged three al-Qa'ida-connected terrorist suspects, pursued charges against Ansar al-Islam leader Mullah Krekar for threatening a public official and inciting terrorism, implemented improved passport security measures, and commenced legal proceedings against a Norwegian-Somali suspected of financing terrorism.

Legislation and Law Enforcement: A new Immigration Act entered into force on January 1, 2010, authorizing the Ministry of Justice (MOJ) to issue instructions to other agencies relating to visa applicants on the EU terror list. The MOJ instructed the Directorate of Immigration, the Immigration Appeals Board, Norwegian foreign missions, and police to issue neither visas nor residence permits to persons who are on the EU terror list, or to persons associated with organizations on the list, before forwarding such visa applications to the MOJ for consideration.

In February 2009, the jury in an appeals court had affirmed a lower court's conviction of Arfan Bhatti for attempted murder and aggravated vandalism; it also affirmed a sentence of eight years imprisonment in the case. Following a retrial in May 2010, the Court of Appeal found Bhatti guilty of causing criminal damage to the synagogue but acquitted him of attempted murder. The court sentenced Bhatti to two years imprisonment on the vandalism charge, but annulled the sentence because he had already spent three years in pretrial custody. The State Prosecutor chose not to appeal the verdict.

In July, three persons with Norwegian citizenship or residency were arrested and charged with conspiracy to commit a terrorist act in Norway. According to open source reports, three were born outside of Norway and had al-Qa'ida connections. The three men, Mikael Davoud, Shawan Bujak, and David Jakobsen, were placed in custody pending further investigation and trial. In September, suspects Davud and Bujak each confessed to plotting a terrorist attack, albeit against different targets. The third suspect, Jakobsen, continued to deny the charges. The Supreme Court ordered Jakobsen released from custody on September 15; the other two suspects remained in pre-trial detention at year's end.

In December, the Oslo District Court acquitted Abdirahman Abdi Osman, a Norwegian citizen of Somali ancestry, of charges of knowingly collecting approximately US$ 34,000 for a terrorist organization and knowingly contributing funds to a terrorist organization. The court found that although a certain amount of the money Osman admitted transferring may have gone to finance al-Shabaab, the money was not earmarked for specific terrorist purposes, and the Norway-based contributors did not control how the money was used. Based on Osman's admission that he transferred money to an armed group, the court fined him US$ 1700 for breaking the UN's weapons embargo on Somalia but also annulled the sum due to time spent in custody. The State Prosecutor has appealed the verdict.

Mullah Krekar (aka Najmuddin Faraj Ahmad), the founder of Ansar al-Islam, an organization on both the U.S. list of designated Foreign Terrorist Organizations and the UN list of entities linked to terrorist activities, resides in Norway. He has been arrested on several occasions in previous years by Norwegian law enforcement. To date, authorities have been unable to collect sufficient evidence to convict him (membership in a terrorist organization is not a criminal offense in Norway). Based on threats he issued against a prominent Norwegian politician during a press conference in Oslo in June, authorities questioned him in court and, in September, initiated preliminary charges against him for threats against public officials, general threats, and incitement to terrorism.

Countering Terrorist Finance: The Government of Norway adopted the Financial Action Task Force's standards and recommendations, including the special recommendations on terrorist financing, and incorporated them into Norwegian law.

Regional and International Cooperation: On February 1, the government ratified the Council of Europe Convention on the Prevention of Terrorism, which entered into force in Norway on June 1.

As of April 6, fingerprint information was required in all newly issued Norwegian passports, consistent with an EU directive on the use of biometrics in EU/Schengen passports. Although not an EU member, Norway was required to implement the EU directive as a signatory of the European Economic Area Agreement and the Schengen agreement. Norway continued to permit the use of passports issued before April 6, as long as they were otherwise valid.

Countering Radicalization and Violent Extremism: In December, the Norwegian government issued an action plan to counter extremist ideology as a key part of its counterterrorism strategy. The plan contained 30 measures that apply from 2010 to 2013 and focuses on four priority areas: 1) increased knowledge and information; 2) strengthened government cooperation; 3) strengthened dialogue and involvement; and 4) support for vulnerable and disadvantaged people.

The Oslo municipality continued its OXLO campaign, "Oslo Extra Large," to facilitate integration and understanding. This year's campaign posters, describing the city as a place that welcomes diversity, were placed at bus and tram stops and metro stations, and school leaders and teachers were encouraged to discuss the campaign with students. In September, government and religious leaders attended the OXLO-Conference 2010, "Dialogue in a Multi-Cultural Society."

RUSSIA

Overview: Russia continued to endure terrorist attacks linked to instability in the North Caucasus. The most visible and largest attacks occurred in two Moscow Metro stations in March. Radical militants calling for a Caliphate within the Caucasus continued to constitute the main terrorist threat. Russia adopted amendments to the Criminal Code on Terrorist Activities to strengthen anti-money laundering efforts and enacted a law on Combating the Finance of Terrorism.

2010 Terrorist Incidents: Terrorist attacks in Russia continued to emanate from the ongoing unrest in the North Caucasus. Officials in mid-December cited 529 terrorist attacks over the course of the year in which 218 victims were killed and 536 injured. Suicide bombings at two Moscow Metro stations on March 29 by two women from Dagestan killed 40 and injured about 100 civilians. Other terrorist attacks occurred in the North Caucasus Federal District, particularly in the republics of Dagestan, Ingushetia, North Ossetia, Chechnya, and Kabardino-Balkaria.

The continuing high level of violence is a chronic problem in the North Caucasus region. The most serious terrorist attacks in the North Caucasus were a March 31 suicide bombing in Kizlyar, Dagestan, which killed 12 and injured 37; a September 9 car bombing at a market in Vladikavkaz, North Ossetia, which killed 18 and injured 140; and a May bombing in Stavropol, which killed seven and injured over 40. While these attacks were designed to cause mass civilian casualties, far more numerous were attacks targeting security forces and government facilities in the region, including an October 19 attack on the Chechen Parliament building in Grozniy, which left three dead and 17 injured. Authorities blamed a splinter group of the Caucasus Emirate for the October 19 Grozniy attack and an August 31 attacks in Tsentoroiy, which killed 11 and wounded 25.

Legislation and Law Enforcement: The 1998 federal law "On Fighting Terrorism" and the 2006 federal law "On Countering Terrorism" remained the principal counterterrorism legal authorities. At year's end, the Federal Assembly was finalizing a controversial new law, "On Police," that would expand police powers to preemptively detain suspected militants. In addition, on December 9, President Medvedev signed the Federal Law "On Amendments to the Criminal Code of the Russian Federation," which increases punishment for perpetrating a terrorist attack, promoting terrorist activities, or inciting the public to terrorist acts. President Medvedev in a mid-November statement cited 60 occasions in which security forces prevented terrorist attacks. Elsewhere, Russian authorities claimed to have conducted 30 counterterrorism operations and killed over 300 militants.

Countering Terrorist Finance: Russia is a member of the Financial Action Task Force (FATF). It is also a leading member, chair, and primary funding source of a similar body known as the Eurasian Group (EAG) on combating money laundering and terrorist financing. Through the EAG, Russia provided technical assistance and funding towards improving legislative and regulatory frameworks and operational capabilities on money laundering and terrorist financing. Russian banks must report suspicious transactions to the Federal Financial Monitoring Service (Rosfinmonitoring), a financial intelligence unit, which reports directly to the Prime Minister and is a member of the FATF and three FATF-style regional bodies: the Egmont Group, Committee of Experts on the Evaluation of Anti-Money Laundering Measures and the Financing of Terrorism (MONEYVAL), and the EAG. The Central Bank and the markets regulator (the Financial Markets Federal Service) can access these transaction reports after requesting them from Rosfinmonitoring.

On July 23, Russia adopted a federal law that made changes to the existing laws "On Combating Money Laundering and Financing of Terrorism (AML/CTF) and the Code of Administrative Infringements." These amendments are based on FATF recommendations and focus on three main areas: expanding AML/CTF jurisdiction, clarifying legal definitions, and improving the administrative oversight for enforcement of AML/CTF legislation. The government expanded AML/CTF jurisdiction. Subsidiaries, representative offices, and affiliates of Russian financial institutions that are located outside the Russian Federation must now comply with Russian AML/CTF regulations. Furthermore, microfinance and short-term loans, which have grown significantly in Russia, are now subject to AML/CTF laws.

Regional and International Cooperation: Russia continued its counterterrorism cooperation within the EU, the G8 Counterterrorism Action Group, the Shanghai Cooperation Organization, and the OSCE; and was an active member of the NATO-Russia Council Counterterrorism Working Group.

In April, Russian President Medvedev attended the Nuclear Security Summit designed to enhance international cooperation to prevent nuclear terrorism. In May, the U.S.-Russia Counterterrorism Working Group (CTWG) was convened; transportation security, countering violent extremism, terrorist finance, and information sharing issues were discussed. In November, the group met again and continued discussions on transportation security, countering violent extremism, coordination on nonproliferation of weapons of mass destruction, and public private partnerships outreach.

The U.S. Federal Bureau of Investigation and Central Intelligence Agency and Russian Federal Security Service and Foreign Intelligence Service continued to cooperate in yearly Intelligence and Law Enforcement CTWG meetings. The most recent discussions were held in October in Washington, DC. In addition, operational and intelligence information related to terrorism-related threats continues to be shared among these four agencies on a regular basis.

Countering Radicalization and Violent Extremism: In December, Prime Minister Putin announced the creation of a Commission for the Socio-Economic Development of the North Caucasus under his chairmanship. As outlined, the program aims to improve economic opportunity in the region, and the central government will back loans of approximately US$ 1.5 billion for projects.

SERBIA

Overview: Serbia's law enforcement and security agencies, particularly the Customs Administration, Criminal Police, Border Police, and Security Information Agency, continued close bilateral counterterrorism cooperation with the United States, while intra-governmental cooperation between these agencies improved, thus increasing their effectiveness. Serbia had two police organizations that operated as counterterrorism tactical response units, the Special Antiterrorist Unit (SAJ) and the Counterterrorist Unit. In addition, the government created a Criminal Investigative Unit for Counterterrorist Investigation within the Interior Ministry's Criminal Investigation Directorate.

Legislation and Law Enforcement: On May 14, the Organized Crime Department of the Belgrade Appellate Court confirmed the convictions of four violent extremists, sentenced in July 2009 to a total of 27 years imprisonment, for conspiracy to commit unconstitutional activity, terrorism, illegal possession of firearms, and attempted murder. On October 22, the National Assembly voted to extend the validity of non-biometric passports until December 31, 2011.

Serbia's close bilateral counterterrorism cooperation with the United States continued across multiple law enforcement and security agencies, with U.S. counterparts providing training and assistance in hostage rescue, terrorist financing, civil aviation security, border security, and document fraud detection.

Countering Terrorist Finance: On November 30, the Parliament adopted a set of amendments to the 2009 Law on the Prevention of Money Laundering and the Financing of Terrorism. The amendments predominantly focus on additional control and supervision of electronic money transfers in accordance with the Council of Europe Committee of Experts on the Evaluation of Anti-Money Laundering Measures and the Financing of Terrorism recommendations.

Regional and International Cooperation: Serbia continued to participate actively in the UN Office on Drugs and Crime Regional Program (2009-2011) of Promoting the Rule of Law and Human Security in South East Europe, with primary emphasis on increasing countries' counterterrorism capacities. In that regard, Serbia established a working group in charge of drafting a law on counterterrorism, which would provide a legal basis for subsequent adoption of a counterterrorism strategy and specific action plans of relevant ministries and agencies.

Serbia organized two successful regional counterterrorism events in 2010. In May, the Interior Ministry held a 10-day counterterrorism seminar at the Regional Special Police Unit Training Center in Kula; the main presenters were experts from the special operations unit of the French Gendarmerie (RAID), and participants included the federal governments of Bosnia and Herzegovina, Montenegro, Croatia, Bulgaria, and Serbia. In October, the SAJ training camp in Batajnica hosted an international counterterrorism seminar with the participation of counterterrorism units from Austria, Slovenia, Bosnia and Herzegovina, Greece, Montenegro, Macedonia, Croatia, Romania, Italy, Bulgaria, the United States (FBI Hostage Rescue Team), and Serbia.

In April, Serbian authorities organized the country's first ever Civil Aviation Security exercise, involving a simulated plane hijacking, with the participation of the Special Anti-Terrorist Unit, Airport and Border Police, and representatives of foreign embassies.

Serbia acceded to the 2005 Protocol on the Suppression of Unlawful Acts against the Safety of Maritime Navigation. Serbia signed bilateral agreements related to counterterrorism with Albania and Bosnia and Herzegovina, and ratified 2009 agreements with Israel and Cyprus.

SPAIN

Overview: Spain continued to confront the dual threat posed by the domestic terrorist group Basque Fatherland and Liberty (ETA) and violent extremists affiliated with al-Qa'ida and its affiliates. Buoyed by strong international cooperation, in particular with France, Spain enjoyed such success in battling ETA, whose aim is to create an independent Basque state, that the weakened terrorist group announced it would halt "offensive actions." Meanwhile, Spain's attention often focused on the fate of the three Spanish aid workers kidnapped by al-Qa'ida in the Islamic Maghreb in late 2009 and released in 2010.

Spain cooperated closely with the United States to counter terrorism. In April, Attorney General Holder signed a Memorandum of Understanding with the Government of Spain to share information and further strengthen bilateral cooperation in the fight against international terrorism. Also in April, the U.S-Spain Agreement to Prevent and Combat Serious Crime, which was signed in 2009, also went into force.

As part of its effort to help close the Guantanamo Bay detention facility, Spain publicly announced its decision to accept five former detainees for resettlement, three of whom have been resettled.

Legislation and Law Enforcement: The Spanish Parliament passed a series of reforms to the country's Penal Code regarding terrorism to better equip the Spanish judiciary to face several realities of violent extremists operating in Spain. The new changes acknowledge that violent extremists in Spain may be inspired by but operate independently of formal terrorist groups such as al-Qa'ida. The reforms criminalized activities such as recruitment, indoctrination, terrorist training, and the facilitation of such activity by sending recruits to training camps. Furthermore, they criminalized the public distribution of messages that are likely to "increase the risk" of others joining a terrorist group or association or perpetrating terrorist attacks. Finally, the new reforms established the financing of terrorism as its own crime.

Spain took steps to improve security and the detection of false documents at its borders. Spain introduced an automated system to read EU passports with biometric data at its two largest airports. Select border control areas have the capacity to scan fingerprints in real time. In July, Spain announced that it would begin testing full-body scanners in one of its airports. Spain deployed a network of radar stations, known as the Integrated External Surveillance System, along its maritime borders. Spain continued its participation in the Megaports and Container Security Initiatives.

Spanish security forces arrested 12 suspected violent extremists, one of whom was accused of managing one of the most influential terrorist websites in the world. In December, police arrested seven suspects (six Pakistanis and one Nigerian) in the greater Barcelona area for allegedly providing false documents, including passports, to terrorist groups. The Spanish police cooperated with the security services in Thailand, where authorities simultaneously detained another three suspects.

In cooperation with international partners, security services also arrested 113 alleged ETA members or associates, including 22 in France and nine in other countries. Spain also arrested 11 individuals for ETA-inspired street violence. Key raids included Spanish cooperation with Portuguese forces in January, when they shut down a large-scale bomb factory and arms cache that ETA had established in Portugal. Spain also arrested an embryonic ETA cell in Catalonia that same month. In February, a joint operation in France resulted in the detention of ETA's latest suspected military leader, whose alleged successor and the successor's would-be replacement were both captured in May during another raid in France.

Spain's judicial system investigated allegations of ETA training camps in Venezuela. In February, a National Court investigating judge issued an arrest warrant for an official in the Venezuelan government. Two ETA suspects arrested in September confessed to having received training from that same official in Venezuela during 2008. (It is not clear whether these individual actions reflect official Venezuelan government support for ETA.)

Countering Terrorist Finance: Spain was a member of the G8 Counterterrorism Action Group and provided technical assistance to other countries to counter terrorist financing. Spain exercised leadership in the Financial Action Task Force to combat money laundering and to take the necessary steps to prevent its financial institutions from engaging in transactions or relationships in support of terrorist activity. In April, Spain enacted Law 10/2010 on Preventing Money Laundering and the Financing of Terrorism.

The government diligently implemented the relevant UNSCRs and has the legal authority to impose autonomous designations.

After the European Parliament voted down an interim agreement on the Terrorist Finance Tracking Program, the Spanish EU Presidency helped secure support for a revised version, which came into effect shortly after the completion of the Spanish presidency. As EU President, Spain hosted numerous conferences and workshops to foster greater international cooperation to confront terrorism, including a U.S-EU workshop on countering terrorist finance.

Regional and International Cooperation: As EU President during the first half of 2010, Spain worked to advance a number of counterterrorism initiatives. In January, weeks after the attempted December 25, 2009 attack on Northwest Flight 253 bound for Detroit, Spain hosted a key meeting of Justice and Home Affairs ministers and helped secured the passage of the "Toledo Resolution" to increase U.S.-EU aviation security. Spain also successfully promoted the EU's adoption of an Internal Security Strategy and built support for strengthening cooperation and information sharing among European counterterrorism coordination centers. Spain signed the Beijing Convention on the Suppression of Unlawful Acts Relating to International Civil Aviation and the Protocol to the Convention for the Suppression of Unlawful Seizure of Aircraft at the conclusion of an International Civil Aviation Organization diplomatic conference in September.

Spain was active in efforts to prevent nuclear materials from falling into the hands of terrorists. President Zapatero attended the Nuclear Security Summit in Washington, DC, which promoted international cooperation to prevent nuclear terrorism. Spain assumed a leading role in the Global Initiative to Combat Nuclear Terrorism (GICNT) and in June was elected to serve as Coordinator of its Implementation and Assessment Group, a working group of technical experts.

Countering Radicalization and Violent Extremism: Spain participated in several international meetings to counter violent extremism and, in its capacity as EU President, hosted a seminar on de-radicalization. Spain's inter-ministerial countering violent extremism (CVE) strategy emphasizes the prevention of radicalization and seeks to counter radical propaganda both online and in other arenas. In addition to promoting international cooperation on these issues, Spanish efforts to counter radicalization are tied closely to the fight against illegal immigration. This strategy seeks the support of civil society and the general public in rejecting violence and extremism. In fulfillment of applicable laws, Spanish penitentiaries employ CVE rehabilitation programs designed to achieve the reintegration of inmates into society.

SWEDEN

Overview: The Swedish Security Service (SAPO), the authority with the main responsibility for countering terrorism, distinguished between attack and activity threats in its annual terrorism report presented in June. According to SAPO, attack threats, which include plans to carry out attacks in Sweden and/or against Swedish interests abroad, remained low during the reporting period, though SAPO had noted the presence of individuals who were planning, supporting, or financing terrorist attacks in areas of conflict and even stated that Swedish nationals were contributing to terrorism in Somalia.

In October, however, SAPO – for the first time ever – raised the National Threat Advisory to "elevated," based on information from the National Center for Terrorism, which discussed an increased threat of potential terrorist attacks towards Sweden and changed activity within certain environments. On December 11, a car bomb device was detonated minutes before Sweden's first ever suicide bomber carried out an attack in a crowded pedestrian area in Stockholm. A few weeks later, on December 29, five individuals were arrested in Sweden and Denmark.

A number of individuals with connections extremist networks – primarily al-Qa'ida (AQ) and al-Shabaab – continued to depart Sweden for training camps in Afghanistan, Pakistan, Somalia, and Iraq.

2010 Terrorist Incidents: Since 2007 when Swedish artist Lars Vilks portrayed the Prophet Mohammed as a cartoon dog, Sweden has become a more prominent target for violent extremists. In November, an al-Shabaab fighter named Abu Zaid appeared in a propaganda video in which he, in fluent Swedish, urged Muslims in Sweden to kill Vilks and to move to Somalia. In May, Vilks' house was attacked with Molotov cocktails and two brothers of Swedish-Kosovarian origin, Mentor and Mensur Alija, were arrested and later convicted of arson.

On December 11, Sweden's first ever suicide bomber, a 28 year-old Swedish citizen of Iraqi descent, Taimour Abdulwahab al-Abdaly, carried out two attacks in a pedestrian shopping area in central Stockholm. In the first explosion, al-Abdaly detonated his abandoned car, slightly wounding two passersby. Authorities believed that al-Abdaly accidently triggered one of the pipe bombs attached to his body, killing himself prematurely on a side street. Shortly before the attack, al-Abdaly sent prerecorded audio clips in Swedish, English, and Arabic to Swedish News Agency TT and to SAPO, in which he cited the presence of Swedish troops in Afghanistan and Lars Vilks as justification for his actions. The investigation was ongoing at year's end.

Legislation and Law Enforcement: On December 1, Sweden's new terrorism legislation came into effect, which criminalizes incitement to recruit and train for terrorism activities. The original legislation from 2003 did not clearly specify these activities.

On December 8, Gothenburg District Court convicted two Swedish citizens of Saudi Arabian and Somali origin of conspiracy to commit terrorist crimes and sentenced both men to four years imprisonment. According to the court, both men are supporters of al-Shabaab and had an agreement to carry out suicide attacks on behalf of the organization in Somalia. Both defendants appealed the verdict on December 29.

On December 29, five individuals were arrested (four in Denmark and one in Sweden) for conspiracy to commit terrorist crimes when planning to attack the newspaper Jyllands-Posten in Denmark.

Countering Terrorist Finance: At the Financial Action Task Force's (FATF) October 2010 Plenary, Sweden was recognized for the "significant progress" it had made in addressing deficiencies identified in its Mutual Evaluation Report. In 2010, the Swedish government allocated extra funds to the Financial Supervisory Authority to continue combating money laundering and terrorism financing. Swedish law does not give the government independent authority to freeze or seize assets, unless in connection with an ongoing criminal investigation. Sweden followed EU decisions on freezing assets of entities and persons listed on the UNSCR 1267 Sanctions Committee (for the Taliban and AQ) list and in accordance with UNSCR 1373.

Regional and International Cooperation: Sweden contributed to counterterrorism capacity building projects through its development aid work carried out by Swedish International Development Agency, the UN, EU, and OSCE. Sweden contributed funds to the Center for Global Counterterrorism Cooperation to arrange a workshop in Jakarta concerning the possible establishment of a regional education center in Dhaka, Bangladesh, which would contribute to regional stability and enhance the region's capacity to prevent and counter terrorism. Together with Germany, Sweden supported a visitors program in Sweden for Afghan representatives as part of the UN Office of Drugs and Crime's training program "Strengthening of the legal sector in the fight against terrorism." Sweden provided trainers to the EU's Training Mission to assist with the training of Somalia's Transitional Federal Government security forces.

Countering Radicalization and Violent Extremism: In February, the Swedish government mandated SAPO to map violent extremism in Sweden. According to the mandate, SAPO was to look into: 1) the existence of violent extremism, 2) the radicalization processes, and 3) tools and strategies needed to counter radicalization. The report was presented December 15 and concluded that there are about 200 individuals in Sweden involved in violent extremist activities. The largest identified threat comes from "returnees" who come to Sweden after being in training camps or participating in attacks abroad. In the past five years, about 30 individuals have traveled abroad, most to Somalia, Pakistan, and Afghanistan, and at least four have died. SAPO continued to work to identify individuals planning to travel to training camps, held dialogues with them to try to prevent their travel, and spoke with persons who were suspected of returning from such travel.

TURKEY

Overview: Domestic and transnational terrorist groups have targeted Turkish nationals and foreigners in Turkey, including on occasion U.S. government personnel, for more than 40 years. Terrorist groups that have operated in Turkey in the past have included Kurdish nationalist, Marxist-Leninist, pro-Chechen, as well as al-Qa'ida and its affiliates. Most prominent among terrorist groups in Turkey is the Kurdistan Workers' Party (PKK). Composed primarily of ethnic Kurds with a nationalist agenda, the PKK operated from bases in northern Iraq and directed its forces to target mainly Turkish security forces. PKK activity was lower in 2009 but increased again in 2010 during a May through October wave of violence. Other prominent terrorist groups in Turkey included the Revolutionary People's Liberation Party/Front (DHKP-C), a militant Marxist-Leninist group with anti-U.S. and anti-NATO views that seeks the violent overthrow of the Turkish state. The Turkish Workers' and Peasants' Liberation Army, though largely inactive, were still considered potential threats by the Turkish government.

Turkish terrorism law defines terrorism as attacks against Turkish citizens and the Turkish state. This definition hampers Turkey's ability to interdict, arrest, and prosecute those who plan and facilitate terrorist acts to be committed outside of Turkey, or acts to be committed against non-Turkish citizens within Turkey. Nonetheless, Turkish counterterrorism cooperation with the United States continued to develop and improve.

2010 Terrorist Incidents: PKK attacks in 2010 once again demonstrated the nation-wide reach of the group. Typical tactics, techniques, and procedures included ambushes on military patrols in the countryside, improvised explosive devices (IEDs) along known military or police routes, and bombings of both security and civilian targets in urban areas. Three attacks received particular attention and condemnation:

- A June bombing of a bus stop in Istanbul that killed five, including a 17-year-old girl, and wounded 13.

- A September attack on a mini-van in Hakkari killed 10 civilians.

- A November suicide-bomb attack in Istanbul's Taksim Square, which killed only the bomber due to an IED malfunction, injured 15 police officers and 17 civilians

Legislation and Law Enforcement: The narrow legal definition of terrorism as an act against the Turkish state in existing Turkish counterterrorism law poses concerns for joint and legal cooperation. In July, the government amended the Anti-Terror Law to prohibit prosecution of minors under the age of 15 under the law. Minors are now tried in juvenile courts rather than in criminal court as adults. Similarly, the Government of Turkey amended the Law on Demonstrations, allowing first time juvenile offenders – those not convicted of an offense involving weapons or arson – to be subject to administrative sanctions rather than sent to prison. These amendments resulted in more than 200 children being released from detention, a development that was welcomed by many human rights groups and ethnic Kurds. Human rights groups continued to allege, however, that overly-broad application of the Anti-Terror Law was still used by the government as a means to stifle legitimate political protest and expression of Kurdish identity or minority viewpoints.

Countering Terrorist Finance: Pursuant to its obligations under UNSCR 1267 and subsequent resolutions, Turkish officials continued to circulate UN-designated names of terrorists to all law enforcement and intelligence agencies and to financial institutions. Turkish officials also distributed U.S.-designated names to the security services for their awareness, although only UN-listed names were subjected to asset freezes enforced through a Council of Ministers decree.

In February, the Financial Action Task Force (FATF) identified Turkey as a jurisdiction with significant anti-money laundering and counterterrorist financing (AML/CTF) vulnerabilities, chief among them was Turkey's incomplete criminalization of terrorist financing and weak national asset freezing mechanisms. In coordination with the FATF's International Cooperation Review Group, the Government of Turkey made a high-level commitment to work with the FATF and adopted an "Action Plan" which committed Ankara to a timeline for implementing new legislation addressing the shortcomings. On June 1, Turkey submitted a report to the FATF plenary along with a draft law on the "Prevention of Terrorism Financing," which was intended to address all CTF deficiencies identified by the FATF with respect to its criminalization of terrorist financing and national asset freezing mechanisms. The draft law was in the Prime Ministry at year's end, where experts within and outside the Prime Minister's office were reviewing it.

Regional and International Cooperation: Turkey has played a critical role as a friendly, neutral, arbiter in Afghanistan and Pakistan, as a regional facilitator, International Security Assistance Force contributor, and bilateral donor. On the development front, Turkey has provided assistance on health, education, and agriculture projects in Afghanistan. Turkey also conceived and continued to support an annual meeting of the Ministers of Interior of the Neighbors of Iraq, which focused on supporting regional stability and security, including counterterrorism and border security issues. Turkey ratified the 2005 Protocol on the Suppression of Unlawful Acts against the Safety of Maritime Navigation.

Countering Radicalization and Violent Extremism: The Government of Turkey has two significant programs in place to counter radicalization and violent extremism. The first, administered by the National Police, is a broad-based outreach program to affected communities, similar to anti-gang activities in the United States. Police worked to reach vulnerable populations before terrorists do, alter the prevailing group dynamics and prevent recruitment. Police also undertook social projects, activities with parents, in-service training for officers and teachers, and utilized social science research. Programs prepared trainers, psychologists, coaches, and religious leaders to intervene to undermine radical messages and prevent recruitment.

The second program, administered by the Religious Affairs Office (Diyanet) of the Government of Turkey, promoted a Hanafi Sunni Islam[3] and worked to undercut the message of radical or violent Islam. In Turkey, all Hanafi Sunni imams are employees of the state's Religious Affairs office (the Diyanet). In support of its message of traditional religious values, Diyanet's over 66,000 imams throughout Turkey conducted individualized outreach to their congregations. Diyanet similarly worked with religious associations among the Turkish diaspora, assisting them to establish umbrella organizations and providing them access to mainstream Hanafi Sunni Islamic instruction. Diyanet supported in-service training for religious leaders and lay-workers through a network of 19 centers throughout Turkey, and has sister-city relationships established with religious authorities abroad.

---

3 *The Diyanet provides services only to the Hanafi Sunni community of Turkey. However, within Turkey's 70 million Muslims there are also 15 to 20 million Alevi (classified as a branch of Shia Islam) and hundreds of thousands of Caferi Shia Muslims.*

The Government of Turkey took steps to follow up on its 2009 Democratic Initiative, also known as the National Unity Project, designed to address the social and economic inequalities that are seen as fueling Kurdish dissent and PKK recruitment. Turkey devised concrete steps within the scope of the initiative to drain the PKK's support, by, for example, liberalizing laws governing the use of the Kurdish language in broadcasting, education, and state buildings; reducing the application of counterterrorism laws to non-violent crimes; and, providing legal incentives to bring members of the PKK who have not engaged in violence back into civil society

UKRAINE

Overview: Ukraine took several steps to mitigate the threat of terrorism. The government installed radiation detection systems at the port of Odesa, enacted amendments that strengthened Ukraine's terrorist financing legislation, and the Ukrainian military participated in regional military counterterrorism exercises.

Legislation and Law Enforcement: Following President Yanukovych's April pledge to eliminate Ukraine's stockpile of highly enriched uranium (HEU) by 2012 at the Nuclear Security Summit in Washington, DC, Ukraine reached a significant milestone in late December with the removal of 50 kilograms of HEU fresh fuel from Kyiv, Kharkiv, and Sevastopol. With this action, Ukraine demonstrated global leadership by ensuring that vulnerable nuclear material does not end up in terrorist hands.

Ukraine completed the installation of radiation detection systems and associated training in conjunction with the U.S. National Nuclear Security Administration's Second Line of Defense (SLD) program at the port of Odesa. The program aims to deter, detect, and interdict illicit trafficking in nuclear and other radioactive materials across international borders and through the global maritime shipping system.

In keeping with the National Biometrics Action Plan, the Ministry of Internal Affairs announced in November plans to introduce biometric passports for Ukrainians traveling abroad. The plan was not yet adopted by the Cabinet of Ministers at year's end, however.

Countering Terrorist Finance: On May 21, President Yanukovych signed into law amendments to Ukraine's anti-money laundering and counterterrorism financing (AML/CTF) legislation. The amendments represented a significant step toward compliance with the recommendations of the Financial Action Task Force (FATF) and the standards of the Council of Europe's Committee of Experts on the Evaluation of Anti-Money Laundering Measures and the Financing of Terrorism (MONEYVAL). The new legislation replaced and significantly improved Ukraine's basic AML/CTF Law, and amended relevant portions of the Criminal Code to bring them into greater compliance with international standards. However, Ukraine has remained on the FATF list of countries with "strategic deficiencies" since February 2010.

Regional and International Cooperation: Ukraine contributed a 20-person Special Operations Task Unit to participate in a multinational special operations counterterrorism exercise that was conducted in Poland in September. U.S. European Command (EUCOM) sponsored the exercise.

UNITED KINGDOM

Overview: The UK continued to play a leading role in global counterterrorism efforts. The new coalition government established a National Security Council; appointed a National Security Adviser; completed a Strategic Defense and Security Review (SDSR); and published a new National Security

Strategy (NSS). The SDSR and NSS reviewed threats to the UK's national security and set out new measures to counter terrorism.

The British government began a review of counterterrorism legislation, measures, and programs with an aim toward balancing liberty and security. In January, the United Kingdom (UK) raised its national threat level to the UK from international terrorism from substantial to severe, meaning that a terrorist attack was highly likely. In September, the UK published for the first time its threat levels from Irish-related terrorism: severe in Northern Ireland, substantial in mainland Britain.

2010 Terrorist Incidents: Throughout the year, dissident republican groups operating in Northern Ireland stepped up their campaigns of terrorism. The Police Service of Northern Ireland (PSNI) reported that between January and November, there were two deaths related to Northern Ireland's security situation, 79 shooting incidents, 87 bombing incidents, 54 casualties resulting from paramilitary-style assaults, and 36 casualties resulting from paramilitary-style shootings. The PSNI estimated a rise of more than 80 percent in bombing incidents in Northern Ireland between January and November compared with 2009.

On October 29, UK police and security services intercepted an explosive device concealed in a computer printer toner cartridge aboard a cargo aircraft at East Midlands Airport in Leicestershire bound for Chicago, believed to have originated in Yemen. The investigation into the "cargo bomb plot" was ongoing through the end of the year, but Home Secretary Theresa May indicated to Parliament in November that the UK government believed al-Qa'ida in the Arabian Peninsula was responsible.

Legislation and Law Enforcement: In April in NI, policing and justice powers were fully transferred from the UK government in London to NI. In November, the Independent Monitoring Commission, a four-commissioner team established by the British and Irish governments in 2004 to support devolution by reporting on paramilitary activity and security, indicated in its annual report that dissidents in Northern Ireland had "steadily increased the number of improvised explosive devises they deployed and the proportion of those that detonated."

In June, Home Secretary Theresa May extended for six months the government's power to hold terrorist suspects for 28 days in pre-charge detention. The provision must be renewed annually or it expires, and May indicated that the government believed the provision should only be temporary. The following month, May announced a broad review of the government's counterterrorism legislation, measures, and programs, and indicated that the pre-charge detention provision would be part of that review. The review also considered the utility of the UK's heavily-debated "control orders." The Prevention of Terrorism Act 2005 empowers the Home Secretary to issue control orders "impos[ing] obligations on [an individual] for purposes connected with protecting members of the public from a risk of terrorism." In practice, control orders have been used to impose near-house arrest and restrict movement and access to the Internet by terrorism suspects who cannot be prosecuted or deported. In undertaking the review, the government cited the need to balance security and civil liberties.

In July, the European Court of Human Rights issued a preliminary ruling blocking the extradition from the UK to the United States of British terrorism suspects Abu Hamza, Babar Ahmad, Seyla Talha Ahsan, and Haroon Rashid Aswat over concerns that the sentences and prison conditions the men could face if convicted in the United States could violate the European Convention on Human Rights. The court asked the UK government to submit further information on these cases. In November, Abu Hamza successfully appealed the government's attempts to strip him of his UK passport.

In July, three men were sentenced to life in prison for their involvement in a 2006 plot to detonate homemade liquid explosives on transatlantic flights. Ibrahim Savant, Arafat Waheed Khan, and Waheed Zaman, who had previously been cleared of involvement in the plot, were found guilty at a retrial of conspiracy to murder. The men were told by the judge that they would serve minimum terms of 20 years.

In response to a decision by the European Court of Human Rights, which found that the UK's police use of stop-and-search powers under Section 44 of the Terrorism Act 2000 were drawn too broadly and failed to protect civil liberties, the Home Secretary announced in July that police would need to rely on Section 43 of the Act, which requires officers to "reasonably suspect [the person] to be a terrorist" before subjecting them to a search. Police retained the authority to search vehicles under Section 44, provided they had reasonable suspicion of terrorist activity.

In October, High Court Judge Lady Justice Hallett opened an inquest into the July 2005 terrorist attacks on London's transport network that left 52 people dead. The inquest will investigate, among other things, whether the security services could have prevented the 2005 attacks. The inquest continued at year's end.

In November, in response to the cargo bomb plot, the government announced a review of airfreight security, imposed temporary restrictions on the transport of large printer cartridges by air, and suspended the transport of unaccompanied airfreight from Yemen and Somalia. The move followed a January decision by the government to suspend all direct flights between the UK and Yemen as part of increased security measures after the attempted Christmas Day 2009 terrorist attack on Northwest Flight 253. After the cargo bomb plot was discovered, the government began working closely with the aviation industry to devise a long-term security screening regime for cargo to mitigate the threats the plot revealed. On December 20, UK police indicated that 12 men between the ages of 17 and 28 were detained on suspicion of the commission, preparation, or instigation of an act of terrorism in the UK. On December 27, nine of the 12 men arrested were charged with conspiracy to cause explosions and preparing acts of terrorism against targets in the UK, allegedly including the U.S. Embassy.

London's Metropolitan Police Service launched an "If You Suspect It, Report It" awareness campaign in December to enlist public support in identifying suspicious activity related to acts of terrorism.

Countering Terrorist Finance: The UK has a comprehensive range of laws aimed at anti-money laundering and counterterrorist financing (AML/CTF). It is a member of the Financial Action Task Force (FATF) and an active participant in FATF-style regional bodies to meet evolving anti-money laundering and counterterrorism financing threats. The UK engages in efforts to freeze the assets of persons who commit terrorist acts, as required by the UN, including through implementation of UNSCRs 1267 and 1373. In January, the UK Supreme Court held that the government had earlier exceeded its authority by imposing asset-freezing orders that went beyond the requirements of UNSCR 1373. The Supreme Court reinstated temporary asset-freezing regulations as an interim measure following the judgment. In December, the UK replaced the temporary provisions with a new legislative framework that contained a higher standard of proof for freezing assets; "reasonable belief" rather than "reasonable suspicion." The legislation was awaiting Royal Assent to enact it at year's end.

To further improve and update Bermuda's anti-money laundering and anti-terrorist financing regulations, in August, Bermuda's Parliament enacted the Proceeds of Crime Regulations (Supervision and Enforcement) Amendment Act that would require the Bermuda Bar Association and the Chartered Accountants in Bermuda to establish jointly a board to regulate law and accountancy firms in order to prevent money laundering and terrorist financing.

Regional and International Cooperation: The UK cooperates with other nations and international organizations to counter terrorism, including in the UN, UNSC, EU, Commonwealth, NATO, Council of Europe, G8, International Atomic Energy Agency, IMF-World Bank, the Global Initiative to Combat Nuclear Terrorism, and Interpol. In January, the UK hosted a conference on Afghanistan that brought over 75 nations and multilateral organizations together to pledge international support for Afghan-led reintegration of former insurgents and transition of full security responsibility to the Afghan leadership. In January, the UK hosted a Friends of Yemen conference in London, which brought together representatives from the Gulf Cooperation Council, G8, UN, EU, Arab League, IMF, World Bank, and other European nations to coordinate international engagement and support for Yemen's efforts to deliver unity, security, and stability. The UK signed the Beijing Convention on the Suppression of Unlawful Acts Relating to International Civil Aviation and the Protocol to the Convention for the Suppression of Unlawful Seizure of Aircraft at the conclusion of an International Civil Aviation Organization diplomatic conference in September.

Countering Radicalization and Violent Extremism: The UK's "Prevent" strategy, launched in 2007 to counter radicalization, outlined a number of objectives, such as support to mainstream voices and increasing community resilience, and involved a range of government actors, particularly the Home Office, The Foreign and Commonwealth Office, the Department of Communities and Local Government, local authorities, and the police. Many of the programs have been run by community organizations, supported by government funding. Examples of Prevent programs include interfaith activities, diversionary programs for youth, professional development for mainstream community and faith leaders, speaking tours by mainstream Islamic scholars, imam training programs, and projects to equip young people with arguments to counter violent extremism. The Research, Information, Communications Unit (RICU), which is physically located in the Home Office, has been responsible for managing counterterrorism communications, including those related to Prevent. The Coalition government has initiated a review of the strategy "to more clearly separate work on preventing violent extremism from work to promote integration," which will determine the future direction of counter-radicalization programs in the UK.

MIDDLE EAST AND NORTH AFRICA OVERVIEW

The Near East region remained one of the most active in terms of terrorist activity in 2010. Multiple terrorist organizations displayed the capability and intent to strike at targets across the region. Al-Qa'ida in the Arabian Peninsula (AQAP) posed an increased risk to stability within Yemen and demonstrated anew its intent to strike the United States. Al-Qa'ida in Iraq (AQI)-despite diminished leadership and capabilities – continued to conduct attacks across Iraq. Al-Qa'ida in the Islamic Maghreb (AQIM) conducted attacks against Algerian government targets and undertook kidnappings elsewhere to extort ransoms. Hizballah in Lebanon continued to pose a significant threat to the stability of Lebanon and the broader region. In Israel and the Palestinian territories, several groups maintained the capability to launch attacks and acquired sophisticated weaponry from outside the country.

Governments across the region improved their own counterterrorism capabilities despite these persistent threats, effectively disrupting the activities of a number of terrorists across the region. The Iraqi government displayed increased capability and effectiveness in targeting multiple Sunni extremist groups as well as a number of Shia insurgents. In Algeria, AQIM became increasingly isolated in limited parts of the country as Algeria increased its already substantial efforts to target the group. While Saudi Arabia remained vulnerable because of the increased instability in Yemen, its efforts to target terrorist activity domestically remained resolute; the Saudi government displayed professionalism in tactical counterterrorism operations and counterterrorist financing, and made some progress on its efforts to counter violent extremist ideology. Israel and the Palestinian Authority also worked to diminish the threat posed by various Palestinian terrorist groups and Hizballah, including targeting weapons smuggling in and around the Gaza Strip and suicide bombers attempting to attack Israel via Gaza and the West Bank.

ALGERIA

Overview: Al-Qa'ida in the Islamic Maghreb (AQIM) continued to pose a significant terrorist threat in the mountainous areas east of Algiers. AQIM primarily targeted Algerian security forces, but civilians were also wounded or killed because of AQIM criminal activity. Algerian security forces isolated AQIM in the north, and the group launched fewer successful terrorist attacks but continued to execute suicide attacks, attacks using improvised explosive devices (IED), and ambushes in the areas east of Algiers.

The government has succeeded in reducing the flow of money to terrorists. Residents of the Kabylie region repeatedly took to the streets to protest kidnappings for ransom, prompting terrorists to release at least five hostages without receiving payment. In August, however, the president (equivalent to a town mayor) of Baghlia commune in Boumerdes was killed near his home, presumably by AQIM retaliating against protests Baghlia residents held earlier in the year to denounce kidnappings.

2010 Terrorist Incidents: AQIM perpetrated notable terrorist attacks in rural areas, including a cross-border attack in the south between Mali and Algeria, the first vehicle-borne suicide bombings since 2008 using of an improvised bomb attack method commonly used in Iraq. As the attacks highlighted below indicate, Algeria experienced a spike in terrorist incidents during the summer and just prior to the start of Ramadan, which began August 11. During Ramadan, there was a brief but significant uptick in AQIM attacks, compared to the same period in 2008 and 2009, possibly triggered by aggressive Algerian counterterrorism operations.

2010 incidents included:

- On June 11, a suicide truck bomb killed five police and wounded 30 others at a paramilitary police barracks in Timizar, 30 miles east of Algiers.

- On July 14, four linked "daisy-chain" IEDs killed four soldiers and wounded 13 others on patrol near Tizi Ouzou, 80 miles east of Algiers. Linking bombs in this fashion was a new technique for AQIM, which has a history of adopting methods of attack used elsewhere by al-Qa'ida or affiliated groups, especially in Iraq.

- On August 31 and September 1, three attacks took place within 24 hours. Terrorists stormed a mosque near Ain Defla, 60 miles southwest of Algiers, killing one and injuring eight. Near Boumerdes, a suicide bomber drove a pickup truck loaded with explosives into a military convoy 45 miles east of Algiers, killing two soldiers and wounding 30 others. A barrage of homemade rockets caused no injuries when they were fired at the judicial police headquarters 40 kilometers north of Tizi Ouzou.

Legislation and Law Enforcement: Algerian security forces – primarily gendarmerie troops under the Ministry of National Defense – conducted periodic sweeping operations in the Kabylie region southeast of the capital, targeting groups of AQIM fighters.

During the year, open source reports indicated that security forces killed or captured approximately 1,175 suspected terrorists. In December, a Boumerdes court sentenced six terrorists in absentia to death on a variety of charges, including murder, attempted murder, and belonging to a terrorist organization. Also in December, authorities suspended consideration of amnesty for 120 terrorists who had applied for amnesty under Algeria's Charter for Peace and National Reconciliation but who had resumed terrorist activity.

Also in December, the Interior Ministry began efforts to disband the communal guard forces, retiring older members and incorporating others into the army and municipal police forces. The Algerian government established the communal guard in 1996 by arming civilians to combat terrorism in the area between the cities of Blida, Algiers, and Medea. As terrorist incidents declined in that area, the government decided to disband the guard but used its forces to bolster counterterrorism units in the army and police.

Algerian law enforcement agencies cooperated with the United States and other foreign governments to prevent terrorist attacks against foreigners. The United States signed a Mutual Legal Assistance Treaty with Algeria in April, creating a framework for increased legal cooperation between Algeria and the United States. The United States provided multiple training courses to Algerian police, judges, and customs officials on cyber crime, bulk cash smuggling, and counterterrorism tactics.

Countering Terrorist Finance: Algeria is a member of the Middle East and North Africa Financial Action Task Force (MENAFATF), a Financial Action Task Force-style regional body, and its mutual evaluation report was adopted by that body in its December MENAFATF Plenary. Algeria has no specific legislation to freeze terrorist assets but maintained that its ratification of international terrorist financing conventions gave it the authority to do so.

In July, a presidential decree mandated that all financial transactions over US$ 6,671 be conducted by credit card, check, or other non-cash method in an effort to increase financial transparency, track illegal financing of terrorism and reduce the possibility of corruption.

Regional and International Cooperation: Algeria continued its efforts to create a viable regional mechanism to deal with AQIM in the countries to its south. It convened three separate meetings of regional foreign ministers, military chiefs of staff, and intelligence chiefs in Algiers to discuss coordinating a response to the threat of terrorism in the trans-Sahara region. Algeria, Mali, Mauritania, and Niger established a combined military command center in Tamanrasset in southern Algeria in September, and later established an intelligence sharing center in Algiers designed to feed information to the command center in Tamanrasset.

Countering Radicalization and Violent Extremism: Beginning in 2010, the Algerian government enlisted religious scholars and former terrorists to appear on its Radio Quran radio station and appeal directly to terrorists still fighting in the mountains. Programs featured Islamic scholars from Algeria and Gulf countries who argued against the doctrines used by AQIM to justify terrorist operations. Former Algerian terrorists appeared on these programs and appealed to terrorists to stop fighting and surrender to Algerian authorities. Other radio programs instructed listeners in various aspects of Islamic law. Algerian newspapers reported that the radio appeals played a major role in convincing scores of terrorists to lay down their arms and take advantage of government amnesty. Under the Charter for Peace and National Reconciliation, the Algerian government has offered amnesty to terrorists who surrender and have not committed major terrorist acts, such as bombings and rape.

The government has the authority to prescreen and approve sermons before they are delivered during Friday prayers. In practice, each province and county employs religious officials to review sermon content. The Ministry of Religious Affairs' educational commission is responsible for establishing policies for hiring teachers at Quranic schools and ensuring that all imams were well-qualified and follow governmental guidelines aimed at stemming violent extremism. The government also has youth outreach programs through the Muslim Scouts.

BAHRAIN

Overview: The Bahraini government worked to actively counter terrorist finance, enhanced border control capability, contributed manpower to international counterterrorism operations, realign internal responsibilities, and successfully prosecuted a number of cases under its 2006 counterterrorism law.

Legislation and Law Enforcement: Key to several Bahraini counterterrorism successes this year was a decision by the King to realign internal intelligence, analytical, and counterterrorism responsibilities in various government ministries under the Bahrain National Security Agency, which has resulted in a clearer delineation of roles and responsibilities allowed for greater capacity building and increased interagency cooperation.

Bahraini law enforcement actions included:

- On January 26, the High Criminal Court convicted and sentenced to five-year prison terms two Bahraini citizens affiliated with al-Qa'ida of plotting a terrorist attack against U.S. diplomatic and naval interests. On May 30, the court's decision was upheld by the Supreme Criminal Appeals Court. Key to the successful prosecution was the digital forensic evidence seized by Bahraini law enforcement.

- On July 5, seven Bahraini citizens were convicted under the 2006 counterterrorism law and sentenced to life imprisonment for their involvement in the March 2009 death of a Pakistani national who was presumed to be a plain clothed police officer at the time of the attack.

- On July 6, two Bahraini citizens were convicted by the High Criminal Court of plotting an April 2009 terrorist attack with a homemade bomb and were each sentenced to a 10-year prison term.

- During August to November, Bahraini law enforcement arrested at least 200 men, including minors, and held many of them under the counterterrorism law for various offenses. Twenty-five Bahraini citizens (including two in absentia) have been charged and the trial was ongoing at year's end. The arrests and subsequent prosecutions have been criticized by local and international human rights organizations as being political in nature, and there have been claims of mistreatment and coerced confessions by some of the detainees' defense counsels.

Countering Terrorist Finance: Bahrain worked actively to counter terrorist finance and hosted the Secretariat for the Middle East and North Africa Financial Action Task Force (MENAFATF), a Financial Action Task Force-style regional body. Bahrain worked cooperatively with its banks on anti-money laundering and counterterrorist finance (AML/CTF) issues. Bahraini law enforcement and customs officials also continued to build AML/CTF capacity through extensive training. In October, Bahrain imprisoned a Syrian national who had been convicted in absentia of terrorist financing by Bahraini courts and sentenced to a five-year prison term in February 2009. Despite progress, Bahrain has yet to adequately amend the law banning money laundering and combating terrorism finance. In addition, Bahrain's designated non-financial businesses and professions remained vulnerable to terrorist financing, due primarily to the non-issuance of legislation for regulating and monitoring the sector. Bahrain was asked to provide MENAFATF a follow up report in 2011 outlining progress.

Regional and International Cooperation: Since formally endorsing the Global Initiative to Combat Nuclear Terrorism in March 2008, Bahrain has worked to expand air, sea, and causeway border control points through increased training, internal cooperation, and staffing the border with officers capable of recognizing and interdicting nuclear proliferation materials such as centrifuges and commercially banned items. Bahrain acceded to the International Convention for the Suppression of Acts of Nuclear Terrorism as well as the Convention on the Physical Protection of Nuclear Material and its 2005 Amendment.

Countering Radicalization and Violent Extremism: Bahrain's efforts to counter radicalization and violent extremism have been spearheaded by the Ministry of Justice and Islamic Affairs (MJIA). The MJIA organized regular workshops and seminars for imams from both the Sunni and Shia sects, and expanded its international scholarship program to include religious schools in Egypt, Jordan, and the United Arab Emirates. It also completed an annual review of schools' Islamic Studies curriculum to evaluate interpretations of religious texts.

EGYPT

Overview: The Egyptian government's strong opposition to violent extremism, together with its effective intelligence and security services, made Egypt an unattractive operating environment for terrorist groups. However, while the government took steps to further secure its borders, Egypt's Northern Sinai region remained a base for the smuggling of arms and explosives into Gaza, and a transit point for Hamas officials and operatives. The smuggling of humans, weapons, cash, and other contraband through the Sinai into Israel and the Gaza Strip has created criminal networks that may be associated with terrorist groups in the region.

2010 Terrorist Incidents: In April and August, rockets were reportedly fired from the Sinai, striking in Jordan and Israel near the cities of Al Aqaba and Eilat, respectively.

Legislation and Law Enforcement: Many of the Egyptian president's far-reaching powers in the realm of counterterrorism come from Egypt's State of Emergency, which has been in force since 1981. Since 2005, former President Mubarak had pledged to lift the State of Emergency and replace it with new counterterrorism legislation, noting that Egypt should follow the example of other countries that have recently passed comprehensive laws to combat terrorism. Counterterrorism legislation had reportedly been drafted, but not submitted to or approved by Egypt's Parliament. Parliament renewed the State of Emergency in May, though it limited its application to terrorism and narcotics cases.

Egypt maintained its strengthened airport security measures and security for the Suez Canal, and instituted more stringent port security measures. The United States provided technical assistance to Egypt in an effort to ensure that the Rafah border crossing is used only for the peaceful and legal movement of people and goods.

In February, an Egyptian state security court began prosecution of 26 men arrested in July 2009 and dubbed the "Zeitun" cell by the media for robbing and murdering a Coptic Christian jeweler to fund terrorism activities. The group was also charged with the February 2009 Khan El Khalili bombing and of having ties with al-Qa'ida. At the end of 2010, the trial had not been completed.

In April, an Egyptian state security court convicted 26 men of belonging to a Hizballah cell that reportedly planned to attack Israeli tourists in the Sinai Peninsula and ships passing through the Suez Canal. Arrested in late 2008, the 26 men were also charged with smuggling weapons and goods through tunnels into the Gaza Strip. Sentences ranged from six months to life in prison. Four of the individuals were tried in absentia.

Countering Terrorist Finance: Over the past eight years, Egypt has tightened its terrorist finance regulations in keeping with relevant UNSCRs. Egypt regularly informed its own financial institutions of any individuals or entities that were designated by the UN 1267 sanctions committee.

Regional and International Cooperation: Egypt actively participated in the Arab League's Counterterrorism Committee. The Egyptian Assistant Deputy Foreign Minister for Counterterrorism was elected chair of this Arab League committee in 2010. Egypt also assisted states in the Middle East, Africa, and South Asia in building counterterrorism capacity.

Countering Radicalization and Violent Extremism: The Egyptian Government sponsored a number of counter-radicalization programs, including a "revision and reintegration program" for members of Al-Gama'a Al-Islamiyya and Egyptian Islamic Jihad who remained in detention. The goal was to further encourage the renunciation of violence through interaction with Egypt's Islamic scholars at Al-Azhar. In addition, the Ministry of Awqaf (Endowments) issued guidance to imams throughout Egypt that included directions to avoid extremism in sermons. Egypt's Al-Azhar University cooperated with Cambridge University on a training program for imams that promoted moderate Islam, inter-faith cooperation, and human rights.

IRAQ

Overview: Iraqi and U.S. security forces worked together and continued to make progress combating al-Qa'ida in Iraq (AQI), affiliated Sunni terrorist organizations, and Shia insurgents. Terrorist attacks primarily targeted Iraqi and U.S. security forces and government officials, but they were also aimed at stirring ethnic tensions among Iraqi sectarian groups and minorities.

AQI adapted to changing conditions and remained capable of large-scale and coordinated attacks. However, the Iraqi Security Forces (ISF) also improved its capabilities in combating terrorist networks with better targeting and capture and detention of terrorists. AQI operated primarily in regions with majority Sunni Arab populations, particularly focusing its efforts in and around Baghdad and Ninewa. The group targeted the ISF, government infrastructure, and sectarian groups in an effort to induce them to emigrate and to erode Iraqi security and governance capabilities.

Sunni leaders in Iraq have overwhelmingly rejected AQI and its extremist ideology. The Sons of Iraq (SOI) who cooperated with the security authorities continued to be a valuable asset in countering AQI. Some of AQI's members have defected, and the group has lost support in key mobilization areas, disrupting its infrastructure. On December 23, the ISF arrested 93 suspects in a crackdown of AQI bases in Anbar province.

Iran continued to fund, train, and provide weapons and ammunition to Shia extremist groups that carried out attacks against Iraqi and U.S. forces. Although attacks by these groups have decreased, their Iranian-supported networks continued to operate throughout Iraq's southern provinces. The Iraqi government pressed senior Iranian leaders to end support for Shia militias, and its national unity efforts to involve Iraqi Shia groups with Iranian ties, such as Asaib ahl al Haq (League of Righteousness), in the political process, have contributed to decreased Shia-linked violence. The ISF also carried out operations throughout southern Iraq and in Baghdad against extremists trained and equipped by Iran, including the Promised Day Brigade and Kata'ib Hezbollah (Brigades of the Party of God).

Jaysh Rijal al-Tariqah al-Naqshabandiyah (JRTN), a Sunni nationalist insurgent group with links to the former Ba'ath Party, also continued attacks during the year. JRTN targeted Iraqi and U.S. forces, Iranians, and Iraqi Shia groups whose members work with Iran.

Foreign fighters, though greatly diminished in number from previous years, continued to enter Iraq, predominantly through Syria. AQI and the group's Sunni extremist partners more often used Iraqi nationals, including women, as suicide bombers. According to Iraqi Ministry of Interior (MOI) security officials, however, four of the five terrorists who attacked the Our Lady of Salvation Church on October 31 were foreigners and 12 other terrorists, mostly foreign, have been implicated in planning the church attack, as well as planning to attack the French Embassy and the Ministry of Planning.

2010 Terrorist Incidents: The deadliest bomb attacks during the year were against security forces, government buildings, and western targets, and included:

- On January 25, suicide bombers struck in quick succession near three Baghdad hotels frequented by Western journalists killing at least 38 people and wounding more than 100.

- On January 26, a suicide car bomber sheared off the front of the main police crime lab in Baghdad, killing 21 and wounding 80.

- On April 4, at least 42 were killed and 249 injured as three bombs struck the Iranian, Egyptian, Syrian, and German embassies.

- On June 13, gunmen and suicide bombers attacked the Central Bank of Iraq, killing at least 18 and wounding dozens.

- On July 18, a suicide bomber killed 32 SOI fighters waiting for paychecks at a center west of Baghdad and wounded 20.

- On August 17, a suicide bomber blew himself up among hundreds of army recruits in Baghdad, killing 60 and wounding 128.

- On August 25, terrorists unleashed a wave of coordinated attacks in 13 towns and cities across Iraq, including hit-and-run shootings, improvised explosive devices (IEDs) and vehicle borne improvised explosive devices (VBIEDs), killing 51.

Major attacks late in the year that also targeted religious and sectarian groups included:

- On October 31, AQI members seized an Our Lady of Salvation Church in Baghdad, killing 58 and wounding 70 with combined IEDs, suicide vests, and small arms fire.

- On November 8, three VBIEDs detonated in the Shia holy cities of Najaf and Karbala killing 19 people and injuring 75, including Iranian pilgrims.

- On December 30, insurgents targeted Christian homes and neighborhoods in Baghdad with IEDs, killing two.

Legislation and Law Enforcement: The Government of Iraq took a number of steps to improve border security. A Council of Ministers' resolution called for a "unity of effort" among all government agencies at all Iraqi ports of entry (POEs). In addition, the MOI and the Minister of Interior for the Kurdistan Regional Government agreed to integrate all POEs in the Iraqi Kurdistan region into the Iraqi government's POE structure. Also, the Iraqi Customs Police returned to duty at the port of Umm Qasr after a two-year absence. Their presence has improved control over imports into Iraq.

The Major Crimes Task Force (MCTF), an agency handling terrorist cases, fostered a collaboration between investigators from Iraq and the United States. The MCTF investigated terrorism, high-profile violent crimes, and murders conducted by terrorists and members of organized criminal enterprises. Iraqi partners conducted complex criminal and counterterrorism investigations, which led to coordinated prosecution of defendants in Iraqi criminal courts. Seventy-two percent of the cases opened and assigned to the MCTF were capital cases involving terrorism.

Iraq continued to face significant challenges moving criminal cases from arrest to trial. The Iraqi government carried out few investigations of alleged sectarian-based crimes; arrests following a murder or other crimes were rare. U.S. and third-country law enforcement officials have trained Iraqi investigators and judges in investigative methodology and forensic evidence collection during the year.

Judicial security was a challenge. Judges investigating and adjudicating terrorism cases faced threats to their personal safety and that of their families. It is likely that some terrorism cases were dismissed due to actual or implied threats. To ameliorate this threat, the Chief Justice of the Higher Judicial Council appointed a cadre of judges to hear terrorism cases; these judges lived in secure apartment blocks. In addition, the government moved several judges hearing terrorism cases from Mosul to Baghdad to protect their safety.

Countering Terrorist Finance: Iraq is a member of the Middle East and North Africa Financial Action Task Force (MENAFATF). The Central Bank of Iraq (CBI) has a Financial Intelligence Unit called the Money Laundering Reporting Office (MLRO), which is still in the early stages of development. Iraq has not yet had a mutual evaluation, a compliance test by the Financial Action Task Force-International Monetary Fund of its anti-money laundering/counterterrorist financing (AML/CTF) regime. While the Director of the MLRO has undergone training on AML/CTF at the Federal Depository Insurance Corporation in the United States, Iraq appeared to have done little to enhance the MLRO to meet international standards. Iraq's AML/CFT legislation neglects to adequately outlaw money laundering and the financing of terrorism and conflicts with other areas of Iraqi legislation. The AML/CFT law was written in 2004 and requires amendment to bring it to international standards.

Regional and International Cooperation: In September, Iraq attended a security meeting held in Bahrain with the interior ministers from Bahrain, Egypt, Iran, Jordan, Kuwait, Saudi Arabia, Syria, and Turkey, as well as the UN, the Organization of Islamic Countries, and the Arab League. The participants issued a joint 20-point statement that stressed the importance of Iraq's internal security to the region and recommended the creation of "cooperative mechanisms" to further address regional security issues. Iraq, Turkey, and the United States continued their formal trilateral security dialogue as one element of ongoing cooperative efforts to counter the Kurdistan Workers' Party in the region.

Countering Radicalization and Violent Extremism: Iraq's MOI initiated a program to counter violent extremism and youth radicalization by making documentaries about terrorists in detention and about victims of terrorism. The Iraqi government also developed programs to counter violent extremist propaganda and to provide local youth positive examples and role models in society. These included USAID projects for at-risk youths and 4H Clubs. The UN Children's Fund in Iraq initiated a project to provide reintegration services for children released from pre/post trial detention. The United States supported a Government of Iraq program to provide local support following the release of militants in order to decrease recidivism and facilitate integration into local communities.

ISRAEL, WEST BANK, AND GAZA

Overview: Israel faced terrorist threats from designated terrorist organizations, such as Hamas and Palestine Islamic Jihad (PIJ) in the Gaza Strip and the West Bank, and Hizballah in Lebanon. Gaza-based Palestinian terrorist organizations continued rocket and mortar attacks into Israeli territory, and skirmished along the security fence surrounding the Gaza Strip. The Government of Israel responded to these terrorist threats as it has in recent years, with operations directed at terrorist leaders, infrastructure, and activities such as rocket launching teams. Israeli officials assessed that Hizballah continued to re-arm following the 2006 Lebanon War. No suicide bombings were carried out against Israeli targets. Israeli law enforcement agencies and courts arrested and sentenced a number of terrorist suspects. The Government of Israel emphasized counterterrorism priorities such as countering terrorist finance and improving aviation security efforts. Israel actively participated in regional and international counterterrorism efforts.

Rocket and mortar fire emanating from the Gaza Strip was the most prevalent form of attack by Palestinian terrorist organizations. The Government of Israel held Hamas, as the dominant organization in effective control of Gaza, responsible for all rocket and mortar attacks emanating from Gaza, even though the majority of such attacks were conducted by Palestinian Islamic Jihad (PIJ) and the Popular Resistance Committees from inside Gaza. Following such attacks, the Israel Defense Forces (IDF) launched reprisal airstrikes targeting terrorist training and weapons facilities, tunnels, and indirect fire launch teams in Gaza. On November 3 and 17, joint IDF/Israel Security Agency (ISA) operations killed two senior leaders of the Army of Islam terrorist group in Gaza. In December, there was a marked increase of rocket and mortar attacks from the Gaza Strip into Israel with a corresponding escalation of IDF reprisals.

Israeli government officials continued to believe that Operation Cast Lead in the Gaza Strip in December 2008-January 2009 helped achieve an increased level of deterrence, as the number of rocket and mortar launches decreased in comparison to years prior to the operation. The number of rocket and mortar launches from Gaza increased, however, during direct peace talks in September. Israeli officials asserted that Palestinian terrorist organizations used the relatively quiet period since Operation Cast Lead to re-arm and reorganize in preparation for any potential future conflict.

The rocket attacks demonstrated technological advancements, allowing groups to continue indigenous manufacturing and stockpiling of rockets at a low cost; the rockets could also be launched from greater distances and with larger warheads. In addition, Iran increased the provision of medium-range rockets. Israeli experts assessed that Hamas successfully smuggled Fajr-5 rockets from the Sinai Peninsula through tunnels into Gaza, and subsequently began producing these rockets in Gaza, which were capable of striking Tel Aviv suburbs. The Israeli Cabinet approved a plan in January to strengthen the Israeli city of Sderot and other communities adjacent to the Gaza Strip against rocket attacks. The Israeli public, however, expressed frustration with the IDF's decision not to deploy permanently the Iron Dome short-range rocket interception system to protect communities within rocket range. The use of a state-of-the-art KORNET anti-tank missile fired at an IDF tank on December 6 demonstrated an increased technological capability for Gaza-based terrorists.

Northern Border: Israeli security officials remained concerned about the terrorist threat posed to Israel from Hizballah and its Iranian and Syrian patrons, arguing that Iran, primarily through the efforts of the Iranian Revolutionary Guard Corps, continued to employ a sophisticated arms smuggling network through Syria to Hizballah in Lebanon. Israeli politicians and security officials pointed to Hizballah's efforts to rebuild and re-arm following the 2006 Lebanon War as evidence that Hizballah remained a threat to Israel. Israeli government officials claimed Hizballah possessed as many as 45,000 rockets and missiles, some of which are capable of striking Israeli population centers including Tel Aviv.

West Bank: The IDF and ISA continued to conduct operations in the West Bank to maintain pressure on Palestinian terrorist organizations and their supporters. Overall, Israeli security services continued the trend of relaxing movement and access measures in the West Bank. Construction on the security barrier in the West Bank and Jerusalem continued at a low level in some areas.

2010 Terrorist Incidents: Israel faced a variety of terrorist attacks and threats in 2010, including drive-by shootings, rocket and mortar fire from the Gaza Strip, skirmishes along the security fence surrounding Gaza, and in one case an attempted roadside bombing against an Israeli diplomatic convoy in Jordan on January 14. Israel also faced several new types of terrorist threats. During the first week of February, Israeli security forces neutralized three barrels containing explosive devices that washed ashore on beaches near Ashkelon, Ashdod, and Rishon Letzion. Israeli authorities believed terrorist organizations released the barrels into the sea from the Gaza Strip. On June 7, the Israeli Navy killed at least four alleged Palestinian terrorists in wetsuits off the coast of Gaza. The IDF claimed the terrorists intended to carry out an amphibious attack on Israel; the al-Aqsa Martyrs Brigade claimed those killed were members of its maritime unit.

Terrorist organizations continued to target Israel with rocket and mortar fire from various locales throughout Gaza. In 2010, it was estimated that between 102 and 200 projectiles landed in Israel.

In addition to rocket and mortar attacks, the IDF estimated approximately 100 terrorist-related incidents took place near the security fence surrounding Gaza since the beginning of 2010. These incidents included attempts to place bombs and IEDs along the fence or infiltrate Israeli territory, exchanges of fire, and rocket-propelled grenade attacks.

Legislation and Law Enforcement: In January, the Israel Airports Authority launched a biometric security system for outbound passengers at Ben Gurion International Airport. The Unipass Airport Management System was being tested before gradual expansion to include within two years all departing passengers who voluntarily register.

In December, the Knesset passed a draft bill that withholds the salary and pensions of any Knesset member suspected of or convicted for committing a terrorist attack. It was named after the former chairman of the Balad Party, Azmi Bishara, who was under investigation on suspicion of aiding Hizballah. The draft bill must pass two more readings before entering into law.

In December, the Ministerial Committee on Legislation approved a draft bill, which would empower courts to suspend attorney access to a terrorist suspect for up to 12 months in cases where suspicion exists that the meeting between the attorney and suspect might be used to coordinate a terrorist attack. The new draft bill may move forward following three readings and subsequent votes in the Knesset. The Minister of Internal Security initiated the draft bill; presently, attorney access to a detained suspect may be suspended for several periods of 21 days up to a maximum total period of three months.

On the law enforcement front, the ISA and Israel National Police (INP) continued to cooperate with U.S. law enforcement agencies on cases involving U.S. citizens killed in terrorist attacks, as well as other counterterrorism initiatives of mutual interest. Highlights included:

- In early January, Israeli security forces arrested two Israeli Arab residents of East Jerusalem at the Beersheva Central Bus Station for allegedly planning terrorist attacks on Israeli territory. According to an ISA investigation, the two men possessed a portable memory card with detailed plans for terrorist attacks against a hospital, hotels, and IDF bus stops in Israel; the men were allegedly recruited by Hamas in Jordan and Dubai.

- On October 12, the IDF Military Appeals Court found a Palestinian member of the al-Aqsa Martyrs' Brigades guilty in the murders of three Israelis – two soldiers and one civilian – in two shooting attacks in 2000 and 2002. The court convicted the defendants of voluntary manslaughter, assistance in voluntary manslaughter, attempted voluntary manslaughter, and shooting a person with live fire.

- On November 6, a Nazareth court indicted an imam from the Shihab al-Din Mosque and another Israeli Arab for supporting terrorist groups and inciting violence

Countering Terrorist Finance: Israel continued to enforce strong measures to prevent the financing of terrorism. Israel's policy of restricting economic activity with the Hamas-controlled Gaza Strip has sought to reduce inflows of funds that could support terrorist activity. The Government of Israel resumed social security payments to eligible Gazans, an indication of strong coordination among relevant authorities. Financing of Hamas through charitable organizations remained a concern for Israeli authorities. Regulation and enforcement of Israel's domestic financial industry is comparable in scope and effect to other highly industrialized and developed nations. Israel has active observer status in the Council of Europe's Select Committee of Experts on the Evaluation Of Anti-Money Laundering Measures (MONEYVAL), a Financial Action Task Force-style regional body. Israel's Money Laundering Prohibition Authority is a member of the Egmont Group.

Regional and International Cooperation: Through the UN Counter-Terrorism Committee Executive Directorate, Israel worked with Kenya and Uganda promoting such issues as border security, countering radicalization, and the "safe cities" concept - a network of cameras sending live footage to a 24-hour monitoring center. Israel also explored areas of counterterrorism cooperation with the Central Asian republics and the Economic Community of West African States. Israel hosted a homeland security conference with a counterterrorism emphasis in November, which was attended by several African nations, including Nigeria.

Israel agreed to join NATO's Partnership Action Plan against Terrorism (PAP-T), and was active in NATO crisis response, consequence management, and civil emergency planning working groups. Israel conducted a seminar on countering terrorist finance under the EU-Israel European Neighborhood Policy Action Plan, and participated in the EU Security Research Initiative to promote technological developments for counterterrorism purposes. Israel also engaged with the EU on transportation and aviation security efforts, including container security. Israelis participated in the OSCE Action against Terrorism Unit, including an October conference in Astana focused on transnational terrorism challenges. Israel was an active member of the Global Initiative to Combat Nuclear Terrorism (GICNT), and hosted a GICNT event in Jerusalem in June. Israel was active in the Megaports Initiative and participated as an observer in the Gaza Counter Arms Smuggling Initiative.

Bilaterally, Israel participated in the annual U.S.-Israel Joint Counterterrorism Group. Israel conducted strategic dialogues, including counterterrorism discussions, with Germany, Canada, Australia, France, Italy, India, Russia, and the United States.

PALESTINIAN TERRITORIES

Overview: The primary Palestinian Authority (PA) security forces in the West Bank were the Civil Police, the National Security Forces (NSF), the Preventive Security Organization, the General Intelligence Service, the Presidential Guard (PG), and the Civil Defense. Much of the PA security forces are under the Interior Minister's operational control and follow the Prime Minister's guidance. Israeli authorities, among others, noted continuing improved capacity and performance of PA security forces as a leading contributor to the improved security environment of the West Bank.

Hamas continued to consolidate its control over Gaza, eliminating or marginalizing potential rivals. Gaza remained a base of operations for several terrorist organizations besides Hamas, such as PIJ; Salafist splinter groups, such as Jund Ansar Allah and Jaysh al-Islam; and clan-based criminal groups that engaged in or facilitated terrorist attacks. Hamas relied on its internal intelligence, police, coastal patrol, border guard, and military-wing "Executive Force" bodies, probably numbering at least 15,000 in total.

2010 Terrorist Incidents: In 2010, there were multiple acts of violence conducted to achieve political goals by different sub-state actors in the West Bank, both Israeli and Palestinian. There were no attacks targeted against Americans. Attacks included:

- On May 4, arson was committed against a mosque south of Nablus in the village of Al Lubban Ash Sharqiya. While perpetrators were never apprehended, it is possible this act was committed in order to stall any political progress related to the Israeli government's 10-month moratorium, imposed in November 2009, on new residential construction in West Bank settlements. This town has no Palestinian Police station and is under Israeli security control.

- On August 31, four Israeli residents of the West Bank settlement of Beit Hagai were killed by gunfire while traveling by car in an area under Israeli security control near Hebron. Hamas spokesmen quickly claimed responsibility for the attack.

- On September 1, two Israeli residents of a Jordan Valley settlement were wounded in a shooting attack near the West Bank settlement of Kokhav Hashahar in an area under Israeli military control, approximately seven miles north-east of Ramallah. Hamas's Izz al-Din al-Qassam Brigades quickly published a "military communique" claiming responsibility.

- On October 4, arson was committed by Israeli citizens against a mosque southwest of Bethlehem in the village of Beit Fajjar, which is under Israeli security control. In addition to fire damage, the mosque was vandalized with Hebrew-language graffiti "revenge" and "price tag."

- On October 20, arson was committed against a Palestinian girls' school building south of Nablus in the village of As Sawiya, which is under Israeli security control. The damaged building also had Hebrew-language graffiti: "regards from the hilltops," suggesting the attack was conducted by Israeli settlers.

Legislation and Law Enforcement: In response to the West Bank shootings that occurred August 31 and September 1, PA security forces and IDF personnel mounted large-scale campaigns throughout the West Bank. By noon on September 1, the PA had detained 283 Hamas supporters for questioning; by September 3 that number had grown to 600. PA President Abbas and Prime Minister Fayyad issued statements condemning each attack. On September 2, President Abbas announced that the PA security forces had tracked down the vehicle used to conduct the August 31 shooting.

The primary limitation on PA counterterrorism efforts in the Gaza Strip remained Hamas' continued control of the area and the resulting inability of PA security forces to operate there. No apparent progress was made in apprehending, prosecuting, or bringing to justice the perpetrators of the October 2003 attack on a U.S. Embassy convoy in Gaza that killed three U.S. government contractors and critically injured a fourth.

Limitations on PA counterterrorism efforts in the West Bank included restrictions on the movement and activities of PA security forces in areas of the West Bank for which the Israeli government retained responsibility for security (some 80 percent of that total land area).

The limited capacity of the PA's civilian criminal justice system also hampered PA counterterrorism efforts. U.S. assistance to police and prosecutors began to have an effect at the local district level in Jenin, where case management improved and backlogs decreased. The PA continued to lack modern forensic capability. Ongoing low-level violence between Israeli settlers and Palestinians in the West Bank tested the limited mandates of PA security forces.

The Palestinian Legislative Council has not functioned since mid-2007, and President Abbas issued no decrees related to counterterrorism. However, a Memorandum of Understanding between police and prosecutors was finalized in 2010 that established best practices for working together, and the Ministry of Justice has begun the first re-write of the penal code in 50 years.

Countering Terrorist Finance: The PA continued its efforts against terrorist financing in the West Bank and Gaza by increasing its capacity to detect, analyze, and interdict suspicious financial activity. The Palestinian financial intelligence unit (referred to locally as the "Financial Follow-up Unit" or FFU) continued to build its capacity. The Palestinian Monetary Authority maintained a staff of roughly 80 in the Gaza Strip to conduct on-site bank examinations, including audits of bank compliance with the PA's 2007 Anti-Money Laundering decree. The PA Ministries of Interior and of Awqaf and Religious Affairs also continued to monitor the charitable sector for signs of abuse by terrorist organizations. PA security forces seized nearly US$10 million in cash from Hamas in 2010, according to PA officials. The PA is an observer to the Middle East and North Africa Financial Action Task Force (MENAFATF), a Financial Action Task Force-style regional body.

Regional and International Cooperation: The United States continued to assist the PA's counterterrorism efforts through the capacity building of PA security forces. As of the end of the year, six NSF battalions and one Presidential Guard battalion had been trained and equipped under the auspices of the U.S. Security Coordinator (USSC). USSC-run training of NSF battalions took place at the Jordan International Police Training Center in Jordan.

Countering Radicalization and Violent Extremism: PA President Mahmoud Abbas and Prime Minister Salam Fayyad consistently condemned acts of violence and reiterated their support for a peaceful, negotiated solution to the Palestinian-Israeli conflict. The PA Minister of Awqaf and Religious Affairs, a former Hamas member who broke with that organization in the 1990s to protest its abuse of religion to justify violence, spoke out publicly against Hamas's rule of Gaza and against attempts to incite violence against non-Muslims. PA efforts to end incitement to violence continued with officials monitoring sermons given in West Bank mosques. There were no such efforts against incitement in Gaza, where the de facto Hamas authorities continued to support and practice incitement in public statements.

JORDAN

Overview: The Jordanian Government responded effectively to several terrorist incidents within the country, and its security forces detected and thwarted several others. Jordan remained committed to a just and durable settlement of the Israel-Palestine dispute and strongly backed President Obama's peace initiatives. In addition to its diplomatic and political assistance to the peace process, Jordan supported the Palestinian Authority and the development of state institutions through its law enforcement training programs at the Jordan International Police Training Center. Jordan was an important voice against violent extremism throughout the region.

2010 Terrorist Incidents:

- On January 14, an Israeli diplomatic vehicle movement was struck by an apparent improvised explosive device (IED) en route to the King Hussein Bridge from Amman. There were no deaths or injuries in the attack.

- On April 22, several rockets were fired at the Red Sea port city of Aqaba. The rockets were allegedly fired from the Sinai Peninsula and may have been targeting the neighboring Israeli city of Eilat. There were no deaths or injuries.

- On August 2, Aqaba again came under rocket attack from the Sinai. Several rockets hit both Eilat and Aqaba, causing one Jordanian fatality and injuring four others.

Local and international media also announced the deaths or arrests of several Jordanian nationals participating in terrorist activities overseas:

- In January, Jordanian al-Qa'ida militant Mahmoud Abu Zeidan was killed in the Afghanistan-Pakistan border region.

- In June, media outlets also reported that two Jordanian violent extremists had been killed in operations against Russian forces in Chechnya.

- In November, local media outlets reported that al-Qa'ida in Iraq (AQI) had confirmed the deaths of four Jordanian terrorists in Iraq in July.

- In December, a Jordanian national was arrested in Yemen in connection with a grenade attack against a U.S. embassy vehicle.

Legislation and Law Enforcement: The first phase of the Joint Border Security Program was completed in September, including the installation of a suite of monitoring and communications equipment along a 50km stretch of Jordan's border with Syria. This border area has historically presented the highest risk of illicit infiltration and smuggling across Jordan's border and it accounted for the greatest number of interdictions by Jordanian law enforcement.

In addition, Jordanian security services remained alert to potential terrorist threats within the country and responded swiftly and effectively to counter identified plots. As a result of their vigilance, several planned attacks were disrupted prior to execution.

The State Security Court (SSC) has primary jurisdiction for terrorism cases and it maintained a substantial caseload during the year. For example:

- In March, three men were sentenced to terms ranging from three years to life for plotting to attack Jordanian security service facilities.

- In March, the SSC convicted six men (including one in absentia) of conspiring to attack Israeli targets during the in 2008-09 Israeli military incursion into the Gaza Strip. The five in custody received sentences of five to 15 years.

- In September, two brothers were arrested and charged with plotting to attack foreign officials in Jordan. According to Jordanian officials, the two had already illegally acquired weapons and attempted to conduct surveillance for their planned assault.

- In October, the SSC convicted 10 men on charges of plotting to attack U.S. individuals and facilities and planning to attack U.S. convoys engaged in resupplying multinational forces in Iraq. One plotter was sentenced to life imprisonment and the other nine received 15-year prison terms.

Countering Terrorist Finance: Jordan remedied a number of significant deficiencies identified by the Middle East and North Africa Financial Action Task Force (MENAFATF) in its mutual evaluation of Jordan, and, by November, had effectively rectified the areas of non- or partial compliance with Financial Action Task Force's core and key recommendations. Jordan implemented these improvements through royal decrees, which were binding and carried the weight of parliamentary legislation. Although the new parliament has the power to pass legislation, the decrees are permanent regardless of parliamentary action. Jordan additionally strengthened its capacity to investigate and prosecute terrorist finance cases. Enhanced legal authorities were matched by improved staffing levels and better physical infrastructure for Jordan's Financial Intelligence Unit (FIU). The Jordanian government participated in several U.S. government-funded training courses, workshops, and technical assistance visits, and hosted a regional anti-money laundering/countering terrorist finance (AML/CTF) seminar aimed at strengthening operational cooperation between regional FIUs. These efforts resulted in significant operational improvements in 2010. The first two indictments for money laundering were brought in Jordan in January and April. In both, the predicate offenses were committed outside of Jordan. One conviction has been achieved to date, involving two defendants and resulting in a sentence of three years' hard labor, a fine of 10,000 Jordanian Dinars (approximately US$ 14,000), and confiscation of the criminal proceeds. In December, Jordan initiated its first domestic prosecution under its strengthened CTF legal regime.

Regional and International Cooperation: Jordan continued to play a constructive role in the process of stabilizing Iraq and integrating it back into the Arab region. Jordan is a member of the Friends of Yemen Working Group, and worked carefully with its international partners and Yemeni counterparts to reform the country's legal and judicial framework. As co-chair of the Rule of Law working group, Jordan hosted a meeting in Amman in July.

Countering Radicalization and Violent Extremism: The Jordanian Government remained firmly committed to combating not just terrorist organizations, but to countering the violent ideology that motivates terrorism. The Royal Aal al-Beit Institute for Islamic Thought, under the patronage of Prince Ghazi bin-Mohammad, continued its sponsorship of ecumenical events promoting interfaith dialogue. Known collectively as "The Common Word" series (after the missive written by Prince Ghazi to Pope Benedict XVI and signed by hundreds of Islamic scholars and Imams), these events sought to promote interreligious and cross-cultural understanding. In a September 25 speech at the UN General Assembly, King Abdullah II successfully proposed UN recognition of "World Interfaith Harmony Week. These interfaith outreach efforts build upon the 2005 Amman Message.

Recognizing the key role that incarceration has played in the radicalization of many terrorists, Jordanian authorities continued their program of theological engagement with suspected radical inmates. This program employed carefully selected and vetted religious scholars and jurists to introduce

Baghdad, Iraq: Iraqis gather at the scene of a car bomb that exploded on April 23, 2010 in the Baghdad district of Sadr City. A series of five car bombs, three during prayers at Shiite mosques in Baghdad, and other attacks across Iraq, killed 58 people. AFP PHOTO/ AHMAD AL-RUBAYE

or reinforce more balanced views, based upon established Islamic jurisprudence and teachings. Jordan segregated extremist prisoners in order to deny them the opportunity to spread their violent ideology among the general inmate population.

KUWAIT

Overview: Despite a lack of legal provisions that deal specifically with terrorism and terrorist financing, the Government of Kuwait maintained its efforts to counter terrorism, notably in the prosecutions of terrorists and terrorism facilitators for other offenses throughout the year.

Legislation and Law Enforcement: The Government of Kuwait lacks a clear legal framework for prosecuting terrorism-related crimes, often having to resort to other legal statues to try suspected terrorists, which hampers enforcement efforts. In February, Kuwait City's head prosecutor commented in *al-Qabas* newspaper that Kuwait needed stronger counterterrorism legislation and a clearer definition of what constituted a terrorist act.

On October 28, an appeals court upheld the May 10 acquittal of eight individuals accused of illegal weapons possession and planning to perform a hostile act against a foreign government, stemming from a plot to carry out attacks on U.S. and Kuwaiti installations at Camp Arifjan in southern Kuwait.

On June 28, a criminal court sentenced 11 defendants to three-year prison terms for a variety of terrorism-related charges, including acts of aggression committed in Afghanistan and possession of weapons training materials. Seven of the convicted were tried in absentia. The disposition of their cases was not known at the end of the reporting period.

On April 26, an appeals court overturned the December 2009 conviction of terrorist facilitator Nasser Ali Snaitan al-Otaibi on charges of collecting funds to commit hostile acts against coalition forces in Afghanistan, and vacated a seven-year prison sentence. The Court of Appeals found that the prosecution had not sufficiently linked funds collected at al-Otaibi's mosque to financing terrorist activity in Afghanistan.

UNSCR 1267 designee Mubarak al-Bathali was detained and released twice during the year. According to press reports, Kuwait State Security detained al-Bathali after he called the Yemeni Ambassador to Kuwait, offering to mediate between the Government of Yemen and al-Qa'ida in the Arabian Peninsula (AQAP). In an alleged recording of the phone call available on *YouTube*, al-Bathali threatened that AQAP's efforts in Yemen would escalate unless Yemen "stopped following American orders." Al-Bathali was detained on September 13 because of a video he posted to *YouTube* on September 11, threatening to "cut the neck" of Shia Member of Parliament Hussain al-Qallaf in response to incendiary comments made by exiled Shia cleric Yasser al-Habib. Al-Bathali was released four days later after making a public apology.

Countering Terrorist Finance: The Kuwaiti government lacked comprehensive legislation that criminalizes terrorist financing. Draft comprehensive anti-money laundering/counterterrorist finance (AML/CTF) legislation was first submitted to the National Assembly in December 2009. Kuwait's parliament rejected the combined bill in November 2010, sending it back to the Council of Ministers with a request to separate terrorist finance from the AML law. By separating terrorist financing from money laundering, Kuwait made measured progress over the past year on its draft AML legislation, which remained under consideration by the Parliament. Despite the lack of adequate legislation, authorities have continued efforts to combat financial crimes, including holding an annual AML/CTF conference to educate government and private sector officials on the issues.

The Ministry of Social Affairs and Labor (MoSAL) and the Ministry of Foreign Affairs (MFA) continued their monitoring and supervision of charities, including enforcing the ban on cash donations except during Ramadan, implementing an enhanced receipt system for Ramadan cash donations, and coordinating closely with the Ministry of Islamic Affairs to monitor and prosecute fraudulent charitable operators. MoSAL reported a continued decline in the number of violations during its 2010 Ramadan audit and an increase in donations, despite more stringent collection regulations. MoSAL added an electronic bank debit option in 2010, allowing charitable funds to move through formal financial channels that can be more easily tracked. MFA and MoSAL officials also worked closely with recipient foreign governments, conducting foreign site visits and audits of selected foreign projects funded by Kuwaiti charities.

Kuwait is a member of MENAFATF, a Financial Action Task Force-style regional body. In late 2010, Kuwait had its on-site visit as part of its mutual evaluation. The report of the evaluation will be discussed in 2011. Kuwait is also a member of the Gulf Cooperation Council, which is a member of the Financial Action Task Force.

Regional and International Cooperation: As in previous years, the Kuwaiti Armed Forces, National Guard, and Ministry of Interior conducted a number of exercises aimed at responding to terrorist attacks, including joint exercises with regional and international partners.

Countering Radicalization and Violent Extremism: Government officials routinely made statements denouncing violent extremism. In his opening remarks to the 31st Gulf Cooperation Council Summit on December 4, the Amir strongly condemned terrorist acts, expressing support for regional and international efforts in the fight against terrorism in all its forms. Kuwaiti television stations ran advertisements discouraging youth from engaging in terrorist activity, emphasizing the negative effects that extremism has on the families and social groups of radicalized youth.

The al-Salam Center, opened by the Government of Kuwait in 2009 – is a treatment facility modeled after the Kingdom of Saudi Arabia's rehabilitation center – to rehabilitate religious extremists, including Kuwaitis repatriated from Guantanamo Bay Detention Center. The facility is located in a secured area within Kuwait's Central Prison and is governed by a board of government officials, medical experts, and a religious scholar.

LEBANON

Overview: The Lebanese government, despite continuous political crisis and the looming threat of armed civil conflict, continued to build its counterterrorism capacity and to cooperate in supporting U.S. counterterrorism efforts. Over the course of the year, Lebanese authorities increased efforts to disrupt suspected terrorist cells before they could act, arrested numerous suspected al-Qa'ida-affiliated militants and Palestinian violent extremists, and uncovered several weapons caches. The Lebanese Armed Forces (LAF), in particular, were credited with capturing wanted terrorist fugitives and containing sectarian violence.

Prime Minister Saad Hariri, despite threats from the Hizballah-led opposition, remained steadfast in his support for the Special Tribunal for Lebanon (STL). The STL was established in May 2007 by UNSCR 1757 to investigate the February 14, 2005, assassination of former Prime Minister Rafik Hariri and others, and it began its work in March 2009. After press reports indicated that the Tribunal planned to indict Hizballah members in the Hariri assassination, Hizballah Secretary General Hassan Nasrallah vehemently denied Hizballah's involvement in the assassinations and vowed to "cut off" any hand that attempted to reach any of the militia's members, and Hizballah officials repeatedly threatened violence should any of the group's members be indicted by the Tribunal. The LAF, concerned about a sectarian conflict, deployed forces in Beirut and other key areas, and LAF commanders publicly voiced their intent to prevent any group from fomenting civil strife.

Several terrorist organizations remained active in Lebanon. Hamas, the Popular Front for the Liberation of Palestine, the Popular Front for the Liberation of Palestine General Command, Asbat al-Ansar, Fatah al-Islam, Jund al-Sham, the Ziyad al-Jarrah Battalions, and several other splinter groups all operated within Lebanon's borders. Al-Qa'ida (AQ)-affiliated extremists and Palestinian extremists operated primarily out of Lebanon's 12 Palestinian refugee camps. The LAF does not have a day-to-day presence in the camps but it occasionally conducted operations in the camps to combat terrorist threats. Hizballah, with deep roots among Lebanon's Shia community, remained the most prominent and influential terrorist group in Lebanon. The Lebanese government views Hizballah, a U.S. Designated Foreign Terrorist Organization, as a legitimate "resistance" group opposing Israeli occupation of Lebanese territory and as a political party that was represented by elected deputies in Lebanon's parliament and has two ministers in the cabinet.

Security along the Syria-Lebanon border remained problematic. In 2010, the Government of Lebanon did not exercise control over parts of the border. Over the course of the year, conflicting reports surfaced of weapons smuggling from Syria and Iran to Hizballah and other militant groups in Lebanon.

Security along the Syria-Lebanon border remained problematic. In 2010, the Government of Lebanon did not exercise control over parts of the border. Over the course of the year, conflicting reports surfaced of weapons smuggling from Syria and Iran to Hizballah and other militant groups in Lebanon. Reports from UN Interim Force in Lebanon (UNIFIL) and the LAF claimed there was no conclusive evidence of arms smuggling to Hizballah in the UNIFIL area of operations south of the Litani River.

On February 15, fighting involved rocket propelled grenades and automatic gunfire broke out in the Ain el-Hilweh Palestinian refugee camp between Fatah and Asbat al-Ansar members, resulting in four deaths and numerous wounded. On June 19, a Spanish UNIFIL patrol discovered 300 kilograms of explosives buried in the ground on the road leading to al-Wazani and Abbasieh villages. On October 26, the LAF Intelligence Bureau discovered a large weapons cache and bomb making materials hidden in a drain near Majdal Anjar.

Legislation and Law Enforcement: Lebanon participated in the Megaports and Container Security initiatives, becoming the first Arab nation to complete the Megaports installation and pass acceptance testing. The Megaports program was officially transferred to the Lebanese government in November.

In 2010, significant law enforcement actions against terrorists and terrorist groups included:

- On January 19, four members of Fatah al-Islam were arrested by the LAF Intelligence Bureau for plotting the prison break of Fatah al-Islam associates held in Roumiyeh prison; 14 Fatah al-Islam members were indicted, including six already in custody.

- On April 19, the military court sentenced 10 extremists to various prison terms ranging from three years hard labor to life in prison for conducting terrorist attacks, forging identification documents, smuggling arms, and committing other crimes.

- On June 1, the military court sentenced 14 Palestinians to life in prison for planning terrorist attacks against UNIFIL.

- On September 6, the military court sentenced members of the al-Qa'ida affiliated Bar Elias terrorist group to terms ranging from one year hard labor to life imprisonment for the 2007 plot to conduct terrorist attacks by firing missiles at the city of Zahle in the Bekaa Valley.

- On November 12, the military court sentenced 54 individuals affiliated with al-Qa'ida and Fatah al-Islam to terms ranging from 18 months hard labor to life in prison.

As described in the 2009 Country Reports on Terrorism, Lebanese authorities maintained that the amnesty for Lebanese individuals involved in acts of violence during the 1975-90 civil wars prevented the government from prosecuting terrorist cases of concern to the United States.

Countering Terrorist Finance: Lebanon is a member of the Middle East and North Africa Financial Action Task Force (MENAFATF). Lebanon's financial intelligence unit is the Special Investigation Commission (SIC), an independent legal entity empowered to investigate suspicious financial transactions, lift banking secrecy, and freeze assets. The SIC is a member of the Egmont Group. From January to November 2010, it investigated 179 cases involving allegations of money laundering, terrorism, and terrorist financing activities. The SIC referred requests for designation or asset freezes regarding Hizballah and affiliated groups to the Ministry of Foreign Affairs, but the Lebanese government did not require banks to freeze these assets because it does not consider Hizballah a terrorist organization. In October, the SIC in collaboration with the IMF and World Bank, hosted a MENAFATF assessor training workshop, providing training to MENAFATF experts to conduct mutual evaluations.

LIBYA

Overview: The Libyan government continued to demonstrate a strong and active commitment to combating terrorist organizations and violent extremism through bilateral and regional counterterrorism and security cooperation, particularly on the issue of foreign fighter flow to Iraq. Domestically, the Government of Libya has continued implementation of a counter-radicalization program focused on rehabilitating former Libyan Islamic Fighting Group (LIFG) leaders and members, as well as other Libyans formerly involved with extremist organizations. Regionally, Libya remained a counterterrorism ally and worked with neighboring countries to counter and respond to terrorist threats stemming from al-Qa'ida in the Islamic Maghreb (AQIM) and other extremist groups.

Legislation and Law Enforcement: Libya maintained long-standing legislation that was used to counter terrorism and terrorist financing. During recent prisoner releases, Saif al-Islam al-Qadhafi, the son of Libyan leader Muammar al-Qadhafi, indicated that some individuals involved in domestic political opposition movements had been wrongly imprisoned on charges of terrorism. New legislation on immigration, ratified during the first half of 2010, contained articles designed to counter the spread of terrorism into Libya.

In 2010, Libya took steps to improve its capacity to monitor its borders and coastlines in an effort to strengthen domestic counterterrorism and security capabilities. The Government of Libya has requested additional support for training of and technical assistance to border guards and security personnel. The government's security ministries and agencies also cooperated with European partners to better train and equip domestic security forces. The government maintained strict port security measures and requested assistance from European nations to expand technical capacity to monitor its 2,000 km desert border.

The Libyan government enforced strict security measures and controls over tourist activity within the country, due to concerns that foreign tourists represented attractive targets for terrorists.

Countering Terrorist Finance: Libya maintained legislation to counter terrorist financing and money laundering. The Libyan Central Bank's Financial Crimes Unit led Libya's efforts to fight terrorist finance and money laundering but lacked the capacity to operate effectively. Libya's largely cash-based economy further complicated regulation and monitoring of domestic financial activity.

Regional and International Cooperation: In September, the heads of state from Libya, Algeria, Mauritania, and Mali met in the coastal city of Sirte to discuss coordination efforts to identify and combat security threats linked to AQIM in the Sahel-Sahara region. Regional governments have publicly confirmed coordination between Libya, Algeria, and Mali on military and intelligence efforts to fight threats from AQIM.

Countering Radicalization and Violent Extremism: In coordination with the Qadhafi International Charity and Development Foundation (QDF), the Libyan government worked to combat domestic terrorist threats through a counter-radicalization program among former members of the LIFG and other terrorist organizations. The goal of the rehabilitation efforts was through dialogue on and exposure to moderate interpretations of Islam, to encourage Libyans formerly involved in terrorist activity to renounce violence and reintegrate into Libyan society.

At a March 24 press conference, QDF chairman and son of Libyan leader Muammar al-Qadhafi, Saif al-Islam, announced the release of 214 prisoners as part of the counter-radicalization program. The released prisoners included the three top LIFG figures, 31 other LIFG members, 100 former members of "radical groups involved in Iraq," as well as 80 individuals charged as associates of "jihadist cells" but whom the Libyan courts had determined were actually prisoners of conscience. Another 37 former LIFG members were released in September as part of the same program. During the press conference, Saif al-Islam claimed that the individuals no longer constituted a threat to Libyan society and would be reintegrated into their communities. The Libyan government and QDF oversee the reintegration process, which includes job training and counseling.

The Libyan government, working with the government-sponsored World Islamic Call Society, QDF, and the government-affiliated Waatesimu Charity Organization, sponsored visits to Libya throughout the last year by a number of moderate Egyptian and Saudi Islamic scholars. The visits were designed to reach out primarily to populations of the country that have historically been politically disenfranchised, as well as to those in detention on terrorism-related charges. The World Islamic Call Society issued guidance to imams throughout Libya that included direction to avoid extremism in sermons.

MOROCCO

Overview: Morocco's counterterrorism efforts were comprehensive in 2010. The Moroccan government emphasized vigilant security measures, regional and international cooperation, and counter-radicalization policies. Indications from Moroccan authorities' disruption of certain groups, and the common characteristics of those groups, continued to support previous analysis that Morocco's threat of terrorist attack stemmed largely from the existence of numerous small "grassroots" extremist cells. These groups, referred to collectively as adherents of Moroccan Salafia Jihadia ideology, remained isolated from one another, small in size, and tactically limited. Their international connections were also limited. The Government of Morocco's counterterrorism efforts have effectively reduced the threat, but the existence of these relatively small groups pointed to the need for continued vigilance.

2010 Terrorist Incidents: Reports of Moroccans either preparing to go or going to terrorist fronts in Somalia, Iraq, and Afghanistan to receive training from al-Qa'ida (AQ) linked facilitators and/or to conduct attacks suggest Morocco remained a source for foreign fighter pipelines. With regard to al-Qa'ida in the Islamic Maghreb (AQIM). The group remained unable to mount a successful terrorist attack in Morocco. Nonetheless, Moroccan authorities remained concerned about the ideological inspiration and knowledge transfer that AQIM may have provided to Moroccan extremists. AQIM repeatedly tried to incite Moroccans to commit violence against their government through website propaganda. The government remained concerned about numbers of veteran Moroccan violent extremists returning from Iraq to conduct terrorist attacks at home. A further cause of concern was Moroccans who were radicalized during their stays in Western Europe, such as those connected with the 2004 Madrid train bombings.

Legislation and Law Enforcement: At a tactical law enforcement level, the Moroccan Directorate General for National Security created a new police special weapons and tactics unit in cooperation with the French government. The new team is based at the Royal Police Academy in Kénitra, and, once operational, its primary responsibilities will be to dismantle terrorist cells and carry out other high-risk urban interventions. With regard to legislation, the Government of Morocco generally accorded terrorist suspects and convicts their rights and due process of law, with more access for defense lawyers and more transparent court proceedings than in previous years.

Morocco's counterterrorism efforts led to the following disruptions of alleged terrorist cells:

- In April, the Moroccan security services arrested 38 members of an AQ-linked terrorist cell who reportedly were planning to send Moroccan volunteers to Somalia, Iraq, and the Sahel. Some cell members, according to the Ministry of Interior, were planning acts of sabotage within Morocco.

- In June, Moroccan authorities arrested 11 members of a Palestinian-led cell that had planned to carry out attacks and assassinations of Moroccan public figures and Jewish people of Moroccan origin, in addition to attacks on tourism sites and police stations.

- In August, Ministry of Interior officials arrested 18 individuals in the Tangier area who were planning to carry out terrorist attacks in several Moroccan cities, with a specific focus on Moroccan military bases and tourist sites that typically attract foreigners.

- In October, Ministry of Interior officials dismantled an international network of cocaine traffickers that reportedly had links with AQIM. The arrests included 34 individuals, at least three of whom were foreigners. The head of the organization in Morocco was included in these arrests and was working closely with another man involved in the network in Mali.

Countering Terrorist Finance: Morocco has a relatively effective system through its Financial Intelligence Unit (FIU), which became operational in late 2009, for disseminating U.S. government and UNSCR terrorist freeze lists to its financial sector and legal authorities. While Morocco is not a regional financial center, it is well integrated into the international financial system. Money laundering was a concern due to the illicit narcotics trade, vast informal sector, trafficking in persons, and large level of remittances from Moroccans living abroad.

The Government of Morocco estimated that Morocco's informal sector accounts for 15 percent of GDP. The predominant use of cash, informal value transfer systems, and remittances from abroad help fuel Morocco's informal sector. Morocco pursued aggressive anti-money laundering legislation and has taken steps to act against violators. Although the legislation targets previously unregulated cash transfers, the country's vast informal sector created conditions for this practice to continue. As of early December, the Moroccan Parliament was debating a new anti-money laundering law that is similar to U.S. anti-money laundering legislation. In addition, Morocco signed an arrangement with the U.S. Department of Treasury to receive technical assistance in the form of a FIU advisor.

Regional and International Cooperation: Moroccan-U.S. cooperation was particularly strong. Moroccan authorities continued to disrupt plots to attack Moroccan, U.S., and other Western-affiliated targets, and aggressively investigated numerous individuals associated with international terrorist groups, often in collaboration with international partners. Morocco and the United States worked together extensively on counterterrorism efforts at the tactical level and made plans to begin joint counter-radicalization programs.

Morocco ratified the International Convention for the Suppression of Acts of Nuclear Terrorism. Morocco has forged solid cooperative relationships with European and African partners by sharing information, conducting joint operations, and participating in training maneuvers. Morocco participates in multilateral peacekeeping operations on the continent and in training exercises. These were important steps, yet the lack of consistent cooperation among countries in the region remained a potential weakness for terrorist groups such as AQIM to exploit. Specifically, while Morocco and Algeria are members of the Trans-Saharan Counterterrorism Partnership, the level of bilateral cooperation on counterterrorism between the two countries did not improve. Morocco was specifically excluded from the Algerian-led Combined Operational Committee (CEMOC), formed at Tamanrasset, Algeria. Algeria and Morocco's political disagreement over the Western Sahara territory remained an impediment to deeper counterterrorism cooperation.

Countering Radicalization and Violent Extremism: In addition to traditional security measures, Morocco's King Mohammed VI has promoted significant efforts to reduce extremism and dissuade individuals from becoming radicalized. At Ramadan, for example, the King hosted a series of religious lectures, inviting Muslim speakers from around the world to promote moderate and peaceful religious interpretations. In the past decade, and specifically following the Casablanca (2003) and Madrid (2004) terrorist bombings, Morocco has increasingly focused on countering youth radicalization, upgrading places of worship, modernizing the teaching of Islam, and strengthening the Ministry of Endowments and Islamic Affairs (MEIA). Begun in 2007 under the MEIA, the pioneering experiment of training and using women as spiritual guides continued. Morocco also formed a Council of Ulema for Europe to train and send Moroccan imams and women spiritual guides to counter extremist messages in Moroccan expatriate communities in Europe. In 2010, the MEIA turned its attention to the medium of television. On June 19, Morocco connected its 2,000 largest mosques to a new television network named "Assadisa," whose goal is to broadcast a tolerant version of Islam as part of the Ministry's drive to fight radicalism.

In 2010, the Moroccan government continued to implement internal reforms aimed at ameliorating the socio-economic factors that terrorists exploit. The National Initiative for Human Development, launched by the King in 2005, is a $1.2 billion program designed to generate employment, combat poverty, and improve infrastructure, with a special focus on rural areas.

With regard to Morocco's efforts to counter youth radicalization, Morocco has accelerated its rollout of education and employment options for youth, and expansion of legal rights and political empowerment for women. The United States worked closely with the Government of Morocco and key Moroccan civil society organizations to support this initiative through innovative assistance programs including a new USAID/INL program to work with youth in prison, recently released from prison, and marginalized youth at-risk of going to prison. The program also included a significant juvenile justice reform component.

OMAN

2010 Terrorist Incidents: There were no terrorist attacks within Oman's land borders in 2010. On July 28, the Japanese tanker M Star was damaged in a terrorist attack by a water borne improvised explosive device (WBIED) while transiting the Strait of Hormuz. All major, navigable shipping lanes in the Strait were in Oman's territorial waters. The Abdullah Azzam Brigade claimed responsibility for the attack, which resulted in no injuries and minor damage to the ship.

Legislation and Law Enforcement: Oman took significant steps during the year to improve border security, as demonstrated by a number of training and border security workshops that were conducted in Oman.

Countering Terrorist Finance: Oman is not a regional or offshore financial center and did not have significant money laundering or terrorist financing concerns. The Omani government is generally transparent regarding its anti-money laundering and counterterrorist financing enforcement efforts. As a charter member of the Middle East and North Africa Financial Action Task Force (MENAFATF), Oman participated in mutual Financial Action Task Force (FATF) evaluations, and enacted anti-money laundering/counterterrorist financing (AML/CTF) legislation largely based on recommendations following a FATF evaluation. Oman's first FATF mutual evaluation was completed in summer 2010. The report had not been released at year's end. Oman is steadily improving its legal system related to AML/CTF. Notable progress was made in 2010, including an overhaul of its AML/CTF legislation. In July, Oman issued Royal Decree number 79/2010, which enacted new comprehensive AML/CTF legislation. This act consolidated Oman's previous AML/CTF laws, created a national committee for combating money laundering and terrorist financing, and codified Oman's "safe harbor", which provides protection to those who provide otherwise confidential banking data to authorities in pursuit of authorized investigations, and mutual legal assistance regulations.

QATAR

Overview: The United States continued to seek improved counterterrorism cooperation and information sharing with the Qatari government. Cooperation with U.S. authorities on counterterrorist finance continued to develop and in April, Qatar passed strong anti-money laundering/counterterrorist finance (AML/CTF) legislation. Still, Qatari efforts to counter terrorist financing outside its borders by private individuals and charitable associations often fell short of recognized international standards. Qatar's leaders maintained political relations with top-ranking Hamas and Hizballah leaders.

Legislation and Law Enforcement: Through a stringent visa and sponsorship regime, Qatar regularly refused entry to and deported foreign residents suspected of extremist sympathies, and monitored extremism in its citizen population. Qatari authorities have indicated that they will increase biometric features on resident ID cards in the near future.

Countering Terrorist Finance: Qatar is a member of the Middle East and North Africa Financial Action Task Force (MENAFATF) and undertook comprehensive MENAFATF assessments of its banking/financial sector and regulatory and enforcement framework in 2010. New AML/CTF legislation purported to meet international legal norms, but no prosecutions for terrorist financing occurred under the new law. Qatar made significant progress on building a financial regulatory framework but did not adequately enforce its laws and international standards to track funds transfers to individuals and organizations (including charities) associated with extremists and terrorist facilitators outside Qatar. Qatar has an increasingly capable Financial Information Unit (FIU) in its Central Bank. Local banks worked with the Central Bank and the FIU on CTF and AML issues.

Countering Radicalization and Violent Extremism: Government authorities were recognized as regional leaders in improving educational standards and curricula, which included civic instruction that criticized violent extremist views. Qatar hosted well-regarded international fora on interreligious dialogue.

SAUDI ARABIA

Overview: The Saudi government continued to build its counterterrorism capacity and its efforts to counter extremist ideology. Over the course of the year, Saudi authorities arrested numerous suspected al-Qa'ida (AQ) associates, uncovered several AQ arms caches, continued to develop a new facilities security force, implemented improved border security measures, and tightened laws to counter terrorist financing. In addition, prominent officials and religious leaders made public comments criticizing extremist ideology. Although Saudi Arabia's capacity to deal with internal threats remained strong, instability in Yemen provided an opportunity for al-Qa'ida in the Arabia Peninsula (AQAP) to recruit members, solicit funds, and plan attacks on Saudi Arabia.

Legislation and Law Enforcement: Saudi Arabia cooperated to prevent acts of terrorism against the U.S. homeland, citizens, and interests. On October 29, international authorities intercepted two mail bombs destined for the United States based on timely information from Saudi authorities.

Saudi Arabia continued to improve border security measures, including installing biometric scanners at entry points throughout the Kingdom. U.S. government officials worked with Saudi officials on a number of border security issues, including the Advance Passenger Information/Passenger Name Record program and compliance with the International Ship and Port Facility Security Code. In April, 12 officials from the Ministry of Interior participated in a customs and border patrol exchange in the United States, and Saudi officials continued to request opportunities to learn about U.S. law enforcement "best practices."

Saudi authorities offer one million Saudi riyals (approximately US$ 270,000) to anyone who supplied information that led to the arrest of a terrorist, and five million riyals (approximately US$ 1.4 million) to anyone who supplied information about a terrorist cell. The reward for anyone supplying information to foil a terrorist attack is seven million riyals (approximately US$ 1.9 million).

<u>Arrests</u>: On March 24, Saudi officials announced the arrest of more than 100 AQ suspects since November 2009. Those arrested were accused of planning attacks against government and oil installations across the Kingdom. They included 47 Saudis, 51 Yemenis, one Somali, one Bangladeshi, and one Eritrean. One of the arrestees, a woman named Haylah Al Qassir, allegedly helped AQ recruit young women and youths, hide fugitives, and plan and finance operations. During the arrests, police seized weapons, ammunition, video recording devices, computers, communication devices, money, and documents. In this operation, security officers also uncovered two six-member suicide bombing cells linked to AQAP. Officers arrested all 12 members as they were in the early stages of planning attacks against oil and security facilities in the Eastern region of Saudi Arabia.

On November 26, Saudi officials announced that 149 AQ suspects had been arrested since April. These suspects had been part of 19 cells across Saudi Arabia and included 124 Saudis. The suspects allegedly planned to poison Saudi officials and journalists with gifts of perfume; to finance operations by robbing banks and companies; and to build explosive devices from mobile phones. They were also accused of sheltering suicide bombers who illegally entered the country from Yemen to attack civilian and military facilities in Saudi Arabia.

Countering Terrorism Finance: Saudi Arabia is a member of the Middle East and North Africa Financial Action Task Force (MENAFATF), a Financial Action Task Force (FATF)-style regional body. Saudi Arabia is also a member of the Gulf Cooperation Council, which itself is a member of the FATF, and its Financial Intelligence Unit is a member of the Egmont Group.

On May 6, Saudi Arabia's Council of Senior Scholars, the country's highest religious body, published, and King Abdullah endorsed, a fatwa criminalizing terrorist acts and the financing, aiding, or abetting of terrorists. The edict declared that these injunctions apply both within Muslim and non-Muslim countries, and it paved the way for comprehensive legislation and implementing regulations for the Saudi Arabian government to prosecute terrorist financing cases.

Saudi Arabia actively participated in the UNSCR 1267 Committee process, proposing individuals for listing and imposing the required asset freeze and travel ban on those listed. The June 2010 Mutual Evaluation Report of Saudi Arabia, conducted as a joint exercise between the FATF and MENAFATF, identified areas of progress and suggested areas for further improvement. According to its mutual evaluation report, Saudi Arabia has not implemented UNSCR 1373.

The Kingdom, due to a large number of transient workers, appeared to be the world's second largest market for remittances. Due to strict rules for banking and remittances in the Kingdom, a considerable part of the remittance sector may be underground. While there is no public data available on illegal remittances in 2010, these underground networks likely still exist.

Regional and International Cooperation: Since 2008, Saudi Arabia has been a member of the Global Initiative to Combat Nuclear Terrorism. Saudi Arabia has security-related bilateral agreements including counterterrorism cooperation with the United States, Italy, the United Kingdom, India, Iran, Turkey, Senegal, Pakistan, Tunisia, Oman, Morocco, Libya, Yemen, Iraq, Jordan, and Sudan. Saudi government officials also issued statements encouraging enhanced cooperation among Arab League states on counterterrorism issues.

Countering Radicalization and Violent Extremism: Countering extremist ideology by ensuring what it calls "ideological security" was a key part of the Saudi government's counterterrorism strategy. The Ministry of Islamic Affairs continued its extensive media campaign to educate young Saudis on the "correct" teachings of Islam to prevent their being drawn to extremist doctrines. The campaign included messages incorporated into Friday sermons at mosques, distribution of literature and tapes, and article postings on the Internet. In 2007, Saudi Arabia issued identification cards to imams and religious leaders to curb instances of unauthorized persons delivering Friday sermons. In 2010, the government continued to monitor these licensed imams and counseled them when necessary. According to the Ministry, they have not dismissed any imams for espousing extremist views since 2008.

As part of coordinated efforts to ensure ideological security, the ministries of Civil Service, Education, and the Interior moved over 2,000 teachers to administrative positions over the past two years for promoting extremist ideology. Over the summer, the Ministry of Education trained school principals and supervisors to report teachers who believed in extremist ideas or lack allegiance to the homeland. Although some overtly intolerant statements were removed or modified, educational textbooks continued to contain such statements against non-Muslim religious groups.

In September, King Abdulaziz University hosted a two-day seminar targeting youth on "The Saudi Moderate Approach." The seminar aimed to instill a culture of tolerance, reduce extremism, and develop patriotism.

The governmental Mohammed Bin Naif Center for Counseling and Care program continued to operate at least nine centers to rehabilitate those with extremist ideologies. These centers employed more than 100 scholars and academics specializing in Islam and Sharia law, and more than 30 psychiatrists and social researchers. Since its inception in 2006, the program has enabled over 300 former extremists, including former Guantanamo detainees, to be re-integrated into Saudi society. The Ministry of Interior estimates recidivism rates for former Guantanamo detainees to be 20 percent and for all other program participants to be less than 10 percent.

In addition to rehabilitation, the Ministry of Interior continued a program of counter-radicalization within the prison system. The Ministry worked with specialists, clerics, and teachers to stop violent extremist groups from recruiting prisoners. Since its inception in 2004, 3,200 prisoners have participated in 5,000 counter-radicalization meetings.

TUNISIA

Overview: The Government of Tunisia placed a high priority on countering terrorism, using tight border and internal security controls to deter the formation of terrorist groups and block any potential for terrorist actions; social programs to reduce the impact of high unemployment and help prevent radicalization; and prosecution to punish potential terrorists. Domestically, the Tunisian government had a strong internal security apparatus through which it provided a tight security net across the country including check points, and unannounced identity document checks. It provided extensive security for those events or persons that could potentially attract terrorist attention, such as the annual Jewish pilgrimage to the island of Djerba, soccer games, and public demonstrations.

Legislation and Law Enforcement: The Tunisian government prosecuted at least 40 separate terrorism-related cases in 2010, many including multiple defendants. Of those cases, two involved people accused of joining a terrorist group outside the country, one case included charges of providing weapons, two cases involved receiving training for terrorist purposes, and several cases included charges of recruiting. The majority of charges, however, related to collecting money without authorization, joining a terrorist group, setting up an illegal group, holding unauthorized meetings, neglecting to inform the authorities of terrorist acts, and/or downloading prohibited material.

Sanaa, Yemen: Yemeni security are seen outside a branch of the U.S. company UPS in Sanaa on October 30, 2010. Yemen launched a probe after explosives were found in air parcels sent to U.S. locations from its territory by suspected al-Qa'ida in the Arabian Peninsula militants. AFP PHOTO/ Mohammad Huwais

Countering Terrorist Finance: Tunisia is a member of the Middle East and North Africa Financial Action Task Force (MENAFATF). The head of Tunisia's Financial Intelligence Unit served as MENA-FATF's President in 2010. The Tunisian government has complied with UNSCRs 1267 and 1373 in many respects, generally concerning the implementation of effective financial controls in Tunisia. There were at least four court cases in 2010 where individuals were charged with collecting or donating money with intent to support terrorist goals.

Regional and International Cooperation: The principal focus of Tunisian government counterterrorism efforts was to secure its territory. Thus, it worked with its neighbors Libya, Algeria, France, and Italy to seek information on migration and smuggling issues and to improve its border security. In December, the Tunisian government signed a new security agreement with Mauritania. Tunisia is a Mediterranean Partner for Cooperation in the OSCE. The Tunisian government participated in the October OSCE Mediterranean Conference on European Security, and in the December OSCE Summit in Kazakhstan. In his presentation at the OSCE Summit, Secretary of State for Maghreb, Arab, and African Affairs Harguem emphasized Tunisia's commitment to countering terrorism, expressed concern that unilateral security measures have reached the limits of their effectiveness, and called for greater international mobilization to create a global response to the phenomena of marginalization, exclusion, and poverty that encourage violent extremism. Tunisia is also host to the Arab League's Arab Interior Ministers' Council, which meets annually. In the December meeting, the ministers focused on combating terrorist use of the Internet. Tunisia acceded to the International Convention for the Suppression of Acts of Nuclear Terrorism, as well as the 2005 Amendment to the Convention on the Physical Protection of Nuclear Material.

Countering Radicalization and Violent Extremism: The Tunisian government continued to maintain tight control over the religious establishment, appointing imams, dictating Friday sermons, closing mosques between prayer times, refurbishing mosques in need of repair, and keeping watch at the local level over who attends services. The Tunisian government promoted a moderate form of Islam through the educational system and the media.

UNITED ARAB EMIRATES

Overview: The United Arab Emirates government continued to build its counterterrorism capacity and worked to strengthen international cooperation to counter terrorism. In 2010, the Government of the United Arab Emirates (UAE) improved border security measures and renewed counterterrorist financing efforts. In addition, prominent officials and religious leaders continued to publicly criticize extremist ideology.

2010 Terrorist Incidents: On October 29, UAE authorities foiled a terrorist plot when authorities in Dubai discovered an explosive device in a package transiting from Yemen to the United States via aircraft. Al-Qa'ida in the Arabian Peninsula claimed responsibility for the plot.

Legislation and Law Enforcement: The UAE participated in the Megaports and Container Security Initiatives (CSI). Under the CSI, which became operational at Port Rashid and Jebel Ali Port in the Emirate of Dubai in 2005, three U.S. Customs and Border Protection officers co-located with the Dubai Customs Intelligence Unit at Port Rashid. In 2010, the UAE Ministry of Interior and the Abu Dhabi Customs Authority signed memoranda of cooperation with Immigration and Customs Enforcement (ICE). These agreements facilitated ICE assistance to provide technical support and instruction in the establishment of two separate training academies to further build Emirati Customs and Police capacity. On May 10, Abu Dhabi Customs signed a memorandum of understanding with ICE to exchange investigation-related information obtained at ports of entry, which was the first U.S. Law Enforcement information-sharing agreement with the UAE.

Countering Terrorist Finance: The UAE continued efforts to strengthen its institutional capabilities to counter terrorist financing, but challenges remained. The Central Bank signed a memoranda of understanding (MOU) with regional financial intelligence units, building on cooperation initiated in 2008, and performed anti-money laundering training both locally and regionally. On October 25, the UAE's Financial Intelligence Unit, the Central Bank's Anti-money Laundering and Suspicious Cases Unit, signed an MOU with the Federal Customs Authority to facilitate information sharing in an effort to improve the UAE's anti-money laundering apparatus.

The UAE is a member of the Middle East and North Africa Financial Action Task Force (MENAFATF), a FATF-style regional body, and its most recent mutual evaluation was adopted by the plenary in 2008. It is also a member of the Gulf Cooperation Council and through this body, the UAE is also a member of the FATF. The UAE hosted the February 2010 FATF plenary meeting. Although the UAE has taken important steps to address hawala remittances, further vigilance is required.

The UAE Central Bank has provided training programs to financial institutions on money laundering and terrorist financing. Continuing initiatives from previous years, the United States and the UAE worked together throughout the year to strengthen efforts to combat Bulk Cash Smuggling (BCS), in particular from countries at higher risk of illicit finance activity. The UAE is an enthusiastic proponent of BCS training and has encouraged MENAFATF members to undertake the training.

Regional and International Cooperation: After the Japanese oil tanker M Star was damaged in the Strait of Hormuz in July, UAE authorities allowed U.S. Navy divers to do a forensic inspection of the ship while docked at the port of Fujairah.

The UAE hosted a plenary meeting for the Global Initiative to Combat Nuclear Terrorism on June 22, which was attended by representatives from 47 countries.

Countering Radicalization and Violent Extremism: In order to prevent extremist preaching in UAE mosques, the General Authority of Islamic Affairs and Endowments provided prescribed guidelines for all Friday sermons and monitored compliance. The UAE worked to keep its education system free of radical influences and emphasized social tolerance and moderation.

YEMEN

Overview: In 2010, resource limitations and unstable security conditions in several parts of the country impeded the Yemeni government's ability to eliminate potential safe havens in Yemen. In addition, counterterrorism efforts were impeded by a lack of legislation. Yemen's vulnerability along it long and weakly protected borders has allowed al-Qa'ida associates to find safe haven in Yemen. Nonetheless, the Government of Yemen continued to build its counterterrorism capacity and deployed its security forces against terrorist threats. The Yemeni government security forces killed or captured numerous suspected al-Qa'ida in the Arabian Peninsula (AQAP) militants, and received assistance in the form of equipment and training from the United States. The Yemeni government's response to the terrorist threat included large-scale kinetic operations against suspected AQAP members in the south. In turn, AQAP attacks against foreign interests, Yemeni government targets, and the Shia Houthi movement in the north increased dramatically in 2010.

2010 Terrorist Incidents: AQAP carried out attacks throughout Yemen, using improvised explosive devices (IEDs), ambushes, and car bombs against government, civilian, and foreign targets, particularly in the South but also within the capital city of Sana'a. Attacks included:

- On April 26, the British Ambassador's vehicle was attacked by a suicide bomber as it approached the British Embassy in Sana'a. The Ambassador escaped unharmed; however, three bystanders were wounded and the bomber died in the attack.

- On June 19, six to eight suspected AQAP gunmen disguised as women staged a daylight attack on a security service headquarters in Aden, killed 12 civilians.

- On July 14, 20 suspected AQAP gunmen staged a coordinated attack on the intelligence and police headquarters in Zinjibar, killing three people.

- On October 6, a vehicle carrying the British Deputy Chief of Mission was attacked with an anti-tank rocket as it was approaching the British Embassy in Sana'a. One Embassy employee and two bystanders were injured.

- On October 29, a plot to send two parcels containing IEDs on two separate flights bound for the United States was discovered. AQAP claimed responsibility.

- On December 15, a man of unknown affiliation detonated a grenade in the bed of an armored pickup truck with four U.S. Embassy personnel aboard outside of a popular restaurant in the Hadda neighborhood of Sana'a. No one was injured. A crowd of Yemenis attacked the man and held him until Yemeni government authorities arrived.

- AQAP also claimed two suicide attacks against Shia Houthis in the north on November 24 and 26 that resulted in 28 dead and many more wounded. Following these attacks, AQAP reportedly ordered the establishment of Salafi brigades to halt the spread of Shiism in Sa'ada governorate.

Legislation and Law Enforcement: Counterterrorism legislation sent to a Parliamentary committee for review in 2008 was not enacted by the end of 2010. For this reason, the Yemeni government must apply other means, including fraudulent document or "membership in an armed gang" laws against foreign fighters intending to go to Afghanistan or elsewhere. Those involved in acts resulting in injury, death, or property destruction may be prosecuted under existing laws. However, terrorism was not defined as a crime per se. As of the end of the year, legal, political, and logistical hurdles hindered an effective detention and rehabilitation program for Guantanamo returnees. The government lacked a legal framework to hold Guantanamo detainees for more than a short period of time. Yemen participated in the Megaports and Container Security Initiatives.

Countering Terrorism Finance: On December 29, 2009, Yemen's Parliament passed long-stalled counterterrorist finance and anti-money laundering legislation, which was signed into law on January 17, 2010, as Law No. 1 of 2010. It provided the government with powers to investigate and prosecute terrorist financial networks operating inside the country. The Financial Action Task Force's International Cooperation Review Group, determined that the law was an improvement but did not yet meet international standards and was not yet effectively implemented. Yemen is a member of the Middle East and North Africa Financial Action Task Force (MENAFATF). There was no information on whether Yemeni authorities have frozen, seized, or demanded forfeiture of other assets related to terrorist financing.

Regional and International Cooperation: The Friends of Yemen process began in 2010 as a forum for two dozen countries, including Yemen, to coordinate a strategic plan of assistance and reform for Yemen. Members have used the forum to advance initiatives such as those related to border security and detainee rehabilitation. Yemen acceded to the International Convention on the Suppression of the Financing of Terrorism.

Countering Radicalization and Violent Extremism: Official and quasi-official media featured messages from President Saleh and other high-level officials and opinion leaders denigrating violent extremism and AQAP. However, Yemeni government messaging did not distinguish between terrorist groups and groups with political opposition to the Yemeni government, and often identified the Southern Movement and the Houthi organizations as "violent extremist" organizations.

SOUTH AND CENTRAL ASIA OVERVIEW

South Asia continued to experience violence in 2010, as terrorists expanded their operations and networks across the region and beyond. In response, the United States worked to increase counterterrorism cooperation with its partners in South Asia. Pakistan remained a critical front. Portions of Pakistani territory remained a safe haven for extremists, including high-level al-Qa'ida leaders. Groups such as the Taliban's Quetta Shura and the Haqqani Network used western Pakistan to plan attacks against American interests in Afghanistan. Tehrik-e-Taliban Pakistan (TTP) continued using Pakistan's tribal belt to plan attacks against the Government of Pakistan and its citizens. Moreover, TTP diversified its target set by seeking to attack the U.S. directly, as demonstrated by its support for the attempted Times Square bombing in May 2010. In other parts of Pakistan, groups such as Lashkar-e-Tayyiba remained a threat to the stability of the region and beyond.

In 2010, Afghanistan experienced a more aggressive and active Taliban-led insurgency with support from affiliated extremist organizations such as the Haqqani Network and Hezb-e-Islami Gulbuddin. These groups increased their use of improvised explosive devices and coordinated attacks using multiple suicide bombers, particularly in the eastern and southern portions of the country, while their leadership remained hiding in their safe havens in Pakistan. Separately, ethnic tensions increased after the Afghan Parliamentary election resulted in Pashtun losses in several provinces.

India continued to be severely impacted by terrorism. Though there were no attacks on the scale of the 2008 Mumbai assault, India suffered a significant number of lower-level terrorist incidents. In response, India has sought not only to improve its own counterterrorism capabilities, but also to improve its coordination with the United States, the international community, and regional partners.

Bangladesh continued to increase its domestic capacity as well as its international and regional counterterrorism cooperation in 2010, working with its partners to increase information sharing and Bangladeshi capacity development. Bangladesh is becoming a positive regional example for its forward-leaning stance and willingness to cooperate both bilaterally and multilaterally.

Despite these successes, there was concern that South Asian nations were susceptible to being used as either transit points or operational hubs for terrorist groups to strike at their neighbors. Moreover, with a few exceptions, information sharing, operational coordination, and other cross-border cooperative efforts remained limited.

Regarding Central Asia, Kazakhstan, Uzbekistan, and Turkmenistan experienced no terrorist attacks, Tajikistan's Rasht Valley remained vulnerable to attacks, and Kyrgystan's political turbulence made it vulnerable to ethnic unrest. As the chair of the Organization for Security and Cooperation in Europe (OSCE), Kazakhstan promoted tolerance through an international conference, although its neighbors used the threat of extremism to maintain restrictive laws on civil liberties, religious expression, and the press.

The Home and Interior Ministers of the South Asian Association for Regional Cooperation (SAARC) have met annually since 2006 to consider and implement measures against the "organization, instigation, financing, and facilitation" of terrorist activities. The June 2010 meeting in Islamabad reaffirmed the need to "extend cooperation to each other against terrorism while remaining within the purview of our national laws and procudres and our international commitments and following the principle of non-interference and non-intervention in each others' affairs."

AFGHANISTAN

Overview: During a year in which it conducted contentious Parliamentary elections and International Security Assistance Force (ISAF) troop numbers surged to over 131,000, Afghanistan continued to confront the challenges of building a stable, democratic government in the face of a sophisticated, multi-faceted insurgency that primarily relied on asymmetric tactics. The insurgency targeted coalition forces, the UN Assistance Mission to Afghanistan (UNAMA), international non-governmental organizations (NGOs), foreign diplomatic missions, Afghan civilians, and Afghan government officials and security forces.

Separate but intertwined and affiliated extremist organizations led by Mullah Omar (Taliban), Sira-juddin Haqqani (Haqqani Network), and Gulbuddin Hekmatyar (Hezb-e-Islami Gulbuddin) increased their use of improvised explosive devices (IEDs) and coordinated attacks using multiple suicide bombers, particularly in the eastern and southern portions of the country. As they did prior to the August 2009 presidential and provincial elections, Taliban militants and other insurgents made a concentrated effort to depress voter turnout during the September 2010 parliamentary elections. A variety of threats, attacks, and intimidation tactics were used to prevent Afghan citizens from voting. Pashtun parliamentary losses in several provinces increased electoral dissatisfaction and ethnic tension.

The Commander of U.S. Central Command maintained command and control of U.S. forces operating in Afghanistan. United States forces targeted insurgent leaders, facilitators, IED networks, the narcotics-insurgent nexus, and insurgent training and logistics centers with the objective of eliminating terrorists and facilitating reconstruction and development. The Afghan National Army (ANA), and to a lesser extent, the Afghan National Police (ANP), continued to lead in the majority of counterterrorism operations in close cooperation with coalition forces. The Afghan National Security Forces (ANSF) continued to work in close partnership with ISAF to develop the capability necessary to assume the lead in security across Afghanistan and take a greater role in planning and execution operations. With support from the international civilian and military community, the ANSF exceeded their recruitment goals for 2010 with an end strength of approximately 150,000 ANA and 117,000 ANP. Notwithstanding the promising growth, key challenges remained: retention and attrition, officer and non-commissioned officer shortages, logistical shortfalls, poor literacy rates, and pay problems.

2010 Terrorist Incidents: IED attacks, direct and indirect fire, and suicide attacks increased in 2010. The increase in ISAF troop presence from 100,000 to 131,730 and their kinetic activities likely led insurgents to increase their activity. There was a 72 percent increase in total kinetic events, with IEDs representing 25 to 40 percent of this activity. According to ISAF, the total number of civilians killed in 2010 exceeded those in 2009, totaling more than 1,408; the vast majority of these deaths were caused by insurgent elements. The UN, which employed a different methodology, reported that, during the first 10 months of the year, more than 2,400 civilians were killed and 3,800 were injured; 76 percent of those casualties were caused by insurgents. The insurgents also continued their attacks on humanitarian workers, with almost 100 killed in 2010.

While insurgent activity occurred daily, high profile attacks included:

- On February 26, 16 were killed, including nine Indian nationals, during an attack on two Indian guesthouses.

- On May 28, the Taliban destroyed one school and threatened two others in the Lakan area of Khost; the attackers demanded the release of certain detainees before they would allow the schools to reopen.

- On July 2, four were killed and 24 were wounded in an attack on the Kunduz office of Development Alternatives Incorporated.

- On August 7, Taliban and Hezb-e-Islami claimed responsibility for killing 10 members of a medical mission team in Badakhshan Province.

- On September 26, a British national who was kidnapped by insurgents was killed during a rescue attempt.

- On October 8, the Kunduz governor Engineer Mohammad Omar, was assassinated.

- On December 19, a suicide attack in Kabul killed five ANA officers.

Legislation and Law Enforcement: The Governments of Afghanistan and the United States investigated a variety of criminal acts, including kidnappings, assassinations, contracting corruption fraud, and other crimes against military and security forces, NGOs, and civilians. U.S. government law enforcement bodies regularly passed actionable information to the Ministry of Interior and the National Directorate of Security and Afghan authorities who then took actions to disrupt, dismantle, and prosecute terrorist suspects based on the information. In 2010, the Afghan Attorney General office received 1170 national security threat cases for prosecution, passing 743 to the courts. The U.S. government often participated in prisoner interviews and debriefings with Afghan authorities of persons suspected of terrorist activity in Afghanistan and persons with connections to the United States.

The implementation of a widespread biometrics program was important to improving the law enforcement environment. Biometric enrollments of the Afghan population would significantly improve the security environment and reduce the ability of extremists and criminals to act anonymously and with impunity. The Afghan Ministry of Interior led the development of a biometrics program called "Afghan 1000", which aimed to enroll 80 percent of the population by late 2012. The Afghan government also considered a National Security Detentions Law that would provide the government with a legal regime better suited to the investigation and prosecution of terrorist and insurgent cases.

Kabul, Afghanistan: Afghan and foreign investigators inspect the site of a suicide attack in Kabul on May 18, 2010. The Taliban, the militia leading a nearly-nine year insurgency against the western-back government and U.S.-led foreign troops, claimed responsibility for the attack, saying they had targeted NATO forces. AFP PHOTO/SHAH Marai

Afghanistan continued to process travelers on entry and departure at Kabul international airport with the Personal Identification Secure Comparison and Evaluation System (PISCES). Afghan authorities reviewed plans for expanded PISCES installations at additional locations.

Countering Terrorist Finance: In 2004, Afghanistan passed two laws to formalize the combating of money laundering and terrorist financing, and established Afghanistan's financial intelligence unit (FIU), the Financial Transactions and Reports Analysis Centre of Afghanistan (FinTRACA). FinTRACA was responsible for collecting "suspicious transaction reports" from banks, analyzing them, and disseminating financial intelligence from this analysis to Afghan law enforcement agencies. FinTRACA also worked closely with other global FIUs and in summer 2010 became a member of the Egmont Group of FIUs, which allowed it to share financial intelligence with, and request financial intelligence from, more than 100 Egmont-member FIUs around the world. Despite these increased efforts by the international community against funding flows, streams of Taliban financing from abroad, along with funds gained from narcotics trafficking and kidnapping, criminal enterprises, and taxing the local population, have allowed the insurgency to strengthen its military and technical capabilities. Narcotics trafficking in particular remained an important financing mechanism of terrorist/insurgent operations.

Regional and International Cooperation: The Government of Afghanistan continued to increase its international cooperation on counterterrorism. In November, Afghanistan joined over 60 countries and the World Customs Organization to partner in the on-going Project Global Shield (PGS), the goal of which is to monitor and curtail the illicit diversion of 14 explosive and drug precursor chemicals used for terrorist purposes. (PGS-targeted precursors were used in insurgent IED attacks targeting civilian, Afghan, and ISAF elements.) The August Summit in Sochi, Russia convened the Presidents of Afghanistan, Russia, Tajikistan, and Pakistan and included discussions of counterterrorism cooperation. The President of Afghanistan and the Prime Minister of Pakistan issued a joint statement after their September 15-16 meeting in Pakistan that recognized the need for close cooperation against terrorism and reaffirmed this commitment in their December 4 meeting in Kabul.

Countering Radicalization and Violent Extremism: The Afghan government supported counter-radicalization programs, mainly by engaging networks of supportive local and traditional leaders that promulgated a tolerant interpretation of Islam. The Ministry of Information, Culture, and Youth and the Ministry of Hajj and Religious Affairs have both convened numerous meetings at both local and national levels to encourage discussion and dialogue on religious issues, including radicalization. Lack of resources and capacity at the Ministry of Hajj and Religious Affairs, however, was a serious impediment to monitoring themes of Friday sermons across the country, and the Ministry lacked the capability to provide guidance to the many thousands of mullahs and imams in the country. The Ministry's Islamic Sciences Research Center produced small books and brochures providing Islamic arguments against terrorism, suicide bombing, and radicalism for distribution throughout the country.

The United States assisted the Afghan government to develop programs to counter radicalization in prisons, as internal prison networks have a great deal of influence on active external terrorist networks. The separation of prisoners who constitute national security threats from common criminals was necessary to prevent insurgent recruitment within prisons.

BANGLADESH

Overview: The Awami League-led government has been committed to combating domestic and transnational terrorist groups since coming into power in January 2009. Bangladesh continued improving its counterterrorism cooperation with its international partners in 2010. The Bangladesh government's ongoing counterterrorism efforts have denied space to and prevented the unfettered operation of transnational terrorists seeking to establish safe havens in Bangladesh. Denying terrorist groups freedom of movement, increased counterterrorism policing, and other law enforcement efforts have hindered terrorist groups from using Bangladesh as a base of operations or transit point from which to attack the country's neighbors.

In October, Bangladesh law enforcement arrested several individuals alleged to have ties to extremist groups including Lashkar-e Tayyiba (LeT) and Harakat ul-Jihad-i-Islami/ Bangladesh (HUJI-B).

Legislation and Law Enforcement: The government passed the Anti-Terrorism Act of 2009 and was in the process of fully implementing the law, including Bangladesh's first counterterrorist finance provisions, during 2010. The government has made numerous well-publicized seizures and arrests of persons alleged to be associated with terrorist organizations including HUJI-B, LeT, Jama'at-ul-Mujahideen Bangladesh, and Hizb-ut Towhid. Few convictions appeared to have resulted from those arrests, however, as the judiciary has continued to work slowly on cases involving terrorism due to a lack of prosecutorial capacity and requisite legal provisions.

Countering Terrorist Finance: The Government of Bangladesh passed new anti-money laundering and counterterrorist finance laws in 2009. In 2010, the government was in the process of implementing these provisions, and examining further areas for legislative improvements to the Money Laundering Prevention Act and the Anti-Terrorism Act, actions that reflected Bangladesh's receptivity to international peer review mechanisms and the Financial Action Task Force (FATF)

International Cooperation Review Group process. In November, the government established the National Coordinating Committee, comprised of all agencies dealing with the anti-money laundering/countering terrorist finance issue, to provide operational level coordination and to develop a national strategy.

Bangladesh is a member of the Asia/Pacific Group against Money Laundering, a FATF-style regional body, and hosted the annual conference in Dhaka. During the typologies conference, the FATF and/or FATF style regional body member countries exchanged information on significant money laundering and terrorist financing cases and operations, and discussed effective countermeasures. Additionally, the Bangladesh Bank (the national bank) and its Financial Intelligence Unit/Anti-Money Laundering Section led the government's effort to comply with the international sanctions regime.

Regional and International Cooperation: U.S. and Bangladeshi law enforcement agencies cooperated well on several cases related to domestic and international terrorism. Bangladesh cooperated with the United States and other international partners to further strengthen control of its borders and land, sea, and air ports of entry. Moreover, the Bangladeshis increased their cooperation with their regional neighbors, most notably with India with whom they increased information sharing, prisoner exchanges, and law enforcement cooperation.

Countering Radicalization and Violent Extremism: The Bangladesh Ministry of Religious Affairs, the Ministry's Islamic Foundation Bangladesh, and USAID have cooperated on Bangladesh's Leaders of Influence (LOI) project. LOI is a four-year old program begun in 2007, designed to enhance the capacity of religious and secular leaders to contribute to national development and democratic reform efforts. In so doing, LOI set out to preserve and promote values of democracy, tolerance, diversity, social harmony, and understanding in Bangladeshi society. Under this program, at least 20,000 community leaders, including at least 10,000 Imams, will have received training and hands-on orientation to programs including democracy and governance, gender equality, health, nutrition, family planning, HIV/AIDS, employment generation, and disaster management. The basic assumption underpinning the program has been that the knowledge of different development aspects, gained through training and exposure, will help these leaders increase tolerance and decrease extremism and opportunities for terrorists to recruit new adherents.

INDIA

Overview: In 2010, India continued to see a reduction in the number of deaths attributable to terrorist violence, as it ramped up its counterterrorism capacity building efforts and increased cooperation with the international community, especially the United States. However, the loss of nearly 1,900 lives (civilian, security forces, and terrorists) still made India one of the world's most terrorism-afflicted countries. Sustained violence in Kashmir over a six-month period and attempted infiltrations from Pakistan across the Line of Control remained serious concerns for the Indian government. In May, an Indian court convicted and sentenced to death the lone surviving attacker of the 2008 Mumbai terrorist attacks. A February bombing in Pune killed 17, and a December improvised explosive device (IED) explosion in Varanasi killed two people. The perpetrators for both attacks remained at large at the end of the year.

The Maoists/Naxalites, whom Prime Minister Singh has called India's greatest internal security threat, were active in 2010, especially in the eastern part of the country. They increasingly directed their attacks at Indian security forces but also used IEDs to blow up railways and other infrastructure projects. Indian security forces successfully ensured security at a number of major events, including the 2010 Hockey World Cup and the 2010 Commonwealth Games, without incident.

Throughout 2010, Indian authorities arrested numerous suspected militants, uncovered several arms caches, continued to develop a new internal security force, implemented improved border security measures mainly along the Pakistani border, and tightened laws to counter terrorist financing. In July, the U.S.-India Counterterrorism Cooperation Initiative was signed, which set the stage for greater cooperation on counterterrorism issues between the two governments.

2010 Terrorist Incidents: On November 22, the Government of India reported that at least 577 civilians had been killed, while more than 260 Special Forces personnel had also lost their lives across the country due to Naxalite violence in 2010. During that same period, at least 137 members of the Communist Party of India (CPI)-Maoist (aka the Naxalites) were killed. Between February 7 and February 9, the CPI-Maoist called a three-day strike. Railway tracks were blown up, railway stations attacked, bombs were placed on railway property, and railway officials were assaulted. Terrorist attacks in 2010 included:

- On February 13, 17 persons, including two foreigners, were killed and over 40 injured in a bomb blast in the popular German Bakery near the Osho Ashram in Pune.

- On April 17, two crude bombs exploded in quick succession outside the M. A. Chinnaswamy cricket stadium in Bangalore, minutes before an Indian Premier League match was to begin, leaving 15 persons injured and creating panic in the packed venue. A third crude bomb was found near another gate to the stadium.

- On May 17, an IED was used to blow up a civilian bus killing 15 civilians and 16 policemen/ Special Police Officers (SPOs) and injuring 12 civilians and an additional 16 policemen/SPOs in district Dantewada, Chhattisgarh.

- On May 28, the Howrah-Kurla-Jnaneshwari Express train was derailed after terrorists removed a portion of the track. The derailment led to a collision with a goods train, leading to the death of 147 persons and injuries to over 150. Maoist/Naxalites were believed responsible for the derailment.

- On September 19, two gunmen on a motorcycle opened fire at the entrance of Jama Masjid, a famous mosque and tourist site in old Delhi, injuring two tourists from Taiwan.

- On December 7, two persons including a woman and an 18-month old child were killed and 30 injured in a blast in Varanasi, Uttar Pradesh. The Indian Mujahedin claimed responsibility for the blast.

Legislation and Law Enforcement: In January, a Delhi court sentenced two Lashkar-e-Tayyiba (LeT) militants to seven years of imprisonment for possession of the explosive RDX in connection with a conspiracy to carry out a suicide attack at the Indian Military Academy in 2005. In May, the Special Sessions Court in Mumbai sentenced to death the lone surviving LeT militant involved in the 2008 Mumbai terrorist attacks, Mohammad Ajmal Amir Kasab.

Throughout the year, India worked to improve its counterterrorism readiness. The Ministry of Home Affairs Annual Report 2009-2010 stated that in response to the November 26, 2008 Mumbai terrorist attacks, Quick Reaction Teams have been set up in four regional hubs (Mumbai, Kolkata, Chennai, and Hyderabad) with 1,086 trained personnel and an additional team on standby at the Delhi airport, ready to deploy during an emergency.

The Indian government continued erecting fences along its borders with Bangladesh and Pakistan.

Countering Terrorist Finance: The on-site visit for India's Financial Action Task Force (FATF) mutual evaluation concluded in December 2009, and the report was adopted by the FATF plenary in June 2010. At the FATF plenary, the FATF also granted India full membership. India presented a detailed action plan covering the period June 2010 to March 2012 to better meet FATF's anti-money laundering/countering terrorist finance standards. FATF concluded that as of October 2010, India was on track with its action plan. India's Financial Intelligence Unit (FIU) is a member of the Egmont Group and regularly shared information with foreign FIUs over the Egmont Secure Web on terrorist financing cases.

Regional and International Cooperation: On July 23, the India-U.S. Counterterrorism Cooperation Initiative was signed. This initiative allows for greater information-sharing, and the sharing of best practices in the areas of investigations, forensic science, countering terrorist finance, cyber security, mass transit and rail security, port and border security, and maritime security.

During his November visit to India, President Obama and Indian Prime Minister Singh announced the establishment of the U.S.-India Homeland Security Dialogue (HSD). The Indian Ministry of Home Affairs and the United States Department of Homeland Security will co-lead the HSD, which will provide a forum for sustained U.S.-India engagement on homeland security issues to facilitate security cooperation.

During the December 2010 visit of French President Nicolas Sarkozy, France and India agreed to enhance their operational cooperation to accelerate the process of extradition requests, combat money laundering for terrorism, and enforce international sanctions regime against terrorist organizations. Both countries reinforced the importance of adhering to sanctions against al-Qa'ida and the Taliban as established by UNSCR 1267.

Countering Radicalization and Violent Extremism: Countering extremist ideology has become an important part of India's counterterrorism strategy. The Ministry of Home Affairs continued its Surrender-cum-Rehabilitation policy, which encouraged misguided youths and militants to surrender, while offering to provide them rehabilitation and assistance in transitioning back into the population. On February 7, Chief Minister of Assam Tarun Gogoi informed Chief Ministers gathered for the Conference on Internal Security that 14,913 militants had surrendered in Assam since 1991. In November, the Manipur State government stated that 128 youth who belonged to a communist party had successfully completed a 90-day behavioral, spiritual, and technical training program allowing them to be placed in reputable companies like the TATA Group, LG, and Hitachi.

KAZAKHSTAN

Overview: Kazakhstan continued to combat domestic and international terrorism and took tangible steps to improve cooperation and information sharing with various countries and international organizations. Although no terrorist incidents occurred in 2010, the Kazakhstani government designated 16 organizations as "terrorist and extremist" groups. The government, acting principally through government-sponsored civil society organizations and state-controlled media, has labeled certain non-violent religious minority groups extremist, though it has not taken action to ban them. Kazakhstani authorities strengthened domestic counterterrorism efforts through reinforced legislation and prosecution of suspected terrorists, and expanded its participation in international and regional counterterrorism partnerships and activities.

Kazakhstan's National Security Committee and Ministries of the Interior, Defense, and Emergency Situations collaborated to strengthen border security, and conducted an increased number of counterterrorism training exercises prior to the December 1-2 OSCE Summit. Kazakhstan also

Puné, India: The dead body of a blast victim lies inside an ambulance outside a hospital in Puné on February 14, 2010. A bomb ripped through the German Bakery restaurant, a destination popular with tourists, late on February 13, killing nine people. AFP PHOTO/ SAJJAD HUSSAIN

completed its plan for the construction of a Material Protection, Control, and Accountability (MPC&A) training center, to be built with support from the U.S. Department of Energy at the Institute of Nuclear Physics near Almaty. In October, Kazakhstan reiterated its intent to establish an additional "Center to Combat the Illegal Use of Nuclear Materials" in Kurchatov to train Kazakhstani rapid response units to combat nuclear terrorism.

Legislation and Law Enforcement: The Kazakhstan government prosecuted suspected terrorists cases, including:

- In January, Kazakhstani officials detained a Tajikistani citizen who belonged to a banned Islamic group and subsequently extradited the detainee to Tajikistan, where he was wanted since 2006 for charges related to extremism and terrorism.

- In February, Kazakhstani authorities detained three men in western Kazakhstan. A Kazakhstani court sentenced the men to jail for supporting terrorist groups in the Russian North Caucasus Republic of Dagestan.

- In May, Kazakhstani authorities detained a Russian citizen wanted by the Russian Federation for smuggling weapons, munitions, and food to Chechen rebels engaged in terrorist activities. In August, Kazakhstan extradited this detainee to the Russian Federation.

- Kazakhstan held 30 asylum seekers from Uzbekistan in detention. The Government of Kazakhstan noted that Uzbekistan had provided strong evidence that the asylum seekers have links to terrorist organizations. By year's end, in full consultation with UN High Commissioner for Refu-

117

gees (UNHCR), the UNHCR mandate refugee status was revoked from the detainees and one of the 30 had been extradited to Uzbekistan. A second was released. Uzbekistan continued to seek the extradition of the remaining 28. At year's end the extradition was pending.

Countering Terrorist Finance: Since 2004, Kazakhstan has been a member of the Eurasian Group (EAG) on combating money laundering and terrorist financing, a Financial Action Task Force-style regional body. As part of a significant effort to enhance the government's ability to combat possible terrorist financing, Kazakhstan adopted a law "On Combating Money Laundering and Financing of Terrorism" in March. The law created a strengthened financial monitoring system with the authority to observe and freeze suspicious financial activities. The government has repeatedly stated that it fully implements all its obligations under UNSCRs 1267 and 1373. The EAG began a mutual evaluation of Kazakhstan's anti-money laundering/countering terrorist finance regime in October 2010.

Regional and International Cooperation: In December, Kazakhstan joined other Commonwealth of Independent States countries in concluding a package of treaties, which included a commitment to develop a cooperative counterterrorism program for 2011-2013. As Chairman-in-Office of the OSCE in 2010, Kazakhstan hosted an October 14-15 international OSCE Conference on Preventing Terrorism. In September, the Global Initiative to Combat Nuclear Terrorism's (GICNT) held its Inaugural Implementation and Assessment Group Meeting and a Conference on Countering the Financing of Nuclear Terrorism in Kazakhstan. In April, Kazakhstan's President Nazarbayev signed into law the Shanghai Cooperation Organization agreement on joint counterterrorism exercises. Kazakhstan also hosted the Shanghai Cooperation Organization's September "Peace Mission 2010" counterterrorism military exercise. In June, Kazakhstan actively participated in the Collective Security Treaty Organization's joint counterterrorism exercise.

Countering Radicalization and Violent Extremism: Kazakhstan actively promoted intercultural and religious dialogue at the international level. In particular, Kazakhstan hosted in Astana the June OSCE Conference on Tolerance and Non-Discrimination. In June, Kazakhstan's President Nazarbayev proposed the establishment of a Tolerance and Non-Discrimination Center in Central Asia. As 2010 Chairman-in-Office of the OSCE, Kazakhstan also advocated strongly for the establishment of an OSCE high commissioner for inter-ethnic and inter-religious tolerance to counteract violent extremism. During the October OSCE Conference on Preventing Terrorism, Kazakhstan's Ambassador-at-Large in charge of OSCE issues, Madina Zharbussynova, responded favorably to a U.S. proposal to help organize an OSCE conference to support the role that women play in countering violent extremism in Central Asia and Afghanistan. However, on the national level the government has generally restricted such dialogue to those religious groups considered "traditional," such as the government-backed Spiritual Association of Muslims of Kazakhstan, the Russian Orthodox Church, the Jewish community, and the Roman Catholic Church.

In October, Kazakhstan hosted the World Forum of Spiritual Culture, which brought together high-ranking leaders from various countries and world religions to foster inter-faith dialogue and collectively condemn violent extremism. In recognition of President Nazarbayev's active role in promoting global interfaith dialogue, the East West Institute awarded President Nazarbayev its 2010 Peace and Preventative Diplomacy Award. However, as noted in the State Department's *Annual Report on International Religious Freedom*, the government continued to restrict Muslim religious groups not affiliated with the government-recognized Spiritual Association of Muslims of Kazakhstan and minority religions seen as "nontraditional."

KYRGYZSTAN

Overview: 2010 was a turbulent year for Kyrgyzstan, with the collapse of the government in April and inter-ethnic clashes in June, which resulted in the deaths of hundreds in the southern cities of Osh and Jalalabad. The Provisional Government successfully organized a Constitutional Referendum in June and Parliamentary elections in October. Following the elections, a new government was formed in December. In spite of the changes in leadership and political system, terrorism remained an important issue for the Government of Kyrgyzstan.

2010 Terrorist Incidents:

- On November 24, police in Bishkek arrested two persons in a car parked near the Central Mosque and seized several improvised explosive devices from the vehicle.

- On November 30 in Bishkek, a bomb exploded outside of the Sports Palace where the trial of former government officials arrested following the April 7 violence was taking place. No one was killed. Two police officers suffered minor injuries.

- On December 25, suspected terrorists parked a vehicle containing an explosive device outside the Bishkek central police station. Security officials discovered the vehicle and defused the bomb before it exploded without injury. The vehicle had been stolen from American citizens during a home invasion and robbery on December 24.

Legislation and Law Enforcement: Following the December terrorist attacks, Kyrgyzstan's security forces arrested a number of terrorist suspects. By year's end, however, none of the suspects were charged with any crimes. The Kyrgyzstan government has significantly expanded the number of uniformed police on the street and increased the number of ID checks of individuals. Due to the events in April and the subsequent dissolution of Parliament, Kyrgyzstan did not pass any new counterterrorism legislation.

Countering Terrorist Finance: Kyrgyzstan is a member of the Eurasian Group (EAG) on Combating Money Laundering and Financing of Terrorism, a Financial Action Task Force (FATF)-style regional body. In November, the EAG Secretariat noted that Kyrgyzstan was partially compliant with eight and non-compliant with eight of the FATF's 16 core anti-money laundering/countering terrorist finance recommendations. It noted that the Kyrgyz Republic had achieved major progress in relation to the financial recommendations since December 2009. The Financial Intelligence Unit of Kyrgyzstan is a member of the Egmont Group. In 2010, Kyrgyzstan did not freeze any terrorist assets, including those called for by UNSCRs 1267 and 1373.

Regional and International Cooperation: As a member state of both organizations, Kyrgyzstan participated in activities of the Collective Security Treaty Organization of the Commonwealth of Independent States and activities of the OSCE.

MALDIVES

Overview: No terrorist incidents occurred in the Maldives in 2010, although there was growing concern about the activities of local violent extremists and their involvement with transnational terrorist groups. There was particular concern about the possibility of young Maldivians joining violent extremist groups in Pakistan, Saudi Arabia, and the Middle East and returning to the Maldives to radicalize their peers and establish violent extremist groups.

The Vice President of the Maldives has publically voiced concerns about young Maldivians being recruited by militant groups in Pakistan and Afghanistan. In February, the government estimated there were 200-300 unregistered Maldivian students in Pakistan. There was an increasing trend, though a relatively small one, of Maldivians joining terrorist organizations, including those with ties to Lashkar-e-Tayyiba. Examples of Maldivians with known terrorist ties included the nine Maldivians arrested by Pakistani authorities for involvement with violent extremist groups in the Waziristan region in March 2009, who were subsequently transferred to the Maldives in 2010 and released. In addition, two of the 2007 Sultan Park bombers incarcerated at Maafushi Prison had their sentences changed from incarceration to three year suspended sentences and were released in August 2010. The Sultan Park bombing was the first recorded terrorist bombing in the Maldives, and resulted in injury to 12 foreign nationals.

Because of concerns about radicalization and extremist ideologies, the government continued to control all religious matters, including religious affiliation, expression, education, and worship. According to government officials, the purpose of this tight control was to maintain a moderate Islamic environment rather than an extremist one.

Legislation and Law Enforcement: The Maldives Police Services led a stakeholder group in drafting a counterterrorism bill, with assistance from INTERPOL and the UN Office on Drugs and Crime. The bill was in the Attorney General's office for review at year's end.

In December, the Immigration Department began installing a new border control system for the airport with biometric capacity and an integrated database.

Countering Terrorist Finance: The Government of Maldives recognized the need for legislation to enhance its ability to prosecute in cases of anti-money laundering/countering terrorist finance (AML/CTF) and fulfillment of UNSCRs. Existing legislation in the Maldives did not criminalize money laundering, apart from a small provision in the Drugs Act. The Maldives Financial Intelligence Unit has taken the lead in drafting an AML/CTF act with IMF assistance. In July, the draft bill was sent to the Attorney General's Office. In November, the Maldives Monetary Authority published for public comment a draft of the Maldives Financial Transactions Reporting regulation. The draft regulation aims to prevent the use of the financial system for money laundering and terrorist financing.

Regional and International Cooperation: The United States and the international community provided counterterrorism training to Maldivian security forces and sponsored Maldivian officials and security force personnel for regional conferences on combating violent extremism.

Countering Radicalization and Violent Extremism: The Ministry of Islamic Affairs ran a religiously-based counter-radicalization program aimed at rehabilitating prisoners jailed for violent extremism-related incidents. The Minister of Islamic Affairs has written books against extremism and brought mainstream scholars from other countries to talk to Muslims in the Maldives.

NEPAL

Overview: Nepal experienced no acts of terrorism during the past year, though the government's limited ability to control the open border with India was of concern, since terrorist groups have used Nepal as a transit point into India. The increased presence of Nepali security services in the southern Terai region led to a decrease in violence there, but the security situation remained problematic, particularly in central and eastern Terai. The United Communist Party of Nepal-Maoist (UCPN-Maoist), designated as a Specially Designated Global Terrorist by the U.S. government under Executive Order 13224, became a partner in the coalition government. The group has not forsworn violence nor has it taken several of the other steps required for delisting, that is it has not renounced violence and terrorism, its youth group has not abandoned violence and reformed, nor has it fully demonstrated a commitment to the peace process by complying with Nepali courts investigating emblematic human rights cases.

Legislation and Law Enforcement: Nepal improved its security monitoring capabilities at official border crossings along the southern border with India and at Kathmandu's Tribhuvan International Airport, while also increasing the Armed Police Force and Nepal Police presence at several crossings along the southern border. Violence in the southern Terai plains decreased due to increased deployment of both the Armed Police Force and the Nepal Police throughout the Terai along with a renewed working relationship with Indian security forces. The government's Special Security Plan, created in July 2009, sought to bridge a gap between the Nepal Police, Armed Police Force, and local communities through promotion of better working relationships, but has fallen short in building sustained public confidence.

Countering Terrorist Finance: Nepal was not a regional financial nexus, and there were no indications that the country was used as a major international money laundering center in 2010. However, government corruption, poorly regulated trade, weak financial sector regulation, and a large informal economy made the country vulnerable to money laundering and terrorist financing. The major sources of laundered proceeds stemmed from tax evasion, corruption, counterfeit currency, smuggling, and invoice manipulation. The Financial Information Unit within the Nepal Rastra Bank (Nepal's Central Bank) continued to investigate money laundering and terrorist financing; however, its efforts were limited by a lack of technical capabilities and government support. Terrorist financing legislation was drafted, and at year's end, the Cabinet was reviewing it before sending it to the legislature. Nepal is a member of the Asia/Pacific Group on Money Laundering, a Financial Action Task Force-style regional body. The Government of Nepal has the authority to freeze suspected terrorist assets and has implemented UNSCR 1373. There was one arrest and conviction for money laundering in 2010.

Regional and International Cooperation: Nepal hosted the U.S.-sponsored "South Asia Conference on the Use of Financial Sanctions in Countering Violent Extremism," which brought together government officials from every country in South Asia to discuss the issues involved with financial sanctions and the importance of maintaining and respecting those sanctions once imposed.

PAKISTAN

Overview: In 2010, Pakistan continued to experience high levels of terrorism and Pakistan-based terrorist organizations continued to threaten internal, regional, and global security. Violence resulted from both political and sectarian conflicts throughout the country, with terrorist incidents occurring in every province. While government authorities arrested many alleged perpetrators of terrorist violence, few convictions resulted. The Pakistani military continued to conduct operations in areas with known terrorist activity but was unable to expand its operations to all areas of concern. Increased sectarian violence between the Sunni and Shia communities and against religious minority communities also resulted in numerous attacks with high casualties. These attacks continued the trend of employing suicide bombers and remotely detonated explosives to perpetrate violence. Attacks using similar methods were also carried out against government and police facilities.

Pakistan, particularly the Federally Administered Tribal Areas region and the Khyber Pakhtunkhwa province, continued to be used as a base for terrorist organizations operating in Pakistan and Afghanistan, and Pakistani security forces undertook substantial efforts to counter these threats. These organizations recruited, trained, and conducted fundraising for terrorist operations in Pakistan, and used Pakistan as a transit point for cross border movement to Afghanistan and abroad. Pakistan's Frontier Corps and military initiated large-scale counterinsurgency operations in Mohmand, Khyber Pakhtunkhwa, and Orakzai, and added one battalion in Khyber Pakhtunkhwa. Pakistan's ability to continue robust operations was negatively impacted by the need to divert resources to provide relief from the 2010 floods, which caused severe, long-term damage in Pakistan. The ability to establish and maintain security in densely populated urban areas or areas with a historically poor security presence also remained a major challenge for Pakistan.

When Pakistan conducted operations to eliminate safe havens in the country, it often lacked the capability to ensure these areas remained under the control of Pakistan's security agencies. Given its inability to pursue the complete elimination of the terrorist presence and fully eliminate terrorist safe havens, Pakistan utilized a strategy to conduct limited operations to "contain" terrorist operatives in known areas of activity. Pakistan's civilian government and military departments cooperated and collaborated with U.S. efforts to identify and counter terrorist activity in Pakistan, and the United States continued to engage Pakistan to ensure it had the will and capacity to confront all extremist elements within its borders.

2010 Terrorist Incidents: The coordination, sophistication, and frequency of suicide and other bombings continued unabated in 2010. Pakistan experienced hundreds of bomb blasts, suicide attacks, and sectarian violence, resulting in more than 2,000 dead and scores more injured. Known terrorist organizations such as Tehrik-e-Taliban (the "Pakistani" Taliban) and Lashkar-e-Jhangvi claimed responsibility for a number of attacks. The Afghan Taliban, Lashkar-e-Tayyiba and al-Qa'ida also have a significant presence in Pakistan and maintained the capability to plan, influence, and assist violent extremist organizations within Pakistan and regionally. 2010 Terrorist Incidents carried out against civil society, religious groups, and government and police officials and offices during 2010 included:

- On February 3, 10 persons were killed and 70 injured when a suicide bomber attacked a Pakistani Frontier Corps convoy en route to an inauguration ceremony for a new school for girls in Maidan in Khyber Pakhtunkhwa.

- On April 28, four policemen were killed and 13 others, including eight policemen, were injured in a suicide car bomb blast in Peshawar at the U.S. Consulate.

- On May 28, over 80 persons were killed and more than 120 injured in Lahore in two separate but simultaneous suicide attacks utilizing assault rifles and grenade attacks. The attacks targeted places of worship of the Ahmadiyya Muslim community.

- On October 2, Dr. Mohammad Farooq Khan, a psychiatrist, religious scholar, and vice-chancellor of Swat Islamic University, was gunned down in his clinic. Farooq was strongly anti-Taliban and frequently took part in television talk shows during which he criticized militants and described suicide attacks as "un-Islamic". The Pakistani Taliban claimed responsibility.

- On December 7, the Chief Minister of Balochistan escaped a suicide attack that injured 10 people but left the Minister unharmed. Three organizations, the Pakistani Taliban, the Baloch Liberation United Front, and Lashkar-e-Jhangvi Alami (Lashkar-e-Jhangvi International), claimed responsibility for the attack.

Legislation and Law Enforcement: While Pakistan's law enforcement community continued to pledge to prosecute those responsible for terrorist acts inside Pakistan, a 2010 review by the United States of Pakistan's Anti-Terrorism Court rulings revealed that Pakistan remained plagued an acquittal rate of approximately 75 percent. The review, in conjunction with information provided by Pakistani law enforcement partners, painted a picture of a legal system almost incapable of prosecuting suspected terrorists. The review determined that the accused in numerous high-profile terrorism incidents involving U.S. victims had all been acquitted by the Pakistani legal system.

The Anti-Terrorism Bill 2010, proposed on July 28, 2010, remained before Pakistan's parliament. It proposes 25 amendments to Pakistan's original anti-terrorism legislation, the Anti-Terrorism Act of 1997, including provisions that broaden the definition of terrorism, expand the authority of law enforcement agencies investigating terrorist incidents, authorize detention of subjects for 90 days before presenting them before a court, and allow increased electronic surveillance and wiretapping.

The U.S. Department of Justice continued to offer assistance to the Government of Pakistan to improve its existing counterterrorism laws. Under the U.S.-Pakistan Strategic Dialogue, Secretary of State Clinton and Pakistan's Foreign Minister Qureshi launched the Law Enforcement and Counterterrorism working group as a platform to discuss ways to increase cooperation. The U.S. Embassy in Islamabad has also implemented a diverse law enforcement training program for federal, provincial, and local law enforcement that included training in crime scene investigation, post blast investigations, and training specifically for counterterrorism personnel and bomb disposal units.

U.S. officials continued to monitor court proceedings involving high-profile terrorist attacks, such as the cases involving seven Pakistanis currently on trial for the 2008 Mumbai attack that killed 166 people, including six Americans; and the three Pakistanis on trial for assisting Faisal Shahzad with the attempted May 1, 2010 bombing of Times Square. The Federal Bureau of Investigation has assisted with the respective prosecutions.

Pakistan continued to process travelers on entry and departure at 13 international airports, five land border sites, four seaports, and two train stations with the Personal Identification Secure Comparison and Evaluation System (PISCES).

Countering Terrorist Finance: Pakistan strengthened its counterterrorist finance regime and committed to making additional improvements. Pakistan's terrorist financing law is ambiguous on key points, however, and the country's implementation of UNSCR 1267 was incomplete.

The informal financial sector continued to play a significant role in Pakistan's legal and illicit economies, but the government has taken substantial steps to curb the role of informal financial service providers in servicing remittances. Through the Pakistan Remittance Initiative, the government has steadily increased the volume of remittances coming through authorized channels during the past three years, improved Pakistan's balance of payments, and enhanced financial transparency. The government has also prosecuted unregistered, illegal money remitters. During the past year, Pakistan took a substantial step toward strengthening its anti-money laundering/countering terrorist finance (AML/CTF) regime. In March, the parliament passed the Anti-Money Laundering Act, which replaced a temporary ordinance and solidified the Financial Monitoring Unit's standing as a national center for the collection and dissemination of suspicious transaction reports related to money laundering and terrorist financing. Pakistan also strengthened financial regulations, in particular the requirements to conduct due diligence and maintain internal controls.

As an active participant in the Asia/Pacific Group on Money Laundering, Pakistan has been under review by the Financial Action Task Force (FATF) because of deficiencies in its AML/CTF regime. In June, the Finance Minister committed Pakistan to an FATF action plan, which outlined a series of steps the government will take to remedy these deficiencies.

Despite progress, deficiencies in Pakistan's AML/CTF regime remained. Notably, the criminalization of the financing of terrorist acts committed against foreign governments and international organizations was ambiguous, as was the criminalization of financing groups that have not been explicitly banned by the government or designated by the UN. Although Pakistan did not make substantial progress toward removing the ambiguity in the law this year, the Government of Pakistan committed to doing so in its FATF action plan.

Another significant concern was Pakistan's weak implementation of UNSCR 1267. UN-designated terrorist organizations were able to skirt sanctions simply by reconstituting themselves under different names. They made little effort to hide their connections to the old groups and gained access to the financial system using new names.

Regional and International Cooperation: Pakistan continued to cooperate in regional and international counterterrorism forums. However, India-Pakistan counterterrorism cooperation was lacking in 2010.

Significant cooperation was documented during the latter part of 2010 in support for Project Global Shield, a World Customs Organization (WCO) Counter Improvised Explosive Device (IED) Project seeking to identify the global movement of precursor chemicals (some dual use) that are used in the manufacture of IEDs. A multi-country conference held at the WCO Headquarters in Brussels in October, launched this project, which commenced on November 1.

As a follow up to the launch of Project Global Shield, the Pakistan Federal Board of Revenue (Customs) and UN Office of Drugs and Crime organized a training conference in Karachi, Pakistan in December, which provided training to customs officers and anti-narcotics officers in the identification and safe handling of precursor chemicals as well as training in the targeting of container shipments that might have inappropriately declared their contents.

In January, the foreign ministers of Pakistan, Afghanistan, and Iran agreed on a roadmap to confront jointly the challenges of violent extremism and terrorism facing the region by signing the Islamabad Declaration, which was described as a guide to stability, security, and development in the region through mutual cooperation. Pakistani Foreign Minister Qureshi said the three sides agreed to confront the common challenges of illicit weapons and drug money through a comprehensive approach. The three nations also agreed to look into the possibilities of developing regional approaches to these challenges.

Countering Radicalization and Violent Extremism: The Government of Pakistan has realized that counter-radicalization through non-military means is a critical component to long-term success against violent extremism, and has initiated certain counter-radicalization efforts in 2010. As part of these efforts, the Ministry of Culture announced plans to set up a TV channel focusing on culture and traditions of the country with the objective of countering violent extremism. The channel reportedly will cover various aspects of Pakistani culture and traditions including folk music, the theatre industry, regional dialects and traditions, archaeological sites, and the history of the region and other areas, according to the Federal Ministry of Culture.

A school in Malakand, run by the Pakistani army, continued to rehabilitate Taliban-influenced youth. The UN Children's Fund-funded school, originally opened in September 2009, provided free religious education and psychiatric counseling to 85 students from Swat, a district heavily influenced by terrorist groups. The students were 13 to 18 years old and few had finished secondary school. The project is the first of its kind in Pakistan.

On July 28, President Asif Ali Zardari called approximately 30 Islamic scholars and representatives of minority communities to his official residence to discuss minority rights and interfaith harmony in the country. The Ministry of Minorities Affairs established interfaith committees at the district level to meet monthly to address issues of religious tolerance and interfaith dialogue.

SRI LANKA

Overview: In 2009, the Government of Sri Lanka announced formally the defeat of the Liberation Tigers of Tamil Eelam (LTTE), a U.S.-designated Foreign Terrorist Organization. While there were no terrorist incidents within Sri Lanka in 2010, there were continuing concerns that the LTTE's international network of financial support might still be functioning; therefore, most counterterrorism activities undertaken by the Sri Lankan government were targeted at countering terrorist finance.

Legislation and Law Enforcement: Legislative efforts were focused on limiting financial support for the remnants of LTTE. Domestically, there was a large budgetary allocation (about four percent of Sri Lanka's GDP) for defense and monitoring of Tamil diaspora activity in coordination with foreign governments. The United States provided training for relevant Sri Lankan government agencies and the banking sector in combating the provision of financial support to the LTTE remnants. The Sri Lankan government implemented the Container Security Initiative and the Megaports program at the Port of Colombo.

Countering Terrorist Finance: In February, Sri Lanka provided a high-level written commitment to work with the Financial Action Task Force (FATF) to implement the following corrective measures: (1) adequately criminalizing money laundering and terrorist financing; and (2) establishing and implementing adequate procedures to identify and freeze terrorist assets. The government was drafting amendments to the 2005-2006 laws on money laundering and terrorist financing, in accordance with FATF recommendations, at year's end.

Regional and International Cooperation: In October, the Financial Intelligence Unit (FIU) of Sri Lanka signed a Memorandum of Understanding (MOU) with the FIU of Bangladesh to share financial information to facilitate the investigation and prosecution of persons suspected of money laundering and terrorist financing. Sri Lanka has already signed MOUs with the Philippines, Nepal, Cambodia, Malaysia, Afghanistan, South Korea, and Indonesia.

Countering Radicalization and Violent Extremism: In order to address lingering resentment in areas that were formerly held by LTTE combatants, the Sri Lankan government was working to restore civil administration, resettle Internally Displaced Persons, provide immediate infrastructure development, encourage private sector participation, and promote the development of industries.

TAJIKISTAN

Overview: Severe weaknesses were exposed in Tajikistan's counterterrorism strategy and its ability to conduct effective counterterrorism operations. Events in the Rasht Valley demonstrated that Tajikistan was vulnerable to an organized insurgency by well-trained and motivated terrorists, both foreign and domestic. The inability of the Government of Tajikistan to police its border with Afghanistan and deal decisively with attacks against government forces emboldened its domestic and foreign enemies. Terrorists, criminals, and fighters of varied allegiances effectively exploited Tajikistan's mountainous terrain and domestic political rivalries.

Nowshera, Pakistan: Pakistani firefighters try to extinguish burning NATO oil tankers following a Taliban attack in Nowshera on October 7, 2010. More than 40 NATO vehicles were destroyed in two separate Taliban attacks in Pakistan on October 6 as the militants stepped up their efforts to disrupt supply routes into Afghanistan. AFP PHOTO/A. Majeed

Tajikistan's counterterrorism policies were focused mainly on controlling Islam in society and increasing the capacity of Tajikistan's military and law enforcement community to conduct tactical operations. The latter was undertaken with support from bilateral assistance programs with the international community. While the government maintained a list of banned groups it considers "extremist", the list included several religious groups – including Jehovah's Witnesses; Tablighi Jamaat, an Islamic missionary organization; and the Salafiya sect – that the government banned despite a lack of any evidence that members engaged in violent extremist activities.

2010 Terrorist Incidents: On September 22, 23 soldiers were killed when militants in the Kamarob Valley (an opposition stronghold just outside of Gharm in the Rasht Valley) ambushed a military convoy. The Ministry of Defense reported that former opposition commanders Mullo Abdullo Rahimov and Ali Bedaki Davlatov led the attack with a contingent of foreign and Tajik fighters that had slipped into Tajikistan from Afghanistan.

On September 3, a Vehicle Born Improvised Implosive Device (VBIED) detonated on the compound of the Regional Department for Combating Organized Crime (UBOP) in the northern city of Khujand, killing two officers and injuring 26 others as they gathered for morning formation. This was the first VBIED attack in Tajikistan since at least the end of the civil war. According to the Ministry of Internal Affairs, the VBIED was detonated by a suicide bomber with possible links to the Islamic Movement of Uzbekistan (IMU). The previously unknown group "Jamatt Ansarullah in Tajikistan" later claimed responsibility. Many speculated that the attack was an act of revenge against UBOP by a local group for the alleged death of a young man in its custody. The driver was reportedly the deceased man's brother. UBOP is notorious for its abusive interrogation methods. Government security operations in the northern Sughd region against suspected IMU members continued throughout the year.

Legislation and Law Enforcement: The Government of Tajikistan used counterterrorism statutes to suppress legitimate political opposition and dissent as well as to prosecute terrorists. Unfortunately, the judicial system in Tajikistan was also plagued by endemic corruption.

An August 23 prison break by suspected insurgents from the Rasht Valley resulted in the death of six police officers and sparked a months-long manhunt. As 2010 drew to a close, more than half of the prisoners had been recaptured or killed. Some were recaptured in Afghanistan with the assistance of Afghan security forces.

Effectively policing the rugged and remote Tajik/Afghan border is a daunting task and the Government of Tajikistan has made progress in improving border security by leveraging bilateral assistance.

Countering Terrorist Finance: Terrorist financing and money laundering were illegal, but existing laws were not comprehensive and did not meet international standards. Despite pressure from the international community, Tajikistan has not taken action to modernize its money laundering criminal code.

Regional and International Cooperation: In September, Tajikistan participated in regional counter-terrorism exercises with Shanghai Cooperation Organization partner nations.

Countering Radicalization and Violent Extremism: Many of the government's measures to counter extremism and radicalization restricted religious freedom. Various initiatives have been undertaken, such as banning the hijab in schools and a recent draft law prohibiting minors from attending mosques. Rather than specifically addressing radicalization and violent extremism, the government sought to marginalize Islam as a whole. Critics claimed that heavy-handed government tactics actually contributed to radicalization rather than deterred it.

TURKMENISTAN

Overview: Turkmenistan adopted new counterterrorism legislation and continued its efforts to improve border security, including training for law enforcement officials. Turkmenistan's border guards, customs service, and law enforcement agencies lacked adequate personnel and remained in need of further training.

Legislation and Law Enforcement: Turkmenistan adopted a revised Criminal Code that went into effect on July 1, 2010. The new Code specifies punishment for terrorism and terrorist financing. Punishment for terrorism ranges from five to 20 years in prison, depending on the seriousness of the terrorist act. Punishment for terrorist financing ranges from four to 15 years in prison and confiscation of property, with the length of the sentence determined by the seriousness of the crime, whether it was premeditated and whether the offender was a government official who misused his position in committing the crime.

The Government of Turkmenistan is in the process of improving its border crossing checkpoints. In 2010, the government purchased modern equipment to enhance detection capacity and renovated checkpoints on the Uzbek and Kazakh borders. In addition, the U.S. government provided new radio equipment to the State Border Service that, together with new trucks provided by the Turkmen government, will improve communications in border areas.

Countering Terrorist Finance: In January, Turkmenistan established a Financial Intelligence Unit under the Ministry of Finance to strengthen the government's efforts to combat money laundering/counterterrorist finance (AML/CTF). In June, Turkmenistan became a full member of the Eurasian Group, a regional AML/CTF organization and part of the Financial Action Task Force (FATF). That month, the FATF placed Turkmenistan on the Improving Global AML/CTF Compliance On-Going Process List stating that while it had demonstrated progress in improving its AML/CTF regime, there remained certain strategic deficiencies that needed to be addressed. Turkmenistan indicated it will implement an action plan to address these deficiencies.

Regional and International Cooperation: Turkmenistan participated in regional and international training programs to bolster its border security. As part of the Border Operations Management Program in Central Asia (BOMCA), the Turkmenistan State Border Service and State Counternarcotics Service sent officers to attend regional training in Tashkent and Almaty on dog handling techniques to search for drugs and explosives. Turkmenistan Migration Service, Customs Service, and Border Service officers participated in BOMCA training programs on integrated border management for the Ashgabat airport and Turkmenbashy seaport. In May, Turkmen officials participated in NATO's Advanced Training Course designed to teach the latest counterterrorism methods and strategies. Turkmenistan is a partner nation in the Global Initiative to Combat Nuclear Terrorism.

UZBEKISTAN

Overview: Despite continued instability in several neighboring countries, and the continued involvement of ethnic Uzbeks and Uzbek nationals in terrorist incidents in other countries, including Afghanistan and Pakistan, no terrorist incidents took place within Uzbekistan. The Government of Uzbekistan continued to exercise tight control over its security situation, convicting an unknown number of people with alleged terrorist ties. As in the past, a lack of reliable information made it difficult to analyze the extent of the terrorist threat in Uzbekistan. It was possible that Uzbekistan security forces neutralized terrorist threats without bringing them to the attention of the press or the international community. It was also well-documented that the government treated many non-violent minority religious groups, such as Nur, Akromiya, and Tablighi Jamaat, as extremist groups that were banned or treated as banned organizations.

Legislation and Law Enforcement: Law enforcement officials continued to arrest, prosecute, and convict an unknown number of people under charges of extremism. It was unclear how many of these defendants would be considered terrorists, as the Government of Uzbekistan has targeted several religious groups that international observers considered to be nonviolent.

On August 14, Uzbek police exchanged fire with four armed men, allegedly religious extremists, near a village in the Tashkent Region. Limited reports on the event stated that one of the armed men was wounded and arrested, while the others escaped.

According to independent media reports, up to 83 people were convicted of charges ranging from anti-constitutional activity to membership in extremist groups and "inciting ethnic and religious animosity" in closed trials during February and March 2010. The trials were allegedly related to several terrorist incidents that took place in 2009, including the assassinations of Khasan Asadov, head of the Uzbek Interior Ministry's directorate for counterterrorism; and Abror Abrorov, the Deputy Director of Kukeldash Madrassah; the attempted murder of Anvar-kori Tursunov, the principal Imam of Tashkent; and a shoot-out that took place in Tashkent in late August 2009. Uzbekistan sought the extradition of 30 Uzbek asylum seekers from detention in Kazakhstan, whose government stated that Uzbekistan provided strong evidence that the asylum seekers had links to terrorist organizations. By year's end, in full consultation with UN High Commissioner for Refugees (UNHCR), UNHCR mandate refugee status was revoked from the detainees and one of the 30 had been extradited to Uzbekistan. A second was released. Uzbekistan continued to seek the extradition of the remaining 28. At year's end the extradition was pending.

Countering Terrorist Finance: Uzbekistan is a member of the Eurasian Group against Money Laundering and Terrorist Financing (EAG). After passing anti-money laundering legislation in 2009, the Government of Uzbekistan did not pass any new legislation or take any new measures against terrorist finance in 2010. The government did not report any efforts to seize terrorist assets. Although terrorist financing was not a significant problem in Uzbekistan, a large and robust black market functioned outside the confines of the official financial system. The unofficial, unmonitored cash-based market created an opportunity for small-scale terrorist money laundering.

Regional and International Cooperation: The Government of Uzbekistan continued to cooperate bilaterally with other foreign governments and multilaterally with several international organizations on general security issues, including border control. In December, the UN Counter-Terrorism Committee Executive Directorate and the OSCE jointly sponsored a conference in Tashkent that focused on countering violent extremism in Central Asia.

Countering Radicalization and Violent Extremism: The Government of Uzbekistan continued to label minority religious groups and Muslim groups operating outside the parameters of State control as extremists. State-controlled media frequently ran programs designed to denigrate terrorist and extremist propaganda, including "documentaries" about extremist groups aired on state-run television, news stories, and opinion columns about the dangers of extremism in state-run newspapers, and public confessions and apologies by alleged extremists who claimed to have seen the error of their ways. However, non-violent religious minorities, including Nur, the Bahais and evangelical Protestants, have been branded as extremists and as threats to society in these "documentaries" and articles.

WESTERN HEMISPHERE OVERVIEW

Terrorist attacks within the Western Hemisphere in 2010 were committed primarily by two U.S.-designated Foreign Terrorist Organizations in Colombia – the Revolutionary Armed Forces of Colombia and the National Liberation Army – and other radical leftist Andean groups elsewhere. The threat of a transnational terrorist attack remained low for most countries in the Western Hemisphere. There were no known operational cells of either al-Qa'ida- or Hizballah-related groups in the hemisphere, although ideological sympathizers in South America and the Caribbean continued to provide financial and moral support to these and other terrorist groups in the Middle East and South Asia.

Overall, regional governments took modest steps to improve their counterterrorism capabilities and tighten border security, but corruption, weak government institutions, insufficient interagency cooperation, weak or non-existent legislation, and reluctance to allocate necessary resources limited progress in many countries. Argentina, Colombia, and Mexico undertook serious prevention and preparedness efforts. Most countries began to look seriously at possible connections between transnational criminal organizations and terrorist organizations.

The United States enjoyed solid cooperation on terrorism-related matters from most hemispheric partners, especially at the operational level, and maintained excellent intelligence, law enforcement, and legal assistance relations with most countries. An important regional focus for this cooperation was the OAS' Inter-American Committee Against Terrorism.

ARGENTINA

Overview: Argentina and the United States cooperated well in analyzing possible terrorist threat information. Argentina continued to focus on the challenges of policing its remote northern and northeastern borders - including the Tri-Border Area (TBA), where Argentina, Brazil, and Paraguay meet - against threats including drug and human trafficking, contraband smuggling, and other international crime.

2010 Terrorist Incidents: According to the Argentine Federal Police, domestic anarchist groups conducted 12 improvised explosive device attacks in Argentina in 2010, resulting in property damage and the loss of one life. Nine of the incidents took place in Buenos Aires Province, two in Rio Negro Province, and one in Neuquen Province. Seven of the targets were banks, two were airline offices, two were police facilities, and one was a telecommunications company. As the explosions were small and took place in the very early morning hours, casualties were limited to one fatality and minor injuries to several individuals.

Legislation and Law Enforcement: The Argentine police have not yet arrested any suspects in the 12 terrorist attacks. On September 30, Argentina granted political asylum to Sergio Apablaza Guerra, a former leader of the Chilean terrorist group Manuel Rodriguez Patriotic Front, wanted by Chile in connection with the 1991 murder of a Chilean senator and the 1991 kidnapping of the son of the owner of a prominent Chilean newspaper.

The Argentine government continued to seek to bring to justice those suspected of the July 18, 1994 terrorist bombing of the Argentine-Jewish Mutual Association in Buenos Aires that killed 85 and injured more than 150 people. At the September UNGA, Argentine President Cristina Fernandez de Kirchner proposed to Iran that the Iranian suspects be tried in a third country. Iran rejected the proposal via a September 28, 2010 note delivered to the UN Secretary General.

Countering Terrorist Finance: The National Coordination Unit in the Ministry of Justice and Human Rights manages the government's anti-money laundering and counterterrorist finance (AML/CTF) efforts and represents Argentina in the Financial Action Task Force (FATF), the FATF Against Money Laundering in South America (GAFISUD), and the OAS Group of Experts of the Inter-American Commission for the Control of the Abuse of Drugs (CICAD). The Government of Argentina underwent a FATF mutual evaluation in November 2009, which was adopted by the FATF plenary in October 2010. The assessment concluded that Argentina had made virtually no progress toward addressing the numerous serious deficiencies identified during the previous assessment and that the legal and preventive AML/CTF measures in place were either inadequate or not being enforced.

Among the many deficiencies noted in the FATF assessment was that the money laundering statute was not effectively implemented. The law provides the legal foundation for Argentina's financial intelligence unit, the Central Bank, and other regulatory and law enforcement bodies to investigate and prosecute money laundering and terrorist finance. The Argentine government and Central Bank claimed to be committed to freezing assets of terrorist groups in Argentine financial institutions identified by the UN; however, measures to freeze terrorist-related funds rely mainly on ordinary criminal procedures, which do not permit timely and effective enforcement in such cases. Argentine authorities have dedicated limited resources to monitoring terrorist financing taking place in the TBA.

Regional and International Cooperation: Argentina participated in the OAS' Inter-American Committee Against Terrorism, MERCOSUR's Special Forum on Terrorism, and the 3+1 Group on Tri-Border Area Security with Paraguay, Brazil, and the United States.

BOLIVIA

Overview: There did not appear to be any credible evidence that international terrorist organizations were present, nor of any plans or intentions within such groups to commit terrorist acts within Bolivia. There were reports that a handful of individuals associated with the Revolutionary Armed Forces of Colombia (FARC) were present. The Peruvian government has made accusations that Tupac Amaru Revolutionary Movement training camps were present in Bolivia. The Government of Bolivia cooperated with the United States only minimally on counterterrorism and did not share counterterrorism information with the U.S. government. In June, President Morales accused the United States of using counterterrorism as an excuse for involvement in other countries' affairs and "to control presidents and governments and the countries' natural resources."

Legislation and Law Enforcement: In March, the Minister of Government reaffirmed the Bolivian government's commitment to a "war against terrorists" operating in Bolivia. The government included terrorist financing measures as part of the Marcelo Quiroga Santa Cruz Anti-Corruption law, which authorizes prison sentences of five to 10 years for such activities.

The Government of Bolivia enacted measures to improve border security by issuing machine-readable passports (though without a biometric chip) to Bolivian citizens.

Countering Terrorist Finance: The Bolivian financial system did not provide strong controls or safeguards for preventing its use by terrorists. Still, there is no evidence that terrorist organizations used Bolivian financial institutions. Bolivia is a member of the Financial Action Task Force Against Money Laundering in South America (GAFISUD), which recommended in 2010 that Bolivia improve its current money laundering legislation to conform with the standards of the Financial Action Task Force. Bolivia has yet to criminalize terrorist financing or allow for the blocking of terrorist assets. Its Financial Investigative Unit lacks the authority to receive, analyze, and communicate information related to terrorist financing.

Regional and International Cooperation: The Government of Bolivia cooperated well with Peru, Colombia, and surrounding countries on counterterrorism.

BRAZIL

Overview: The Brazilian government cooperated in countering terrorism-related activities, including investigating potential terrorism financing, document forgery networks, and other illicit activity. Operationally, security forces of the Brazilian government worked with U.S. officials to pursue investigative leads provided by U.S. authorities regarding terrorist suspects.

Although Brazil has no official list of terrorist groups and does not recognize the Colombian Revolutionary Armed Forces (FARC) as one, former President Luiz Inacio Lula da Silva and current President Dilma Rousseff have been critical of the FARC's use of violence and publicly called on the group to desist its armed struggle against the Colombian government.

Legislation and Law Enforcement: The Government of Brazil's counterterrorism strategy consisted of deterring terrorists from using Brazilian territory to facilitate attacks or raise funds, while monitoring and suppressing transnational criminal activities that could support terrorist actions. It accomplished this through coordination among its law enforcement entities and through cooperation with the United States and other partners in the region.

The Brazilian government is achieving visible results thanks to recent investments in border and law enforcement infrastructure that were made with a view to control the flow of goods—legal and illegal—through the Tri- Border Area (TBA) of Brazil, Argentina, and Paraguay, whose proceeds could be diverted to support terrorist groups. The inspection station at the Friendship Bridge in the TBA that was completed by the Brazilian customs agency (Receita Federal) in 2007 continued to take effective action to reduce the smuggling of drugs, weapons, and contraband goods along the border with Paraguay. From January to November 2010, Receita Federal seized more than US$ 716 million in contraband goods, including drugs, weapons, and munitions.

As a result of the effective crackdown on the Friendship Bridge, most smuggling operations now take place through the Parana River and Lago Itaipu, and some have migrated to other sections of the border, such as the towns of Guiara and Ponta Pora. The Federal Police has special maritime police units in both Foz de Iguacu and Guaira that patrol the maritime border areas, but because of the scale and complexity of the endeavor to curtail smuggling and trafficking activities through the waterways, Brazil is considering using an unmanned aerial vehicle to assist law enforcement in monitoring the border, a development that could further improve border security. In the meantime, the State of Parana has paired with the Federal Police to create a Border Operations Independent Company consisting of roughly 120 officers.

The Container Security Initiative in Santos continued in 2010.

Countering Terrorist Finance: Brazil is a member of the Financial Action Task Force (FATF) and is also a member of the FATF of South America (GAFISUD). Brazil seeks to play an active leadership role in GAFISUD and has offered technical assistance to Argentina to implement FATF recommendations. The relevant executive branch agencies in Brazil view FATF recommendations as a top priority. The government has created a working group, chaired by the Ministry of Justice, to incorporate these recommendations into proposed legislation and regulation, however, Congress had not acted by year's end.

Terrorist financing is not an autonomous offense in Brazil. Terrorist financing is, however, an established predicate offense for money laundering. A 2008 draft terrorist financing bill passed the Brazilian Senate and was awaiting approval by the lower chamber at year's end. The bill would facilitate greater law enforcement access to financial and banking records during investigations, criminalize illicit enrichment, allow administrative freezing of assets, and facilitate prosecutions of money laundering and terrorist financing cases.

Brazil monitored domestic financial operations and effectively used its financial intelligence unit, the Financial Activities Oversight Council (COAF), to identify possible funding sources for terrorist groups. Through COAF, which is a largely independent entity under the authority of the Finance Ministry (Fazenda), Brazil has carried out name checks for persons and entities on the UNSCR 1267 list, but it has so far not reported any assets, accounts, or property in the names of persons or entities on the UN lists. The Brazilian government has generally responded to U.S. efforts to identify and block terrorist-related funds.

In December, the United States designated Bilal Mohsen Wehbe, Hizballah's chief representative in South America, under Executive Order 13224. Wehbe has been involved in transferring funds collected in Brazil to Hizballah in Lebanon. COAF has reported that Wehbe's name was placed in their database for continued monitoring. COAF does not have the authority to unilaterally freeze assets without a court order. The FATF has recommended that COAF create a standard operating procedure for freezing funds, which COAF has prioritized for next year's actions.

Regional and International Cooperation: Brazil participated in regional counterterrorism fora, included the Union of South American Nations and Mercosur's working group on terrorism and the sub-working group on financial issues, the latter of which covers terrorist financing and money laundering among the Mercosur countries. Brazil signed the Beijing Convention on the Suppression of Unlawful Acts Relating to International Civil Aviation and the Beijing Protocol to the Convention for the Suppression of Unlawful Seizure of Aircraft at the conclusion of an International Civil Aviation Organization diplomatic conference in September.

CANADA

Overview: Canada remained one of the United States' closest counterterrorism partners. Testifying before a Parliamentary committee on May 11, Canadian Security Intelligence Service (CSIS) Director Richard Fadden said, "confronting the threat from al-Qa'ida, its affiliates, and its adherents" remained the "number one priority" of his organization. Canada continued to face threats to both Canadian interests abroad and domestically.

Legislation and Law Enforcement: The Canadian government introduced several counterterrorism-related bills in 2010, all of which were still under consideration at year's end:

- Bill C-17, Combating Terrorism Act, provides for investigative hearings and bail with conditions.

- Bill C-42, Strengthening Aviation Security Act, provides legal authority for Canadian officials to share information with the United States for the purposes of the Secure Flight program.

- Bill C-53, Fair and Efficient Criminal Trials Act, aims to improve criminal procedure to cut the number of long, drawn-out trials, according to the government.

- Bill S-7, An Act to deter Terrorism and Amend the State Immunity Act, will allow terrorism victims to sue terrorists and terrorist entities for loss or damage suffered as a result of their acts. It will also allow victims of terrorism, in certain circumstances, to sue foreign states that have supported terrorist entities, which have committed such acts.

- On October 26, the government reintroduced legislation (S-13) to implement the Framework Agreement on Integrated Cross-Border Maritime Law Enforcement Operations ("Shiprider") between the Canada and the United States. The agreement will allow the exchange of cross-designated officers (ship riders) to create seamless maritime law enforcement operations across the U.S.-Canadian maritime border.

- On December 15, An Act to Amend the Criminal Code (Suicide Bombings) (S-215) became law. The bill clarifies that suicide bombings fall within the definition of "terrorist activity" in the Criminal Code.

On June 16, Commissioner John Major delivered the final Report of the Commission of Inquiry into the Investigation of the 1095 Bombing of Air India Flight 182 [4]. In its response to the report, the government said, "The Commission identified numerous mistakes that were committed around the time of the bombing, including as regards the treatment of the victims' families." The government pledged to "recognize these shortcomings and work consistently to prevent another such tragedy." The government introduced an action plan for implementing the recommendations of the Major Commission. The plan builds on legislative initiatives already in progress in Parliament.

[4] Air India Flight 182 was an Air India flight operating on the Montréal-London-Delhi route. On June 23, 1985, it was blown up by a bomb while in Irish airspace and crashed into the Atlantic Ocean, killing 329 people, including 280 Canadian citizens, mostly of Indian birth or descent, and 22 Indians. The incident was the largest mass murder in modern Canadian history and the deadliest act of air terrorism before 9/11.

Lima, Peru: Mario Sifuentes aka "Sergio" (C), second in command of Peru's Shining Path terrorist group, is taken into custody at the Police airport in Lima, on December 30, 2010. Sifuentes was captured in Alto Huallaga as a result of an intelligence operation, police said. AFP PHOTO/ Ernesto Benavides

On August 25 and 26, Royal Canadian Mounted Police (RCMP) officers arrested three individuals in Ottawa in relation to an alleged terrorist plot. Federal prosecutors charged Misbahuddin Ahmed, Hiva Alizadeh, and Dr. Khurram Sher with conspiracy to knowingly facilitate a terrorist activity, probably in Canada. RCMP seized over 50 circuit boards that could be used for remote-controlled triggers for improvised explosive devices (IEDs) as well as schematics, videos, drawings, instructions, books and electrical components designed specifically for the construction of IEDs. Prosecutors laid further charges against Ahmed and Alizadeh for possessing an explosive substance with intent to harm, and Alizadeh faces a charge of providing property or financial services for the benefit of a terrorist group. In September, Ahmed was released pending trial and Alizadeh remained detained.

On August 30, a Federal Court judge granted Abousfian Abdelrazik, a Montreal man who was stranded in Sudan for six years, permission to continue his suit against the federal government and Foreign Affairs Minister Lawrence Cannon. In 2009, a federal court judge ruled the Canadian government violated Abdelrazik's rights by refusing to allow him to return home because of travel ban provisions relating to his listing at the UN's 1267 Committee. The government expressed disagreement with the ruling but did not appeal, bringing Abdelrazik back to Canada in June 2009.

Canadian prosecutors secured a number of convictions in terrorism cases in 2010:

- On May 14, Prapaharan Thambithurai, the first person convicted under Canada's anti-terrorism law for knowingly raising money to benefit a terrorist group, pled guilty in a Vancouver, BC court to raising money for the Liberation Tigers of Tamil Eelam. The judge imposed a six-month sentence on Thaambithurai, who was arrested in 2008 and subsequently admitted to raising $600 and collecting pledges for another $2,000 from local Sri Lankans.

- On December 7, an Ontario provincial judge sentenced Roger Clement, a retired federal civil servant, to three-and-a-half years in prison for firebombing an Ottawa bank.

- On December 9, the Federal Court of Canada upheld an immigration security certificate against alleged al-Qa'ida terrorist Mohamed Harkat. Justice Simon Noel ruled that the government had reasonable grounds to believe that Harkat constituted a threat to national security and deemed him inadmissible under Canada's immigration law. Pending deportation, authorities may continue to monitor Harkat, who has claimed that he faces a risk of torture if deported to his native Algeria.

- In a separate ruling, the federal court upheld the constitutionality of the revised security certificate process implemented in 2008. Two other security certificates remained in place against alleged terrorist suspects Mahmoud Jaballah and Mohamed Zeki Mahjoub.

- In a separate ruling on December 17, the Ontario Court of Appeal dismissed the appeal of Piratheepan Nadarajah and Suresh Sriskandarajah regarding their extradition order to the United States to stand trial on charges of offering to purchase surface to air missiles and other weaponry in the United States for the Liberation Tigers of Tamil Eelam.

- During 2010, of the 18 individuals originally charged in the 2006 Toronto 18 case, seven pled guilty, and courts found four others guilty. In December, the courts increased the severity of the sentences against two of the convicted adult Toronto 18 individuals to send a strong message about the gravity of the offences. (The Toronto 18 planned to bomb several Canadian targets, including Parliament Hill, RCMP headquarters, and nuclear power plants.)

Countering Terrorist Finance: Canada is a member of the Financial Action Task Force (FATF) as well as the Asia/Pacific Group on Money Laundering (APG), and is a supporting nation of the Caribbean Financial Action Task Force (CFATF); both APG and CFATF are FATF-style regional bodies. Canada is also an observer in the Council of Europe's Select Committee of Experts on the Evaluation Of Anti-Money Laundering Measures (MONEYVAL).

The Government of Canada designated suspected terrorists and terrorist organizations on the UN 1267 Sanctions Committee's consolidated list. The Anti-Terrorism Act provides measures for the Government of Canada to create a list of entities. Listed entity's property can be the subject of seizure, forfeiture, or both. In addition, financial institutions such as banks and brokerages are subject to reporting requirements with respect to an entity's property and must not allow those entities to access the property nor may these institutions deal or otherwise dispose of the property. Canada recently completed a two-year review of the 42 entities on its domestic terrorist list and all 42 remained on the list. In 2010, Canada domestically listed al-Qa'ida in the Arabian Peninsula and al-Shabaab.

Regional and International Cooperation: Canada has been an important partner with the United States in the UN and other multilateral counterterrorism efforts. Canada and the United States cooperate bilaterally through the Cross Border Crime Forum sub-group on counterterrorism and the Bilateral Consultative Group on Counterterrorism.

Countering Radicalization and Violent Extremism: Canadian officials spoke out frequently on the need for all Canadians to remain engaged and vigilant in the fight against violent extremism in Canada. The government worked with non-governmental partners and concerned Canadian communities to deter violent extremism through preventative programming and community outreach. The

RCMP's National Security Community Outreach program promoted interaction and relationship-building with communities at risk. The Cross-Cultural Roundtable on Security fostered dialogue on national security issues between the government and community leaders.

CARIBBEAN BASIN

The political will of Caribbean nations to counter terrorism remained strong, despite limited resources and capabilities. Primary counterterrorism objectives for the Caribbean included: preventing terrorists or terrorist organizations from entering or transiting the Caribbean en route to other countries, particularly the United States; increasing countries' awareness of the potential threat from terrorists or terrorist organizations; preventing terrorists or terrorist organizations from operating or developing safe havens in the Caribbean; and increasing countries' capabilities to prevent terrorists from attacking targets of opportunity.

JAMAICA: Jamaican-U.S. counterterrorism cooperation included the Container Security Initiative and law enforcement cooperation. Jamaica also worked closely with the immigration and security agencies of countries such as Canada and the United Kingdom, both of which have sizeable Jamaican émigré communities and serve as transit points for travelers to Jamaica from many world regions.

Jamaica is a member of the Caribbean Financial Action Task Force. Jamaica has supported implementation of UNSCRs 1267 and 1373.

Jamaica is a member of the regional organizations Caribbean Community (CARICOM) and the OAS. Within the OAS, Jamaica is an active member of the Inter-American Committee Against Terrorism. Jamaica also actively supports efforts to improve regional security through the Caribbean Basin Security Initiative. The CARICOM Council of Ministers of National Security meets regularly to discuss regional threats to security, including terrorism. Jamaica's Minister of National Security, Dwight Nelson, hosted the most recent such meeting on December 1, 2010 in Montego Bay.

TRINIDAD AND TOBAGO: Trinidad and Tobago faced a number of challenges related to border control and limited law enforcement capacity. A small number of Trinidadians also have connections to radical elements outside the country. The Government of Trinidad and Tobago continued to partner with U.S. law enforcement authorities, making efforts to improve its ability to detect, deter, and investigate acts of terrorism.

The Government of Trinidad and Tobago has canceled the purchase of certain offshore patrol vessels described in prior reports and is now seeking to increase domestic security though improved radar and aerial capacity and more effective coastal patrols in an effort to counter transnational trafficking and bolster border security. Trinidad and Tobago participated in the Advanced Passenger Information System.

Although the mandate of Trinidad and Tobago's Financial Intelligence Unit (FIU), established in late 2009, covered terrorist finance, the FIU was not fully operational in 2010 because it lacked supervisory powers and thus did not successfully pursue any terrorist finance cases. With respect to the most recent Caribbean Financial Action Task Force progress report on Trinidad and Tobago, the government was urged to take immediate action to implement adequate procedures to identify and freeze terrorist assets. Additionally, effective implementation of new measures dealing with both listing terrorists and their entities and freezing terrorist property was required. Another key recommendation was implementation of adequate procedures permitting the confiscation of funds derived from money laundering.

Trinidad is a member of CARICOM and the OAS Inter-American Committee Against Terrorism, and has received funds through the Caribbean Basin Security Initiative.

CHILE

Overview: Chile's major legislative accomplishments this year included reforming the counterterrorism law in response to a hunger-strike by indigenous Mapuche activists protesting the application of the law in land dispute cases and passing a law increasing the penalty for financing terrorism. In August, Chile adopted a new security plan that increases border protection to counter drug and human trafficking, and a new requirement that businesses report suspicious financial transactions. Chile was not considered a major destination for international terrorist activity. Domestic anarchist groups engaged in several small-scale bomb attacks.

2010 Terrorist Incidents: Approximately 80 improvised explosive devices (IEDs) were detonated, deactivated, or found in 2010. Officials believed that these IEDs were tied to anarchist activity. The majority of the bombs were small and crudely built and most of the attacks in the first half of the year took place late at night and did not appear to be designed to kill or injure people. A slight change in modus operandi was seen from July to October, however, as anarchist bomb makers began placing IEDs in areas more likely to injure passersby during times of high traffic at both restaurants and near malls. These IEDs did not injure anyone as passersby saw and reported them, and they were consequently deactivated by the Chilean special police unit (GOPE). Since the arrest of 14 anarchist bomb makers in September and October, only one IED has been reported or found.

Chilean law enforcement agencies confronted sporadic low-level violence related to indigenous land disputes throughout the year. A group of indigenous Mapuches staged a demonstration against the Chilean state and staged a sit-in of the UN building. The demonstration was part of a larger protest, including a massive hunger strike, against the application of a counterterrorism law to prosecute some Mapuche activists. The Coordinadora Arauco Malleco (CAM), a group seeking recovery of former Mapuche indigenous lands, sometimes through radical means, claimed responsibility for several arson attacks during the year.

Legislation and Law Enforcement: On October 8, several significant changes to Chile's anti-terrorism law entered into effect; modifications to existing articles included redefining what constitutes a terrorist act and regulating how the defense can cross-examine protected witnesses (whose identities are secret). The legislative changes were a direct result of a hunger strike by 32 Mapuche prisoners, the majority of whom were in pretrial detention, protesting their prosecution under the anti-terrorism law and the military justice system for charges relating to their protest over the disputed lands, which included destruction of property, attacks on farms, or confrontations with police.

On May 10, Pakistani citizen Mohammed Saif Ur Rehman Khan was detained after a security check at the U.S. Embassy revealed traces of explosive residue on his clothes and personal belongings. Chilean law enforcement officials investigated Khan for suspected terrorist activity and terrorist ties. On December 1, the Public Prosecutor's Office announced it was ending its investigation as it did not have sufficient evidence to bring the case to court.

Chilean authorities also detained Chilean citizen Manuel Francisco Olate Cespedes for suspected involvement with the Revolutionary Armed Forces of Colombia following an extradition request from the Colombian government. Olate faces several charges in Colombia, including terrorist financing, aiding and abetting a crime with terrorist ends, and administration of resources related to terrorist activities.

Countering Terrorist Finance: Chile has a large and well-developed banking and financial sector with an established anti-money laundering and counterterrorist financing regime. All banks, financial institutions, and companies involved in money transfers are required to report suspicious transactions. Chile is a member of the Financial Action Task Force (FATF) of South America (GAFISUD) and the Egmont Group of Financial Intelligence Units. Chile complied with UNSCRs 1267 and 1373 and supported efforts to freeze terrorist assets.

Regional and International Cooperation: Chile was actively involved in the UN, OAS, and APEC, and incorporated those groups' recommendations into its security strategy. Chile also collaborated on bilateral and sub-regional activities to prevent terrorism through the Southern Common Market (MERCOSUR), and participated on international initiatives such as the Global Initiative to Combat Nuclear Terrorism. Chile ratified the International Convention for Suppression of Acts of Nuclear Terrorism.

COLOMBIA

Overview: The Colombian government continued its vigorous military, law enforcement, intelligence, and economic measures against the Revolutionary Armed Forces of Colombia (FARC), the National Liberation Army (ELN), and remaining elements of the demobilized United Self-Defense Forces of Colombia (AUC). Colombia continued to increase its international counterterrorism cooperation and training efforts. As of October 31, the Colombian government reported that more than 2,000 members of the FARC and ELN demobilized in 2010, more than 1,500 were captured, and more than 400 were killed in military or police operations.

2010 Terrorist Incidents: Despite its weakened state, the FARC still numbered approximately 8,000 members, and continued terrorist attacks, extortion, and kidnapping. The group increased its use of land mines, ambushes, snipers, and improvised explosive devices (IEDs). The FARC also used non-uniformed militia members to carry out terrorist attacks, especially in more populated areas. The FARC continued narcotics trafficking activities, bombed military and civilian targets in urban areas, and targeted rural outposts, police stations, infrastructure, and local political leaders. The Colombian government reported that 391 members of the military and police forces were killed in the first 10 months of 2010, while 1,681 were injured and another 211 were injured or killed by land mines. Some independent Colombian organizations reported higher 2010 public security force casualty figures.

Examples of 2010 terrorist activity attributed to the FARC included:

- On February 13, the FARC ambushed gubernatorial candidate Jose Alberto Perez near San Jose de Guaviare, injuring him and killing four police officers.

- On March 24, the FARC detonated a powerful car bomb on a crowded street in downtown Buenaventura, Valle del Cauca Province, next to the offices of the prosecutor general and the mayor. Ten were killed in the attack, and more than 50 were wounded.

- On March 25, the FARC convinced an unsuspecting 12-year-old to carry an explosive device to a police station in Charco, Nariño Province. The FARC detonated the bomb, killing the child and wounding five others, including two police officers.

- On August 12, the FARC detonated a powerful car bomb in north Bogota in front of the Caracol Media Building, injuring nine civilians and causing significant property damage.

- On September 1, a sophisticated FARC roadside IED attack and ambush killed 14 Colombian National Police officers and wounded nine others unit near Doncello, Caqueta Province.

- On November 30, the FARC tricked a bus driver into carrying a powerful bomb in Vegalarga, Huila, and detonated the explosive while it was parked in front of a police station, killing the driver, and wounding 10 police officers and a civilian.

The ELN remained active with approximately 1,250 fighters, but with diminished resources and a reduced capability. Still, the ELN continued to inflict numerous casualties on the Colombian military through use of land mines and ambushes. The ELN financed its operations through drug trafficking, kidnapping, and extortion. Reaffirming their pact of non-aggression announced in December 2009, there was some increase in the FARC and ELN level of cooperation against Colombian security forces in 2010, but long-existing rivalries remained in many areas.

Legislation and Law Enforcement: The Colombian government continued vigorous military, law enforcement, intelligence, and economic measures against the FARC, ELN, and remaining elements of the demobilized AUC. Extradition to the United States remained an important tool for bringing drug traffickers and terrorists to justice. Colombia extradited 148 defendants to the United States in 2010 for prosecution, and 1,200 have been extradited since July 4, 1991; most were Colombian nationals. The Colombian government sought to extend the legislation allowing for individual demo-bilizations from these terrorist groups, and proposed legislation to address legal issues associated with the earlier demobilization of approximately 17,000 of the over 32,000 demobilized members of the AUC.

On September 23, the Colombian government announced that FARC Secretariat member and Eastern Bloc commander Victor Julio Suarez Rojas (alias "Mono Jojoy") was killed in a joint police and military operation. Mono Jojoy had more than a dozen convictions and 60 orders for capture for terrorism, murder, drug trafficking, kidnapping, and forcible recruitment of minors. He had also been indicted for the March 1999 killing of three U.S. citizens (Ingrid Washinawatch, Kah'ena'e Gay, and Terence Freitas). On June 13, Colombian forces rescued three Colombian police and one Army hostage who had been held captive by the FARC for nearly 12 years. Although the FARC's supreme commander, Guillermo León Sáenz (alias "Alfonso Cano"), evaded capture, Colombian security forces also captured or killed a number of mid-level FARC leaders during the year.

Public forces continued to debrief terrorist group deserters for detailed information on their respec-tive units, and reduced the amount of territory where terrorists could freely operate. The Colombian military and police destroyed caches of weapons and supplies, and reduced the groups' financial resources through counternarcotics operations.

Colombia participated in the Megaports and Container Security Initiatives.

Countering Terrorist Finance: Colombia cooperated with the United States to block terrorists' assets, and Colombian authorities and police carried out several operations during the year to arrest and charge financial support networks of the FARC. Aerial and manual eradication of illicit drugs in Colombia destroyed approximately 143,000 hectares of illegal drug crops as of December 3, thus depriving terrorist groups of potentially huge profits. All Colombian financial institutions immedi-ately close drug trafficking and terrorism-related accounts on Colombian government orders or in response to sanctions designations by the United States. The Colombian financial sector is proac-tive in the filing of Suspicious Activity Reports (SARs) with the Colombian Financial Intelligence Unit (UIAF), and the Colombian government has now extended its SAR requirements to casinos, public notaries, and other non-financial sectors.

The United States carried out two major designation actions against over 100 financial targets associated with narcotics traffickers and money launderers tied to the FARC pursuant to the Foreign Narcotics Kingpin Designation Act. Both actions were tied to ongoing Colombian money laundering investigations of the same targets. In June, UIAF hosted the annual Egmont plenary for more than 100 member financial intelligence units worldwide in Cartagena, Colombia, which recognized Colombia's global role and regional leadership in efforts to investigate and analyze money laundering and terrorist financing cases.

Regional and International Cooperation: The Colombian government expanded its role as a regional leader in counterterrorism, continued to seek enhanced regional counterterrorism cooperation to eliminate terrorist safe havens in vulnerable border areas, and provided counterterrorism training to officials from partner countries across the region. Colombia and Mexico significantly increased joint training and operations against narco-terrorist organizations operating in both countries. Colombia enjoyed positive relations with and cooperated on border security with Panama, Peru, and Brazil.

Colombia and Ecuador formally restored diplomatic relations in December, which Ecuador had broken in March 2008 following a Colombian military attack against a FARC camp inside Ecuadorean territory. Relations with Venezuela deteriorated in the first half of 2010, with Colombia publicly accusing the Venezuelan Government of harboring and aiding top FARC and ELN leaders in its territory. Relations with Venezuela were restored, however, after Colombian President Juan Manuel Santos took office in August. In November, the Venezuelan government extradited one FARC and two ELN members to Colombia.

Countering Radicalization and Violent Extremism: The Colombian government maintained strategic communications aimed at countering terrorist propaganda and sought to increase individual demobilizations. The government proposed potentially transformative legislative agenda on victims and land restitution, and began implementing an initial plan to return and formalize land for 130,000 families.

The Colombian government continued to process and investigate demobilized AUC members under the Justice and Peace Law (JPL), which offers judicial benefits and reduced prison sentences for qualifying demobilizing terrorists. The law requires all participants to confess fully to their crimes as members of a terrorist group and to return all illicit profits. More than 32,000 rank-and-file ex-AUC members who did not commit serious crimes have demobilized, and many were receiving benefits through the government's reintegration program, including psychosocial attention, education, healthcare, and career development opportunities. Three senior leaders of the AUC have been convicted and sentenced to eight years in prison under the JPL process. Over 160,000 victims have registered under JPL, although Colombian government efforts to create measures to provide reparations to victims stalled. Some former paramilitaries continued to engage in criminal activities after demobilization, mostly in drug trafficking. The Colombian government refers to these criminal groups as criminal bands, and estimated their membership at more than 3,500, while non-governmental organizations estimate membership at 6,000 or more.

ECUADOR

Overview: Ecuador's greatest counterterrorism and security challenge remained the presence of Colombian narcotics and criminal and terrorist groups in the extremely difficult terrain along its porous 450-mile border with Colombia. Ecuador continued its response to this threat, although it faced resource constraints and limited capabilities. The Correa Administration, while still maintaining that the Colombian conflict was mainly Colombia's responsibility, repeated its opposition to encroachments by armed groups across its borders and increased its military presence in the north to discourage incursions by these groups. Ecuador's security forces continued operations against Revolutionary Armed Forces of Colombia (FARC) training and logistical resupply camps along the northern border.

2010 Terrorist Incidents: On November 22, an undetonated bomb was found in the office of the rector at the University of Guayaquil. The Popular Combatants Group (PCG), which had been dormant for the last few years, claimed responsibility for the bomb. The PCG said that it had placed the device in support of the leftist student movement University Students of Daniel Cuellar to influence the upcoming elections for the national Federation of University Students of Ecuador. The Daniel Cuellar movement disavowed the action and said it had no ties with the PCG. Other fragments of the PCG claimed the device was placed by "rightist" police forces to discredit the organization.

Legislation and Law Enforcement: Until September 7, 2010, Ecuadorean immigration officials allowed almost all travelers to enter the country for 90 days without a visa, including travelers from countries of concern for terrorism, drug smuggling, and illegal immigration, based on a visa-free travel policy enacted in June 2008. On September 7, the Ministry of Foreign Affairs revised this policy to require that citizens from nine countries – Afghanistan, Bangladesh, Eritrea, Ethiopia, Kenya, Nepal, Nigeria, Pakistan, and Somalia – obtain visas prior to entering the country. Active smuggling rings in Ecuador that focused on moving aliens continued to raise concerns about the transit of individuals with terrorism connections.

Ecuador's judicial institutions remained weak, susceptible to corruption, and heavily backlogged with pending cases. While the military and police made numerous arrests, the judicial system had a poor record of achieving convictions in all types of criminal cases.

Countering Terrorist Finance: Ecuador is a member of the Financial Action Task Force (FATF) of South America (GAFISUD). In February, the Financial Action Task Force (FATF) included Ecuador on the list of countries that pose a high-risk to the international financial system due to strategic anti-money laundering and counterterrorism finance deficiencies. Following Ecuador's demonstration of a high level political commitment to work with FATF and GAFISUD to address these deficiencies in June, FATF moved Ecuador to the ongoing review list of countries that have developed a FATF action plan. On November 5, Ecuador's National Assembly voted to approve a bill reforming the existing anti-money laundering (AML) law. Ecuador's new AML law is the "Law of Prevention, Detection, and Eradication of the Crime of Money Laundering and the Financing of Crimes." The bill added an article to the Penal Code criminalizing the financing of any of the acts listed in the Penal Code's section under "Crimes of Sabotage and Terrorism." Ecuador is not yet a member of the Egmont Group of Financial Intelligence units, as terrorist finance legislation is a requirement for Egmont membership.

The Ecuadorean government sought to strengthen controls over money laundering through the Financial Intelligence Unit, established under a 2005 Money Laundering Law and further strengthened in the AML passed in November. This unit, which under the new law is now called the Financial Analysis Unit, continued to improve cooperation with the Anti-Narcotics Police Directorate's Financial Crimes Unit, the Superintendent of Banks, the Attorney General, the courts, and the private banker association to identify suspicious transactions and develop information for the prosecution of cases.

Regional and International Cooperation: Ecuador restored diplomatic relations with Colombia in December 2010, which it had broken in March 2008 following a Colombian military attack against a FARC camp inside Ecuadorean territory. Restoration of these ties permitted closer security and political cooperation on northern border issues.

Countering Radicalization and Violent Extremism: The Government of Ecuador is working to improve access to government services and economic development in the northern border region to reduce the incentive to work with or for illegal armed groups.

MEXICO

Overview: The Mexican government remained vigilant against domestic and international terrorist threats and continued its efforts to disrupt and dismantle the transnational criminal organizations responsible for unprecedented drug-trafficking-related violence. It worked with its neighbors to increase control of its northern and southern borders. No known international terrorist organization had an operational presence in Mexico and no terrorist group targeted U.S. interests and personnel in or from Mexican territory. There was no evidence of ties between Mexican criminal organizations and terrorist groups, nor that the criminal organizations had aims of political or territorial control, aside from seeking to protect and expand the impunity with which they conduct their criminal activity.

2010 Terrorist Incidents: The Animal Liberation Front claimed responsibility for using propane and gasoline-based bombs to cause property damage at banks and commercial sites in Mexico City. Police arrested several alleged members. The People's Revolutionary Army (EPR), which has resorted to violence in the past, threatened to reemploy violent measures to force a response to its demands for a government investigation into the disappearance of two of its members.

Legislation and Law Enforcement: Mexican security forces improved their operational effectiveness, information sharing, and interagency coordination as part of a government-wide campaign to combat organized crime, reduce violence, and prevent terrorism. As part of this effort, the United States supported the Mexican government's efforts by providing training to Mexican federal law enforcement and security agencies, and promoting interagency law enforcement cooperation at the federal and state levels. President Calderon proposed legislation to clarify national security roles and responsibilities, streamline control of non-federal police forces, and prevent money laundering and terrorist financing. Although these efforts were primarily aimed at organized crime groups, they also supported government preparedness against domestic or international terrorism. The Mexican government has nearly doubled spending on public and national security over the past four years.

The United States and Mexico worked closely to address border security challenges along Mexico's southern and northern borders. U.S. Homeland Security Secretary Napolitano signed arrangements with Mexican Interior and Public Security departments to share information about transnational threats; promote law enforcement information and intelligence sharing; produce joint strategic plans; deploy enhanced airport screening technologies; and strengthen passenger information sharing. On the U.S.-Mexico border, officials increased coordination of patrols and inspections and improved communications across the border. U.S. and Mexican officials also improved cooperation on investigations of aliens who may raise terrorism concerns. Mexico implemented biometric controls and other measures to reduce smuggling on its border with Guatemala and Belize.

Countering Terrorist Finance: There was no indication that terrorist organizations used Mexico as a conduit for illicit activities. Nevertheless, Mexico's limited capacity to counter money laundering suggested a potential vulnerability. In order to counter the illegal movement of funds, Mexican financial institutions are required to follow international standards advocated by the Financial Action Task Force, of which Mexico holds the 2010-2011 presidency. Furthermore, Mexican financial institutions are required to follow the Law of Credit Institutions, as ordered by the Mexican Treasury and supervised by the National Bank and Securities Commission. This law requires banks to consult international and country lists of individuals involved in terrorism or other illicit activities and submit a suspicious activities report within 24 hours to the Mexican Department of Treasury's Financial Intelligence Unit on the activities of any individual on that list.

Regional and International Cooperation: As 2009-2010 chair of the Inter-American Committee Against Terrorism, Mexico worked to strengthen the capacities of OAS member countries to prevent terrorism by promoting consultation and by strengthening border controls. Mexico signed the Beijing Convention on the Suppression of Unlawful Acts Relating to International Civil Aviation and the Beijing Protocol to the Convention for the Suppression of Unlawful Seizure of Aircraft at the conclusion of an International Civil Aviation Organization diplomatic conference in September.

PANAMA

Overview: The most direct counterterrorism challenge facing Panama is a unit of the Revolutionary Armed Forces of Colombia (FARC), which used the remote Darien Region as a safe haven. The safety of the Panama Canal continued to benefit from the Government of Panama's solid stewardship and support of the annual PANAMAX exercise, a multinational security training exercise tailored to the defense of the canal, perhaps the region's most important infrastructure component.

Legislation and Law Enforcement: The Government of Panama's determination to exercise its sovereignty in the Darien through more aggressive patrolling by security forces has increasingly brought FARC combatants in direct contact with Panamanian forces. In January, three FARC members were killed and two were captured during a confrontation with Panamanian border police in the Darien, and in June two border police were injured by improvised explosive devices (IEDs), presumably placed by the FARC. Eight local Panamanians were subsequently arrested for collaborating with the FARC. In October, the Colombian military bombed a FARC camp near the Panamanian border, killing one mid-level commander and several other members. Finally, in December, Panama brought to trial three presumed members of the FARC 57th front captured after a February 2008 confrontation with border police in the Darien; the trial is one of the first held in Panama specifically on terrorism charges.

The United States and Panama continued to plan for incidents that could potentially shut down transit through the Panama Canal. In September, Panama co-hosted the annual PANAMAX exercise, a multinational security training exercise initiated in 2003 that focuses on the security of the canal. The exercise replicates real world threats and includes specific exercises designed to counter terrorist attacks. Several U.S. government agencies participated in the exercise.

In November, U.S. Department of Homeland Security Secretary Napolitano signed a memorandum of understanding with Panama to collect and interpret Advance Passenger Information System (APIS) data to target potentially dangerous and criminal passengers on all flights in and out of Panama, complementing data already being shared between Panama and the United States.

Panama continued its participation in the Container Security Initiative at Balboa and Manzanillo, and the Evergreen Colon Container Terminal. The U.S. Southern Command (SOUTHCOM) sponsored Combating Terrorism Fellowship Program (CTFP) has supplemented instructional training and professional development with Mobile Training Teams and conferences.

Countering Terrorist Finance: The factors that have contributed to Panama's growth and financial sophistication– the large number of offshore banks and shell companies, the presence of the world's second-largest free trade zone, the growth in ports and maritime industries, and the use of the U.S. dollar as the official currency – also provided the infrastructure for significant money laundering activity. While Panama has taken extensive measures to counter money laundering in the banking system, the Colon Free Trade Zone's significant revenue turnover and cash-intensive transactions left the area vulnerable to money laundering and terrorist financing. In October, Panama passed Law 67, which among other actions now requires the declaration of cash or merchandise valued at $10,000 or over when leaving the country, consistent with FATF Special Recommendation IX. The Government of Panama cooperated fully in reviewing terrorist finance lists.

Regional and International Cooperation: Panama hosted a September meeting on terrorism legislation sponsored by the UN Office of Drugs and Crime, and participated actively in meetings sponsored by the OAS/Inter-American Committee Against Terrorism and the FATF. In October, Panama attended a regional demobilization conference in Bogota sponsored by Ameripol, an association of Latin American police forces. Panama signed the Beijing Convention on the Suppression of Unlawful Acts Relating to International Civil Aviation and the Beijing Protocol to the Convention for the Suppression of Unlawful Seizure of Aircraft shortly after the conclusion of an International Civil Aviation Organization diplomatic conference in September.

PARAGUAY

Overview: Increased activity by an internal insurgent group and the resulting public demands for action brought terrorism to the policy forefront. President Fernando Lugo responded to threats by mobilizing the military in April and passing terrorism legislation in June. Though Paraguay enhanced its counterterrorism efforts, it remained hampered by ineffective immigration, customs, and law enforcement controls along its porous borders, particularly the Tri-Border Area (TBA) with Argentina and Brazil. The June arrest of alleged Hizballah financier Moussa Ali Hamdan in Ciudad del Este, Paraguay, demonstrated the area's permissive environment for terrorist financing activity. Limited resources, sporadic interagency cooperation, and corruption within customs, the police, the public ministry, and the judicial sector, impeded the government's law enforcement initiatives throughout the country.

Since 2008, the leftist Paraguayan People's Army (EPP) has been active in the northern departments of Paraguay, abutting the Brazilian border. Membership statistics for the EPP are difficult to establish, but it is believed to be a small, decentralized group operating mainly in Concepcion Department. The Paraguayan government classified the EPP as an internal terrorist organization based on several kidnappings and multiple shootouts with the police and military. The EPP claimed responsibility for a 2009 explosion and a December 2010 bomb threat, both at the Palace of Justice, though neither claim was verified.

Legislation and Law Enforcement: On June 23, President Fernando Lugo signed a new terrorism bill into law that defines and criminalizes terrorist activities and aids governmental counterterrorism efforts, particularly in relation to terrorism financing, when paired with Paraguay's 2009 anti-money laundering law. The law established sentencing guidelines from five to 30 years for terrorism-based crimes.

In May, five U.S. Border Patrol and Customs and Border Protection (CBP) Officers conducted an assessment of Paraguay's porous eastern border with Brazil and Argentina. Based on its assessment, the CBP and Border Patrol conducted a three-week training session in September to assist Paraguayan Customs Officials and Police in better confronting smuggling and related crimes in areas known as sources of terrorist financing.

Countering Terrorist Finance: The new counterterrorism law includes a terrorist financing provision stipulating prison sentences of five to 15 years for financial assistance, interaction, or connection with terrorist organizations and/or individuals. Paired with 2009's anti-money laundering law, the new legislation provides Paraguay's Secretariat for the Prevention of Money Laundering (SEPRELAD) better tracking, reporting, and enforcement powers.

Paraguay is a member of the Financial Action Task Force (FATF) against Money Laundering in South America (GAFISUD). Paraguay assumed GAFISUD's rotating Presidency in December 2010. As a member of the Egmont Group, SEPRELAD exchanges information with other members of the Egmont Group, including the United States.

Paraguayan law does not provide for freezing or seizure of many criminally derived assets. Authorities can only freeze assets of persons under investigation for a crime in which the state risks loss of revenue from furtherance of a criminal act, such as tax evasion. In December, SEPRELAD's Minister submitted a draft bill to the Presidency that requests SEPRELAD be given administrative power to freeze suspected money laundering and terrorism-related assets.

Regional and International Cooperation: In March, Paraguay signed an agreement with Colombia to fight terrorism and organized crime. Paraguay's strongest regional partner in counterterrorism and law enforcement activities was Brazil. In October, Brazilian and Paraguayan ministers met in Asuncion and announced a plan to coordinate activities along the border to counter arms and narcotics trafficking, though no agreement has been signed.

Paraguay signed the Beijing Convention on the Suppression of Unlawful Acts Relating to International Civil Aviation and the Beijing Protocol to the Convention for the Suppression of Unlawful Seizure of Aircraft at the conclusion of an International Civil Aviation Organization diplomatic conference in September.

PERU

Overview: Peru's primary counterterrorism concern remained Sendero Luminoso (Shining Path or SL), a U.S.-designated Foreign Terrorist Organization that wreaked havoc on the country in the 1980s and 1990s in a conflict that claimed more than 69,000 lives. SL elements in the Upper Huallaga River Valley (UHV) sought to regroup and replenish their ranks following significant setbacks in recent years. Separately, the rival SL faction in the Apurimac and Ene River Valley (VRAE) maintained its influence in that area. Implementation of the government's Plan VRAE, which in its security component called for 2,000 troops and 19 counterterrorism bases under a central command, was still evolving in 2010. Plans for new health, education, and infrastructure investment in these isolated communities were not fully implemented, but authorities made some improvements to roadways and rural electrification.

Although Peru nearly eliminated SL in the 1990s, the organization, now entwined with narcotics trafficking, remained a threat. Because of the nature of the threat and SL's close ties to narcotics trafficking, counterterrorism efforts are often, but not always, intrinsically tied to counter-narcotics; some analysts refer to SL as "narco-terrorists." In 2010, the U.S. State Department added the leaders of both SL factions to its Narcotics Rewards Program, and offered up to US$ five million each for information leading to the arrest and/or conviction of Florindo Eleuterio Flores-Hala (aka "Artemio," of the UHV) and Victor Quispe Palomino (aka "Jose," of the VRAE).

SL forcibly recruited young children. Digital cameras found at an SL camp in the VRAE raided by Peruvian authorities in October contained numerous photos of about 50 children of ages five to 16, many of them carrying automatic weapons or reading Maoist literature. The children apparently formed part of a group led by "Alipio," a high ranking leader known for leading some of the bloodiest ambushes in the VRAE. Some of the children were thought to have been kidnapped from local towns or indigenous communities, while others may be the children of SL members.

The Revolutionary Armed Forces of Colombia (FARC) continued to use remote areas along the Colombian-Peruvian border to regroup and make arms purchases. Peruvian government experts believed the FARC continued to fund coca cultivation and cocaine production among the Peruvian population in border areas.

2010 Terrorist Incidents: The two factions of the SL (UHV and VRAE) together carried out 136 terrorist acts that killed police and civilians (mostly individuals perceived by SL in the UHV as police informants or collaborators), and members of the military in 2010. The Peruvian Army's 2008 offensive in the Vizcatan region, called "Operation Excellence 777," continued haltingly, with the military maintaining a number of small provisional bases in the area. Confrontations generally consisted of SL members attacking Peruvian patrols or incoming supply helicopters, but in several cases SL attacked a military base.

Legislation and Law Enforcement: Government efforts to improve interagency cooperation, especially in intelligence, and to strengthen prosecutorial capacity were somewhat successful. Police units specializing in counterterrorism and counternarcotics conducted some joint operations with the Peruvian Army in the UHV, where police captured two high-ranking SL terrorists. Peru has counterterrorism legislation and applied it consistently to arrest and convict terrorists. No new counterterrorism legislation was passed in 2010, and there was no movement on President Garcia's 2006 proposal calling for the death penalty for those convicted of acts of terrorism.

Police detained over 121 suspected terrorists during the year, including Edgar Mejia Ascencio (aka "Izula"), believed to be the UHV faction's number two leader, and later Mario Antonio Sifuentes Sandoval (aka "Sergio), who had succeeded Mejia as number two. In November, police arrested 43 people during a raid in the UHV as part of its "Operation Eclipse." The detainees, several of whom were prominent coca farmer leaders and local elected officials, faced drug trafficking, terrorism, falsification of documents, homicide, money laundering, and other charges. Some of the detainees had been filmed meeting with Artemio in April, demonstrating an alliance between coca growers and SL.

Authorities also killed five SL members in clashes with SL columns, including Victor Raul Vasquez Santa Cruz (aka "Ruben"), who was reputed to have assassinated political leaders in the UHV and to be in Artemio's inner circle. SL founder and leader Abimael Guzman and key accomplices remained in prison serving life sentences on charges stemming from crimes committed during the 1980s and 1990s. Many others have been released in recent years, having completed their sentences or been released on parole for good behavior.

Peruvian authorities installed body scanners for drug detection at the border crossings with Chile and two international airports. Authorities collected no biometrics information, and citizens of neighboring countries were allowed to travel to Peru by land using national identification cards alone. There is no visa requirement for citizens of most countries in Western, Central, and Eastern Europe.

Countering Terrorist Finance: Peru is a member of the Financial Action Task Force (FATF) Against Money Laundering in South America (GAFISUD), which held its XXI Plenary Session in Lima in July. Peru's Superintendent of Banks served as Chair of GAFISUD during 2010. Peru was ranked as 'partially compliant' in the GAFISUD 3rd Evaluation Report (2008) on the Ratification and Implementation of UN Instruments and the Special Recommendation Freezing and Confiscating Terrorist Assets. As a result, the Superintendent of Banking issued a resolution in September establishing guidelines for financial and insurance entities to implement the UN resolutions to prevent and suppress the financing of terrorism.

Regional and International Cooperation: Peru is an active member of the OAS, the Union of South American Nations, and the Andean Community. On October 21, senior military commanders from Colombia, Peru, and Brazil met in Leticia, Colombia to discuss joint actions, including aircraft monitoring against drug trafficking and guerrillas along their common tri-border area in the Amazon jungle. Previously, the countries had conducted bilateral operations; this will mark the first tripartite effort to address drug trafficking and terrorism.

Countering Radicalization and Violent Extremism: While the Government of Peru does not have a systematic program to counter radicalization and violent extremism, aspects of Plan VRAE (improvements in education, infrastructure, health, and security) are designed to increase the state's presence and improve governance. The official position of the National Penitentiary Institute is that prison is meant to rehabilitate and reintegrate prisoners, especially terrorists, and therefore a psychological assessment that indicates such change has taken place is required before a terrorist can be granted parole. This benefit is also meant to encourage prisoners to change, rather than to continue in conflict with the state. Many observers have expressed concern that convicted terrorists are not, in fact, rehabilitated, and many return to SL after they complete sentences and are released. Comrade "Sergio," for example, completed a 12-year prison sentence for terrorism charges in 2004, and promptly returned to SL to become Artemio's number two leader in 2010 before being re-arrested in December.

VENEZUELA

Overview: In May 2010, for the fifth consecutive year, the U.S. Department of State determined that Venezuela was not cooperating fully with U.S. antiterrorism efforts pursuant to section 40A of the Arms Export Control Act. Throughout the year, President Chavez rejected allegations that he or his government supported terrorism and instead accused the United States of sponsoring terrorism. Several times during the year, the Colombian government publicly accused the Venezuelan government of harboring members of the Revolutionary Armed Forces of Colombia (FARC) and the National Liberation Army (ELN) on its territory. It alleged that these groups used Venezuelan territory to rest and regroup, engage in narcotics trafficking, and extort protection money and kidnap Venezuelans to finance their operations. In a July 22 special session of OAS Permanent Council, the Colombian Permanent Representative presented alleged evidence of FARC training camps in Venezuela and proposed an international verification commission to investigate the presence of FARC and ELN members in Venezuela.

In response to these charges, the Venezuelan government broke diplomatic relations with Colombia, and on July 25, President Chavez denied that "a foreign paramilitary or military guerrilla force has taken over even the smallest millimeter squared of our sovereign territory." On August 10, newly-inaugurated Colombian President Juan Manual Santos and President Chavez met in Santa Marta,

Colombia, and announced the restoration of diplomatic relations, including the establishment of a bilateral commission with five working groups, including one on security. Since then, there have been ministerial-level meetings to discuss bilateral security issues.

During the year, the Spanish government asked Venezuela for information regarding allegations that it was providing support to Basque Fatherland and Liberty (ETA). Although President Chavez initially said that Venezuela "has nothing to explain," the two governments later issued a statement that "condemned terrorism in all its forms" and promised police and judicial cooperation. There was no information publicly available about the results of that cooperation.

In October, the Spanish government requested the extradition of Arturo Cubillas Fontan, a naturalized Venezuelan citizen and employee of the Venezuelan National Land Institute, on several charges, including murder, in connection with an ongoing investigation in Spain about ETA-FARC links in Venezuela. Two former ETA members accused Cubillas in a Spanish court of having given training to ETA members in weapons and explosives in an undisclosed training camp in Venezuela in 2008. President Chavez "dismissed and denied" the accusations on October 4, 2010, which he claimed were the result of a "permanent international conspiracy" against his "Bolivarian revolution." The Venezuelan prosecutor general said the constitution prohibited the extradition of Venezuelan nationals.

The Venezuelan government took no action against government and military officials linked to the FARC or ELN. General Hugo Armando Carvajal Barrios, who was designated by the United States in September 2008 for materially assisting the narcotics trafficking activities of the FARC, remained Director of the Military Intelligence Directorate. In November, President Chavez promoted another official also designated by the United States in 2008 for materially assisting the FARC, Henry Rangel Silva, Chief of the Armed Force's Strategic Operation Command, to the four-star equivalent General in Chief. The prosecutor general also awarded Rangel Silva with a Citizen's Merit Medal for his "service in defense of the interests of the country and the constitution."

President Chavez has continued to strengthen Venezuela's relationship with state sponsor of terrorism Iran. In October 2010, President Chavez met President Ahmadinejad during a two-day visit to Iran. During the visit, Chavez condemned international sanctions against Iran over its nuclear program and signed cooperation agreements in areas including oil and gas, trade, and construction.

We remain concerned about Hizballah's fundraising activities in Venezuela.

Legislation and Law Enforcement: The Government of Venezuela took the following actions in connection with individuals allegedly connected to terrorist organizations:

- In July, Venezuelan officials arrested and extradited the Salvadoran Francisco Chavez Abarca in connection with the bombings of Cuban hotels in 1997.

- On November 17, the Venezuelan government extradited to Colombia two suspected members of the ELN and one of the FARC.

Countering Terrorist Finance: Venezuela is a member of the Caribbean Financial Action Task Force (CFATF) and its Financial Intelligence Unit is a member of the Egmont Group; it also participates in the Money Laundering Experts Working Group of the OAS Inter-American Commission on Drug Abuse Control. In March, Venezuela hosted a five-day CFATF training workshop on "The Legal Framework against Money Laundering."

Regional and International Cooperation: As a member of the Union of South American Nations, Venezuela publicly condemned the terrorist action of those behind the August 12 car bomb attack in Bogota, Colombia.

CHAPTER 3.
STATE SPONSORS OF TERRORISM

In order to designate a country as a State Sponsor of Terrorism, the Secretary of State must determine that the government of such country has repeatedly provided support for acts of international terrorism. Once a country has been designated, it continues to be a State Sponsor of Terrorism until the designation is rescinded in accordance with statutory criteria. A wide range of sanctions are imposed as a result of a State Sponsor of Terrorism designation, including:

1. A ban on arms-related exports and sales.

2. Controls over exports of dual-use items, requiring 30-day Congressional notification for goods or services that could significantly enhance the terrorist-list country's military capability or ability to support terrorism.

3. Prohibitions on economic assistance.

4. Imposition of miscellaneous financial and other restrictions.

More information on State Sponsor of Terrorism designations may be found online at http://www.state.gov/s/ct/c14151.htm.

CUBA

Overview: Designated as a State Sponsor of Terrorism in 1982, the Government of Cuba maintained a public stance against terrorism and terrorist financing in 2010, but there was no evidence that it had severed ties with elements from the Revolutionary Armed Forces of Colombia (FARC) and recent media reports indicate some current and former members of the Basque Fatherland and Liberty (ETA) continue to reside in Cuba. Available information suggested that the Cuban government maintained limited contact with FARC members, but there was no evidence of direct financial or ongoing material support. In March, the Cuban government allowed Spanish Police to travel to Cuba to confirm the presence of suspected ETA members.

Cuba continued to denounce U.S. counterterrorism efforts throughout the world, portraying them as a pretext to extend U.S. influence and power.

Cuba has been used as a transit point by third-country nationals looking to enter illegally into the United State. The Government of Cuba is aware of the border integrity and transnational security concerns posed by such transit and investigated third country migrant smuggling and related criminal activities. In November, the government allowed representatives of the Transportation Security Administration to conduct a series of airport security visits throughout the island.

Legislation and Law Enforcement: Cuba did not pass new counterterrorism legislation in 2010. The Cuban government continued to aggressively pursue persons suspected of terrorist acts in Cuba. In July, Venezuela extradited Salvadoran national Francisco Antonio Chavez Abarca to Cuba for his alleged role in a number of hotel and tourist location bombings in the mid to late 1990s. In December, a Cuban court convicted Chavez Abarca on terrorism charges and sentenced him to 30 years in prison. Also in December, the Cuban Supreme Court commuted the death sentences of two Salvadorans, René Cruz León and Otto René Rodríguez Llerena, who had been convicted of terrorism, and sentenced them both to 30 years.

Regional and International Cooperation: Cuba did not sponsor counterterrorism initiatives or participate in regional or global operations against terrorists in 2010.

IRAN

Overview: Designated as a State Sponsor of Terrorism in 1984, Iran remained the most active state sponsor of terrorism in 2010. Iran's financial, material, and logistic support for terrorist and militant groups throughout the Middle East and Central Asia had a direct impact on international efforts to promote peace, threatened economic stability in the Gulf, and undermined the growth of democracy.

In 2010, Iran remained the principal supporter of groups implacably opposed to the Middle East Peace Process. The Qods Force, the external operations branch of the Islamic Revolutionary Guard Corps (IRGC), is the regime's primary mechanism for cultivating and supporting terrorists abroad. Iran provided weapons, training, and funding to Hamas and other Palestinian terrorist groups, including the Palestine Islamic Jihad (PIJ) and the Popular Front for the Liberation of Palestine-General Command (PFLP-GC). Since the end of the 2006 Israeli-Hizballah conflict, Iran has assisted Hizballah in rearming, in direct violation of UN Security Council Resolution 1701. Iran has provided hundreds of millions of dollars in support of Hizballah in Lebanon and has trained thousands of Hizballah fighters at camps in Iran.

Iran's Qods Force provided training to the Taliban in Afghanistan on small unit tactics, small arms, explosives, and indirect fire weapons, such as mortars, artillery, and rockets. Since at least 2006, Iran has arranged arms shipments to select Taliban members, including small arms and associated ammunition, rocket propelled grenades, mortar rounds, 107mm rockets, and plastic explosives. Iran has shipped a large number of weapons to Kandahar, Afghanistan aiming to increase its influence in the country.

Despite its pledge to support the stabilization of Iraq, Iranian authorities continued to provide lethal support, including weapons, training, funding, and guidance, to Iraqi Shia militant groups that target U.S. and Iraqi forces. The Qods Force continued to supply Iraqi militants with Iranian-produced advanced rockets, sniper rifles, automatic weapons, and mortars that have killed Iraqi and Coalition Forces, as well as civilians. Iran was responsible for the increased lethality of some attacks on U.S. forces by providing militants with the capability to assemble explosives designed to defeat armored vehicles. The Qods Force, in concert with Lebanese Hizballah, provided training outside of Iraq as well as advisors inside Iraq for Shia militants in the construction and use of sophisticated improvised explosive device technology and other advanced weaponry.

2010 Terrorist Incidents: Jundallah, a terrorist organization that operated primarily in the province of Sistan va Balochistan of Iran, has engaged in numerous terrorist attacks within Iran. Jundallah's primary target is the Iranian regime; however, it has also attacked many civilians. Since its inception in 2003, these attacks have resulted in the death and maiming of scores of Iranian civilians and government officials. Jundallah has used a variety of terrorist tactics, including suicide bombings, ambushes, kidnappings, and targeted assassinations. Following the February 2010 capture and execution by Iranian authorities of Jundallah's leader, Abdul Malik Rigi, the group selected a new leader, Mohammed Dhahir Baluch, and confirmed its commitment to continue its terrorist activities. In July, Jundallah attacked the Grand Mosque in Zahedan, killing approximately 30 and injuring hundreds. On December 15, Jundallah claimed credit for another attack in the Southeastern city of Chabahar, where two suicide bombs killed at least 39 and wounded more than 100 people. In November, the United States designated Jundallah as a Foreign Terrorist Organization. (See Chapter 6, *Foreign Terrorist Organizations*, for more information on Jundallah.)

Legislation and Law Enforcement: In 2010, Iran remained unwilling to bring to justice senior al-Qa'ida (AQ) members it continued to detain, and refused to publicly identify those senior members in its custody. Iran has repeatedly resisted numerous calls to transfer custody of its AQ detainees to their countries of origin or third countries for trial.

In June, Iranian authorities executed former Jundallah leader Abdul Malik Rigi. In December, Iranian authorities executed 11 members of Jundallah reportedly connected to the July mosque attack.

SUDAN

Overview: Designated as a State Sponsor of Terrorism in 1993, Sudan remained a cooperative partner in global counterterrorism efforts against al-Qa'ida (AQ) in 2010. During the past year, the Government of Sudan worked actively to counter AQ operations that posed a potential threat to U.S. interests and personnel in Sudan. Sudanese officials have indicated that they viewed continued cooperation with the United States as important and recognized the potential benefits of U.S. training and information-sharing.

2010 Terrorist Incidents: The Sudanese government has taken steps to limit the activities of foreign terrorist groups within Sudan and has worked hard to disrupt foreign fighters' use of Sudan as a logistics base and transit point for violent extremists going to Iraq. Nonetheless, elements of designated Foreign Terrorist Organizations, including al-Qa'ida-inspired terrorists, remained in Sudan, as gaps remained in the Sudanese government's knowledge of and ability to identify and capture these individuals as well as prevent them from exploiting the territory for smuggling activities. Some evidence suggested that individuals who actively participated in the Iraqi insurgency have returned to Sudan, and may be in a position to use their expertise to conduct attacks within Sudan or to pass on their knowledge. Sudanese officials continued to view Hamas members as representatives of the Palestinian Authority. Hamas members conducted fundraising in Sudan, and Palestine Islamic Jihad (PIJ) maintained a presence in Sudan.

The Lord's Resistance Army (LRA) continued to operate in the region, though there was no reliable information that corroborated allegations that the Government of Sudan provided support to the LRA. Operating in small cells, the LRA carried out attacks in areas where the borders of the Democratic Republic of the Congo, Central African Republic, and Southern Sudan intersect. The UN estimated that in 2010, LRA attacks displaced 25,000 southern Sudanese. In October, the African Union (AU) announced that Uganda, Sudan, the Democratic Republic of the Congo and the Central African Republic will form an AU-backed joint brigade to pursue the LRA.

Legislation and Law Enforcement: On June 11, four Sudanese men sentenced to death for the January 1, 2008, killing of two U.S. Embassy staff members escaped from Khartoum's maximum security Kober prison. One police officer was reportedly killed and another was injured in an exchange of fire at a checkpoint following the breakout. Police subsequently intercepted the getaway car and arrested the driver, but the four fugitives escaped on foot. On June 22, Sudanese authorities confirmed that one of the four convicts was recaptured. The whereabouts of the other three convicts remained unknown at year's end. The Sudanese government cooperated with the United States in efforts to bring the four to justice.

Countering Terrorist Finance: The Central Bank of Sudan and its financial intelligence unit circulated to financial institutions a list of individuals and entities that have been included on the UN 1267 al-Qa'ida and Taliban sanctions committee's Consolidated List. Through increasing cooperation with the Financial Action Task Force (FATF), Sudan took steps in 2010 to meet international standards in combating money laundering and terrorist financing. The most significant achievement was passage of the Money Laundering and Terrorism Financing Act of 2010, approved by the Council of Ministers in January 2010 and ratified by Parliament in June 2010. Sudan continued its cooperation with the U.S. government in investigating financial crimes related to terrorism.

Regional and International Cooperation: Sudanese officials regularly discussed counterterrorism issues with U.S. counterparts. Sudan was generally responsive to the international community's concerns on terrorism and was generally supportive of international counterterrorism efforts.

SYRIA

Overview: Designated in 1979 as a State Sponsor of Terrorism, Syria in 2010 continued its political support to a variety of terrorist groups affecting the stability of the region and beyond. Syria provided political and weapons support to Hizballah in Lebanon and allowed Iran to resupply the terrorist organization with weapons. The external leadership of Hamas, the Palestine Islamic Jihad (PIJ), the Popular Front for the Liberation of Palestine (PLFP), and the Popular Front for the Liberation of Palestine-General Command (PFLP-GC), among others, were based in Damascus and operated within Syria's borders. Statements supporting terrorist groups like Hamas and Hizballah consistently permeated government speeches and press statements.

President Bashar al-Asad continued to express public support for Palestinian terrorist groups as elements of the resistance against Israel. Damascus historically has allowed exiled individuals safe haven in Syria and Hamas Politburo head Khalid Meshaal and his deputies continued to reside in Syria, while the Syrian government provided Meshaal security escorts for his motorcades. Though the Syrian government claimed periodically that it used its influence to restrain the rhetoric and activities of Palestinian groups, Meshaal freely traveled around Damascus and the Syrian government allowed Meshaal's use of the Syrian Ministry of Information as the venue for press conferences. Open source reports indicated that Hamas used Syrian soil as training grounds for its militant fighters.

Added to the terrorist operatives calling Damascus home, in 2010, Iraqi Baathists continued to congregate in the Syrian capital and some of them call for violence against the Iraqi government, Iraqi civilian targets, and American and coalition forces within Iraq. Al-Rai Television, a television station owned by Iraqi Baathist Mishaan al-Jaburi and broadcast from a suburban Damascus location, transmitted violent messages in support of terrorism in Iraq throughout the year.

2010 Terrorist Incidents: The Syrian government stressed its success in achieving security and stability within its borders, and terrorist attacks on Syrian soil remained rare. However, a string of incidents over the past several years have increased concerns that militant groups can strike Syrian targets and have caused the authorities to strengthen their efforts to prevent attacks. Especially following a September 27, 2009 bombing near a Syrian security installation that killed 17, the regime has attempted to portray Syria as a victim of terrorism rather than a purveyor of it. In July 2010, the Syrian security services conducted a series of raids that netted operatives of the Kurdistan Workers' Party (PKK), accused of plotting and implementing terrorist attacks in neighboring Turkey.

Legislation and Law Enforcement: Syria has laws on the books pertaining to counterterrorism and terrorism financing/money laundering, but largely used these legal instruments against only those groups perceived as a threat to the regime or country. Opponents of the regime, including Islamist activists and Kurdish separatists, were frequently charged with violating counterterrorism statutes. Furthermore, these laws were not enforced against Hamas, Hizballah, or the various Palestinian rejectionist groups based in Damascus.

Countering Terrorist Finance: Syria remained a source of concern regarding terrorist financing. Industry experts reported that 60 percent of all business transitions were conducted in cash and that nearly 80 percent of all Syrians did not use formal banking services. Despite Syrian legislation that required money-changers to be licensed by the end of 2007, many money-changers in 2010 continued to operate illegally in Syria's vast black market, estimated to be as large as Syria's formal economy. Regional "hawala" networks remained intertwined with smuggling and trade-based money laundering, facilitated by notoriously corrupt customs and immigration officials, raising significant concerns that some members of the Syrian government and the business elite were complicit in terrorist financing schemes.

Regional and International Cooperation: Syria continued its strong partnership with fellow state sponsor of terrorism Iran in 2010. Throughout the year, the countries exchanged frequent high-level visitors. Iranian President Ahmedinejad visited Damascus in February and September and President Assad visited Tehran in October. The Iranian National Security Advisor, Defense Minister, Foreign Minister, and Intelligence Chief all visited Damascus within the last year. Syria also allowed leaders of Hamas and other Palestinian groups resident in Syria to visit Tehran. Asad continued to be a staunch defender of Iran's policies, including Iran's nuclear ambitions.

Syria exhibited a mixed record on Iraq. Syria increased border monitoring activities, instituted tighter screening practices on military-age Arab males entering its borders, and expressed a desire to increase security cooperation with Iraq. These activities likely contributed to a decrease in Iraq-bound foreign fighters. At the same time, however, Syria remained a key hub for foreign fighters en route to Iraq and a safe haven for Iraqi Baathists expressing support for terrorist attacks against Iraqi government interests and coalition forces.

Attacks against coalition and Iraqi security forces and Iraqi citizens continued to have a destabilizing effect on Iraq's internal security. While Syria and Iraq returned their ambassadors to Baghdad and Damascus, respectively, in the autumn of 2010, Syrian and Iraqi security cooperation has been largely inactive since Iraqi Prime Minister Nouri al-Maliki in August 2009 accused Baathists harbored by Syria of fomenting terrorism in Iraq.

CHAPTER 4.
THE GLOBAL CHALLENGE OF CHEMICAL, BIOLOGICAL, RADIOLOGICAL, AND NUCLEAR (CBRN) TERRORISM

THE MATERIAL THREATS

Chemical. Preventing chemical terrorism is particularly challenging since terrorists can use toxic industrial chemicals and other commonly available chemical agents and materials as low-cost alternatives to traditional chemical weapons and delivery systems. Today's chemical terrorism threat ranges from the potential acquisition and dissemination of chemical warfare agents with military delivery systems to the production and use of toxic industrial chemicals or improvised dissemination systems for chemical agents. The growth and sophistication of the worldwide chemical industry, including the development of complex synthetic and dual-use materials, makes the task of preventing and protecting against this threat more difficult.

Biological. Bioterrorism involves the deliberate dispersal of pathogens (viruses, fungi, and bacteria) through inhalation, ingestion, injection vectors to cause disease. Even though the necessary technical skills are not beyond the expertise of motivated scientists with university-level training, developing a mass-casualty bioterrorism capability presents some scientific and operational challenges. International laboratories that store and work with dangerous pathogens are often not adequately secured. Moreover, many Select Agent pathogens, such as anthrax, are widely available in nature. Equipment suitable for cultivating and disseminating such materials is almost entirely dual-use and is widely employed for legitimate purposes.

Radiological. Radioactive materials are used widely in industrial, medical, and research applications. They may be employed in devices used for power supply in remote locations, cancer therapy, food and blood irradiation, and radiography. Their widespread use in nearly every country makes these materials much more accessible for deployment in a radiological dispersal device (RDD), often referred to as a "dirty bomb," than the fissile materials required for nuclear weapons.

Nuclear. The diffusion of scientific and technical information regarding the assembly of nuclear weapons – some of which is now available on the Internet – has increased the risk that a terrorist organization in possession of sufficient fissile material could develop its own crude nuclear weapon. The complete production of a nuclear weapon strongly depends on the terrorist group's access to special nuclear materials as well as significant engineering and scientific expertise.

Dual Use Materials, Equipment, and Technologies. Dual-use materials, equipment, and technologies have legitimate commercial applications but may be used in the development of weapons of mass destruction (WMD) and advanced conventional capabilities. Terrorists have shown an interest in acquiring sophisticated dual-use technologies to advance their own weapons programs and are taking advantage of the availability of such material and expertise and diverting it to illicit end-uses. As a result, reducing the risk of terrorist access to and exploitation of dual-use science remains a critical challenge.

The United States regulates export, re-export, transit, transshipment, and brokering of dual-use goods based on its international commitments in the multilateral export control regimes. The United States also maintains unilateral controls on a wide range of dual-use items predominantly for antiterrorism reasons. Effective partnerships with private sector organizations, industry, academia, and governmental scientific communities, play an important role in mitigating the risk of dual-use capabilities falling into the wrong hands.

STATE SPONSORSHIP OF TERRORISM: A KEY CONCERN

A state that directs CBRN resources to terrorists or does not secure dual-use resources poses a grave CBRN terrorism threat. Although terrorist organizations will continue to seek a CBRN capability independent of state programs, the sophisticated CBRN knowledge and resources of a state could enable a terrorist capability. State sponsors of terrorism and all nations that fail to live up to their international counterterrorism and nonproliferation obligations deserve continued scrutiny as potential facilitators of CBRN terrorism.

NON-STATE FACILITATORS: AN EMERGING THREAT

State sponsors of terrorism with CBRN programs represent just one facet of the overall risk of CBRN terrorism. The non-governmental entities (terrorist groups and smugglers) state sponsors use to facilitate their CBRN programs have emerged as a growing proliferation threat in recent years that could eventually provide terrorists with access to materials and expertise particularly hard to acquire.

ADDRESSING THE INTERNATIONAL NUCLEAR THREAT

The first Nuclear Security Summit was held in Washington, April 12-13, 2010. Forty-six nations were invited to participate; all accepted, and the United Nations, the International Atomic Energy Agency, and the European Commission also participated. The United States was very pleased with the outcome of the 2010 Summit, which helped develop a common understanding of the threat posed by nuclear terrorism and achieved broad political agreement on effective measures to secure nuclear material and prevent nuclear smuggling and nuclear terrorism. The Summit's Joint Communiqué and detailed Work Plan articulate a common commitment among countries to evaluate the threat, improve security as conditions change, and continually exchange information, best practices, and practical security solutions.

PARTNERSHIPS TO COMBAT CBRN TERRORISM

Since September 11, 2001, the international community has made significant strides in responding to the threat of CBRN terrorism. States are working together bilaterally and multilaterally to address these threats and protect their populations. Through a variety of multinational initiatives such as the Global Threat Reduction Initiative, the Proliferation Security Initiative (PSI), and the Global Initiative to Combat Nuclear Terrorism (GICNT), the United States has taken a leadership role in reducing the threat of CBRN terrorism. Some of these efforts are focused on preventing threats from non-state actors and terrorists; others aim at preventing the proliferation of weapons of mass destruction to states as well as non-state actors.

UN Security Council Resolution 1540: In 2004, the UN Security Council unanimously adopted Resolution 1540, which requires states to take measures to prevent the spread of weapons of mass destruction, including adopting and enforcing laws to prohibit the transfer of WMD and related materials to non-state actors. While the Resolution is legally binding on all UN Member States, universal compliance with the resolution has not yet been achieved. Several states lack the capacity to comply with the resolution's requirements and need assistance to do so. The United States is one of the leading providers of such assistance. Several programs are in place to help countries develop their abilities to combat illicit trafficking in WMD and related materials. Other sources of assistance include other developed nations, international organizations such as the International Atomic Energy Agency (IAEA), and the Organization for the Prohibition of Chemical Weapons (OPCW), and a variety of non-government organizations (NGOs).

The Proliferation Security Initiative (PSI): Announced in 2003, the PSI has led to a number of important interdictions over the last eight years and is an important tool in the overall global effort to combat WMD proliferation to both state and non-state actors. In its eighth year, the PSI is a cooperative global effort that aims to stop the trafficking of WMD, their delivery systems, and related materials to and from states and non-state actors of proliferation concern. The PSI relies on voluntary actions by states, using existing national and international legal authorities to put an end to WMD-related trafficking. PSI partners take steps to strengthen those legal authorities as necessary, share information, and cooperate on interdiction activities. States that wish to participate in the PSI endorse its Statement of Interdiction Principles, by which states commit to undertake specific actions to halt the trafficking of WMD and related materials. As of December 31, 2010, 98 states have endorsed the Statement. Each year, PSI endorsers conduct a series of activities, including exercises, workshops, and expert's group meetings, to improve operational capabilities to conduct interdictions, share information, and develop new operational concepts.

The Global Initiative to Combat Nuclear Terrorism (GICNT): The GICNT, which is co-chaired by the United States and Russia, is a cross-cutting strategic framework of 82 partners and four observers who are determined to strengthen individual and global capacity to prevent, detect, and respond to a nuclear terrorist event. These partners have endorsed a set of core nuclear security principles encompassing the full spectrum of deterrence, prevention, detection, and response objectives. Partners utilize multilateral activities and exercises to share best practices and lessons learned in order to strengthen individual and collective capacity to combat nuclear terrorism. To date, partners have conducted over 40 multilateral activities and six senior-level meetings in support of these nuclear security goals. Through these activities, partners have improved international understanding in emerging nuclear detection technologies, emergency response and preparedness practices, and anti-smuggling assistance programs. The Initiative is open to nations that share in its common goals and are committed to combating nuclear terrorism on a determined and systematic basis.

Nuclear Smuggling Outreach Initiative (NSOI): The NSOI seeks to enhance partnerships with key countries around the world to strengthen capabilities to prevent, detect, and respond to incidents of nuclear smuggling. It focuses on both bilateral partnerships to improve such capabilities and donor partnerships to support these improvements. In its bilateral partnerships, NSOI engages those countries seen to be most important to the global effort to combat smuggling of nuclear or highly radioactive materials. In its donor partnerships, NSOI engages those countries that have resources or expertise that can be provided to improve the capabilities of other countries. The NSOI team works with the governments of potential donor partners to identify their particular interests and assets for such assistance. NSOI has to date completed Joint Action Plans and developed anti-nuclear smuggling cooperative projects with Ukraine, Kazakhstan, Georgia, the Kyrgyz Republic, Armenia, and the Democratic Republic of the Congo. It has engaged several additional bilateral partners with whom it plans to complete such documents soon, and it plans to engage several more over the coming years. NSOI has also developed donor partnerships with ten countries and three international organizations and hopes to create more such partnerships over the coming years.

Export Control and Related Border Security Program (EXBS): The EXBS program is the U.S. government's premier initiative to assist other countries in improving their strategic trade control systems. EXBS seeks to prevent the proliferation of weapons of mass destruction and their delivery systems, as well as destabilizing accumulations of advanced conventional weapons by helping to build effective national export control systems in countries that possess, produce, or supply strategic items as well as in countries through which such items are most likely to transit. EXBS is directed by the Office of Export Control Cooperation in the Bureau of International Security and Nonproliferation at the Department of State (ISN/ECC), which also leads the U.S. government interagency working group that seeks to coordinate U.S. government nonproliferation export and border control assistance and ensure EXBS is harmonized with and complements the Department of Homeland Security's Container Security Initiative, the Department of Energy's Second Line of Defense Program, the Megaports Initiative, and other international donor assistance programs. EXBS programs improve partner countries' capabilities to combat proliferation threats and fulfill their commitments as part of the Proliferation Security Initiative, the Global Initiative to Combat Nuclear Terrorism, and UNSCR 1540. EXBS currently has 23 Program Advisors stationed globally and is active in over 60 countries.

Second Line of Defense (SLD): Under its SLD Program, the Department of Energy's National Nuclear Security Administration (DOE/NNSA) cooperates with partner countries to provide radiation detection systems and associated training to enhance partner nation capabilities to deter, detect, and interdict illicit trafficking of special nuclear and other radiological materials across international borders. The SLD Program includes two components: the Core Program and the Megaports Initiative. The Core Program focuses on providing equipment to land border crossings, feeder seaports, and international airports. This work originally began in Russia and has since expanded to include former Soviet states, the Caucasus, Eastern Europe, and other key regions. Mobile detection equipment is also provided to selected countries for use at land borders and internal checkpoints.

Global Threat Reduction (GTR): GTR programs work globally to prevent terrorists from acquiring CBRN expertise, materials, and technology. GTR is actively engaged in a variety of countries including the front line countries of Pakistan, Iraq, Yemen, and Afghanistan. GTR programs have expanded to meet emerging CBRN proliferation threats worldwide and focus on promoting biological, chemical, and nuclear security in those countries where there is a high risk of CBRN terrorism or proliferation. The programs also engage scientists with WMD and WMD-applicable skills. By engaging biological, chemical, and nuclear, scientists with dual-use expertise, and helping to secure dual-use material, GTR seeks to keep CBRN and dual-use materials, technology, and expertise away from terrorists who would use these materials against the US homeland.

The Global Threat Reduction Initiative (GTRI): The goal of GTRI, announced by the United States on May 26, 2004, in Vienna, Austria, is to secure, remove, or facilitate the conversion of final arrangements for disposal of materials as expeditiously as possible, including nuclear and radioactive materials in civilian applications around the world that have been identified as vulnerable or posing a potential threat to the international community. GTRI focuses on minimizing the use of highly enriched uranium in research reactors and isotope-production processes around the world as well as protecting or removing unwanted or unused plutonium and high-activity radioactive sources. Approximately one hundred international partners cooperate with GTRI programs under this initiative.

Biological Weapons Convention Intersessional Work Program: In response to a proposal from the United States, the States Parties to the Biological Weapons Convention (BWC) in 2002 embarked on a series of expert exchanges aimed at raising awareness, sharing best practices, and facilitating assistance on topics related to implementation of the BWC and reducing the threat of BW use, with a new emphasis on the terrorist threat. Work has included exchanges on national legislative and regulatory frameworks; laboratory biosecurity; outreach to promote responsible conduct by members of the scientific community; and investigation of and response to suspect attacks.

National Strategy for Countering Biological Threats: In November 2009, President Obama approved a new national strategy to provide greater policy cohesion and coordination for U.S. efforts to prevent state or non-state actors from acquiring or using biological weapons. (Efforts to mitigate the consequences of use are dealt with through other policy/strategy frameworks). Federal agencies have developed detailed implementation plans and are actively coordinating efforts in support of the Strategy's seven key objectives, which are to:

1. Promote global health security

2. Reinforce norms of responsible/beneficent conduct

3. Obtain timely/accurate insight on current/emerging risks

4. Take reasonable steps to reduce potential for exploitation

5. Expand capability to disrupt, apprehend and attribute

6. Communicate effectively with all stakeholders

7. Transform international dialogue on biological threats

CHAPTER 5.
TERRORIST SAFE HAVENS
(UPDATE TO 7120 REPORT)

5.1A TERRORIST SAFE HAVENS

Terrorist safe havens described in this report include ungoverned, under-governed, or ill-governed physical areas where terrorists are able to organize, plan, raise funds, communicate, recruit, train, transit, and operate in relative security because of inadequate governance capacity, political will, or both. For further informations on the countries in this section and their cooperation with U.S. counterterrorism efforts, see *Chapter 2, Country Reports on Terrorism*.

AFRICA

Somalia. With its long unguarded coastline, porous borders, continued political instability, and proximity to the Arabian Peninsula, Somalia provides opportunities for terrorist transit and remains a major safe haven. Al-Shabaab, a clan-based insurgent and terrorist group, has grown stronger with sustained financing and become more dangerous over the past year. Several senior al-Shabaab leaders have publicly proclaimed loyalty to al-Qa'ida (AQ), and these leaders have established and supported a number of training camps in southern Somalia for young Somali and foreign recruits to al-Shabaab. In some camps, AQ-affiliated foreign fighters often led the training and indoctrination of the recruits. The majority of al-Shabaab fighters, however, are clan-based militias primarily interested in defeating the Somali government and African Union Mission in Somalia forces.

According to independent sources and non-governmental organizations engaged in demining activities on the ground, there was little cause for concern for the presence of WMDs in Somalia in 2010.

The Trans-Sahara. The primary terrorist threat in this region was al-Qa'ida in the Islamic Maghreb (AQIM). AQIM was historically based primarily in northeastern Algeria, but factions also operated from a safe haven in northern Mali, from which they transited areas of the Maghreb and Sahel, especially Mali, Niger, and Mauritania. AQIM continued to conduct small scale ambushes and attacks on Algerian security forces in northeastern Algeria, but in recent years, the group has not been able to conduct large attacks on the scale of the 2007 bombings of the UN and Algerian government buildings in Algiers. AQIM factions based in northern Mali used the area to conduct kidnappings – some of which have resulted in the murder of Western hostages – and limited attacks on Nigerien and Mauritanian security personnel. While regional governments took steps to counter AQIM operations, there was a need for foreign assistance in the form of law enforcement and military capacity building.

Trafficking of WMD and related materials could be of concern in this region, given the porous borders.

EAST ASIA AND PACIFIC

The Sulu/Sulawesi Seas Littoral. In Southeast Asia, the terrorist organizations Jemaah Islamiya and Abu Sayyaf Group have sought safe haven in the vicinity of the Sulawesi Sea and the Sulu Archipelago. The numerous islands in the area make it a difficult region for authorities to monitor, and a range of licit and illicit activities that occur there, such as worker migration, tourism, and trade, pose additional challenges to identifying and countering the terrorist threat. Indonesia, Malaysia, and the Philippines have improved efforts to control their shared maritime boundaries, including through the U.S.-funded Coast Watch System radar network, which is intended to enhance domain awareness in the waters south of Mindanao. Nevertheless, the expanse remained difficult to control. Surveillance was improved but remained partial at best, and traditional smuggling and piracy groups have provided an effective cover for terrorist activities, such as movement of personnel, equipment, and funds.

WMD trafficking, proliferation, and the spread of WMD-applicable expertise have been concerns in this region, given the high volume of global trade that ships through the region as well as the existence of proliferation networks looking to exploit vulnerabilities in states' export controls.

The Southern Philippines. Terrorist operatives have sought safe haven in areas of the southern Philippines, specifically in the Sulu archipelago and Mindanao. Philippine government control and the rule of law in this area are weak due to rugged terrain, poverty, and local Muslim minority resentment of central governmental policies. Jemaah Islamiya fugitives and Abu Sayyaf Group constituted the primary terrorist presence in the southern Philippines, although the Rajah Solaiman Movement and the New People's Army also maintained a presence there.

THE MIDDLE EAST

Iraq. With heightened capabilities and the continued support of U.S. force, the Iraq Security Force (ISF) continued to make progress against al-Qa'ida in Iraq (AQI), some Shia violent extremists, and other groups. AQI is no longer supported by many Sunni populations. Iraqis in Baghdad, Anbar, and Diyala Provinces, and elsewhere, continued to oppose the group and cooperated with the Iraqi government and U.S. forces to defeat it. The Baghdad Security Plan, along with assistance from primarily Sunni tribal and local groups, succeeded in reducing violence levels and disrupting and diminishing AQI leadership, financing, supply, and traditional strongholds. Throughout Iraq, the ISF has increased its effectiveness in rooting out terrorist cells and eliminating potential safe haven locations.

The U.S. government is working with Iraq to implement comprehensive strategic trade controls and improve security at facilities that house biological and chemical materials. In October 2010, the United States hosted a senior Iraqi delegation in Washington, DC, to discuss the threat of proliferation of WMD, critical elements of effective strategic trade controls, and international strategic trade control best practices. In addition, the United States provided border security assistance focused on detecting and interdicting strategic goods to Iraqi enforcement agencies. Furthermore, Iraq has established a radioactive source regulatory infrastructure, the Iraq Radioactive Source Regulatory Authority (IRSRA). The U.S. government has an ongoing program to assist IRSRA with securing dangerous radioactive sources used in medical oncology programs. The Department of Energy has also provided Iraq with hand detection devices that are being used to detect radiological material at border crossings in a program established by IRSRA. Iraq has developed a draft strategic trade control legislation, which was pending parliamentary approval at year's end.

Lebanon. Hizballah remained the most prominent and powerful terrorist group in Lebanon, with deep roots among Lebanon's Shia community, which composes at least one third of Lebanon's population. The Lebanese government continued to recognize Hizballah, a U.S.-designated Foreign Terrorist Organization, as a legitimate "resistance group" and political party. Hizballah maintained offices in Beirut and military-style bases elsewhere in the country and was represented by elected deputies in parliament.

AQ associated extremists also operated within the country, though their presence was small compared to that of rejectionist Palestinian groups not aligned with AQ operating in refugee camps. While the Lebanese security services do not have a day-to-day presence within 11 of the 12 camps, they have at times conducted operations in the camps to combat terrorist threats.

Lebanon is not a source country for WMD components, but the primary concern is that Lebanon's porous borders will make the country vulnerable to being used as a transit/transshipment hub for proliferation-sensitive transfers. To address these concerns, the U.S. government hosted a senior Lebanese delegation in Washington, DC in November 2010 to initiate discussion about the need to adopt comprehensive strategic trade controls, international best practices, and steps Lebanon has to take to comply with international standards. Hizballah's continued ability to receive sophisticated munitions via Iran and Syria requires that we continue to aggressively monitor this issue.

Yemen. Yemen's lack of a government presence in much of the country and porous borders has allowed terrorists to establish safe haven within the country. The establishment of al-Qa'ida in the Arabian Peninsula (AQAP) in January 2009 provided a network and hierarchy that could absorb incoming terrorists to Yemen. As Saudi security forces continued to put pressure on extremists in their country, terrorists and foreign fighters returning from Afghanistan and Pakistan, sought safe haven within Yemen. Al-Qa'ida in the Arabian Peninsula (AQAP) continued to plan, execute, and attack targets within Yemen and the greater Arabian Peninsula as well as against the United States. While the Government of Yemen increased counterterrorism cooperation with the United States in 2010, and its capacity to address terrorist threats has improved, resource limitations and political instability in various parts of the country have impeded its ability to eliminate terrorist safe havens.

Yemen's current political instability makes the country vulnerable for use as a transit point for WMD-related materials. In the past three years, progress in developing strategic trade controls has been undermined by ongoing civil unrest, protests, and economic problems.

SOUTH ASIA

Afghanistan. The Government of Afghanistan, in concert with the International Security Assistance Force and the international community, continued its efforts to eliminate terrorist safe havens and build security, particularly in the country's south and east where insurgents threatened stability. Many insurgent groups, including Taliban elements, the Haqqani Network, Hezb-e-Islami Gulbuddin, al-Qa'ida (AQ), and Lashkar-e-Tayyiba, continued to use territory across the border in Pakistan as a base from which to plot and launch attacks within Afghanistan and beyond. AQ leadership in Pakistan maintained its support to militants conducting attacks in Afghanistan and provided funding, training, and personnel to facilitate terrorist and insurgent operations. Anti-Coalition organizations continued to operate in coordination with AQ, Taliban, and other insurgent groups, primarily in the east.

The potential for WMD trafficking and proliferation is a concern in Afghanistan because of its porous borders and the presence of terrorist groups. The U.S. government is working with Afghanistan to implement comprehensive strategic trade controls. In late 2010, the U.S. government provided legislation development assistance to Afghan government officials in drafting comprehensive strategic trade controls legislation. In addition, the Export Control and Related Border Security Assistance (EXBS) program contributed to strengthening Afghanistan's enforcement capacity through participation in a regional cross-border enforcement exercise.

Pakistan. Despite efforts by Pakistani security forces, al-Qa'ida (AQ) terrorists, Afghan militants, foreign insurgents, and Pakistani militants continued to find safe haven in portions of Pakistan's Federally Administered Tribal Areas (FATA), Khyber Paktunkhwa (KPK), and Baluchistan. AQ and other groups such as the Haqqani Network used Pakistani safe havens to launch attacks in Afghanistan, plan operations worldwide, train, recruit, and disseminate propaganda. The Pakistani Taliban (Tehrik-e-Taliban or TTP) also used the FATA to plan attacks against civilian and military targets across Pakistan and abroad. Outside the FATA, the Quetta-based Afghan Taliban and separate insurgent organizations such as Hizb-e-Islami Gulbuddin used the areas in Baluchistan and the KPK for safe haven. Violent extremist groups and many local tribesmen in the FATA and the KPK continued to resist the government's efforts to improve governance and administrative control. In spite of Pakistani military operations throughout FATA and KPK, TTP, AQ, and other extremist groups remained dangerous to Pakistan and the international community.

Despite international condemnation for its November 2008 attacks in Mumbai, Lashkar-e-Tayyiba (LT) continued to plan regional operations from within Pakistan. While the Government of Pakistan has banned LT, the United States continued to urge further action against this group and its front organizations.

The potential for WMD trafficking and proliferation remained of concern in Pakistan due to the porous borders and the difficult security situation. Export Control and Related Border Security Assistance (EXBS) has enabled Pakistani officials to gain expertise in properly classifying items of proliferation concern and learn about export licensing best practices.

WESTERN HEMISPHERE

Colombia's borders with Venezuela, Ecuador, Peru, Panama, and Brazil include rough terrain and dense forest cover, which coupled with low population densities and historically weak government presence, created potential safe havens for insurgent and terrorist groups, particularly the Revolutionary Armed Forces of Colombia (FARC). The FARC, retreating in the face of Colombian military pressures, has operated with relative ease along the fringes of Colombia's borders, and used areas in neighboring countries along those borders to rest and regroup, procure supplies, and stage and train for terrorist attacks. The FARC elements in these border regions often engaged the local population in direct and indirect ways, including relying on them for recruits and logistical support. This is seemingly less so in Brazil and Peru where potential safe havens were addressed by stronger government actions. Both Ecuador and Panama appeared to be strengthening their efforts against Colombian narcotics trafficking and terrorist groups.

Trafficking of WMD and related materials could be a potential concern in this region, given the high volume of global trade that ships through, and the existence of proliferation networks looking to exploit vulnerabilities in states' export controls.

Venezuela. During the year, the Colombian government continued to accuse the Venezuelan government of harboring the Revolutionary Armed Forces of Colombia (FARC) and the Colombian National Liberation Army (ELN) in its territory. More specifically, Colombian authorities alleged that these groups used Venezuelan territory to rest and regroup, engage in narcotics trafficking, extort protection money, and kidnap Colombians to finance their operations. In a July 22 special session of the OAS Permanent Council, the Colombian Permanent Representative presented purported evidence of FARC training camps in Venezuela and proposed an international verification commission to investigate the presence of FARC and ELN members in Venezuela. The Venezuelan government didn't take effective steps to investigate such allegations and ensure that such groups did not operate with impunity in Venezuelan territory. Nor did it take action to investigate or remove senior Venezuelan officials allegedly linked to the FARC or ELN.

The Tri-Border Area (Argentina, Brazil, and Paraguay). No credible information showed that Hizballah, HAMAS, or other Islamist extremist groups used the Tri-Border Area for terrorist training or other operational activity, but the United States remained concerned that these groups used the region to raise funds from local supporters. The Argentine, Brazilian, and Paraguayan governments have long been concerned with arms and drugs smuggling, document fraud, money laundering, trafficking in persons, and the manufacture and movement of contraband goods through the Tri-Border Area.

As two of a handful of countries with uranium enrichment capabilities, Brazil and Argentina have the potential to serve as a source of WMD-related equipment, materials, and proliferation-sensitive nuclear fuel cycle expertise. The goal of the Export Control and Related Border Security Assistance (EXBS) Program in Brazil and Argentina is to encourage strengthening and greater the transparency of their strategic trade control systems and to foster their regional leadership by providing nonproliferation training and technical expertise to their neighbors. With EXBS cooperation, Brazil was quick to develop a Commodity Identification Training (CIT) course to train enforcement officials in identification of proliferation-sensitive goods and is now conducting domestic training without EXBS support. Likewise, Argentina has worked with EXBS on WMD violation training for judges and prosecutors to help enforce criminal and administrative sanctions and has also begun providing CIT training to neighboring countries.

5.1B STRATEGIES, TACTICS, AND TOOLS FOR DISRUPTING OR ELIMINATING SAFE HAVENS

I. COUNTERING TERRORISM ON THE ECONOMIC FRONT

In 2010, the Department of State designated four new Foreign Terrorist Organizations (FTOs), and amended one FTO designation to include a new alias for Lashkar-e Tayyiba. In addition, the Department listed 16 organizations and individuals under Executive Order (EO) 13224, including groups such as al-Qa'ida in the Arabian Peninsula, Harakat-ul Jihad Islami, Tehrik-e Taliban Pakistan, Jundallah, and the Falah-i-Insaniat Foundation. Individuals listed under E.O. 13224 include Nayif al-Qahtani, Qasim al-Rimi, Nasir al-Wahishi, Said al-Shihri, Eric Breininger, Mohamed Belkalem, Taleb Nail, Doku Umarov, Hakimullah Mehsud, Wali Ur Rehman, and Fahd al-Quso. The Department of the Treasury also designates organizations and individuals under EO 13224.

Key FTO designations:

- On January 19, the Department of State designated al-Qa'ida in the Arabian Peninsula (AQAP) as a Foreign Terrorist Organization. *(See Chapter 6, Foreign Terrorist Organizations, for further information on AQAP.)*

- On August 6, the Department of State designated Harakat-ul Jihad Islami (HUJI) as a Foreign Terrorist Organization. In tandem with the HUJI designation, the Department of the Treasury also designated HUJI leader Mohammad Ilyas Kashmiri who is wanted for terrorism-related offenses in connection with an attack against the Jyllands-Posten newspaper in Denmark. *(See Chapter 6, Foreign Terrorist Organizations, for further information on HUJI.)*

- On September 1, the Department of State designated Tehrik-e Taliban Pakistan (TTP) as a Foreign Terrorist Organization. *(See Chapter 6, Foreign Terrorist Organizations, for further information on TTP.)*

- On November 3, the Department of State designated Jundallah, a violent extremist organization that operates primarily in the Iranian province of Sistan va Balochistan. *(See Chapter 6, Foreign Terrorist Organizations, for further information on Jundallah.)*

- On November 24, the Department of State amended the designation of Lashkar-e-Tayyiba (LeT) to include the addition of Falah-i-Insaniat Foundation (FIF) as an alias of LeT. FIF is a Pakistan-based charitable organization that is closely connected to banned terrorist group LeT and its former humanitarian front, Jamaat-ud-Dawa (JUD

Key E.O. 13224 designations:

- On January 19, the Department of State also designated AQAP senior leaders Nasir al-Wahishi and Said al-Shihri. Nasir al-Wahishi proclaimed himself as the leader of AQAP in January 2009. Since then, Al-Wahishi has provided significant support for AQAP terrorist operations and has worked with AQAP operatives to facilitate attacks. Said Ali al-Shihri was publicly identified in January 2009 as the deputy leader of AQAP.

- On May 11, the Department of State designated AQAP's senior military commander Qasim al-Rimi. Rimi has played a key role in reviving AQAP, which is the regional franchise of al-Qa'ida (AQ). In 2007, he and AQAP Emir Nasir al-Wahishi announced the emergence of al-Qa'ida in Yemen (AQY)—AQAP's predecessor group.

- On May 26, the Department of State designated al-Qa'ida in the Islamic Maghreb (AQIM) leaders Mohamed Belkalem and Taleb Nail. Mohamed Belkalem plays a key operational role in AQIM and has participated in terrorist attacks such as the 2005 assault on a Mauritanian military barracks and the kidnapping of two Austrian tourists in 2008. Belkalem is wanted by the Algerian government and was sentenced by the Government of Algeria, in absentia, to death for forming a terrorist organization. Also wanted by the Algerian government, Taleb Nail has been involved in numerous terrorist attacks in the Trans-Sahara region, including a 2005 assault on Mauritanian military barracks.

- On June 23, the Department of State designated Doku Umarov, leader of the Russia-based extremist group Caucasus Emirates. Umarov transformed Chechnya's insurgent separatist and nationalist fight into a movement that sought to establish an Islamic Emirate throughout the North Caucasus with himself as its Emir. Umarov claimed responsibility for masterminding attacks in and around Moscow and throughout the North Caucasus region, and claimed responsibility for the 2009 Nevsky Express train derailment, which killed 28 people, and the 2010 Moscow subway bombings, which killed 40.

- On July 16, the Department of the Treasury designated AQAP senior leader Anwar al-Aulaqi, who plays a major role in setting the strategic direction for AQAP and has recruited individuals to join AQAP, facilitated training at camps in Yemen in support of acts of terrorism, and helped focus AQAP's attention on planning attacks on U.S. interests. Since late 2009, al-Aulaqi has taken on an increasingly operational role in the group, including preparing Umar Farouk Abdulmutallab, who attempted to detonate an explosive device aboard a Northwest Airlines flight from Amsterdam to Detroit on December 25, 2009, for his operation.

- On July 22, the Department of the Treasury designated Nasiruddin Haqqani, emissary for the Haqqani Network (HQN) and brother of HQN leader Sirajuddin Haqqani. Nasiruddin collects funds for HQN through donations from the Gulf region, trafficking drugs, and receiving payments from AQ. Nasiruddin has also participated in raising funds for the Taliban.

- On September 1, the Department of State designated Tehrik-e Taliban Pakistan's senior leaders Hakimullah Mehsud and Wali Ur Rehman. Hakimullah Mehsud has been the leader of TTP since August 2009 and Wali Ur Rehman is the TTP Emir in South Waziristan. Rehman has participated in cross-border attacks in Afghanistan against U.S. and NATO personnel, as well as attacks against Pakistani security forces.

- On November 24, the Department of the Treasury designated Mohammad Naushad Alam Khan, a key financial facilitator for LET who supports the organization through an international counterfeit currency operation and smuggling network.

- On December 7, the Department of State designated AQAP operative Fahd al-Quso. Prior to the formation of AQAP, al-Quso was associated with AQ elements in Yemen and was involved in the 2000 USS Cole bombing in the Port of Aden, which killed 17 U.S. citizens. For his involvement in the attack, al-Quso was jailed in Yemen in 2002 but released from prison in 2007. In May 2010, al-Quso appeared in an AQAP video in which he threatened to attack the U.S. homeland, as well as U.S. embassies and naval vessels abroad.

II. MULTILATERAL EFFORTS TO COUNTER TERRORISM

International Instruments related to Counterterrorism. In 2010, the 2005 Protocol to the Convention for the Suppression of Unlawful Acts Against the Safety of Maritime Navigation and the 2005 Protocol to the Protocol for the Suppression of Unlawful Acts Against the Safety of Fixed Platforms entered into force. Furthermore, a diplomatic conference held under the auspices of the International Civil Aviation Organization concluded the Beijing Convention on the Suppression of Unlawful Acts Relating to International Civil Aviation and the Beijing Protocol to the Convention for the Suppression of Unlawful Seizure of Aircraft. Both instruments modernize the international legal regime to cover new and emerging threats to the safety of civil aviation. The United States signed both the Beijing Convention and Beijing Protocol at the conclusion of the conference.

The UN. Sustained and strategic engagement at the UN on counterterrorism issues is a priority for the United States as it is an important forum for setting global counterterrorism norms and building counterterrorism partnerships and capacities. The United States engaged with a wide range of UN actors on counterterrorism in 2010, including the three counterterrorism related committees of the Security Council: the Counter-Terrorism Committee; the 1267 Committee; and the 1540 Committee.

The Counter-Terrorism Committee. The United States welcomed adoption of UN Security Council resolution 1963 (December 2010), which renewed the mandate of the UN Counterterrorism Executive Directorate (CTED) for another three years. In 2010, CTED conducted several visits to countries in the Horn of Africa, the Sahel, South Asia, and Europe to assess the implementation of UNSCR 1373.

CTED has proven itself to be uniquely suited to bring together local officials from countries in the region to identify practical solutions to common counterterrorism challenges. The United States supported CTED by co-funding and participating in a workshop in New York in December 2010, which brought together senior prosecutors from across the globe with experience in handling high-profile terrorism cases. The United States also participated in CTED's October 2010 regional workshop in Sarajevo, Bosnia and Herzegovina on national coordination and regional cooperation and its December 2010 regional workshop in Tashkent, Uzbekistan on terrorism prevention and countering violent extremism.

The UNSC 1267 Committee. In 2010, to ensure that current listings remained appropriate, the committee completed a review pursuant to UNSCR 1822 of all 488 individuals and entities on the Consolidated List at the time of the adoption of that resolution (June 30, 2008). The resolution mandated the committee complete this review by June 30. The review resulted in the removal of 45 listings, including 24 individuals and 21 entities. Updated identifying information was submitted for the remaining entries, and Narrative Summaries explaining the reasons for listing were posted publically on the UN 1267 website. Pursuant to Resolution 1904, the Secretary-General, in close consultation with the committee, appointed an ombudsperson in 2010 to assist the committee in its review of petitions received by or on behalf of individuals and entities seeking removal from the Consolidated List to help ensure the delisting procedures are fair and transparent.

The UNSC 1540 Committee. See Chapter 4, *The Global Challenge of Chemical, Biological, Radiological, and Nuclear (CBRN) Terrorism.*

The Counterterrorism Implementation Task Force (CTITF). Since the adoption of the UN Global Counterterrorism Strategy in 2006, the Task Force–comprised of all UN member states and 30 UN entities across the UN system and Interpol–has become the focal point for UN efforts to support implementation of the global framework. In 2010, the United States supported CTITF efforts by funding a series of workshops aimed at raising awareness of the Strategy in key regions. The first workshop was held in Bali, Indonesia in November. CTITF also supported the Integrated Assistance for Countering Terrorism (I-ACT) initiative, which seeks to enhance information sharing and coordination of technical assistance delivery with partnering governments and the different entities of the UN. I-ACT visited Nigeria in August.

The UN Interregional Crime and Justice Research Institute (UNICRI). In June, the Counterterrorism Implementation Task Force welcomed the opening of the UNICRI's "Centre on Policies to Counter the Appeal of Terrorism," which will analyze different policies and programs on detection and prevention of pathways into terrorism, early intervention efforts against terrorist recruitment, and rehabilitation initiatives. With U.S. support, UNICRI is bringing together national practitioners from key countries to share experiences and identify best practices in the rehabilitation of terrorists.

The International Civil Aviation Organization (ICAO). Member States endorsed a Declaration on Aviation Security at the triennial ICAO Assembly in September/October, which outlined areas of cooperation designed to promote and strengthen aviation security. The Assembly also endorsed the ICAO Comprehensive Aviation Security Strategy, a new approach composed of seven focus areas. In addition, Member States gave unanimous support for the continuation of the Universal Security Audit Program. In September, at a diplomatic conference held in Beijing, two treaties to further criminalize acts of unlawful interference against civil aviation were adopted. In December, the ICAO Council amended the aviation security annex to the Convention on International Civil Aviation to strengthen global air cargo security measures.

The UN Office on Drugs and Crime's (UNODC's) Terrorism Prevention Branch (TPB). The TPB and its Global Program Against Money Laundering continued to provide assistance to countries in the legal and related aspects of counterterrorism. In 2010, the United States supported UNODC/TPB through its pledge of US $1.25 million, including funding to train national prosecutors and judges in Yemen on counterterrorism best practices.

The International Atomic Energy Agency (IAEA). The IAEA continued to implement its Nuclear Security Plan (2010-2013) for countering the threat of terrorism involving nuclear and other radioactive material. The United States has been working to enhance security for vulnerable nuclear and other radioactive materials within the IAEA's 152 member states to reduce the risk that such materials could be used in a terrorist event.

Group of Eight (G8) Counterterrorism Actions. Canada, which held the G8 presidency, hosted the 2010 annual G8 Summit in Muskoka where its leaders committed to work cooperatively on transportation security; border security and identity integrity (including biometrics, to ensure the legitimacy and validity of travel and identity documents); preventing chemical, biological, nuclear, and radiological terrorism; counterterrorist financing; countering violent extremism and radicalization leading to violence; and terrorist recruitment. They also reiterated their commitment to further develop initiatives that assist victims and survivors of terrorism.

Counterterrorism Action Group (CTAG). CTAG's membership includes the G8 and Australia, Spain, and Switzerland. Officials from relevant UN bodies and regional and functional organizations are also invited to participate in these meetings. In October 2010, under Canada's Presidency, the CTAG organized its first regional meeting in Bamako, Mali, which focused on building counterterrorism capacity and cooperation in the Sahel region.

Financial Action Task Force (FATF) and FATF-Style Regional Bodies (FSRBs). In 2010, the U.S. delegation supported the Plenary on issues of policy, conducting mutual evaluations, and participating in the Working Groups on issues of implementation. The United States continued its co-chair role with Italy on the International Cooperation Review Group (ICRG). The U.S. delegation increased its engagement in this process by emphasizing Special Recommendation III, a provision regarding the freezing and confiscation of assets. It also participated as part of the core project team in major FATF typologies work, focusing on kidnapping for ransom and maritime piracy for ransom. In 2010, additional work contributed by the United States included the evaluation and revision of selected recommendations and criteria, outreach to the private sector, public-private partnerships, and the development of guidance for non-financial businesses and professions.

The United States played a similar and equally active role in the FSRBs, supporting FSRB-executed training and workshops, as well as providing technical assistance to both members and the Secretariats. In addition to providing them with training, the United States also provided advice with an eye to increasing the capacity and transparency of the Secretariats. Additionally, the United States took part in Contact and Expert Review Groups.

EU. The EU Counterterrorism Coordinator (CTC), Gilles de Kerchove, along with counterterrorism officials in the European Commission and the newly established European External Action Service, participated in regular dialogues with U.S. counterparts. In November, the CTC presented an action plan to the European Council calling for specific measures to address vulnerabilities and challenges associated with transport security, terrorist travel, cyber security, external counterterrorism efforts, and the fight against discrimination and social marginalization. Specific developments included:

- In January, the Toledo Joint Statement on Aviation Security pledged to increase efforts to identify individuals and illicit materials that pose a security risk as soon as possible in order to prevent entry of such passengers and/or cargo on to aircraft.

- In February, the U.S.-EU Extradition and Mutual Legal Assistance Agreements and the conforming bilateral agreements with Member States came into force.

- In June, a joint U.S.-EU countering violent extremism (CVE) seminar explored the nature of violent extremism in the United States, the EU, and third countries. Thematic workshops on counter-radicalization and de-radicalization were held as were geographical workshops on Yemen/Sahel and South Asia.

- In August, the U.S.-EU Terrorist Finance Tracking Program (TFTP) agreement entered into force.

- In December, the US and EU launched negotiations for a new PNR agreement to replace the 2007 pact that was provisionally in force. PNR is the data a traveler provides an airline and may include an itinerary, payment method and contact information. PNR data analysis can help DHS identify watchlisted individuals, non-watchlisted co-travelers, and terrorists or criminals adopting known illicit travel patterns. PNR data proved key in the three most high profile terrorist investigations in 2009-2010.

The November 2010 U.S.-EU Summit pledged further collaboration on CVE and the establishment of a U.S.-EU Working Group on Cybersecurity and Cybercrime to tackle new threats to global security. It also reaffirmed the leaders' commitment to develop a common set of data privacy principles and work towards negotiating a comprehensive agreement on data protection for our law enforcement authorities to enhance cooperation, while ensuring full protection for U.S. and EU member-state citizens.

OSCE. The OSCE was chaired by Kazakhstan in 2010, marking the first time that a Central Asian state has led the OSCE, which brought special attention to the need to address transnational threats in the Central Asian region. The United States supported this through active participation in an October counterterrorism conference and the OSCE Summit in December, both held in Astana, Kazakhstan. U.S. counterterrorism efforts in the OSCE focused on critical energy infrastructure protection, travel document security, cyber security, non-proliferation, and countering violent extremism. In particular, a U.S.-sponsored seminar and tabletop exercise in early 2010 on critical energy infrastructure protection for all 56 participating States provided a valuable forum for greater awareness of shared challenges and opportunities throughout the region.

NATO. NATO led International Security Assistance Force (ISAF) stability operations against insurgents in Afghanistan. ISAF, in support of the Government of Afghanistan, conducted operations in Afghanistan to degrade the capability and will of the insurgency, support the growth in capacity and capability of the Afghan National Security Forces, and facilitate improvements in governance and socio-economic development to provide a secure environment for sustainable stability. For details regarding ISAF contributions by country, please see http://www.isaf.nato.int/troop-numbers-and-contributions/index.php.

NATO also continued Operation Active Endeavor, a naval mission that aimed to counter terrorism by monitoring Mediterranean maritime traffic. In 2010, NATO established a new organizational unit, the Emerging Security Challenges Division, to address a broad range of counterterrorism issues, including cyber security and critical infrastructure protection. Through NATO's Defense Against Terrorism program, the Alliance was also developing a range of new cutting-edge technologies to protect troops and civilians against terrorist attacks.

The new NATO Strategic Concept, adopted in Lisbon at the NATO Summit, resulted in a commitment to intensify efforts to deny terrorists access to weapons of mass destruction (WMD) and their means of delivery and to strengthen the capacity to detect and defend against international terrorism through enhanced analysis of the threat, more consultations with our partners, and the development of appropriate military capabilities, including to help train local forces to fight terrorism themselves. At the NATO-Russia Council (NRC) Summit in Lisbon, leaders affirmed the Joint Review of 21st Century Common Security Challenges ("Joint Review"). The Joint Review identifies combating terrorism as one of the five priority areas for concrete NRC cooperation over the next year and beyond.

The African Union (AU). AUC Chairperson Jean Ping published the Report of the Chairperson on the Commission on Measures to Strengthen Cooperation in the Prevention and Combating of Terrorism in November 2010. The report included sections on Africa's vulnerabilities to terrorism, the AU's legal instruments to fight terrorism, an update on the AU's Plan of Action, and a discussion of the AU's recent counterterrorism efforts. The report indicated that key determinants of the terrorist threat in Africa were activities in two regions led by two organizations: al-Qa'ida in the Islamic Maghreb (AQIM) in North and West Africa, and al-Shabaab in East Africa.

With the approval of the UN in Somalia, the AU operated the African Union Mission in Somalia (AMISOM), which conducts a Peace Support Operation to stabilize Somalia's security situation and create a safe and secure environment so that leadership can be transferred to the UN. The United States actively supports AMISOM with training and supplies. AMISOM is mandated to support transitional governmental structures, implement a national security plan, train the Somali security forces, and assist in creating a secure environment for the delivery of humanitarian aid.

The first-ever AU Special Representative for Counterterrorism, appointed in 2010, was tasked to coordinate AU efforts to ensure the effective implementation of the relevant AU legal instruments. The Special Representative's efforts also focused on the mobilization of the international community in support of Africa's counterterrorism efforts.

In 2010, the AUC completed its Anti-Terrorism Model Law for use by member states to enact more robust domestic counterterrorism legislation. The AUC provided guidance to its 53-member states and coordinated limited technical assistance to cover member states' counterterrorism capability gaps. The African Center for the Study and Research on Terrorism, based in Algiers, Algeria, served as the AU's central institution to collect information, studies, and analyses on terrorism and terrorist groups and to develop CT training programs, serving as a forum for discussion, cooperation, and collaboration among AU member states.

Association of Southeast Asian Nations (ASEAN). In 2010, the United States worked closely with ASEAN to enhance counterterrorism cooperation. In an October meeting with ASEAN Senior Officials on Transnational Crime, the United States called for increased international cooperation in combating terrorism and suggested possible new areas for U.S. engagement with ASEAN to bolster the capabilities of member countries to address terrorism and other transnational criminal threats. The United States actively participated in counterterrorism-related activities of the 27-member ASEAN Regional Forum (ARF), including the annual meetings on counterterrorism and transnational crime (CTTC) as well as providing substantial support in capacity building through ARF institutions. In support of the CTTC work plan, which focuses ARF efforts on three priority areas of biological terrorism, narcotics trafficking, and cyber security and terrorism, the United States proposed to establish the ARF Transnational Threat Information-sharing Center to utilize and deepen existing regional mechanisms that specialize in information-sharing and capacity building.

Asia Pacific Economic Cooperation (APEC). The United States actively led APEC initiatives to strengthen aviation and maritime security, which included implementing capacity building work-shops to enhance air cargo security and introducing tools for assessing and planning against risks to port facilities. The United States supported APEC efforts to implement the Financial Action Task Force Special Recommendations on Terrorist Financing. The United States led capacity building work to counter terrorist threats against the food supply, implementing follow on activities with Peru and Thailand under the APEC Food Defense Program.

OAS Inter-American Committee against Terrorism (CICTE). In March, at the Tenth Regular Session of CICTE in Washington DC, the 33 member states adopted the Declaration on Public-Private Partnerships in the Fight against Terrorism. The CICTE Secretariat conducted 114 activities, training courses and technical assistance missions, which benefited more than 3,500 participants through nine programs in five areas: border controls; critical infrastructure protection; counterter-rorism legislative assistance and terrorist financing; strengthening strategies on emerging terrorist threats (crisis management); and international cooperation and partnerships. The United States is a major contributor to CICTE's training programs and directly provided funding and/or expert trainers for capacity building programs focused on maritime security, aviation security, travel document secu-rity and fraud prevention, cybersecurity, counterterrorism legislation, and efforts to counter terrorism financing.

III.   LONG-TERM PROGRAMS/ACTIONS DESIGNED TO REDUCE CONDITIONS THAT ALLOW TERRORIST SAFE HAVENS TO FORM.

Countering Violent Extremism (CVE). The State Department's strategic counterterrorism efforts flow from our recognition that terrorism cannot be defeated by law enforcement and military means alone. The key elements of CVE are:

1.   Promoting Alternatives: We must provide positive alternatives to persons at risk of recruitment into violent activity in hotspots of radicalization.

2. Undermining the al-Qa'ida (AQ) narrative: We must undermine AQ's extremist rhetoric and support credible moderate voices.

3. Building Capacity: We must improve partners' capacity – both civil society and government – to address grievances, provide alternatives to joining extremist groups, and counter the AQ narrative.

In 2010, our CVE work focused on:

Countering the Narrative: The Center for Strategic Counterterrorism Communication (CSCC) is a new interagency unit set up within the Department of State to coordinate, orient, and inform communications activities targeted against al-Qa'ida and its affiliates and weaken their ability to recruit and gain support overseas. Among the Center's main activities is a Digital Outreach Team operating in Arabic and Urdu to counter extremist messaging on the Internet.

Countering Extremist Voices: The State Department's Bureau of Public Affairs and Public Diplomacy and USAID collaborated to increase the reach of alternative voices into at risk populations by investing in cell, radio, and television transmission towers. With increased capacity to carry content into at-risk areas we were increasingly able to work with host nations and other local actors to drown out extremists by flooding the market with a more diverse set of programming and voices.

USAID: USAID currently has CVE-related programs that focus on youth empowerment, non-formal education, local government, and community based media.

Hotspots of Radicalization: We have seen distinct patterns and clusters of radicalization in particular localities. The Office of the Coordinator for Counterterrorism has partnered with colleagues in the interagency to identify hotspots of radicalization, determine local grievances, and establish attitudinal baselines to measure the effectiveness of programming. The purpose of this assessment effort is to ensure that our programs are grounded in solid research.

Ambassador's Fund Programs: The Ambassador's Fund for Counterterrorism provides U.S. embassies with the resources necessary to implement small-scale, locally-relevant counter-radicalization projects. These include a variety of activities and are focused on engaging at-risk youth within their communities. In FY 2010, we provided US$ 2.5 million for these small grants through projects that challenged violent extremist narratives, empowered mainstream voices, built trust between youth and law enforcement, and engaged at-risk youth in a variety of locales.

Somali Diaspora: The State Department is working with the National Counterterrorism Center and the Department of Homeland Security to reach out to Somalis in Europe, Canada, and elsewhere, so that they will have a better and deeper understanding of the risks that violent extremism present to themselves and their families in Somalia.

International CVE Conferences: The Office of the Coordinator for Counterterrorism convened its second conference in June 2010 with international partners to discuss CVE issues, share best practices, and ensure coordinated approaches. A third meeting was hosted by the Netherlands in November.

Victims' Narratives: Victims of terrorism may play an important role in countering violent extremism by presenting powerful stories that delegitimize violent extremist narratives, including false claims by terrorist groups that they do not target innocents.

Capacity Building Programs. As the terrorist threat has evolved and grown more geographically diverse in recent years, it has become clear that our success depends in large part on the effectiveness and ability of our partners. To succeed over the long-term, we must increase the number of countries capable of and willing to take on this challenge. We have had important successes in Indonesia and Colombia, but we must intensify efforts to improve our partners' law enforcement and border security capabilities to tackle these threats. Our current CT capacity building programs – Antiterrorism Assistance, Counterterrorist Financing, Counterterrorism Engagement, TIP/PISCES, and transnational activities under the Regional Strategic Initiatives – are all critically important and work successfully every day to build capacity and improve political will. (For information on the Antiterrorism Assistance (ATA) Program; the Terrorist Interdiction Program/Personal Identification Secure Comparison and Evaluation System Program (TIP/PISCES); the Counterterrorist Finance Program; and the Ambassador's Fund for Counterterrorism; we refer you to the Annual Report on Assistance Related to International Terrorism, Fiscal Year 2010 at http://www.state.gov/s/ct/rls/other/rpt/161418.htm.

The Regional Strategic Initiative. Denying safe haven to terrorists plays a major role in undermining their capacity to operate effectively and forms a key element of U.S. counterterrorism strategy. The State Department's Office of the Coordinator for Counterterrorism has developed the Regional Strategic Initiative (RSI) in key terrorist theaters of operation to collectively assess the threat, pool resources, and devise collaborative strategies, action plans, and policy recommendations. In 2010, RSI groups were in place for South East Asia, Iraq and its neighbors, the Eastern Mediterranean, the Western Mediterranean, East Africa, the Trans-Sahara, South Asia, and Latin America.

INTERNATIONAL CONVENTIONS AND PROTOCOLS

1. **CONVENTION ON OFFENCES AND CERTAIN OTHER ACTS COMMITTED ON BOARD AIRCRAFT**
   Signed in Tokyo on September 14, 1963.
   Convention entered into force on December 4, 1969.
   Status: 185 Parties

2. **CONVENTION FOR THE SUPPRESSION OF UNLAWFUL SEIZURE OF AIRCRAFT**
   Signed in The Hague on December 16, 1970.
   Convention entered into force on October 14, 1971.
   Status: 185 Parties

3. **CONVENTION FOR THE SUPPRESSION OF UNLAWFUL ACTS AGAINST THE SAFETY OF CIVIL AVIATION**
   Signed in Montreal on September 23, 1971.
   Convention entered into force on January 26, 1973.
   Status: 188 Parties

4. **CONVENTION ON THE PREVENTION AND PUNISHMENT OF CRIMES AGAINST INTERNATIONALLY PROTECTED PERSONS, INCLUDING DIPLOMATIC AGENTS**
   Adopted in New York on December 14, 1973.
   Convention entered into force on February 20, 1977.
   Status: 173 Parties

5. **INTERNATIONAL CONVENTION AGAINST THE TAKING OF HOSTAGES**
   Adopted in New York on December 17, 1979.
   Convention entered into force on June 3, 1983.
   Status: 168 Parties

6. **CONVENTION ON THE PHYSICAL PROTECTION OF NUCLEAR MATERIAL**
   Signed in Vienna on October 26, 1979.
   Convention entered into force on February 8, 1987.
   Status: 144 Parties

7. **PROTOCOL FOR THE SUPPRESSION OF UNLAWFUL ACTS OF VIOLENCE AT AIRPORTS SERVING INTERNATIONAL CIVIL AVIATION, SUPPLEMENTARY TO THE CONVENTION FOR THE SUPPRESSION OF UNLAWFUL ACTS AGAINST THE SAFETY OF CIVIL AVIATION**
   Signed in Montreal on February 24, 1988.
   Protocol entered into force on August 6, 1989.
   Status: 171 Parties

8. **CONVENTION FOR THE SUPPRESSION OF UNLAWFUL ACTS AGAINST THE SAFETY OF MARITIME NAVIGATION**
   Done in Rome on March 10, 1988.
   Convention entered into force on March 1, 1992.
   Status: 157 Parties

9. PROTOCOL FOR THE SUPPRESSION OF UNLAWFUL ACTS AGAINST THE SAFETY OF FIXED PLATFORMS LOCATED ON THE CONTINENTAL SHELF

Done in Rome on March 10, 1988.
Protocol entered into force on March 1, 1992.
Status: 146 Parties

10. CONVENTION ON THE MARKING OF PLASTIC EXPLOSIVES FOR THE PURPOSE OF DETECTION

Done in Montreal on March 1, 1991.
Convention entered into force on June 21, 1998.
Status: 147 Parties

11. INTERNATIONAL CONVENTION FOR THE SUPPRESSION OF TERRORIST BOMBINGS

Adopted in New York on December 15, 1997.
Convention entered into force on May 23, 2001.
Status: 164 Parties

12. INTERNATIONAL CONVENTION FOR THE SUPPRESSION OF THE FINANCING OF TERRORISM

Adopted in New York on December 9, 1999.
Convention entered into force on April 10, 2002.
Status: 173 Parties

13. INTERNATIONAL CONVENTION FOR THE SUPPRESSION OF ACTS OF NUCLEAR TERRORISM

Adopted in New York on April 13, 2005.
Convention entered into force on July 7, 2007.
Status: 77 Parties

14. 2005 AMENDMENT TO THE CONVENTION ON THE PHYSICAL PROTECTION OF NUCLEAR MATERIAL

Not yet entered into force
Status: Forty-seven States have deposited instruments of ratification, acceptance or approval with the depositary.

15. PROTOCOL OF 2005 TO THE CONVENTION FOR THE SUPPRESSION OF UNLAWFUL ACTS AGAINST THE SAFETY OF MARITIME NAVIGATION

Not yet entered into force
Status: Ten States have deposited instruments of ratification, acceptance or approval with the depositary.

16. PROTOCOL OF 2005 TO THE PROTOCOL FOR THE SUPPRESSION OF UNLAWFUL ACTS AGAINST THE SAFETY OF FIXED PLATFORMS LOCATED ON THE CONTINENTAL SHELF

Not yet entered into force
Status: Eight States have deposited instruments of ratification, acceptance or approval with the depositary.

Name of the country	1	2	3	4	5	6	7	8	9	10	11	12	13	14	15	16
Afghanistan	15/04/1977	29/08/1979	26/09/1984	24/09/2003	24/09/2003	12/09/2003		23/09/2003	23/09/2003	01/10/2003	24/09/2003	24/09/2003				
Albania	01/12/1997	21/10/1997	21/10/1997	22/01/2002	22/01/2002	05/03/2002	29/04/2002	19/06/2002	19/06/2002	20/10/2004	22/01/2002	10/04/2002				
Algeria	12/10/1995	06/10/1995	06/10/1995	07/11/2000	18/12/1996	30/04/2003	06/11/1995	11/02/1998	30/06/2006	14/11/1996	08/11/2001	08/11/2001	03/03/2011	25/04/2007	25/04/2011	25/04/2011
Andorra	17/05/2006	23/09/2004	22/05/2006	23/09/2004	23/09/2004	27/06/2006	22/05/2006	17/07/2006	17/07/2006	17/05/2006	23/09/2004	22/10/2008				
Angola	24/02/1998	12/03/1998	12/03/1998				16/01/2008									
Antigua and Barbuda	19/07/1985	22/07/1985	22/07/1985	19/07/1993	06/08/1986	04/08/1993	12/07/2010	12/10/2009	12/10/2009	18/03/2011	24/09/2009	11/03/2002	01/12/2009	17/12/2009		
Argentina	23/07/1971	11/09/1972	26/11/1973	18/03/1982	18/09/1991	06/04/1989	12/02/1992	17/08/1993	26/11/2003	08/03/1999	25/09/2003	22/08/2005	22/08/2005			
Armenia	23/01/2003	10/09/2002	10/09/2002	18/05/1994	16/03/2004	24/08/1993	10/09/2002	08/06/2005	08/06/2005	22/07/2005	16/03/2004	16/03/2004	22/09/2010			
Australia	22/06/1970	09/11/1972	12/07/1973	20/06/1977	21/05/1990	22/09/1987	23/10/1990	19/02/1993	19/02/1993	26/06/2007	09/08/2002	26/09/2002	07/06/2007	17/07/2008		
Austria	07/02/1974	11/02/1974	11/02/1974	03/08/1977	22/08/1986	22/12/1988	28/12/1989	28/12/1989	28/12/1989	31/05/1999	06/09/2000	15/04/2002	14/09/2006	18/09/2006	18/06/2010	18/06/2010
Azerbaijan	05/02/2004	03/03/2000	15/03/2000	02/04/2001	29/02/2000	19/01/2004	23/03/2000	26/01/2004	26/01/2004	04/07/2000	02/04/2001	26/10/2001	28/01/2009			
Bahamas	12/06/1975	13/08/1976	27/12/1984	22/07/1986	04/06/1981	21/05/2008	02/05/2008	25/10/2005	25/10/2005	21/05/2008	05/05/2008	01/11/2005	04/05/2010	09/06/2010		
Bahrain	09/02/1984	20/02/1984	20/02/1984	16/09/2005	16/09/2005	10/05/2010	12/02/1996	21/10/2005	21/10/2005	30/01/1996	21/09/2004	21/09/2004				
Bangladesh	25/07/1978	28/06/1978	28/06/1978	20/05/2005	20/05/2005	11/05/2005	27/06/2005	09/06/2005	09/06/2005	16/08/2005	20/05/2005	26/08/2005	07/06/2007			
Barbados	04/04/1972	02/04/1973	06/08/1976	26/10/1979	09/03/1981		12/09/2002	06/05/1994	06/05/1994	12/09/2002	18/09/2002	18/09/2002				
Belarus	03/02/1988	30/12/1971	31/01/1973	05/02/1976	01/07/1987	09/09/1993	01/05/1989	04/12/2002	04/12/2002	06/02/2002	01/10/2001	06/10/2004	13/03/2007			
Belgium	06/08/1970	24/08/1973	13/08/1976	19/05/2004	16/04/1999	06/09/1991	20/04/1999	11/04/2005	11/04/2005	16/04/2007	20/05/2005	17/05/2004	02/10/2009			
Belize	19/05/1998	10/06/1998	10/06/1998	14/11/2001	14/11/2001		10/06/1998				14/11/2001	01/12/2003				
Benin	30/03/2004	13/03/1972	19/04/2004	31/07/2003	31/07/2003		19/04/2004	31/08/2006	31/08/2006	30/03/2004	31/07/2003	30/08/2004				
Bhutan	25/01/1989	28/12/1988	28/12/1988	16/01/1989	31/08/1981		26/08/2005			26/08/2005		22/03/2004				
Bolivia	05/07/1979	18/07/1979	18/07/1979	22/01/2002	07/01/2002	24/01/2002	01/02/2002	13/02/2002	13/02/2002	01/02/2002	22/01/2002	07/01/2002	07/01/2002			
Bosnia and Herzegovina	07/03/1995	15/08/1994	15/08/1994	01/09/1993	01/09/1993	30/06/1998	15/08/1994	28/07/2003	28/07/2003	03/05/2004	11/08/2003	10/06/2003		21/06/2010		
Botswana	16/01/1979	28/12/1978	28/12/1978	25/10/2000	08/09/2000	19/09/2000	30/10/2000	14/09/2000	14/09/2000	19/09/2000	08/09/2000	08/09/2000				
Brazil	14/01/1970	14/01/1972	24/07/1972	07/06/1999	08/03/2000	17/10/1995	09/05/1997	25/10/2005	25/10/2005	04/10/2001	23/08/2002	16/09/2005	25/09/2009			
Brunei Darussalam	04/10/1989	20/10/1977	16/04/1986	13/11/1997	18/10/1988	23/02/2007	20/12/2000	08/12/2003	08/12/2003	09/07/2009	14/03/2002	04/12/2002				
Bulgaria	11/06/1991	01/07/1991	01/07/1991	18/07/1974	10/03/1988	10/04/1984	26/03/1991	08/07/1999	08/07/1999	08/09/1999	12/02/2002	15/04/2002	19/02/2008	17/03/2006	07/10/2010	07/10/2010
Burkina Faso	06/06/1969	19/10/1987	19/10/1987	01/10/2003	01/10/2003	13/01/2004	08/12/1998	15/01/2004	15/01/2004	07/07/2004	01/10/2003	01/10/2003				
Burundi	14/07/1971		11/02/1999	17/12/1980									24/09/2008			
Cambodia	22/10/1996	08/11/1996	08/11/1996	27/07/2006	27/07/2006	04/08/2006	08/11/1996	18/08/2006	18/08/2006		31/07/2006	12/12/2005				
Cameroon	24/03/1988	14/04/1988	11/07/1973	08/06/1992	09/03/1988	29/06/2004	13/03/2003			03/06/1998	21/03/2005	06/02/2006				
Canada	07/11/1969	20/06/1972	19/06/1972	04/08/1976	04/12/1985	21/03/1986	02/08/1993	18/06/1993	18/06/1993	29/11/1996	03/04/2002	19/02/2002				
Cape Verde	04/10/1989	20/10/1977	20/10/1977	10/09/2002	10/09/2002	23/02/2007	12/09/2002	03/01/2003	03/01/2003	04/11/2002	10/05/2002	10/05/2002	12/03/2007			
Central African Republic	11/06/1991	01/07/1991	01/07/1991	19/02/2008	09/07/2007	20/02/2008	01/07/1991				19/02/2008	19/02/2008	19/02/2008		07/10/2010	
Chad	30/06/1970	12/07/1972	12/07/1972		01/11/2006											
Chile	24/01/1974	02/02/1972	28/02/1974	21/01/1977	12/11/1981	27/04/1994	15/08/1989	22/04/1994	22/04/1994	02/08/2000	10/11/2001	10/11/2001	27/09/2010	12/03/2009		
China	14/11/1978	10/09/1980	10/09/1980	05/08/1987	26/01/1993	10/01/1989	05/03/1999	20/08/1991	20/08/1991		13/11/2001	19/04/2006	08/11/2010	14/09/2009		
Colombia	06/07/1973	03/07/1973	04/12/1974	16/01/1996	14/04/2005	28/03/2003	14/01/2004				14/09/2004	14/09/2004				
Comoros	23/05/1991	01/08/1991	25/09/2003	25/09/2003	25/09/2003	18/05/2007	10/03/2008	06/03/2008	06/03/2008		25/09/2003	25/09/2003	12/03/2007			
Congo	13/11/1978	24/11/1989	19/03/1987													
Congo (Democratic Republic of the)	20/07/1977	06/07/1977	06/07/1977	25/07/1977		21/09/2004							23/09/2010			

Name of the country	1	2	3	4	5	6	7	8	9	10	11	12	13	14	15	16
Cook Islands	12/04/2005	14/04/2005	14/04/2005				14/04/2005	12/03/2007	25/03/2003			04/03/2004			12/03/2007	
Costa Rica	24/10/1972	09/07/1971	21/09/1973	02/11/1977	24/01/2003	02/05/2003	22/04/2003	25/03/2003	25/03/2003	12/07/2005	20/09/2001	24/01/2003				
Côte d'Ivoire	03/06/1970	09/01/1973	09/01/1973	13/03/2002	22/08/1989						13/03/2002	13/03/2002	13/03/2002			
Croatia	05/10/1993	08/06/1993	08/06/1993	12/10/1992	23/09/2003	29/09/1992	08/06/1993	18/08/2005	18/08/2005	24/02/2005	02/06/2005	01/12/2003	30/05/2007	11/09/2006		
Cuba	12/02/2001	27/11/2001	31/10/2001	10/06/1998	15/11/2001	26/09/1997	31/10/2001	20/11/2001	20/11/2001	30/11/2001	15/11/2001	15/11/2001	17/06/2009			
Cyprus	31/05/1972	05/07/1972	27/07/1973	24/12/1975	13/09/1991	23/07/1998	23/04/2002	02/02/2000	02/02/2000	20/09/2002	24/01/2001	30/11/2001	28/01/2008			
Czech Republic	25/03/1993	14/11/1994	14/11/1994	22/02/1993	22/02/1993	24/03/1993	25/03/1993	10/12/2004	10/12/2004	25/03/1993	06/09/2000	27/12/2005	25/07/2006	30/12/2010		
Denmark	17/01/1967	17/10/1972	17/01/1973	01/07/1975	11/08/1987	06/09/1991	23/11/1989	23/08/1995	23/08/1995	05/10/1998	31/08/2001	27/08/2002	20/03/2007			
Djibouti	10/06/1992	24/11/1992	24/11/1992	01/06/2004	01/06/2004	22/06/2004	11/06/2004	09/06/2004	09/06/2004	11/06/2004	01/06/2004	13/03/2006		19/05/2010		
Dominica		26/07/2005	26/07/2005	24/09/2004	09/09/1986	08/11/2004	26/07/2005	31/08/2001	12/10/2004		24/09/2004	24/09/2004				
Dominican Republic	03/12/1970	22/06/1978	28/11/1973	08/07/1977	03/10/2007	30/04/2009		03/07/2008	12/08/2009	09/05/2011	21/10/2008	04/09/2008	11/06/2008		09/03/2010	09/03/2010
Ecuador	03/12/1969	14/06/1971	12/01/1977	12/03/1975	02/05/1988	17/01/1996	04/03/2004	10/03/2003	10/03/2003	15/12/1995		09/12/2003				
Egypt	12/02/1975	28/02/1975	20/05/1975	25/06/1986	02/10/1981		25/07/2000	08/01/1993	08/01/1993	19/07/1993	09/08/2005	01/03/2005				
El Salvador	13/02/1980	16/01/1973	25/09/1979	08/08/1980	12/02/1981	15/12/2006	08/04/1996	07/12/2000	07/12/2000	18/02/2000	15/05/2003	15/05/2003	27/11/2006			
Equatorial Guinea	27/02/1991	02/01/1991	02/01/1991	07/02/2003	07/02/2003	24/11/2003	14/01/2004	14/01/2004	14/01/2004	14/01/2004	07/02/2003	07/02/2003				
Eritrea										01/12/1994						
Estonia	31/12/1993	22/12/1993	22/12/1993	21/10/1991	08/03/2002	09/05/1994	22/12/1993	15/02/2002	28/01/2004	05/03/1996	10/04/2002	22/05/2002		24/02/2009	16/05/2008	16/05/2008
Ethiopia	27/03/1979	26/03/1979	26/03/1979	16/04/2003	16/04/2003	06/09/1991	15/12/1999	06/11/1990	06/11/1990	16/04/2003	16/04/2003					
Fiji	31/01/1972	27/07/1972	05/03/1973	15/05/2008	15/05/2008	23/05/2008	21/09/1992	21/05/2008	21/05/2008	11/07/2008	15/05/2008	15/05/2008	15/05/2008	22/06/2008	21/05/2008	21/05/2008
Finland	02/04/1971	15/12/1971	13/07/1973	31/10/1978	14/04/1983	22/09/1989	03/04/1998	12/11/1998	28/04/2000	05/12/2001	28/05/2002	28/06/2002	13/01/2009			
France	11/09/1970	18/09/1972	30/06/1976	26/08/2003	09/06/2000	06/09/1991	06/09/1989	02/12/1991	02/12/1991	21/05/1997	19/08/1999	07/01/2002				
Gabon	14/01/1970	14/07/1971	29/06/1976	14/10/1981	19/04/2005	19/02/2008	13/08/2003				10/03/2005	10/03/2005	01/10/2007	20/03/2008		
Gambia	04/01/1979	28/11/1978	28/11/1978				16/06/2000	01/11/1991		20/06/2000						
Georgia	16/06/1994	20/04/1994	20/04/1994	18/02/2004	18/02/2004	07/09/2006	15/02/1999	11/08/2006	11/08/2006	25/04/2000	18/02/2004	27/09/2002	23/04/2010			
Germany	16/12/1969	11/10/1974	03/02/1978	25/01/1977	15/12/1980	06/09/1991	25/04/1994	06/11/1990	06/11/1990	17/12/1998	23/04/2003	17/06/2004	08/02/2008	21/10/2010		
Ghana	02/01/1974	12/12/1973	12/12/1973	25/04/1975	10/11/1987	16/10/2002	15/07/1997	01/11/2002	01/11/2002	22/04/1998	06/09/2002	06/09/2002	13/01/2009			
Greece	31/05/1971	20/09/1973	15/01/1974	03/07/1984	18/06/1987	06/09/1991	25/04/1991	11/06/1993	11/06/1993	30/10/1995	27/05/2003	16/04/2004				
Grenada	28/08/1978	10/08/1978	10/08/1978	13/12/2001	10/12/1990	09/01/2002	15/01/2002	09/01/2002	09/01/2002	15/01/2002	13/12/2001	13/12/2001				
Guatemala	17/11/1970	16/05/1979	19/10/1978	18/01/1983	11/03/1983	23/04/1985	11/10/1994	26/08/2009	26/08/2009	26/11/1997	12/02/2002	12/02/2002	12/02/2002			
Guinea	18/01/1994	02/05/1984	02/05/1984	22/12/2004	22/12/2004	29/11/2005	01/10/1998	01/02/2005	01/02/2005	23/01/2004	07/09/2000	14/07/2003				
Guinea-Bissau	17/10/2008	20/08/1976	20/08/1976	06/08/2008	06/08/2008	08/10/2008	17/10/2008	14/10/2008	14/10/2008	08/10/2008	06/08/2008	19/09/2008	06/08/2008			
Guyana	20/12/1972	21/12/1972	21/12/1972	12/09/2007	12/09/2007	13/09/2007	19/06/2002	02/01/2003	02/01/2003	13/12/2007	12/09/2007	12/09/2007				
Haiti	26/04/1984	09/05/1984	09/05/1984	25/08/1980	17/05/1989											
Holy See												13/01/2010				
Honduras	08/04/1987	13/04/1987	13/04/1987	29/01/2003	01/06/1981	28/01/2004	20/01/2004	17/05/2005	17/05/2005	18/02/2004	25/03/2003	25/03/2003				
Hungary	03/12/1970	13/08/1971	27/12/1972	26/03/1975	02/09/1987	04/05/1984	07/09/1988	09/11/1989	09/11/1989	11/01/1994	13/11/2001	14/10/2002	12/04/2007	04/12/2008		
Iceland	16/03/1970	29/06/1973	29/06/1973	02/08/1977	06/07/1981	18/06/2002	09/05/1990	28/05/2002	28/05/2002	24/05/2002	15/04/2002	15/04/2002				
India	22/07/1975	12/11/1982	12/11/1982	11/04/1978	07/09/1994	12/03/2002	22/03/1995	15/10/1999	15/10/1999	16/11/1999	22/09/1999	22/04/2003	01/12/2006	19/09/2007		
Indonesia	07/09/1976	27/08/1976	27/08/1976			05/11/1986					29/06/2006	29/06/2006				
Iran (Islamic Republic of)	28/06/1976	25/01/1972	10/07/1973	12/07/1978	20/11/2006		14/02/2002	12/10/2009	30/10/2009					27/05/2010		
Iraq	15/05/1974	03/12/1971	10/09/1974	28/02/1978			31/01/1990									
Ireland	14/11/1975	24/11/1975	12/10/1976	30/06/2005	30/06/2005	06/09/1991	26/07/1991	10/09/2004	10/09/2004	15/07/2003	30/06/2005	30/06/2005				
Israel	19/09/1969	16/08/1971	30/06/1972	31/07/1980		22/01/2002	02/04/1993	06/01/2009	06/01/2009		10/02/2003	10/02/2003				

Name of the country	1	2	3	4	5	6	7	8	9	10	11	12	13	14	15	16
Italy	18/10/1968	19/02/1974	19/02/1974	30/08/1985	20/03/1986	06/09/1991	13/03/1990	26/01/1990	26/01/1990	26/09/2002	16/04/2003	27/03/2003				
Jamaica	16/09/1983	15/09/1983	15/09/1983	21/09/1978	09/08/2005	16/08/2005	18/08/2005	17/08/2005	19/08/2005	18/08/2005	09/08/2005	16/09/2005				
Japan	26/05/1970	19/04/1971	12/06/1974	08/06/1987	08/06/1987	28/10/1988	24/04/1998	24/04/1998	24/04/1998	26/09/1997	16/11/2001	11/06/2002	03/08/2007			
Jordan	03/05/1973	18/11/1971	13/02/1973	18/12/1984	19/02/1986	07/09/2009	18/09/1992	02/07/2004	02/07/2004	23/05/1996		28/08/2003		07/10/2009		
Kazakhstan	18/05/1995	04/04/1995	04/04/1995	21/02/1996	21/02/1996	02/09/2005	18/05/1995	24/11/2003	24/11/2003	18/05/1995	06/11/2002	24/02/2003	31/07/2008	26/04/2011		
Kenya	22/06/1970	11/01/1977	11/01/1977	16/11/2001	08/12/1981	11/02/2002	05/10/1995	21/01/2002	21/01/2002	22/10/2002	16/11/2001	27/06/2003	13/04/2006	01/08/2007		
Kiribati				15/09/2005	15/09/2005		19/07/1995	17/11/2005	17/11/2005		15/09/2005	15/09/2005	26/09/2008			
Korea (Democratic People's Republic of)	09/05/1983	28/04/1983	13/08/1980	01/12/1982	12/11/2001		19/07/1995									
Korea (Republic of)	19/02/1971	18/01/1973	02/08/1973	25/05/1983	04/05/1983	07/04/1982	27/06/1990	14/05/2003	10/06/2003	02/01/2002	17/02/2004	17/02/2004				
Kuwait	27/11/1979	25/05/1979	23/11/1979	01/03/1989	06/02/1989	23/04/2004	08/03/1989	30/06/2003	30/06/2003	18/03/1996	19/04/2004					
Kyrgyzstan	28/02/2000	25/02/2000	25/02/2000	02/10/2003	02/10/2003		28/02/2000			14/07/2000	01/05/2001	02/10/2003	02/10/2007			
Lao People's Democratic Republic	23/10/1972	06/04/1989	06/04/1989	22/08/2002	22/08/2002	29/09/2010	07/10/2002				22/08/2002	29/09/2008				
Latvia	10/06/1997	23/10/1998	13/04/1997	14/04/1992	14/11/2002	06/11/2002	13/04/1997	04/12/2002	04/12/2002	17/08/1999	25/11/2002	14/11/2002	25/07/2006	23/11/2010	16/11/2009	16/11/2009
Lebanon	11/06/1974	10/08/1973	23/12/1977	03/06/1997	04/12/1997	16/12/1997	27/05/1996	16/12/1994	16/12/1994	26/11/1997			13/11/2006			
Lesotho	28/04/1972	27/07/1978	27/07/1978	06/11/2003	05/11/1980	18/08/2010	08/06/2010			10/11/2009	12/11/2001	12/11/2001	22/09/2010			
Liberia	10/03/2003	01/02/1982	01/02/1982	30/09/1975	05/03/2003		10/03/2003	05/10/1995	05/10/1995		05/03/2003	05/03/2003				
Libyan Arab Jamahiriya	21/06/1972	04/10/1978	19/02/1974	25/09/2000	25/09/2000	18/10/2000	26/07/1996	08/08/2002	08/08/2002	10/10/2002	22/09/2000	09/07/2002	22/12/2008	19/07/2006		
Liechtenstein	26/02/2001	23/02/2001	23/02/2001	28/11/1994	28/11/1994	25/11/1986	26/02/2001	08/11/2002	08/11/2002	04/12/2002	26/11/2002	09/07/2003	25/09/2009	13/10/2009	28/08/2009	28/08/2009
Lithuania	21/11/1996	04/12/1996	04/12/1996	23/10/2002	02/02/2001	07/12/1993	04/12/1996	30/01/2003	30/01/2003	21/11/1996	17/03/2004	20/02/2003	19/07/2007	19/05/2009		
Luxembourg	21/09/1972	22/11/1978	18/05/1982	10/05/2006	29/04/1991	06/09/1991	14/11/2003	05/04/2011	05/04/2011	06/11/2006	06/02/2004	05/11/2003	02/10/2008			
Macedonia (The former Yugoslav Republic of)	30/08/1994	07/01/1998	04/01/1995	12/03/1998	12/03/1998	20/09/1996	04/01/1995	07/08/2007	07/08/2007	21/09/1998	30/08/2004	30/08/2004	19/03/2007			
Madagascar	02/12/1969	18/11/1986	18/11/1986	24/09/2003	24/09/2003	28/10/2003	30/03/1998	15/09/2006	15/09/2006	23/12/2003	24/09/2003	24/09/2003				
Malawi	28/12/1972	21/12/1972	21/12/1972	14/03/1977	17/03/1986						11/08/2003	11/09/2003	07/10/2009			
Malaysia	05/03/1985	04/05/1985	04/05/1985	24/09/2003	29/05/2007		08/09/2006			27/11/2007	24/09/2003	29/06/2007	29/06/2007			
Maldives	28/09/1987	01/09/1987	01/09/1987	21/08/1990			22/03/1999			22/03/1999	07/09/2000	20/04/2004	20/04/2004			
Mali	31/05/1971	29/09/1971	24/08/1972	12/04/2002	08/02/1990	07/05/2002	31/10/1990	29/04/2002	29/04/2002	28/09/2000	28/03/2002	28/03/2002	05/11/2009	27/01/2010		
Malta	28/06/1991	14/06/1991	14/06/1991	11/11/2001	11/11/2001	16/10/2003	14/06/1991	20/11/2001	20/11/2001	15/11/1994	11/11/2001	11/11/2001				
Marshall Islands	15/05/1989	31/05/1989	31/05/1989	27/01/2003	27/01/2003	07/02/2003	30/05/1989	29/11/1994	16/10/1995	06/02/2003	27/01/2003	27/01/2003	27/01/2003		09/05/2008	09/05/2008
Mauritania	30/06/1977	01/11/1978	01/11/1978	09/02/1998	13/03/1998	29/01/2008	08/07/2003	17/01/2008	17/01/2008	24/05/2011	30/04/2003	30/04/2003	28/04/2008	28/02/2008		
Mauritius	05/04/1963	25/04/1983	25/04/1983	24/09/2003	17/10/1980		17/08/1989	03/08/2004	03/08/2004	24/01/2003	24/01/2003	14/12/2004	14/12/2004			
Mexico	18/03/1969	19/07/1972	12/09/1974	22/04/1980	28/04/1987	04/04/1988	11/10/1990	13/05/1994	13/05/1994	09/04/1992	20/01/2003	20/01/2003	27/06/2006			
Micronesia (Federated States of)			19/03/2003	06/07/2004	06/07/2004		19/03/2003	10/02/2003			23/09/2002	23/09/2002				
Moldova (Republic of)	20/06/1997	21/05/1997	21/05/1997	08/09/1997	10/10/2002	07/05/1998	20/06/1997	12/10/2005	12/10/2005	01/12/1997	10/10/2002	10/10/2002	18/04/2008	22/12/2008		
Monaco	02/06/1983	03/06/1983	03/06/1983	27/11/2002	16/10/2001	09/08/1996	22/12/1993	25/01/2002	25/01/2002	14/05/1998	06/09/2001	10/11/2001				
Mongolia	24/07/1990	08/10/1971	14/09/1972	08/08/1975	09/06/1992	28/05/1986	22/09/1999	22/11/2005	22/11/2005	22/09/1999	07/09/2000	25/02/2004	06/10/2006			
Montenegro	20/12/2007	20/12/2006	20/12/2006	23/10/2006	23/10/2006	21/03/2007	20/12/2006	03/06/2006	03/06/2006		23/10/2006	23/10/2006	23/10/2006			
Morocco	21/10/1975	24/10/1975	24/10/1975	09/01/2002	09/05/2007	23/08/2002	15/02/2002	08/01/2002	08/01/2002	26/05/1999	09/05/2007	19/09/2002	31/03/2010			
Mozambique	06/01/2003	16/01/2003	16/01/2003	14/01/2003	14/01/2003	03/03/2003	16/01/2003	08/01/2003	08/01/2003	15/03/2006	14/01/2003	14/01/2003				
Myanmar	23/05/1996	22/05/1996	22/05/1996	04/06/2004	04/06/2004		22/05/1996	19/09/2003	19/09/2003	01/09/2004	12/11/2001	16/06/2006				

Name of the country	1	2	3	4	5	6	7	8	9	10	11	12	13	14	15	16
Namibia	19/12/2005	04/11/2005	04/11/2005			02/10/2002	04/11/2005	20/07/2004	07/09/2005							
Nauru	17/05/1984	17/05/1984	17/05/1984	02/08/2005	02/08/2005	12/08/2005	19/08/2005	11/08/2005	11/08/2005	03/04/2006	02/08/2005	24/05/2005	24/08/2010	14/06/2010	29/04/2010	29/04/2008
Nepal	15/01/1979	11/01/1979	11/01/1979	09/03/1990	09/03/1990											
Netherlands	14/11/1969	27/08/1973	27/08/1973	06/12/1988	06/12/1988	06/09/1991	11/07/1995	05/03/1992	05/03/1992	04/05/1998	07/02/2002	07/02/2002	30/06/2010			
New Zealand	12/02/1974	12/02/1974	12/02/1974	12/11/1985	12/11/1985	19/12/2003	02/08/1999	10/06/1999	10/06/1999	19/12/2003	04/11/2002	04/11/2002			30/05/2011	
Nicaragua	24/08/1973	06/11/1973	06/11/1973	10/03/1975	24/09/2003	10/12/2004	25/04/2002	04/07/2007	04/07/2007	10/01/2006	17/01/2003	14/11/2002	25/02/2009			
Niger	27/06/1969	15/10/1971	01/09/1972	17/06/1985	26/10/2004	19/08/2004	23/12/2008	30/08/2006	30/08/2006	06/03/2009	26/10/2004	30/09/2004	02/07/2008	28/05/2009		
Nigeria	07/04/1970	03/07/1973	03/07/1973			04/04/2007	25/03/2003	24/02/2004	10/05/2002	10/05/2002	16/06/2003	16/06/2003	30/09/2004	04/05/2007		
Niue	23/06/2009	30/09/2009	30/09/2009	22/06/2009	22/06/2009	19/06/2009	30/09/2009	22/06/2009	22/06/2009	01/12/2009	22/06/2009	22/06/2009		20/08/2009		
Norway	17/01/1967	23/08/1971	01/08/1973	28/04/1980	02/07/1981	15/08/1985	29/05/1990	18/04/1991	18/04/1991	09/07/1992	20/09/1999	15/07/2002				
Oman	09/02/1977	02/02/1977	02/02/1977	22/03/1988	22/07/1988	11/06/2003	27/11/1992	24/09/1990	24/09/1990	13/12/2001						
Pakistan	11/09/1973	28/11/1973	24/01/1974	29/03/1976	08/09/2000	12/09/2000	26/09/2000	20/09/2000	20/09/2000		13/08/2002	17/06/2009				
Palau	12/10/1995	03/08/1995	03/08/1995	14/11/2001	14/11/2001	24/04/2007	12/10/1995	04/12/2001	04/12/2001	30/11/2001	14/11/2001	14/11/2001				
Panama	16/11/1970	10/03/1972	24/04/1972	17/06/1980	19/08/1982	01/04/1999	10/04/1996	03/07/2002	03/07/2002	12/04/1996	05/03/1999	03/07/2002	21/06/2007		25/05/2011	25/05/2011
Papua New Guinea	15/12/1975	15/12/1975	15/12/1975	30/09/2003	30/09/2003		11/07/2002				30/09/2003	30/09/2003				
Paraguay	09/08/1971	04/02/1972	05/03/1974	24/11/1975	22/09/2004	06/02/1985	23/07/2002	12/11/2004	12/11/2004	15/10/2004	22/09/2004	30/11/2004	29/01/2009			
Peru	12/05/1978	28/04/1978	28/04/1978	25/04/1978	06/07/2001	11/01/1995	07/06/1989	19/07/2001	19/07/2001	07/02/1996	10/11/2001	10/11/2001	29/05/2009			
Philippines	26/11/1965	26/03/1973	26/03/1973	26/11/1976	14/10/1980	22/09/1981	17/12/2003	06/01/2004	06/01/2004	17/12/2003	07/01/2004	07/01/2004				
Poland	19/03/1971	21/03/1972	28/01/1975	14/12/1982	25/05/2000	05/10/1983	12/08/2004	25/06/1991	25/06/1991	26/09/2006	03/02/2004	26/09/2003	08/04/2010	01/06/2007		
Portugal	25/11/1964	27/11/1972	15/01/1973	11/09/1995	06/07/1984	06/09/1991	18/12/2001	05/01/1996	05/01/1996	09/10/2002	10/11/2001	18/10/2002		26/11/2010		
Qatar	06/08/1981	26/08/1981	26/08/1981	03/03/1997		09/03/2004	17/06/2003	18/09/2003	18/09/2003	09/11/1998	27/06/2008	27/06/2008				
Romania	15/02/1974	10/07/1972	15/08/1975	15/08/1978	17/05/1990	23/11/1993	03/09/1998	02/06/1993	02/06/1993	21/09/1998	29/07/2004	09/01/2003	24/01/2007	06/02/2007		
Russian Federation	03/02/1988	24/09/1971	19/02/1973	15/01/1976	11/06/1987	25/05/1983	31/03/1989	04/05/2001	04/05/2001	19/09/2007	08/05/2001	27/11/2002	20/01/2007	19/09/2008		
Rwanda	17/05/1971	03/11/1987	03/11/1987	29/11/1977	13/05/2002	28/06/2002	16/05/2002				13/05/2002	13/05/2002				
Saint Kitts and Nevis		03/09/2008	10/09/2008	28/07/2008	17/01/1991	29/08/2008	03/09/2008	17/01/2002		09/05/2002	16/11/2001	16/11/2001			29/03/2007	05/07/2010
Saint Lucia	31/10/1983	08/11/1983	08/11/1983				11/06/1990	20/05/2004	20/05/2004							
Saint Vincent and the	18/11/1991	29/11/1991	29/11/1991	12/09/2000	12/09/2000		29/11/1991	09/10/2001	09/10/2001	14/07/2010	15/09/2005	28/03/2002	08/07/2010		05/07/2010	
Grenadines																
Samoa	09/07/1998	09/07/1998	09/07/1998			09/07/1998	18/05/2004			09/07/1998		27/09/2002				
San Marino											12/03/2002	12/03/2002				
Sao Tome and Principe	04/05/2006	08/05/2006	08/05/2006	12/04/2006	23/08/2006		08/05/2006	05/05/2006	05/05/2006		12/04/2006	12/04/2006				
Saudi Arabia	21/11/1969	14/06/1974	14/06/1974	01/03/2004	08/01/1991	07/01/2009	21/02/1989	02/02/2006	02/02/2006	11/07/1996	31/10/2007	23/08/2007	11/07/1996	21/01/2011		
Senegal	09/03/1972	03/02/1978	03/02/1978	07/04/2006	10/03/1987	03/11/2003	24/03/2003	09/08/2004	08/08/2004	11/02/2004	27/10/2003	24/09/2004				
Serbia	06/09/2001	23/07/2001	23/07/2001	12/03/2001	12/03/2001	27/04/2002	06/09/2001	03/06/2005	03/06/2006	22/06/2006	31/07/2003	10/10/2002	26/09/2006		08/07/2010	
Seychelles	04/01/1979	29/12/1978	29/12/1978	29/05/1980	12/11/2003	13/08/2003	21/05/2004	24/01/1989	24/01/1989	14/08/2003	22/08/2003	30/03/2004	30/03/2004	09/01/2006		
Sierra Leone	09/11/1970	13/11/1974	20/09/1979	26/09/2003	26/09/2003						26/09/2003	26/09/2003				
Singapore	01/03/1971	12/04/1978	12/04/1978	02/05/2008	22/10/2010		22/11/1996			20/01/2003	31/12/2007	30/12/2002				
Slovakia	20/03/1995	13/12/1995	06/03/1995	28/05/1993	28/05/1993	10/02/1993	20/03/1995	08/12/2000	08/12/2000	20/03/1995	08/12/2000	13/09/2002	23/03/2006			
Slovenia	18/12/1992	27/05/1992	27/05/1992	06/07/1992	06/07/1992	07/07/1992	27/05/1992	18/07/2003	18/07/2003	05/06/2000	25/09/2003	23/09/2004	17/12/2009	01/09/2009		
Solomon Islands	23/03/1982	13/04/1982	13/04/1982								24/09/2009	24/09/2004	24/09/2009			
Somalia																
South Africa	26/05/1972	30/05/1972	30/05/1972	23/09/2003	23/09/2003	17/09/2007	21/09/1998	08/07/2005	08/07/2005	01/12/1999	01/05/2003	01/05/2003	09/05/2007			

Name of the country	1	2	3	4	5	6	7	8	9	10	11	12	13	14	15	16
Spain	01/10/1969	30/10/1972	30/10/1972	08/08/1985	26/03/1984	06/09/1991	08/05/1991	07/07/1989	07/07/1989	31/05/1994	30/04/1999	09/04/2002	22/02/2007	09/11/2007	16/04/2008	16/04/2008
Sri Lanka	30/05/1978	30/05/1978	30/05/1978	27/02/1991	03/09/2000		11/02/1997	04/09/2000		11/10/2001	23/03/1999	08/09/2000	27/09/2007			
Sudan	25/05/2000	18/01/1979	18/01/1979	10/10/1994	19/06/1990	18/05/2000	15/05/2000	22/05/2000	22/05/2000	25/05/2000	08/09/2000	05/05/2003				
Suriname	10/09/1979	27/10/1978	27/10/1978		05/11/1981		27/03/2003			27/03/2003						
Swaziland	15/11/1999	27/12/1999	27/12/1999	04/04/2003	04/04/2003	17/04/2003		17/04/2003	17/04/2003	13/05/2003	04/04/2003	04/04/2003				
Sweden	17/01/1967	07/07/1971	10/07/1973	01/07/1975	15/01/1981	01/08/1980	26/07/1990	13/09/1990	13/09/1990	05/04/2007	06/09/2001	06/06/2002				
Switzerland	21/12/1970	14/09/1971	17/01/1978	05/03/1985	05/03/1985	09/01/1987	09/10/1990	12/03/1993	12/03/1993	03/04/1995	23/09/2003	23/09/2003	15/10/2008	15/10/2008	15/10/2008	15/10/2008
Syrian Arab Republic	31/07/1980	10/07/1980	10/07/1980	25/04/1988			18/07/2002	24/03/2003	24/03/2003	29/09/2004		24/04/2005				
Tajikistan	20/03/1996	29/02/1996	29/02/1996	19/10/2001	06/05/2002	11/07/1996	29/02/1996	12/08/2005	12/08/2005	18/07/2006	29/07/2002	16/07/2004				
Thailand	06/03/1972	16/05/1978	16/05/1978	23/02/2007	02/10/2007		14/05/1996			25/01/2006	12/06/2007	29/09/2004				
Timor-Leste								02/12/2005								
Togo	26/07/1971	09/02/1979	09/02/1979	30/12/1980	25/07/1986	07/06/2006	09/02/1990	10/03/2003	10/03/2003	22/07/2003	10/03/2003	10/03/2003				
Tonga	13/02/2002	21/02/1977	21/02/1977	09/12/2002	09/12/2002	24/01/2003	10/12/2002	06/12/2002	06/12/2002	10/12/2002	09/12/2002	09/12/2002				
Trinidad and Tobago	09/02/1972	31/01/1972	09/02/1972	15/06/1979	01/04/1981	25/04/2001	03/04/2001	27/07/1989	27/07/1989	03/04/2001	02/04/2001	23/09/2009				
Tunisia	25/02/1975	16/11/1981	16/11/1981	21/01/1977	18/06/1997	08/04/1993	07/06/1994	06/03/1998	06/03/1998	28/05/1997	22/04/2005	10/06/2003	28/09/2010	07/06/2010		
Turkey	17/12/1975	17/04/1973	23/12/1975	11/06/1981	15/08/1989	27/02/1985	07/07/1989	06/03/1998	06/03/1998	14/12/1994	30/05/2002	28/06/2002			19/07/2010	
Turkmenistan	30/06/1999	25/05/1999	25/05/1999	25/06/1999	25/06/1999	07/01/2005	25/05/1999	08/06/1999	08/06/1999	14/01/2005	25/06/1999	07/01/2005	28/03/2008	22/09/2005		
Tuvalu																
Uganda	25/06/1982	27/03/1972	19/07/1982	05/11/2003	05/11/2003	10/12/2003	17/03/1994	11/11/2003		02/07/2004	05/11/2003	05/11/2003				
Ukraine	29/02/1988	21/02/1972	26/01/1973	20/01/1976	19/06/1987	06/07/1993	03/01/1990	21/04/1994	21/04/1994	18/03/1999	26/03/2002	06/12/2002	25/09/2007	24/12/2008		
United Arab Emirates	16/04/1981	10/04/1981	10/04/1981	25/02/2003	24/09/2003	16/10/2003	09/03/1989	15/09/2005	15/09/2005	21/12/1992	23/09/2005	23/09/2005	10/01/2008	31/07/2009		
United Kingdom	29/11/1968	22/12/1971	25/10/1973	02/05/1979	22/12/1982	06/09/1991	15/11/1990	03/05/1991	03/05/1991	28/04/1997	07/03/2001	07/03/2001	24/09/2009	08/04/2010		
United Republic of Tanzania	12/08/1983	09/08/1983	09/08/1983		22/01/2003	24/05/2006	09/03/2004	11/05/2005	18/02/1999	11/02/2003	22/01/2003	22/01/2003				
United States of America	05/09/1969	14/09/1971	01/11/1972	26/10/1976	07/12/1984	13/12/1982	19/10/1994	06/12/1994	06/12/1994	09/04/1997	26/06/2002	26/06/2002				
Uruguay	26/01/1977	12/01/1977	12/01/1977	13/06/1978	04/03/2003	24/10/2003	03/12/1998	10/08/2001	10/08/2001	14/06/2001	10/11/2001	08/01/2004				
Uzbekistan	31/07/1995	07/02/1994	07/02/1994	19/01/1998	19/01/1998	09/02/1998	07/02/1994	25/09/2000	25/09/2000	09/06/1999	30/11/1998	09/07/2001	29/04/2008			
Vanuatu	31/01/1989	22/02/1989	06/11/1989				09/11/2005			25/01/2006		31/10/2005			20/08/2008	20/08/2008
Venezuela (Bolivarian Republic of)	04/02/1983	07/07/1983	21/11/1983	19/04/2005	13/12/1988						23/09/2003	23/09/2003				
Viet Nam	10/10/1979	17/09/1979	17/09/1979	02/05/2002			25/08/1999	12/07/2002	12/07/2002			25/09/2002				
Yemen	26/09/1986	29/09/1986	29/09/1986	09/02/1987	14/07/2000	30/06/2000	05/01/2007	30/06/2000	30/06/2000	04/07/2007	23/04/2001	03/03/2010				
Zambia	14/09/1971	03/03/1987	03/03/1987							31/05/1995						
Zimbabwe	08/03/1989	06/02/1989	06/02/1989													

2. SUPPORT TO PAKISTAN

We refer you to http://www.state.gov/s/special_rep_afghanistan_pakistan/133902.htm for the Pakistan Country Assistance Strategy.

3. COUNTERTERRORISM COORDINATION WITH SAUDI ARABIA

The United States and Saudi Arabia have a strong bilateral relationship. Multiple high-level visits in 2010 deepened this relationship at the personal and institutional level and enabled senior officials from both countries the chance to discuss means of improving coordination. Secretaries Clinton, Gates, Napolitano, and Chu each visited Saudi Arabia in 2010, meeting with King Abdullah and other Saudi leaders. From the Saudi side, King Abdullah visited President Obama in Washington in June 2010. These visits also allowed leaders and senior officials to communicate to the people of both countries the importance and focal points of the relationship.

Intelligence and security cooperation in the fight against terrorism is a pillar of our bilateral relationship. We continued to enjoy strong coordination with our Saudi partners on these issues through regular high-level discussions and close working-level collaboration. Symbolic of this coordination was the assistance Saudi authorities provided in relation to the attempt by al-Qa'ida in the Arabian Peninsula terrorists to carry out an attack using package bombs in October. The major arms sale of F-15s and helicopters notified to Congress in October also illustrated our commitment to supporting Saudi Arabia's legitimate security needs, including the fight against terrorism.

Saudi Arabia made progress in its campaign to counter extremist ideology in Saudi Arabia and internationally. Examples of progress include a historic fatwa issued by Saudi Arabia's Council of Senior Scholars (the country's highest religious body) and endorsed by King Abdullah criminalizing terrorist acts and the financing, aiding, or abetting of terrorists; the removal from the classroom of over 2,000 teachers over the past two years for promoting extremist ideology; and continued domestic and international efforts to promote religious and cultural tolerance and moderation. The U.S. also continued to press for further progress in key areas, including revision of school textbooks to eliminate passages that seem to promote intolerance or incite violence. For more detailed information on Saudi efforts to counter extremist ideology and areas where further steps are needed, please see the following reports: the 2010 Human Rights Report and the 2010 International Religious Freedom Report.

Like other countries in the region, Saudi Arabia sought to find meaningful economic and civic opportunities for its people, over 70 percent of whom are under 30 years old. The King has clearly enunciated an economic reform agenda. Saudi Arabia made progress in implementing this agenda in 2010, particularly in the closely related area of education, yet significant challenges remain. While the Saudi government welcomes certain forms of volunteerism and civic participation, its reform agenda in these areas is less clearly enunciated. The United States continued to support the Saudis in the reforms they are undertaking by facilitating Saudis studying in the United States and other educational exchanges; by encouraging increased bilateral trade and investment and urging Saudi Arabia to take actions necessary to attract job-creating partnerships with U.S. companies; and by targeted programming in areas that include judicial reform, local governance, and women's entrepreneurship. The United States encouraged the Saudi government to take concrete steps to increase opportunities for civic participation in 2011, including holding previously delayed municipal council elections and allowing women to participate in those elections.

U.S.-Saudi collaboration was not confined to bilateral issues: we consulted closely with the Saudi government on regional stability in the Arab and Islamic worlds, for example in Yemen and on Middle East peace. The United States welcomed the Saudi government's decision to host a Friends of Yemen ministerial meeting and the additional budget support it provided in October 2010 to the Palestinian Authority. Saudi Arabia has shown a desire to improve relations with an inclusive Iraqi government, and the United States encouraged all of Iraq's neighbors, including Saudi Arabia, to increase the scope and scale of their relationships with Iraq.

4. BROADCASTING BOARD OF GOVERNORS INITIATIVES: OUTREACH TO FOREIGN MUSLIM AUDIENCES

Four of the five broadcast entities under the supervision of the Broadcasting Board of Governors: the Voice of America (VOA), the Middle East Broadcasting Networks (Alhurra TV and Radio Sawa), Radio Free Europe/Radio Liberty (RFE/RL), and Radio Free Asia provided programming for Muslim audiences.

- Eighteen of RFE/RL's broadcast languages – almost two-thirds of the total – are directed to regions where the majority populations are Muslim, including Iran, Iraq, Afghanistan, Azerbaijan, Kosovo, Kazakhstan, Kyrgyzstan, Tajikistan, Turkmenistan, and Uzbekistan, as well as the majority Muslim populations of Tatarstan, Bashkortostan, and the North Caucasus in the Russian Federation.

- VOA's Persian News Network (PNN), the top international broadcaster to Iran, reached 19.6 percent of the adult population watching at least once weekly, with the majority of those surveyed indicating the network has increased their understanding of events in the Mideast, Iran, and the United States.

- The Middle East Broadcasting Networks (MBN) broadcast throughout the Middle East, to a Muslim population estimated at 315 million, according to Pew Research Center.

- VOA's Indonesian Service reached more than 26 million Indonesians each week.

- VOA and RFE/RL provided news and information to Afghanistan and the Afghanistan-Pakistan border region in Dari and Pashto; together RFE/RL and VOA reached 65 percent of Afghan adults each week.

- Radio Free Asia broadcast to the more than 16 million Uighur Muslims in the Xinjiang Uighur Autonomous Region of northwestern China and Central Eurasia.

The BBG used the latest communications technologies to combat jamming and to reach new audiences through digital and other communications tools, such as webchats, blogs, and other applications featured on comprehensive websites.

The Middle East

Arabic. In 2010, Radio Sawa, a 24/7 network of stations designed to reach the Arabic-speaking population under the age of 35, broadcast 325 newscasts per week providing news about the Middle East, the United States and the world. Radio Sawa also offered discussion and informational programs such as the *Sawa Chat* interactive feature and the *Free Zone,* a weekly review and discussion of democracy and freedom. According to international research firms such as ACNielsen, Radio Sawa has a weekly reach of 17.6 million people.

Radio Sawa broadcast on FM in:

- Morocco (Rabat, Casablanca, Tangier, Meknes, Marrakesh, Agadir, and Fes)

- Jordan (Amman and Ajlun)

- The Palestinian Territories (Ramallah and Jenin)

- Kuwait (Kuwait City)

- Bahrain (Manama)

- Qatar (Doha)

- United Arab Emirates (Abu Dhabi and Dubai)

- Iraq (Baghdad, Nasiriya, Basra, Mosul, Kirkuk, Sulimaniya, Fallujah, Ramadi, Al-Hilla, Tikrit, Amara, Najaf, Samawa, and Erbil)

- Lebanon (Beirut, North Lebanon, South Lebanon, and Bekaa Valley)

- Djibouti

Radio Sawa also broadcast on medium wave to Egypt, Yemen, Saudi Arabia, and throughout Sudan; it was available on the Arabsat, Nilesat, and Eutelsat satellite systems.

Alhurra Television covered 21 countries in the Middle East via the same satellites used by major indigenous Arabic channels. In the last three years, Alhurra consistently averaged approximately 26 million weekly viewers and was the only Arabic-language network to have dedicated correspondents at the White House, State Department, Congress, and the Pentagon.

The network launched three new programs:

- *Stories with Akram Khuzam:* a weekly documentary series examining social and cultural issues in Arab countries.

- *FOCUS:* in-depth news features from around the world, and some of the best stories from the archives of the critically acclaimed *PBS NewsHour* translated into Arabic.

- *Almajalla:* showcases the best in American culture and society.

Iraq. Every week, 73 percent of Iraqi adults—some 9.5 million people—listened to or watched one of the four BBG broadcasters serving the country: Alhurra TV, Radio Sawa, Radio Free Europe/Radio Liberty's Radio Free Iraq, and Voice of America (VOA) Kurdish. Alhurra was the leading TV channel among hundreds available by satellite and locally with 32 percent daily and 64 percent weekly reach. Radio Sawa had 28.7 percent weekly reach and was the number one radio station for Iraqis. Radio Free Iraq, with 10 percent weekly reach, was among the top five radio stations for news. VOA Kurdish reached 12 percent of its target audience weekly.

Radio Free Iraq. In 2010, Radio Free Iraq (RFI) concentrated on three major themes: the aftermath of the March 7 elections and the subsequent effort to form a new government; the security situation before and after the withdrawal of US combat troops from Iraq; and, the national census as a step toward steady political development.

Kurdish. VOA's Kurdish Service is the only international broadcaster that speaks to Iraq's Kurds in their main dialects, Sorani and Kurmanji. Although the target audience is the Iraqi Kurd population, the Kurdish Service regularly covers developments in neighboring Iran, Turkey, and Syria, all of which have sizable Kurdish minorities. The Service broadcast three hours of radio programming seven days a week via FM transmitters in the cities of Sulaimania, Kirkuk, Mosul, and Erbil. During the parliamentary elections in Iraq, VOA's Kurdish Service utilized stringers in Baghdad, Sulaimania, Kirkuk, Mosul, and Dohuk, and interviewed 30 candidates from different parties and coalitions. The Kurdish Service increased the number of video reports produced for Internet audiences, and postings on YouTube, Facebook, and Twitter increased the number of visitors to the service's Sorani and Kurmanji sites. A 2010 survey indicated an increase of 1.3 percent over the 2009 weekly listening rate of six percent of Kurdish adults in Iraq.

Iran

VOA Persian News Network. VOA's Persian News Network (PNN) continued to expand its reach through television, with about 13.6 million adults watching the broadcasts weekly. PNN is the top international broadcaster to Iran with 19.6 percent of the adult population watching at least once weekly. The PNN website is one of VOA's most active with an average of 1.7 million visits per month. PNN also oversaw 12 *Facebook* sites, five blogs, and a *YouTube* channel.

PNN's popular show, *Parazit*, attracted more than 17-million *Facebook* page views last month. YouTube recorded another 3.5 million uploaded views of the show. *Static*, the highly popular weekly 30-minute satirical program, has more *Facebook* fans than any other *Facebook* page in Iran.

Radio Free Europe/Radio Liberty's **Radio Farda**'s programs include newscasts at the top of each hour, followed by reports, features, interviews, and regular segments on youth, women, culture, economy, and politics. Radio Farda's 2010 highlights included:

- The launch of a live one-hour, five-day-a-week, satirical-political show, Radio Pasfara, which had over 25,000 listeners.

- The introduction of a one-hour weekly program about U.S.-Iran relations with the aim of providing listeners, especially younger Iranians, with unbiased information.

- The launch of a daily 90-minute program, *Breakfast with News*, providing listeners early morning news, music, and political, economic, and cultural reports.

- *Your Voice, Farda's Voice*, featured interactive radio programming presenting news and entertainment segments. It reached significant audiences in Iran in spite of the government's consistent jamming.

- Radio Farda's *Facebook* page made web-based content available to more than 67,000 fans. Each month, the webpage was visited five million times, and averaged 4,000 comments per month. Farda received on average 13,000 phone calls, emails, and text messages monthly.

Europe

Azerbaijan. As a result of the ban by the Azerbaijani authorities on affiliation between local and international broadcasters, the Internet was the main platform of delivery for RFE/RL's Azerbaijan service. A multimedia web portal was updated daily with additional materials on tolerance. The audio and video products of the Service were delivered via three short-wave frequencies and satellite to audiences in Azerbaijan and the neighboring provinces of Iran.

Turkey. VOA's Turkish Service covered U.S.-Turkish relations and U.S. institutions and values. The Service's web site, updated with top news seven days a week, offered English teaching programs, a daily web radio program, video and audio clips, and the ability to post comments by users. It was also accessible by web-enhanced mobile phones and similar devices and content was distributed on *YouTube*, *Twitter,* and *Facebook*. In response to strong demand from its TV affiliate, TGRT News Network in Turkey (one of the top five all-news networks in Turkey), the service increased the frequency of its 15-minute live TV news and analysis broadcasts from three to four times per week. VOA Turkish also produced a weekly 30-minute magazine show that was aired on TGRT.

South Asia

Radio Free Afghanistan. According to research by InterMedia, Radio Free Europe/Radio Liberty's (RFE/RL) Radio Free Afghanistan (Radio Azadi) was the most trusted and most listened-to radio broadcaster in Afghanistan. Afghanistan is the only country in RFE/RL's broadcast region where U.S. government-funded broadcasters are the dominant media outlets. Radio Azadi provided breaking news, in-depth reporting and analysis, and programming emphasizing the promotion of democracy, the rights of women, and minority and religious tolerance. Radio Azadi provided live and extensive coverage of major national events, including the 2010 presidential and parliamentary elections, the international conference held in July in Kabul, and the consultative peace Jirga of June. The Service's Dari and Pashto websites increased viewership by 500%, while the *Facebook* and *Twitter* pages were visited 2000 times per day. The Service also launched SMS and citizen journalism projects and Intelligent Voice Recognition (IVR) and MMS projects with the help of the Etisalat telecommunications company in Afghanistan. Radio Azadi received an average of 250 SMS messages daily.

Voice of America (VOA) Ashna TV. VOA's Afghan Service increased its efforts to reach out to Muslim audiences with the debut of "Karwan," a 30-minute weekly TV show aimed at Afghans under age 25. Daoud Seddiqi, a popular Afghan personality, hosted the program and solicited feedback from viewers through *Facebook* and *YouTube*. TV Ashna's programs have explored topics such as the proposed construction of an Islamic Center near the 9/11 site and the increasing political activism of Muslim Americans. On the lighter side, the Service produced a piece on a new comic book, with a Muslim Super-Hero, inspired by President Obama's 2009 Cairo speech.

VOA Ashna Radio. With more than five million listeners across Afghanistan, VOA's Ashna radio maintained its competitive edge among the top ranking media. Ashna covered all of the major news in Afghanistan through reports from its stringers and interviews with analysts and government officials in Afghanistan. Live coverage of the September 18 parliamentary elections was one of the most important stories of the year. VOA's Managing Editors visited the polling stations, providing live reports regarding allegations of election fraud. Full coverage of press conferences held by the Elections Commission and protests by the candidates were included in VOA coverage. The service made progress using its website as a hub for all of its TV and radio programming in the Dari and Pashto languages – website hits increased to an average of 2,000 daily in the last quarter of the 2010, compared to 1,500 in 2009.

VOA Urdu. VOA Urdu TV's weekly 30-minute show, in English and Urdu, profiled a variety of American Muslims, and tackled myths and realities of American life. Positive comments from viewers in Pakistan and around the world were posted on VOA's *YouTube* and *Facebook* pages, as well as the Service website, which opened a "Comments" application in 2010 to support viewer feedback.

The Urdu TV service ran other long-format shows on local Pakistan network, GEO. Segments included *Hello America*, a video Q&A show between Pakistani and American citizens; *Campus*, a weekly spot plus blog on the experiences of Pakistani students when they study at U.S. universities; and *Melting Pot*, which highlighted multicultural life in the United States.

VOA Urdu's 12/7 *Radio Aap ki Dunyaa (Your World)* broadcast on shortwave, medium wave, and on 11 FM frequencies operated by the Pakistan Broadcasting Corporation.

The Pakistan/Afghanistan Border Region. VOA Deewa Radio's daily nine-hour broadcast provided accurate, timely news to over 30 million Pashtuns in an area dominated by state-controlled media and the Taliban-run Mullah Radio. The radio station reached its target audience via radio, internet, and available social media tools, attracting at least 1000 callers everyday to its four interactive call-in shows. Research performed through InterMedia showed Deewa Radio leading the BBC and other international media in audience share in target region. Deewa's network of 30 stringers helped provide listeners with reports on Pakistan's devastating floods; U.S. assistance for the flood victims; Pakistan's military campaign against Taliban forces; and the challenge of hundreds of thousands of internally displaced persons.

On January 15, RFE/RL launched Radio Mashaal ("Torch" in Pashto), a broadcast service directed to Pakistan and the Afghanistan/Pakistan border region. Radio Mashaal provided breaking news and in-depth coverage of developments in the Pashtun region, and focused on issues of religious tolerance, culture, countering terrorism, and promoting understanding. Interaction with the audience through call-in shows and message recording was emphasized.

Bangladesh. In 2010, VOA Bangla produced numerous radio and television features on Muslim youth, Islamic centers in the United States, and other topics. The Service's television program, Washington Barta, broadcast special coverage from Ground Zero on the 9/11 anniversary, and a feature on women-led Eid prayers at a local Mosque. The Eid feature stoked a strong response, driving YouTube numbers higher than any other feature aired. The Service ran interviews with U.S. and Bangladeshi officials, including one with the first member of the House of Representatives who is of Bangladeshi descent, Rep. Hansen Clarke.

Central Asia

Kazakhstan. RFE/RL's Kazakh Service is delivered primarily through its Internet platform, continuing radio programming for one hour in the evening with a one-hour repeat in the morning. This web strategy helped to attract a younger audience to this bilingual (Kazakh and Russian) site, providing more opportunities for interactivity and exploring new genres such as video reporting. The Kazakh government's continuous effort to block internet resources that host what it believed were hostile blogs left a number of young bloggers in the country without a platform. In response, the service offered "Blogistan", a blog platform on RFE/RL's web site (under RFE/RL editorial control) that began with a handful of young bloggers and became a social platform for bloggers who regularly post on RFE/RL's "Radio Azattyq" site. In December, a collection of the best blogs on Blogistan was published as a book and distributed.

Kyrgyzstan. RFE/RL's Kyrgyz Service radio and TV programs were the first to return to the air nationwide, just one day after the April 7 anti-government uprising in Kyrgyzstan. A December survey conducted by the Kyrgyz State National University showed that the service was considered the most reliable Kyrgyz-language media information source. A new three-day-a-week "hard news" radio talk show provided straightforward discussion on religion, politics, and culture. Twice monthly, the service organizes "Chaihana" (Tea House) roundtables at its Bishkek bureau where five to seven guests engage on a variety of topics such as Islam and democracy and the Kyrgyz mentality.

Tajikistan. Radio Free Europe/Radio Liberty's (RFE/RL) Tajik Service is the largest independent media outlet in Tajikistan and the top international broadcaster in the country. As the country's only source for unbiased information, the Tajik service was repeatedly criticized by the Tajik government for its coverage.

Uzbekistan. Lacking a local bureau since it was closed in 2005, and operating in adverse conditions, Radio Free Europe's Uzbek Service continued to provide news coverage and supported democracy promotion in Uzbekistan. Its TV program and daily 30-minute radio broadcast featured interviews with U.S. and international sources on such topics as terrorism, religious extremism, and U.S.-Uzbek relations. The Uzbek Service launched uzmobil.com, distributing Voice of America (VOA) news to mobile phone subscribers in Uzbekistan. VOA Uzbek reports were also accessible on Twitter, YouTube, and Facebook.

East Asia and Pacific

China. Radio Free Asia's (RFA) Uighur language service is the only international radio service providing impartial news and information in the Uighur language to the potential audience of more than 16 million Uighur Muslims in Western China and Central Eurasia. Consistent with RFA's mandate, the Uighur service acted as a substitute for indigenous media reporting on local events in the region. The service broadcast two hours daily, seven days a week. Programs included breaking news, analysis, interviews, commentary, a weekly news review, and feature stories. News and stories featured interviews with various U.S. and international sources, including Chinese and Uighur dissidents worldwide. RFA's Uighur service well-trafficked website streamedthe daily RFA broadcast in Uighur and offering ongoing coverage of events in the XUAR in text, image, and video.

RFA confronted Chinese jamming of RFA broadcasts and the blocking of its website by broadcasting on multiple short-wave frequencies and regularly e-mailing instructions on accessing the banned www.rfa.org through proxy web servers. RFA provided users with instructions on how to directly access the RFA website through anti-censorship software.

Indonesia. VOA's weekly audience in Indonesia grew from 10.5 to 16.2 percent, or more than 26 million people, largely because of the placement of short program segments on popular national TV stations. VOA Indonesian TV products were regularly seen on eight of Indonesia's 11 national stations, in addition to more than 20 local and regional stations. In 2010, the Service launched a new radio program on the Radio Dangdut Indonesia network. During Ramadan, VOA produced a special series on Islam in the United States, which was carried by national stations. The Service produced eight hours daily of original radio programming for a network of more than 230 affiliate FM and medium wave stations across the country. Radio programming included five-minute *Headline News* reports, aired 32 times a day, seven days a week.

The Russian Federation

Throughout 2010, VOA's Russian Service has systematically addressed issues related to Islam in the target area. A special section on the website, dealing specifically with developments in the North Caucasus region, was launched.

Tatarstan/Bashkortostan. The Tatar and Bashkir communities are the two largest Muslim communities in Russia. Radio Free Europe/Radio Liberty's (RFE/RL) Tatar/Bashkir Service is the only major international broadcaster in the Tatar and Bashkir languages; it provided listeners with objective news and analysis. The service's web page has become a virtual meeting place for people to discuss these issues. VOA Russian also targeted these communities, who largely rely on Russian language for their news and information. Since May 2010, there were over 100,000 visits to VOA's Russian website Tatarstan and Bashkortostan.

Africa

Nigeria. Broadcasts of Voice of America's (VOA) Hausa Service reached most of the estimated 90 million Muslims in Nigeria and Niger. In Nigeria, where the language is spoken by over 75 million people, VOA has a 36 percent weekly audience share. In January, the service covered the violence between Muslims and Christians in Plateau State. A forum with call-in programs for listeners to discuss ways to promote harmony between the two communities was provided and in January, the Service conducted two town hall meetings in the Nigerian states of Adamawa and Taraba, which were attended by thousands of people. Throughout the year, VOA Hausa engaged Muslim audiences with a weekly program called *Islam in the United States*, while its web site posted "Eid" listener greetings to mark the end of the Holy Month of Ramadan.

Ethiopia and Eritrea. VOA's Horn of Africa Service broadcast 17 hours a week in three languages: seven 60-minute broadcasts in Amharic, five 30-minute broadcasts in Tigrigna, and five 30-minute broadcasts in Afan Oromo. In addition to shortwave, these languages now air live on VOA24, a 24/7 channel on Arabsat satellite television.

Somalia. The Somali Service broadcast to an almost all-Muslim audience estimated 16 million people in the Horn of Africa, including 10 million in Somalia. Service broadcasts were heard on short wave, as well as on FM affiliate stations in Somalia, Kenya, and Djibouti. The Somali Service web site reached an estimated two million Somali speakers outside the Horn region.

In late 2010, the Service ran a five-part series on young Muslim women. An October town-hall meeting, held in Nairobi, focused on Somali radicalism and its effects on East Africa.

Swahili. VOA's Swahili Service broadcast to large Muslim populations in Tanzania, Kenya, as well as to significant Muslim communities in Uganda, Burundi, and the Democratic Republic of the Congo's Manema province.

French to Africa. VOA's French to Africa Service broadcast 23 hours weekly on radio via shortwave and to an array of affiliates across the region to the 250 million French speakers in Africa, many of whom live in predominantly Muslim countries such as Senegal, Mali, Burkina Faso, Niger, and Chad. A weekly interactive program, "Dialogue of Religions," featured guest experts on issues of concern to Muslims and took listener calls. VOA's French to Africa service also broadcast a 30-minute weekly television program.

5. ECONOMIC REFORM

In countries with predominantly Muslim populations, the pursuit of economic growth is a method of achieving sustainable social benefits – such as increased rates of education, health, and employment – that ultimately can minimize the pressures that can lead to radicalization. USAID activities often focused on improving the regulatory or business enabling environment, so that the power of private sector investment, both domestic and foreign, could be leveraged to increase business activity and trade. A battery of program interventions were designed and implemented to pursue measurable results in the commercial, legal, and regulatory framework that would significantly lower the costs, obstacles, and time required for doing business.

GLOBAL TRADE CAPACITY BUILDING

Albania. The United States provided technical assistance and training in information technologies, trade knowledge and skills, technological innovations, business management, and compliance with international regulations and standards.

Egypt. USAID/Egypt provided assistance to Egyptian government ministries to develop their institutional capacity regarding trade reform, by providing technical assistance by local and expatriate professionals, training, mentoring, and information technology.

Indonesia. The Enterprise and Agribusiness Development Activity/Competitiveness Program (SENADA) attempted to generate growth, jobs, and income by increasing the competitiveness of at least five labor-intensive manufacturing industries: furniture, auto parts, garments, home accessories, and information and communications technology.

The Indonesia Trade Assistance Project (ITAP) provided assistance to the Ministry of Trade to build and strengthen capacity related to the analysis, negotiation, and implementation of bilateral and multilateral trade agreements. ITAP helped the Ministry to implement institutional reforms and to strengthen inter-Ministerial and inter-Agency frameworks that were expected to better equip Indonesia to further compete in international markets. The objective of these reforms was to fuel growth, trade, and employment.

Iraq. U.S. assistance helped Iraq prepare positions on four of the 12 World Trade Organization (WTO) Global Agreement on Trade and Services (GATS) sectors: Tourism, Financial Services, Telecom/Postal and Courier, and Computers/Research and Development Services. After helping to establish the National Investment Commission, the U.S. government assisted the Commission in developing by-laws and implementing regulations for investment law, and created a one-stop-shop to promote international investment in Iraq. The U.S. government also provided aid to revise the Investor Guide and the Investor Road Map in preparation for the October Iraq Investment Conference.

Jordan. The United States provided technical assistance to the Government of Jordan in its negotiations to accede to the WTO Government Procurement Agreement, and actively engaged to improve the trade and investment climate in Jordan through training sessions for Jordanian government officials in Intellectual Property Rights and export assistance. Services funded by the U.S. government to small and medium enterprises included the development of human resource systems, financial systems, strategic planning, market research, developing interactive websites, customer relations management systems, and conducting training on information, communication technologies, and trade-related advice.

Kazakhstan. USAID programs provided assistance in trade capacity building in Kazakhstan. USAID efforts were expected to simplify and accelerate trading across borders as well as decrease costs to businesses.

Kyrgyz Republic. USAID's trade capacity building support in Kyrgyzstan focused on ongoing efforts to reduce investment constraints and facilitate trade by providing assistance for Kyrgyzstan to meet its WTO obligations, to develop trade services for importers and exporters, and to reduce barriers to cross-border trade.

Morocco. U.S. assistance helped Moroccan producers access international markets through the introduction of improved management of production and processing techniques in order to meet international standards. Through the USAID Economic Growth program, U.S. government assistance improved trade knowledge and skills among Moroccan companies for more effective export planning. The New Business Opportunities Program helped export-oriented Moroccan firms to take advantage of new possibilities for entry and expansion in the United States created by the Morocco-U.S. Free Trade Agreement.

Nigeria. Trade capacity building activities increased due to the startup of several activities under the Global Food Security Response (GFSR) initiative. Increased support to the agriculture sector resulted in increased yields, better links between producers and processors, and ultimately improved access to domestic, regional, and international markets. New activities included work on improving the legal and regulatory framework for customs, an assessment of the main north-south trade corridor, and capacity building for trade facilitation with the Ministry of Commerce and Industry. New GFSR resources allowed U.S. government activities to have a greater impact in areas such as customs reform and trade corridor improvement. Work with the Nigeria Customs Service (NCS) included a full review of the legal framework and enabling legislation for NCS.

Pakistan. The USAID Pakistan Trade Project (PTP) addressed factors that impeded trade, such as the need for customs reform, harmonized border procedures, and simplified trade processes. The USAID Pakistan Firms, helped Pakistani businesses become internationally competitive so they could capture new export opportunities. Together these activities focused on assisting sectors that offered the greatest opportunity for growth and new employment.

Tajikistan. Four USAID projects and the Export Control and Related Border Security (EXBS) program worked to build trade capacity in Tajikistan. USAID's Economic Reforms to Enhance Competitiveness project helped reorganize the Tax Committee to create a more tax-friendly environment for traders by improving administration procedures and clearly defining national and local taxes. The Regional Trade Liberalization and Customs project provided advice, analysis, and recommendations to the government to bring its legislation into compliance with World Trade Organization agreements. The project also worked to reduce barriers to trade, transport, transit, custom clearance, and border crossing through mechanisms consistent with international standards. The Business Environment Improvement (BEI) project helped develop a more enabling environment for small and medium enterprises (SMEs), including small traders, and more specifically helped the government inventory all licenses and permits. With BEI support, the government performed a legal analysis of the legislation "On Special Economic Zones" (SEZ) in Tajikistan and helped with the creation of the Sughd SEZ. BEI was also active in alleviating local administrative barriers throughout Tajikistan. EXBS assistance to Tajikistan enhanced its capacity to establish an effective strategic trade control system and effectively control its border.

West Bank and Gaza. USAID's trade facilitation activities helped improve the speed, efficiency, and security of the movement and access of people and goods within the West Bank and between the West Bank and Gaza and Israel. The Trade Facilitation Project helped boost trade in the West Bank and Gaza by building capacity within the Palestinian Authority and private sector counterparts, promoting Palestinian-Israeli cooperation on border management and security, and conducting analyses to facilitate the movement of people and goods. These undertakings resulted in almost $3.5 million in private sector cost savings over the fiscal year.

INTRAREGIONAL TRADE

Central Asia Regional Program. "Trade Capacity Building" support in Central Asia had two primary goals. The first was to provide on-going advice, analysis, and recommendations to the Governments of the Central Asian Republics in reviewing their legislation for compliance with World Trade Organization agreements and regulations associated with trade. The second goal was to facilitate the implementation of a Single Window and Single Administrative Document processes for customs in Kazakhstan, Kyrgyzstan, and Tajikistan.

Middle East Partnership Initiative (MEPI). MEPI economic programming focused on region-wide economic and employment growth driven by private sector expansion and entrepreneurship, providing the kind of economic opportunity that created more stable, prosperous communities. Examples of MEPI's collaborations with people in the region include entrepreneur training exchange projects, technical assistance in support of free trade agreements, promotion of international labor standards, and reform of banking regulations and lending processes to encourage business growth.

The Department of Commerce's Commercial Law Development Program (CLDP) supported the implementation of U.S. Free Trade Agreements. Assistance included legislative reform, bilateral training in international commercial law, workshops aimed to reduce technical barriers to trade, and technical assistance with bankruptcy, title, collateral, World Trade Organization dispute resolution, and alternative dispute resolution.

The USAID Africa Regional Bureau program fostered policy, legal, and regulatory action to spur trade and investment and build capacity. Business enabling environment assessments were completed for Burundi and Uganda. East Africa Regional Analyses for trade and credit were produced as part of an ongoing collaboration with The Common Market for Eastern and Southern Africa and USAID/East Africa. Regional Intellectual Property Protection Workshops were conducted in West Africa (Ghana) and Southern Africa, with the cooperation of the Economic Community of West African States, the Southern Africa Development Community, U.S. Customs, the U.S. Department of Justice, and the U.S. Patent and Trademark Office. The workshop in Ghana trained 150 participants from fifteen countries of West Africa and 10 Ghanaian intellectual property agencies and industry representatives.

Assistance was provided for energy projects in Botswana and Nigeria. Significant results were the World Bank Board of Directors signing of an International Development Association loan agreement for US$ $200 million and commitment to US$ 400 million of Partial Risk Guarantees to support the sale of natural gas by independent oil companies to three electricity sector projects in Nigeria. The Information and Communications Technology (ICT) program provided capacity building to a network of six software development centers at universities in sub-Saharan Africa, facilitated capacity building of the West Africa Telecom Regulatory Association, and established an ICT and Business Center in Malawi.

The USAID ASEAN Competitiveness Enhancement program worked to increase intra-ASEAN trade and global competitiveness within two of ASEAN's 12 priority sectors: textiles/apparel and tourism. Together with the ASEAN Federation of Textile Industries, the program launched the Source ASEAN Full Service Alliance. This strategy created alliances of stakeholders along the supply chain that offer a one-stop shop for international apparel buyers.

6. BASIC EDUCATION IN MUSLIM MAJORITY COUNTRIES

In 2010, USAID/Asia and Middle East Bureau's total basic education assistance for the region was approximately US$ 583 million, of which approximately US$ 550 million was targeted in predominantly Muslim countries or in Muslim majority populations within a country, including Afghanistan, Bangladesh, Egypt, India, Indonesia, Jordan, Lebanon, Morocco, Pakistan, Philippines (Mindanao), West Bank/Gaza, Yemen, and the Central Asian Republics. USAID/Europe and Eurasia Bureau's education assistance benefitted Kosovo and Macedonia and totaled approximately US$ six million. USAID/Africa Bureau's total education assistance for the region was approximately US$ 223 million in Basic Education, of which US$ 48.4 million benefitted Muslim populations in Djibouti, Ethiopia, Kenya, Mali, Nigeria, Senegal, Somalia, Tanzania, Uganda, and through regional programs in several other countries.

Coordination of the International Effort. USAID collaborated closely with the State Department's Middle East Partnership Initiative (MEPI) and the U.S. Department of Education on literacy reform. As a result of the June 2009 broader Middle East and North Africa (BMENA) Community and Technical College Workshop in Amman, 10 awards ranging between US $100,000 and US $150,000, each for 18-months' partnerships between U.S. community colleges and community and technical colleges in the BMENA region, were awarded.

Leveraging Contributions from the Private Sector and Civil Society Organizations. USAID's Global Development Alliances, also known as public-private partnerships, are tailored to country-specific needs and the private sector partners' interests. In 2010, Partners For A New Beginning was established to broaden and deepen engagement between the United States and international Muslim communities by building public-private partnerships that advance economic opportunity, science and technology, education, and exchange.

U.S. Government Coordination to Reduce Duplication and Waste. MEPI and USAID coordinate to avoid potential duplication of efforts and investments and to maximize results. A modest number of MEPI-funded education programs, notably the support for the Arab Civitas network, are implemented in conjunction with USAID. In Yemen, USAID and MEPI work together to increase community and student engagement in school management.

Innovation and Technology. USAID/India Technology Tools for Teaching and Training (T4) employed educational technologies to educate poor and disadvantaged children studying in public schools in Karnataka, Chhattisgarh, Madhya Pradesh, Jharkhand, and Bihar states. By combining technology tools with sound pedagogy and effective teacher training, USAID and its partners developed interactive radio, video, and computer programs that simplified the teaching of difficult concepts in various subjects, including language, math, science, and social studies. T4 reached more than 24 million children. In addition, USAID/India's Youth Skill Development Initiative provided education in basic life and employability skills to deprived out-of-school youth, effectively linking their education to the skills demanded by the new economy. The program provided training to these youth in market-oriented skills, such as computer usage, spoken English, and communication and customer relations to make participants more employable. Over 38,000 youth were trained in the states of Delhi, Jharkhand, and Maharashtra. Seventy-five percent of the trainees received employment and many opted for further studies. Designed as a public-private initiative, 50 percent of the program costs came from non-USAID sources. Finally, USAID/India implemented a program in over 500 madrassas in Hyderabad, West Bengal, and Andra Pradesh that introduced formal curricula, enrolled and retained out-of-school children, improved the quality of education, and prepared madrassas to meet government standards. Over 50,000 Muslim children were provided with formal education in the two states.

In **Afghanistan,** USAID's basic education program totaling US$ 72,844,000 continued to build the skills of Afghan partners to deliver basic education and literacy training for out-of-school youth and adults. U.S. assistance increased access to quality basic education by improving learning materials and instructional quality; offering community-based education opportunities, youth, and adult literacy programs; and by renovating and building schools. To support U.S. government stabilization goals, USAID initiated emergency education activities for over 20,000 children affected by conflict in the south and east. U.S. assistance provided low-literate and unemployed youth in two provinces with access to vocational training and second-chance primary education programs. Community-based education reached over 60,000 children in areas with no government schools, and a youth and adult literacy program provided learning opportunities for over 151,000 learners, 60 percent of whom were female. U.S. government in-service teacher training, the printing of 21.5 million textbooks, and assistance with school materials and security have strengthened educational programs that reached 2.3 million (one third) of Afghan school children. The training of 40,850 teachers and over 3,800 literacy teachers was complemented by follow-up classroom support to help improve the quality of basic education programs. Programs on pedagogy, instructional content, and research methods updated teaching skills for over 700 education professors involved in pre-service education of secondary school instructors.

Community participation in education significantly expanded in 2010. More than 4,200 U.S.-trained school management committees monitored classes and teacher performance, contributed furnishings and materials, aided teacher recruitment, and collaborated with district and provincial officials. Small grants made capital improvements at local schools. U.S. assistance also strengthened Ministry of Education employee recruitment and performance evaluation systems, and established an electronic database for employees.

In **Bangladesh**, the focus was on early childhood development to improve enrollment, retention, and performance in primary schools. USAID funded the Promoting Talent through Early Education program to develop a pre-school curriculum and increase learning skills and access to educational opportunities for 39,710 pre-schoolers. In 2010, USAID trained over 1,700 primary school teachers in targeted areas on interactive teaching methodologies that included health, nutrition, and sanitation components. The $8.3 million USAID-supported Sisimpur, the Bangladesh version of Sesame Street, aired 181 times and was the most widely viewed children's television show in Bangladesh, reaching over 10 million children on a weekly basis.

In **India,** USAID's basic education activities benefited 43 million students and 361,959 teachers in eleven states. Programs promoted the use of technology to improve teaching and learning in the classroom and interventions that linked education to employment. The skills development technology and madrassa programs attracted nearly a 2:1 match for every dollar invested. This amounted to a $1.8 million private sector investment, which was 80 percent in capital and 20 percent in-kind support for market surveys, curriculum development, training, and placements. In FY 2010, activities benefitted over 100,000 Muslim children in approximately 1,200 madrassas. Strong government ownership in Andhra Pradesh ensured continued support to mainstream basic education in the targeted madrassas.

In **Indonesia,** the Decentralized Basic Education initiative resulted in 76 district governments officially budgeting for USAID Basic Education programs in more than 10,000 schools across seven target provinces benefiting more than 57,388 educators, 22,998 administrators, and 468,312 students. USAID also supports Jalan Sesama, the Sesame Street Workshop that reached 7.5 million children to help them succeed in primary school. In FY 2010, the Opportunities for Vulnerable Children program assisted children with special needs to attend inclusive education programs.

In **Kyrgyzstan,** USAID launched a youth aid for education initiative, which provided 1,042 pre-school children with a 100-hour school preparation program, and an additional 723 children with school supplies and support to enroll in school. USAID trained 2,091 school administrators, representing 386 secondary schools, to meet the development and emotional needs of children, teachers, and parents affected by the civil unrest in April and June in southern Kyrgyzstan. USAID worked directly with three in-service teacher training institutes and developed six in-service training programs that trained teachers to encourage higher order thinking. USAID also supported a Development Credit Authority student loan program and the American University of Central Asia. The student loan program increased access to higher education and vocational training for students, particularly those from rural areas, by creating a replicable, private-sector tuition financing model.

In **Tajikistan,** USAID's program expanded access to quality primary and secondary education. Five new training programs for competency in Tajik language, math, chemistry, and biology were developed and adopted by the government. In FY 2010, over 1,500 primary and secondary teachers and 100 school principals were trained with USAID resources on modern teaching and learning approaches. Technical assistance was provided to the Ministries of Education and Finance to reform education financing using a per capita model that the government expanded nationwide in all 68 districts. USAID also supported 86 schools in Vakhsh and Kulob.

In **Egypt,** USAID's assistance focused on K-12 schools in underprivileged urban areas in Cairo and Alexandria, and the five Upper Egypt governorates of Aswan, Qena, Beni Suef, Minya, and Fayoum. Specific USAID interventions continued to reform the "Teacher Cadre" law that established a revolutionary system for hiring, training, and promoting teachers; improving student assessment and developing the National Education Standards; strengthening the education management information systems; and using technology in schools to enhance teaching, learning, and school management. The program built 98 schools that included computer centers serving over 44,000 students in underserved communities; provided over 24 million books for libraries and classrooms in all 39,000 public primary, preparatory, and secondary schools in Egypt; and supported Alam Simsim, the Egyptian Sesame Street, which is viewed by 85 percent of Egyptian children.

In **Jordan,** the Government of Jordan's Education Reform for a Knowledge Economy started its second phase (2010-2020) to deliver quality education to Jordan's children. In FY 2010, and on target, three of 28 schools were completed and opened for the 2010-11 school year. Also in 2010, over 4,000 teachers and educators received training on the use of new technologies, quality assurances for the delivery of sound kindergarten education, school-to-career activities, the school as a community center, and school counseling. At the end of FY 2010, procurement was completed for a small project to provide assistance for small-to-medium private schools to be ready to receive and repay loans from micro finance institutions. USAID established 26 Community Parent School Coalitions where new schools were being constructed or where rehabilitations and expansions are taking place. Finally, USAID/Jordan supported a program called Drive to Read that has reached 5,000 children in disadvantaged neighborhoods in Amman and Zarqa. Hikayat Simsim, the Jordanian Sesame Street, reached approximately 10,000 children through its outreach component and the distribution of educational materials.

In **Lebanon,** USAID launched a new basic education program in 2010 to develop rehabilitation assistance to public schools and provided professional development opportunities for teachers. The program targeted all of Lebanon's 1,300 public schools and aimed to enhance student achievement through interventions such as bolstering learning environments through physical repairs and provision of equipment; increase learning opportunities through in-service teacher training and extracurricular activities; and increase stakeholder engagement in public schools. Additionally, USAID/ Lebanon provided financially disadvantaged students with scholarship assistance at the American Community School and the International College.

In **Morocco,** USAID launched a new education and youth program in 2010 to address school quality issues and to work with students who dropped out of school prematurely. The project targets middle schools, where there is a critical shortage of teachers, an increasing student population, and high drop-out rates. The Out-of-School Youth Development program provided educational services for out-of-school youth, developed policies to facilitate coordination of such service delivery, and built institutional networks to strengthen the youth development field in selected regions of the country.

In **Pakistan,** the State Department and USAID worked to improve both access and quality of education opportunities to give at-risk youth greater opportunities. USAID trained 222 master trainers and 405 education managers, improved administration and academic supervision, and supported federal, provincial, and district education officials for school management and planning, including procuring and training for the National Education Management Information System. In the underserved areas of Baluchistan and Sindh, USAID improved the teaching skills of 42 percent of public primary school teachers. By the end of 2009, 399 schools emphasized critical-thinking curricula, 3,770 teachers were trained in interactive teaching and learning skills, and 67,000 library books were donated to 15 schools, benefiting 6,000 students. USAID assisted the Ministry of Education in the formulation of a strategic framework for teacher certification and accreditation. USAID's Strengthening Teacher Education in Pakistan Initiative developed national standards for teacher certification and accreditation and improved networking among government teacher training institutions. Under the FATA School Rehabilitation and Construction Program, USAID supported the rehabilitation and furnishing of 58 public schools and two Government Colleges of Elementary Teachers in FATA. The schools were completed and handed over to the FATA authorities. The State Department targeted English language teaching programs to Pakistan's most marginalized communities in an effort to increase their access to education, jobs, and participation in other U.S. government programs.

In the **West Bank and Gaza,** USAID assisted the Palestinian Authority to codify its priorities in the education sector as demonstrated by the Palestinian Education Development Strategic Plan for 2008-2012. USAID constructed and rehabilitated classrooms to improve the teaching and learning environment and sustain the current percentage of basic education school enrollment at 100%. In 2010, USAID supported the Model Schools Network to encourage professional networking among schools and linkages between schools and their communities in order to foster communities of learning. USAID also promoted positive educational messages that are both entertaining and educational to pre-school children through the Palestinian Sesame Street, *Shara' Simsim*, with episodes that focused on numeracy, literacy, tolerance, and non-violence.

In **Yemen,** USAID worked at the central, governorate, and community-district levels to strengthen the capacity of communities, schools, and the Ministry of Education to sustain educational improvements. USAID's education program activities included school renovations, adult literacy support, support to increase community participation in school management, and teacher professional development in reading, writing, and mathematics. The program established baseline data on target student competencies in math and science.

In **Kosovo,** the $2,190,000 program improved access and education quality for primary and secondary schools resulting in a reduction of shifts from four to three in some areas and from three to two in others with a goal of achieving no more than two shifts by the end of 2012. The FY

2010 target of 225 classrooms was exceeded by 15 classrooms, resulting in over 26,000 students experiencing improved learning environments in their schools. The government of Kosovo provided matching contributions of $1.6 million.

Sub-Saharan Africa

The Africa Bureau supported a US$ 100 million East Africa Counterterrorism Initiative that provided basic education opportunities in marginalized Muslim communities, particularly in Kenya, Uganda, Tanzania, and Ethiopia.

In **Ethiopia,** activities in Muslim-dominated areas in Somali, Afar, Benishangul, Gumuz, and Oromia regions included teacher training to improve the quality of primary education; provision of capacity building training for Parent-Teacher Associations and community members to increase parent and community involvement in school management; grants to schools to enhance learning and teaching, building the capacity of education officers to improve the planning and management of the education system; and establishment and expansion of alternative basic education centers to provide non-formal primary education to children, especially girls; and adult literacy classes for illiterate Muslim men and women.

In **Kenya,** USAID's Education for Marginalized Children concentrated on the North Eastern and Coast Provinces; nearly 470,000 children were reached in the two provinces in FY 2010. Approximately 250 Early Childhood Development Centers were supported and over 4,000 teachers were trained in child-centered teaching methods. The School Infrastructure Program successfully built 107 classrooms, three dining halls, eight dormitories, and 2000 desks. The program expanded from seven to 15 districts, providing assistance in every district of both Provinces. USAID/Kenya's Education Office also oversees the Garissa Youth Project, which provided livelihood and workforce readiness programs for ethnic-Somali youth susceptible to recruitment by Somali terrorist organization al-Shabaab. The program addressed underlying conditions in the Garissa region that are thought to contribute to the local Muslim population's experience of marginalization. The youth program partnered with USAID's Office of Military Affairs to pilot the District Stability Framework, a tool to gauge the level of instability within Garissa and to help coordinate an inter-agency response, as well as action by the youth themselves through an $800,000 youth fund. This was the first pilot of the Framework outside of Iraq, Afghanistan, or Yemen.

Tanzania. USAID/Tanzania signed a Memorandum of Understanding for a Global Development Alliance with Cisco, Intel, Microsoft, and two local partners—UhuruOne and Zantel—to support a $49 million 21st Century Basic Education Program. USAID/Tanzania enhanced service delivery in Zanzibar, while adding two pilot districts (Lindi Urban and Mtwara Urban) on the southern Tanzanian mainland. Over 30,000 secondary-, 230,000 primary-, and 26,000 pre-primary school students benefitted from U.S. government support targeting education delivery systems at local, district, and regional levels. In addition, innovative radio instruction activity focused on pre-primary and primary-level education and established 180 informal learning centers in two districts in Zanzibar as well as piloted radio instruction in 246 primary-school classrooms. Isolated communities in rural areas established 95 Community Learning Centers in seven districts in mainland Tanzania providing equitable access to education for 23,500 children.

In **Uganda,** USAID supported the Aga Kahn Foundation's Madrassa Early Childhood Development Program, which targets poor districts and allowed communities to establish and manage their own pre-schools. In 2010, 53 community pre-schools and 527 primary schools participated in the program. A total of 108 sub-county officials and 1,965 School Management Committee and Parent-Teacher Association members received training, and a total of 2,760 pre-school children and 93,126 students in lower primary school benefited from the program.

In **Mali,** USAID conducted diverse activities in support of the Trans-Sahara Counterterrorism Partnership. USAID/Mali's basic education program focused on supporting moderate Islamic schools and improving the quality of primary education for Mali's predominantly Muslim population. Assistance ($1,279,000 from 2008 to 2010) supported the training of 1,600 madrassa teachers and principals in the use of Interactive Radio Instruction programs; produced daily broadcast and practice in the reading and writing of French and didactic materials for French language learning, and assisted the teachers with techniques of balanced literacy instruction to reinforce students' reading and writing skills. In the three northern regions of the country, USAID provided scholarships for over 6,000 disadvantaged girls.

In **Senegal,** the USAID Basic Education Program provided support to 21,324 vulnerable and out-of-school youth to either enroll them in improved Quranic schools (called daraas) or return them to the formal education system. USAID also supported the rehabilitation of 51 daara, including classroom spaces, bathrooms, access to water, and provision of hygiene kits as well as training for management committees and Quranic teachers on hygiene and health. USAID also supported the development, testing, and implementation of three-year curriculums in French and math for vulnerable children in 71 daaras reaching 3,658 children (688 girls). The program, taught by 212 volunteer teachers, prepares children in religious schools with the basic skills needed to transition into the formal education system. The program also supported the development of an on-line professional development web portal. Last year, USAID tested a model to integrate information communication and technology (ICT) into teaching and learning practices in 15 schools. The private sector, including Intel and Microsoft, contributed more than $198,000 in cost-share for ICT-related products for this pilot. Finally USAID trained education officials and administrators as well as elected officials, community based organizations, and parent-teacher associations in effective education planning, budgeting, and management at the local level.

In **Somalia,** USAID improved the overall educational environment in at least 250 communities, through improvements to infrastructure, water and hygiene, management and instructional quality, as well as through targeted technical assistance to government education officials over three years. Through Mercy Corps, USAID was able to complete work in 11 schools in South Central Somalia in addition to its work in 18 schools in Somaliland and 27 schools in Puntland. The program rehabilitated 303 existing classrooms and constructed 144 new classrooms and provided 1,584 desks, and distributed 13,478 school kits in 51 schools, thereby increasing access for 23,896 students. The program also trained 210 educators, supported 58 Community Education Committees, rehabilitated and constructed 331 school latrines, installed 142 hand-washing facilities, improving access to water and sanitation for the 23,896 students mentioned above and 14,280 community members. Finally, the program provided training to 101 Ministry of Education officials in education management and planning. As a result, 45% of ministry officials reported new education management skills. USAID also provides Interactive Radio Instruction programs, particularly to out-of-school learners and internally displaced children.

In **Sudan,** formal and non-formal programs focused on primary and girls' education, teacher training and institutional development, and targeted out-of-school youth, women, girls, pastoralist communities, returnees, and other vulnerable groups. The USAID education programs had a tremendous impact on enrollment and retention. 136,705 children have been reached in primary schools in Southern Sudan and the Three Areas, and 16,449 students are enrolled in secondary school (5,528 girls). A total of 2,380 teachers and 1,135 education administrators were trained to improve the quality of education and 24,093 teaching and learning materials were distributed to teachers and learners. The programs expedited the provision of primary education and adult literacy through radio-based instruction to 9,885 adults. Conflict resolution, recovery, and prevention were integrated to support the peace process.

In **Djibouti,** USAID's education program included: decentralized teacher training; strategic planning and budgeting; enhanced community participation; improving the Education Management Information System; and increasing learning for out-of-school youth. The program trained 1,100 teachers and administrators in childhood literacy and numeracy. Host country strategic information capacity was improved through support to a software application that accurately captures statistical data and training in the use of this data for more informed planning and policy decision making. To address Djibouti's chronically high unemployment and enable the Djiboutian people to leverage their own skills for continued economic growth, the program expanded education and training for employment for out-of-school youth and dropouts. A girls' scholarship program also benefited girls and a small number of boys from needy families who otherwise could not afford to send their children to school. In addition to its bilateral program, USAID/Djibouti implemented the Ambassador's Girls' Scholarship program benefitting over 1,200 recipients. Scholarships include supplies, mentoring, clothing, hygiene kits, tutorials, payment for school fees, and HIV/AIDS awareness training. The Teachers' for Africa program provided highly skilled volunteers to assist in the decentralized teacher training program.

Nigeria. In FY 2010, U.S. government resources were focused on two Northern states, Sokoto and Bauchi, to improve the state and local government competency in: teacher training, placement and remuneration; financial planning and management; transparent data collection and use in planning and evaluation; student assessment; and community involvement. One hundred and seventy administrators were trained in various education systems strengthening areas dealing with financial management, teacher training and community involvement. A total of 64,640 learners were enrolled in U.S. government-supported primary schools and 342 individuals were trained in operational research, in support of the transparent collection of education data. Otherwise, the USAID program focused on increased quality of primary education, especially girls' education, and teacher education and information management policy reforms. Working at the community level, the education programs ensured access to basic educational materials, improved teaching techniques, and improved pupil performance in numeracy and literacy.

CHAPTER 6.
FOREIGN TERRORISM ORGANIZATIONS

Foreign Terrorist Organizations (FTOs) are designated by the Secretary of State in accordance with section 219 of the Immigration and Nationality Act (INA). FTO designations play a critical role in the fight against terrorism and are an effective means of curtailing support for terrorist activities.

LEGAL CRITERIA FOR DESIGNATION UNDER SECTION 219 OF THE INA AS AMENDED:

1. It must be a *foreign organization*.

2. The organization must *engage in terrorist activity*, as defined in section 212 (a)(3)(B) of the INA (8 U.S.C. § 1182(a)(3)(B)), or *terrorism,* as defined in section 140(d)(2) of the Foreign Relations Authorization Act, Fiscal Years 1988 and 1989 (22 U.S.C. § 2656f(d)(2)), *or retain the capability and intent to engage in terrorist activity or terrorism.*

3. The organization's terrorist activity or terrorism must threaten the security of U.S. nationals or the national security (national defense, foreign relations, or the economic interests) of the United States.

U.S. GOVERNMENT DESIGNATED FOREIGN TERRORIST ORGANIZATIONS

Abu Nidal Organization (ANO)
Abu Sayyaf Group (ASG)
Al-Aqsa Martyrs Brigade (AAMB)
Al-Qa'ida (AQ)
Al-Qa'ida in the Arabian Peninsula (AQAP)
Al-Qa'ida in Iraq (AQI)
Al-Qa'ida in the Islamic Maghreb (AQIM)
Al-Shabaab (AS)
Ansar al-Islam
Asbat al-Ansar
Aum Shinrikyo (AUM)
Basque Fatherland and Liberty (ETA)
Communist Party of Philippines/New People's Army (CPP/NPA)
Continuity Irish Republican Army (CIRA)
Gama'a al-Islamiyya (IG)
Hamas
Harakat ul-Jihad-i-Islami (HUJI)
Harakat ul-Jihad-i-Islami/Bangladesh (HUJI-B)
Harakat ul-Mujahideen (HUM)
Hizballah
Islamic Jihad Union (IJU)
Islamic Movement of Uzbekistan (IMU)
Jaish-e-Mohammed (JEM)
Jemaah Islamiya (JI)
Jundallah

Kahane Chai
Kata'ib Hizballah (KH)
Kurdistan Workers' Party (PKK)
Lashkar e-Tayyiba (LT)
Lashkar i Jhangvi (LJ)
Liberation Tigers of Tamil Eelam (LTTE)
Libyan Islamic Fighting Group (LIFG)
Moroccan Islamic Combatant Group (GICM)
Mujahadin-e Khalq Organization (MEK)
National Liberation Army (ELN)
Palestine Liberation Front – Abu Abbas Faction (PLF)
Palestine Islamic Jihad – Shaqaqi Faction (PIJ)
Popular Front for the Liberation of Palestine (PFLP)
Popular Front for the Liberation of Palestine-General Command (PFLP-GC)
Real IRA (RIRA)
Revolutionary Armed Forces of Colombia (FARC)
Revolutionary Organization 17 November (17N)
Revolutionary People's Liberation Party/Front (DHKP/C)
Revolutionary Struggle (RS)
Shining Path (SL)
Tehrik-e Taliban Pakistan (TTP)
United Self-Defense Forces of Colombia (AUC)

ABU NIDAL ORGANIZATION

aka ANO; Arab Revolutionary Brigades; Arab Revolutionary Council; Black September; Fatah Revolutionary Council; Revolutionary Organization of Socialist Muslims

Description: The Abu Nidal Organization (ANO) was designated as a Foreign Terrorist Organization on October 8, 1997. The ANO was founded by Sabri al-Banna (aka Abu Nidal) after splitting from the Palestine Liberation Organization (PLO) in 1974. In August 2002, Abu Nidal died in Baghdad. Present leadership of the organization remains unclear. ANO advocates the elimination of Israel and has sought to derail diplomatic efforts in support of the Middle East peace process.

Activities: The ANO has carried out terrorist attacks in 20 countries, killing or injuring almost 900 persons. The group has not staged a major attack against Western targets since the late 1980s. Major attacks included those on the Rome and Vienna airports in 1985, the Neve Shalom synagogue in Istanbul, the hijacking of Pan Am Flight 73 in Karachi in 1986, and the City of Poros day-excursion ship attack in Greece in 1988. The ANO is suspected of assassinating PLO Deputy Chief Abu Iyad and PLO Security Chief Abu Hul in Tunis in 1991. In 2008, a Jordanian official reported the apprehension of an ANO member who planned to carry out attacks in Jordan. The ANO did not successfully carry out attacks in 2009 or 2010.

Strength: Current strength is unknown.

Location/Area of Operation: The group has not launched an attack in recent years, although former and current ANO associates are presumed present in Lebanon.

External Aid: The ANO's current access to resources is unclear, but it is likely that the decline in support previously provided by Libya, Syria, and Iran has had a severe impact on its capabilities.

ABU SAYYAF GROUP

aka al Harakat al Islamiyya

Description: The Abu Sayyaf Group (ASG) was designated as a Foreign Terrorist Organization on October 8, 1997. ASG is the most violent of the terrorist groups operating in the southern Philippines and claims to promote an independent Islamic state in western Mindanao and the Sulu Archipelago, though the goals of the group appear to have vacillated over time between criminal objectives and a more ideological intent. The group split from the much larger Moro Islamic Liberation Front (MILF) in the early 1990s under the leadership of Abdurajak Abubakar Janjalani, who was later killed in a clash with Philippine police in December 1998. His younger brother, Khadaffy Janjalani, replaced him as the nominal leader of the group. In September 2006, Khadaffy Janjalani was killed in a gun battle with the Armed Forces of the Philippines. Radullah Sahiron is assumed to be the ASG leader.

Activities: The ASG engages in kidnappings for ransom, bombings, beheadings, assassinations, and extortion. The group's stated goal is to promote an independent Islamic state in western Mindanao and the Sulu Archipelago, areas in the southern Philippines heavily populated by Muslims. The group's first large-scale action was a raid on the town of Ipil in Mindanao in April 1995. In April 2000, an ASG faction kidnapped 21 people, including 10 Western tourists, from a resort in Malaysia. In May 2001, the ASG kidnapped three U.S. citizens and 17 Filipinos from a tourist resort in Palawan, Philippines. Several of the hostages, including U.S. citizen Guillermo Sobero, were murdered. A Philippine military hostage rescue operation in June 2002 freed U.S. hostage Gracia Burnham, but her husband Martin Burnham, also a U.S. national, and Filipina Deborah Yap were killed.

U.S. and Philippine authorities blamed the ASG for a bomb near a Philippine military base in Zamboanga in October 2002 that killed a U.S. serviceman. In February 2004, the ASG bombed SuperFerry 14 in Manila Bay, killing at least 116 people, making this one of the most destructive acts of maritime violence to date. In March 2004, Philippine authorities arrested an ASG cell whose bombing targets included the U.S. Embassy in Manila. In 2006, the Armed Forces of the Philippines began "Operation Ultimatum," a sustained campaign that disrupted ASG forces in safe havens on Jolo Island in the Sulu archipelago, and that resulted in the killing of ASG leader Khadaffy Janjalani in September 2006 and his deputy, Abu Solaiman in January 2007. During 2009, the ASG staged multiple kidnappings, beheadings, and assassinations, including the January kidnappings of three Red Cross workers in the southern Philippines who were later released.

The group increased its activities in 2010, which included multiple attacks on civilians, humanitarian organizations, a church, and military and police personnel. There were six reported kidnapping incidents targeting Christians and other civilians. ASG's most complex attack occurred on the island of Basilan in April 2010 when the group launched a synchronized assault including the use of a vehicle borne improvised explosive device (VBIED) which resulted in at least 11 deaths and 10 injured. In the attack, armed operatives detonated two VBIEDs and fired weapons at several targets. A third improvised explosive device (IED) targeting a judge was later disarmed by police. There is an alarming trend of indiscriminate ASG attacks directed at civilians as exemplified by the February 2010 shooting that resulted in at least 11 deaths in a small village in the island of Basilan. In December 2010, Madhatta Asagal Haipe, a founding member of Abu Sayyaf, was extradited to the United States and sentenced in U.S. District Court, Washington, DC, to 23 years in prison for his role in a 1995 kidnapping of U.S. citizens.

Strength: ASG is estimated to have approximately 200 to 400 members.

Location/Area of Operation: The ASG was founded in Basilan Province and operates primarily in the provinces of the Sulu Archipelago, namely Basilan, Sulu, and Tawi-Tawi. The group also operates on the Zamboanga peninsula, and members occasionally travel to Manila. The group expanded its operational reach to Malaysia in 2000 with the abduction of foreigners from a tourist resort there. In mid-2003, the group started operating in Mindanao's city of Cotobato and on the provincial coast of Sultan Kudarat, Mindanao. The ASG was expelled from Mindanao proper by the MILF leadership in mid-2005.

External Aid: The ASG is funded through kidnappings and extortion, and may receive funding from external sources such as remittances from overseas Filipino workers and Middle East-based extremists. The ASG also receives funding from regional terrorist groups such as Jemaah Islamiya (JI), whose operatives have provided training to ASG members and helped to facilitate several ASG terrorist attacks. In October 2007, the ASG appealed for funds and recruits on YouTube by featuring a video of the Janjalani brothers before they were killed.

AL-AQSA MARTYRS BRIGADE

aka al-Aqsa Martyrs Battalion

Description: The al-Aqsa Martyrs Brigade was designated as a Foreign Terrorist Organization on March 27, 2002. The al-Aqsa Martyrs Brigade comprises an unknown number of small cells of Fatah-affiliated activists that emerged at the outset of the second Palestinian uprising, or al-Aqsa Intifada, in September 2000. Al-Aqsa's goal is to drive the Israeli military and West Bank settlers from the West Bank in order to establish a Palestinian state loyal to the Fatah.

Activities: Al-Aqsa employed primarily small-arms attacks against Israeli military personnel and settlers as the intifada spread in 2000, but by 2002 they turned increasingly to suicide bombings against Israeli civilians inside Israel. In January 2002, the group claimed responsibility for the first female suicide bombing inside Israel. After the June 2007 Hamas takeover of Gaza, al-Aqsa Martyrs cells in Gaza stepped up rocket and mortar attacks against Israel. In 2010, AAMB launched numerous rocket attacks on communities in Israel, including the city of Sederot and areas of the Negev desert. Al-Aqsa has not pursued a policy of targeting U.S. interests as a policy, although its anti-Israeli attacks have killed dual U.S.-Israeli citizens.

Strength: A few hundred members.

Location/Area of Operation: Most of al-Aqsa's operational activity is in Gaza but the group also planned and conducted attacks inside Israel and the West Bank. The group also has members in Palestinian refugee camps in Lebanon.

External Aid: Iran has exploited al-Aqsa's lack of resources and formal leadership by providing funds and guidance, mostly through Hizballah facilitators.

AL-QA'IDA

Variant spelling of al-Qa'ida, including al Qaeda; translation "The Base"; Qa'idat al-Jihad (The Base for Jihad); formerly Qa'idat Ansar Allah (The Base of the Supporters of God); the Islamic Army; Islamic Salvation Foundation; the Base; The Group for the Preservation of the Holy Sites; The Islamic Army for the Liberation of the Holy Places; the World Islamic Front for Jihad Against Jews and Crusaders; the Usama Bin Ladin Network; the Usama Bin Ladin Organization; al-Jihad; the Jihad Group; Egyptian al-Jihad; Egyptian Islamic Jihad; New Jihad

Description: Al-Qa'ida (AQ) was designated as a Foreign Terrorist Organization on October 8, 1999. AQ was established by Usama bin Ladin in 1988 and originally consisted of members who fought in Afghanistan against the Soviet Union. The group helped finance, recruit, transport, and train Sunni Islamist extremists for the Afghan resistance. AQ's strategic objectives include uniting Muslims to fight the United States and its allies, overthrowing regimes it deems "non-Islamic," and expelling Westerners and non-Muslims from Muslim countries. Its ultimate goal is the establishment of a pan-Islamic caliphate throughout the world. AQ leaders issued a statement in February 1998 under the banner of "The World Islamic Front for Jihad against the Jews and Crusaders," saying it was the duty of all Muslims to kill U.S. citizens, civilian and military, and their allies everywhere. AQ merged with al-Jihad (Egyptian Islamic Jihad) in June 2001.

Activities: AQ is the most significant terrorist threat to the United States and it developed stronger relationships with its affiliates in the Middle East, North Africa, and Europe in 2010. AQ, its allies, and those inspired by the group were involved attacks in Africa, Europe, the Middle East, and South Asia including suicide bombings and vehicle-borne improvised explosive devices in Iraq, Afghanistan, and Pakistan.

AQ and its supporters claim to have shot down U.S. helicopters and killed U.S. servicemen in Somalia in 1993, and to have conducted three bombings that targeted U.S. troops in Aden in December 1992. AQ also carried out the August 1998 bombings of the U.S. Embassies in Nairobi and Dar es Salaam, killing up to 300 individuals and injuring more than 5,000. In October 2000, AQ conducted a suicide attack on the USS Cole in the port of Aden, Yemen, with an explosive-laden boat, killing 17 U.S. Navy sailors and injuring 39.

On September 11, 2001, 19 AQ members hijacked and crashed four U.S. commercial jets – two into the World Trade Center in New York City, one into the Pentagon near Washington, DC; and the last into a field in Shanksville, Pennsylvania – leaving over 3,000 individuals dead or missing.

In November 2002, AQ carried out a suicide bombing of a hotel in Mombasa, Kenya that killed 15. AQ probably provided financing for the October 2002 Bali bombings by Jemaah Islamiya that killed more than 200. In 2003 and 2004, Saudi-based AQ operatives and associated extremists launched more than a dozen attacks, killing at least 90 people, including 14 Americans in Saudi Arabia. Bin Ladin's deputy al-Zawahiri claimed responsibility on behalf of AQ for the July 7, 2005 attacks against the London public transportation system. AQ likely played a role in the 2006 failed plot to destroy several commercial aircraft flying from the United Kingdom to the United States using liquid explosives.

The Government of Pakistan accused AQ, along with Tehrik-e Taliban Pakistan (TTP), of being responsible for the October 2007 suicide bombing attempt against former Pakistani Prime Minister Benazir Bhutto that killed at least 144 people in Karachi, Pakistan. The Government of Pakistan stated that Baitullah Mehsud, a now-deceased TTP leader with close ties to AQ, was responsible for Bhutto's December 27, 2007 assassination.

In January 2009, Bryant Neal Vinas – a U.S. citizen who traveled to Pakistan, allegedly trained in explosives at AQ camps, and was eventually captured in Pakistan and extradited to the United States – was charged with providing material support to a terrorist organization and conspiracy to commit murder. Vinas later admitted his role in helping AQ plan an attack against the Long Island Rail Road in New York and confessed to having fired missiles at a U.S. base in Afghanistan. In September 2009, Najibullah Zazi, an Afghan immigrant and U.S. lawful permanent resident, was charged with conspiracy to use weapons of mass destruction, to commit murder in a foreign country, and with providing material support to a terrorist organization as part of an AQ plot to attack the New York subway system. Zazi later admitted to contacts with AQ senior leadership, suggesting they had knowledge of his plans. In February 2010, Zazi pled guilty to charges in the United States District Court for the Eastern District of New York. U.S. officials have described the alleged bombing plot as one of the most serious terrorist threats to the United States since the 9/11 attacks.

Strength: AQ's organizational strength is difficult to determine in the aftermath of extensive counterterrorism efforts since 9/11. The arrests and deaths of mid-level and senior AQ operatives have disrupted communication, financial, facilitation nodes, and a number of terrorist plots. Additionally, supporters and associates worldwide who are "inspired" by the group's ideology may be operating without direction from AQ central leadership; it is impossible to estimate their numbers. AQ serves as a focal point of "inspiration" for a worldwide network that is comprised of many Sunni Islamic extremist groups, including some members of the Gama'at al-Islamiyya, the Islamic Movement of Uzbekistan, the Islamic Jihad Union, Lashkar i Jhangvi, Harakat ul-Mujahadin, the Taliban, and Jemaah Islamiya. TTP also has strengthened its ties to AQ.

Location/Area of Operation: AQ was based in Afghanistan until Coalition Forces removed the Taliban from power in late 2001. Since then, they have resided in Pakistan's Federally Administered Tribal Areas. AQ has a number of regional affiliates, including al-Qa'ida in Iraq (AQI), al-Qa'ida in the Arabian Peninsula, and al-Qa'ida in the Islamic Maghreb.

External Aid: AQ primarily depends on donations from like-minded supporters as well as from individuals who believe that their money is supporting a humanitarian cause. Some funds are diverted from Islamic charitable organizations. In addition, parts of the organization raise funds through criminal activities; for example, AQI raises funds through hostage-taking for ransom, and members in Europe have engaged in credit card fraud. U.S. and international efforts to block AQ funding have hampered the group's ability to raise money.

AL-QA'IDA IN THE ARABIAN PENINSULA

aka al-Qa'ida in the South Arabian Peninsula, al-Qa'ida in Yemen, al-Qa'ida of Jihad Organization in the Arabian Peninsula, al-Qa'ida Organization in the Arabian Peninsula, Tanzim Qa'idat al-Jihad fi Jazirat al-Arab, AQAP, AQY

Description: Al-Qa'ida in the Arabian Peninsula (AQAP) was designated as a Foreign Terrorist Organization on January 19, 2010. In January 2009, the leader of al-Qa'ida in Yemen (AQY), Nasir al-Wahishi, publicly announced that Yemeni and Saudi al-Qa'ida operatives were working together under the banner of AQAP. This announcement signaled the rebirth of an al-Qa'ida franchise that carried out attacks under this name in Saudi Arabia between 2004 and 2006. AQAP's self-stated goals include establishing a caliphate in the Arabian Peninsula and the wider Middle East as well as implementing Sharia law.

Activities: AQAP has claimed responsibility for numerous terrorist acts against both internal and foreign targets since its inception in January 2009. Attempted attacks against foreign targets include a March 2009 suicide bombing against South Korean tourists in Yemen, the August 2009 attempt to assassinate Saudi Prince Muhammad bin Nayif, and the December 25, 2009 attempted attack on Northwest Airlines Flight 253 from Amsterdam to Detroit, Michigan. AQAP was responsible for an unsuccessful attempt to assassinate the British Ambassador in April 2010 and a failed attempt to target a British embassy vehicle with a rocket in October. Also in October 2010, AQAP claimed responsibility for a foiled plot to send explosive-laden packages to the United States via cargo plane. The parcels were intercepted in the United Kingdom and in United Arab Emirates.

Strength: AQAP is estimated to have several hundred members.

Location/Area of Operation: Yemen

External Aid: AQAP primarily depends on donations from like-minded supporters.

AL-QA'IDA IN IRAQ

aka al-Qa'ida Group of Jihad in Iraq; al-Qa'ida Group of Jihad in the Land of the Two Rivers; al-Qa'ida in Mesopotamia; al-Qa'ida in the Land of the Two Rivers; al-Qa'ida of Jihad in Iraq; al-Qa'ida of Jihad Organization in the Land of The Two Rivers; al-Qa'ida of the Jihad in the Land of the Two Rivers; al-Tawhid; Jam'at al-Tawhid Wa'al-Jihad; Tanzeem Qa'idat al Jihad/Bilad al Raafidaini; Tanzim Qa'idat al-Jihad fi Bilad al-Rafidayn; The Monotheism and Jihad Group; The Organization Base of Jihad/Country of the Two Rivers; The Organization Base of Jihad/Mesopotamia; The Organization of al-Jihad's Base in Iraq; The Organization of al-Jihad's Base in the Land of the Two Rivers; The Organization of al-Jihad's Base of Operations in Iraq; The Organization of al-Jihad's Base of Operations in the Land of the Two Rivers; The Organization of Jihad's Base in the Country of the Two Rivers; al-Zarqawi Network

Description: Al-Qa'ida in Iraq was designated as a Foreign Terrorist Organization on December 17, 2004. In the 1990s, Abu Mus'ab al-Zarqawi, a Jordanian-born militant, organized a terrorist group called al-Tawhid wal-Jihad as an opposition to the presence of U.S. and Western military forces in the Islamic world and also the West's support for and the existence of Israel. He traveled to Iraq during Operation Iraqi Freedom and led his group against U.S. and Coalition forces there until his death in June 2006. In late 2004 he joined al-Qa'ida and pledged allegiance to Usama bin Ladin. After this al-Tawhid wal-Jihad became known as al-Qa'ida in Iraq (AQI), and al-Zarqawi was given the al-Qa'ida title, "Emir of al-Qa'ida in the Country of Two Rivers."

In January 2006, in an attempt to unify Sunni extremists in Iraq, AQI created the Mujahidin Shura Council (MSC), an umbrella organization meant to encompass the various Sunni terrorist groups in Iraq. AQI claimed its attacks under the MSC until mid-October 2006, when Abu Mus'ab al-Zarqawi's successor, Abu Ayyub al-Masri, took the first step toward al-Qa'ida's (AQ's) goal of establishing a caliphate in the region by declaring the "Islamic State of Iraq" (ISI), under which AQI now claims its attacks. Iraqis comprise over 90 percent of the group's membership. While a disproportionate percentage of AQI's senior leadership was foreign-born earlier in the organizational history, today AQI leadership is predominantly Iraqi. In an attempt to give AQI a more Iraqi persona, the AQI-led ISI was created with Iraqi-national Abu Umar al-Baghdadi named its leader. Al-Baghdadi and AQI's other top leader Abu Ayyub al-Masri were killed in a raid in April 2010, after which AQI subsequently named Abu Baker al-Baghdadi al-Husseini al-Qurashi as ISI's head and Abu Ibrahim al-Issawi as his Minister of War.

Activities: AQI's predecessor group, led by al-Zarqawi, was established in 2003 and swiftly gained prominence, striking numerous Iraqi, Coalition, and relief agency targets such as the Red Cross. In August 2003, AQI carried out major terrorist attacks in Iraq when it bombed the Jordanian Embassy in Baghdad, which was followed 12 days later by a suicide vehicle-borne improvised explosive device (VBIED) attack against the UN Headquarters in Baghdad that killed 23, including the Secretary-General's Special Representative for Iraq, Sergio Vieira de Mello. Since its founding, AQI has conducted high profile attacks, including improvised explosive device (IED) attacks against U.S. military personnel and Iraqi infrastructure throughout 2004, videotaped beheadings of Americans Nicholas Berg (May 11, 2004), Jack Armstrong (September 22, 2004), and Jack Hensley (September 21, 2004), suicide bomber attacks against both military and civilian targets, and rocket attacks. AQI perpetrates the majority of suicide and mass casualty bombings in Iraq, using foreign and Iraqi operatives.

AQI, acting through its front organization ISI, was highly active in 2010, perpetrating almost daily attacks on Coalition forces, Iraqi civilian targets, and military assets. Many of these attacks had significant casualty counts. For example, on October 31 and November 2, 2010 alone, ISI attacked locations in Baghdad using mortars, VBIEDs, and IEDs, resulting in 122 deaths and 430 wounded. In all, ISI either claimed responsibility for, or was suspected of, being responsible for almost 350 attacks inside Iraq in 2010.

Strength: Membership is estimated at 1,000-2,000, making it the largest, most potent Sunni extremist group in Iraq.

Location/Area of Operation: AQI's operations are predominately Iraq-based, but it has perpetrated attacks in Jordan. The group maintains a logistical network throughout the Middle East, North Africa, Iran, South Asia, and Europe. In Iraq, AQI currently conducts the majority of its operations in Ninawa, Diyala, Salah ad Din, and Baghdad provinces and is working to re-establish its capabilities in Al Anbar.

External Aid: AQI probably receives most of its funding from a variety of businesses and criminal activities within Iraq.

AL-QA'IDA IN THE ISLAMIC MAGHREB

aka AQIM; Group for Call and Combat; GSPC; Le Groupe Salafiste Pour La Predication Et Le Combat; Salafist Group for Preaching and Combat

Description: The Salafist Group for Call and Combat (GSPC) was designated as a Foreign Terrorist Organization on March 27, 2002. After the GSPC officially merged with al-Qa'ida (AQ) in September 2006 the organization became known as al-Qa'ida in the Islamic Maghreb (AQIM). On February 20, 2008, the Department of State amended the GSPC designation to reflect the change and made AQIM the official name for the organization. Some senior members of AQIM are former Armed Islamic Group (GIA) insurgents. AQIM remains largely a regionally-focused terrorist group. It has adopted a more anti-Western rhetoric and ideology and has aspirations of overthrowing "apostate" African regimes and creating an Islamic Caliphate. AQIM numbers under a thousand fighters and is significantly constrained by its poor finances and lack of broad general appeal in the region. Abdel-malek Droukdel, aka Abu Mus'ab Abd al-Wadoud, is the leader of the group.

Activities: In 2007, AQIM bombed the UN building and an Algerian government building just outside of Algiers killing over 60 people. In 2008 and 2009, even as it was under significant pressure by Algerian security forces, AQIM continued to conduct small scale attacks and ambushes in northeastern Algeria against Algerian security forces and regularly used improvised explosive devices there. In June 2010, an AQIM attack resulted in the death of 11 Algerian soldiers and the kidnapping of a customs official who was later executed by the organization. Also in June, AQIM was responsible for a detonation of a vehicle-borne improvised explosive device (VBIED) at a police checkpoint, which resulted in the death of seven national police officers and three civilians. In Niger, the group conducted its first vehicle-borne suicide attack in March and in August used similar tactics in an attack on a Mauritanian military base. In total, AQIM attacks in Algeria, Mali, Mauritania, and Niger resulted in the deaths of over 80 people in 2010.

AQIM factions in the northern Sahel (northern Mali, Niger, and Mauritania) conducted kidnap for ransom operations and conducted small scale attacks and ambushes on security forces. The targets for kidnap for ransom are usually Western citizens from governments or third parties that have established a pattern of making concessions in the form of ransom payments or the release of operatives in custody. In April 2010, AQIM kidnapped French aid worker Michel Germaneau in Niger, later moving him to Mali. In July, Germaneau was killed in retaliation for the death of six AQIM operatives during a failed attempt by France and Mauritania to free him. In September, AQIM claimed responsibility for the kidnapping of seven people, including five French nationals working at a mine in Niger. At year's end, the hostages had not been released.

Strength: AQIM has under a thousand fighters operating in Algeria with a smaller number in the Sahel.

Location/Area of Operation: Northeastern Algeria (including but not limited to the Kabylie region) and northern Mali, Niger, and Mauritania.

External Aid: Algerian expatriates and AQIM members abroad, many residing in Western Europe, provide limited financial and logistical support. AQIM members engage in hostage-taking for ransom and criminal activity to finance their operations.

AL-SHABAAB

aka The Harakat Shabaab al-Mujahidin; al-Shabab; Shabaab; the Youth; Mujahidin al-Shabaab Movement; Mujahideen Youth Movement; Mujahidin Youth Movement

Description: Al-Shabaab was designated as a Foreign Terrorist Organization on March 18, 2008. Al-Shabaab was the militant wing of the former Somali Islamic Courts Council that took over parts of southern Somalia in the second half of 2006. In December 2006 and January 2007, Ethiopian forces routed the Islamic Court militias in a two-week war, which became a protracted insurgency over the next two years. Since the end of 2006, al-Shabaab and disparate clan militias have led a violent insurgency using guerrilla warfare and terrorist tactics against the Transitional Federal Government (TFG) of Somalia. Several senior al-Shabaab leaders have publicly proclaimed loyalty to AQ. These leaders founded and supported a number of training camps in southern Somalia for young national and international recruits to al-Shabaab. In some camps, AQ-affiliated foreign fighters often led the training and indoctrination of the recruits. Rank and file militia fighters from multiple clan and sub-clan factions that are aligned with al-Shabaab are predominantly interested in indigenous issues. In

January 2010, the organization announced its support for militants in Yemen. In December, despite past clashes over territory, al-Shabaab entered into a tenuous merger with a severely weakened, nearly defunct faction of Hizbul Islam, another clan-based insurgent group fighting against the TFG.

Activities: Al-Shabaab has used intimidation and violence to undermine the Somali government, forcibly recruit new fighters, and kill activists working to bring about peace through political dialogue and reconciliation. The group has claimed responsibility for several high profile bombings and shootings throughout Somalia targeting African Union troops and TFG officials. It has been responsible for the assassination of numerous civil society figures, government officials, and journalists. Al-Shabaab fighters or those who have claimed allegiance to the group have conducted violent attacks and targeted assassinations against international aid workers and nongovernmental organizations. During 2010, al-Shabaab carried out multiple attacks, including a number in Mogadishu against the TFG and African Union Mission in Somalia. Among the most deadly were a series of attacks in March, which killed at least 60 people and wounded 160 more; and a string of attacks in late August, which killed at least 87 people and wounded 148. Also in August, al-Shabaab suicide bombers entered the Muna Hotel in Mogadishu and killed 31 people, including six members of parliament and four other government officials, when they detonated their explosives on the roof of the hotel. In the organization's first attack outside of Somalia, al-Shabaab was responsible for the July 11 suicide bombings in Kampala, Uganda during the World Cup, which killed nearly 80 people, including one American citizen. In total, al-Shabaab is estimated to be responsible the death of over 900 people in 2010.

Location/Area of Operation: Ethiopian troops left Somalia in late January 2008 and the subsequent security vacuum in parts of central and southern Somalia has led divergent factions to oppose al-Shabaab and its extremist ideology. However, hardcore al-Shabaab fighters and allied militias conducted bold attacks in Mogadishu and other outlying areas, primarily in South-Central Somalia, causing the organization's area of control to expand in 2010. In May, al-Shabaab launched a major offensive in Mogadishu, gaining control over parts of the capital. Al-Shabaab – by understanding the historical conflict between the Ogadeni and Marehan sub-clans of the Darood – gained primary control over the southern port of Kismayo in late 2009. Al-Shabaab's victories can also be tied to their ability to play upon clan fissures and the military weakness of the Somali Government. Furthermore, July's attack in Uganda demonstrates al-Shabaab's desire to expand operations outside of Somalia.

Strength: Precise numbers are unknown, but al-Shabaab is estimated to have several thousand members when augmented by foreign fighters and allied clan militias.

External Aid: Because al-Shabaab is a multi-clan entity, it received significant donations from the global Somali diaspora; however, the donations were not all specifically intended to support terrorism. Rather, the money was also meant to support family members. Al-Shabaab leaders and many rank and file fighters have successfully garnered significant amounts of money from port revenues and through criminal enterprises, especially in Kismayo.

ANSAR AL-ISLAM

aka Ansar al-Sunna; Ansar al-Sunna Army; Devotees of Islam; Followers of Islam in Kurdistan; Helpers of Islam; Jaish Ansar al-Sunna; Jund al-Islam; Kurdish Taliban; Kurdistan Supporters of Islam; Partisans of Islam; Soldiers of God; Soldiers of Islam; Supporters of Islam in Kurdistan

Description: Ansar al-Islam (AI) was designated as a Foreign Terrorist Organization on March 22, 2004. It's goals include expelling the western interests from Iraq and establishing an independent Iraqi state based on Sharia law. AI was established in 2001 in Iraqi Kurdistan with the merger of two Kurdish extremist factions that traced their roots to the Islamic Movement of Kurdistan. AI has ties to al-Qa'ida (AQ) central leadership and to al-Qa'ida in Iraq (AQI). Since Operation Iraqi Freedom, AI has become one of the most prominent groups engaged in anti-Coalition attacks in Iraq behind AQI.

Activities: AI has conducted attacks against a wide range of targets including Iraqi government and security forces, and U.S. and Coalition forces. AI has also conducted numerous kidnappings, executions, and assassinations of Iraqi citizens and politicians. One of the more notable attacks was a March 2008 bombing at the Palace Hotel in As Sulamaniyah that killed two people. The group has either claimed responsibility or was believed responsible for a total of 13 attacks in 2010 that killed 15 and wounded at least 39. On January 7, six Iraqi civilians, including a child, were killed along with one Iraqi police officer in an improvised explosive device (IED) attack in al-Anbar Province, Iraq, for which AI was believed responsible. On May 17 and 18, seven Iraqi civilians died in IED attacks in Mosul and Baghdad for which AI claimed responsibility.

Strength: Although precise numbers are unknown, AI is considered one of the largest Sunni terrorist groups in Iraq.

Location/Area of Operation: Primarily northern Iraq but maintained a presence in western and central Iraq.

External Aid: AI received assistance from a loose network of associates in Europe and the Middle East. .

ASBAT AL-ANSAR

aka Asbat al-Ansar; Band of Helpers; Band of Partisans; League of Partisans; League of the Followers; God's Partisans; Gathering of Supporters; Partisan's League; AAA; Esbat al-Ansar; Isbat al-Ansar; Osbat al-Ansar; Usbat al-Ansar; Usbat ul-Ansar

Description: Asbat al-Ansar was designated as a Foreign Terrorist Organization on March 27, 2002. Asbat al-Ansar is a Lebanon-based Sunni extremist group composed primarily of Palestinians with links to al-Qa'ida (AQ) and other Sunni extremist groups. Some of the group's goals include thwarting perceived anti-Islamic and pro-Western influences in the country. Asbat al-Ansar's leader, Ahmad Abd al-Karim al-Sa'di, a.k.a. Abu Muhjin, remained at large despite being sentenced to death in absentia for the 1994 murder of a Muslim cleric.

Activities: Asbat al-Ansar first emerged in the early 1990s. In the mid-1990s, the group assassinated Lebanese religious leaders and bombed nightclubs, theaters, and liquor stores. The group has also plotted against foreign diplomatic targets. In October 2004, Mahir al-Sa'di, a member of Asbat al-Ansar, was sentenced in absentia to life imprisonment for his 2000 plot to assassinate then-U.S. Ambassador to Lebanon, David Satterfield. Asbat al-Ansar-associated elements have been implicated in Katyusha rocket attacks against Israel occurring in December 2005 and June 2007.

Asbat al-Ansar has no formal ties to the AQ network, but the group shares AQ's ideology and has publicly proclaimed its support for al-Qa'ida in Iraq. Members of the group have traveled to Iraq since 2005 to fight Coalition Forces. Asbat al-Ansar has been reluctant to involve itself in operations in Lebanon due in part to concerns over losing its safe haven in Ain al-Hilwah. However, according to the Lebanese press, a woman was killed by a rocket propelled grenade on February 15, 2010 during a clash between Asbat al-Ansar and another militant group in Ain al-Hilwah.

Strength: The group has fewer than 2,000 members, mostly of Palestinian descent.

Location/Area of Operation: The group's primary base of operations is the Ain al-Hilwah Palestinian refugee camp near Sidon in southern Lebanon. The group is also present in Iraq where the group has engaged in fighting U.S. forces.

External Aid: It is likely that the group receives money through international Sunni extremist networks.

AUM SHINRIKYO

aka A.I.C. Comprehensive Research Institute; A.I.C. Sogo Kenkyusho; Aleph; Aum Supreme Truth

Description: Aum Shinrikyo (Aum) was designated as a Foreign Terrorist Organization on October 8, 1997. Shoko Asahara established Aum in 1987, and the cult received legal status in Japan as a religious entity in 1989. The Japanese government revoked its recognition of Aum as a religious organization following Aum's deadly sarin gas attack in Tokyo in March 1995. Despite claims of renunciation of violence and Ashara's teachings, members of the group continue to adhere to the violent and apocalyptic teachings of its founder.

Activities: In March 1995, Aum members simultaneously released the chemical nerve agent sarin on several Tokyo subway trains, killing 12 people and causing up to 6,000 to seek medical treatment. Subsequent investigations by the Japanese government revealed the group was responsible for other mysterious chemical incidents in Japan in 1994, including a sarin gas attack on a residential neighborhood in Matsumoto that killed seven and hospitalized approximately 500. Japanese police arrested Asahara in May 1995, and in February 2004, authorities sentenced him to death for his role in the 1995 attacks. In September 2006, Asahara lost his final appeal against the death penalty and the Japanese Supreme Court upheld the decision in October 2007. In February 2010, the death sentence for senior Aum member Tomomitsu Miimi was finalized by Japan's Supreme Court. This would bring the number of Aum members on death row for their crimes related to the sarin gas attack to 10.

Since 1997, the cult has recruited new members, engaged in commercial enterprises, and acquired property, although it scaled back these activities significantly in 2001 in response to a public outcry. In July 2001, Russian authorities arrested a group of Russian Aum followers who had planned to set off bombs near the Imperial Palace in Tokyo as part of an operation to free Asahara from jail and smuggle him to Russia.

Although Aum has not conducted a terrorist attack since 1995, concerns remain regarding its continued adherence to the violent teachings of founder Asahara that led them to perpetrate the 1995 sarin gas attack.

Strength: According to a study by the Japanese government issued in December 2009, Aum Shinrikyo/Aleph membership in Japan is approximately 1,500 with another 200 in Russia. The study said that Aum maintained 31 facilities in 15 Prefectures in Japan and continued to possess a few facilities in Russia. At the time of the Tokyo subway attack, the group claimed to have as many as 40,000 members worldwide, including 9,000 in Japan and 30,000 members in Russia.

Location/Area of Operation: Aum's principal membership is located in Japan; while a residual branch of about 200 followers live in Russia.

External Aid: Funding primarily comes from member contributions.

BASQUE FATHERLAND AND LIBERTY

aka ETA, Askatasuna; Batasuna; Ekin; Euskal Herritarrok; Euzkadi Ta Askatasuna; Herri Batasuna; Jarrai-Haika-Segi; K.A.S.; XAKI

Description: Basque Fatherland and Liberty (ETA) was designated as a Foreign Terrorist Organization on October 8, 1997. ETA was founded in 1959 with the aim of establishing an independent homeland based on Marxist principles encompassing the Spanish Basque provinces of Vizcaya, Guipuzcoa, and Alava; the autonomous region of Navarra; and the southwestern French territories of Labourd, Basse-Navarre, and Soule. Spain and the EU have listed ETA as a terrorist organization. In 2002, the Spanish Parliament banned the political party Batasuna, ETA's political wing, charging its members with providing material support to the terrorist group. The European Court of Human Rights in June 2009 upheld the ban on Batasuna. In September 2008, Spanish courts also banned two other Basque independence parties with reported links to Batasuna. In 2010, Batasuna continued to try to participate in regional politics and splits between parts of ETA became publicly apparent in deciding a way forward. Spanish and French prisons together are estimated to hold a total of more than 750 ETA members.

Activities: ETA primarily has conducted bombings and assassinations. Targets typically have included Spanish government officials, businessman, politicians, judicial figures, and security and military forces, but the group also targeted journalists and tourist areas. The group is responsible for killing more than 800 civilians and members of the armed forces or police and injuring thousands since it formally began a campaign of violence in 1968.

In March 2006, days after claiming responsibility for a spate of roadside blasts in northern Spain that caused no injuries, ETA announced that it would implement a "permanent" ceasefire. On December 30, 2006, however, ETA exploded a massive car bomb that destroyed much of the covered parking garage outside the Terminal Four of Madrid's Barajas International Airport.

Between 2007 and 2010, more than 400 ETA members were arrested. Since 2008, Spanish and French authorities have apprehended six of ETA's top leaders, and have seized ETA arms caches containing more than 800 kilos of explosives, 15 complete limpet bombs, and weapons and ammunition. Despite these law enforcement efforts, ETA has continued to carry out attacks resulting in extensive damage and casualties.

In March 2010, a Spanish judge charged ETA and Revolutionary Armed Forces of Colombia members of terrorist plots, including a plan to assassinate Colombian President Alvaro Uribe. On March 16, ETA claimed responsibility for killing a police officer outside of Paris, France. In August, a suspected ETA supporter in the Basque Country injured two police officers in an arson attack. In September, a small improvised bomb went off in an industrial zone of Vitoria, the Basque capital, with no reports of injuries. Police suspected an ETA support group planted the bomb despite an ETA ceasefire announced 11 days earlier.

Strength: ETA's exact strength is unknown, but current estimates by Spanish authorities and scholars put membership between approximately 100-300 operational personnel.

Location/Area of Operation: ETA operated primarily in the Basque autonomous regions of northern Spain and southwestern France, but has attacked Spanish and French interests elsewhere. Most recently, ETA safe houses have been identified and raided in Portugal.

External Aid: ETA financed its activities primarily through bribery and extortion of Basque businesses. In the past, it has received training in Libya and Lebanon, although there is no indication that such training continues. Some ETA members have allegedly fled to Cuba and Mexico, while others reside in South America.

COMMUNIST PARTY OF PHILIPPINES/NEW PEOPLE'S ARMY

aka CPP/NPA; Communist Party of the Philippines; the CPP; New People's Army; the NPA

Description: The Communist Party of the Philippines/New People's Army (CPP/NPA) was designated as a Foreign Terrorist Organization on August 9, 2002. The military wing of the Communist Party of the Philippines (CPP), the New People's Army (NPA), is a Maoist group formed in March 1969 with the aim of overthrowing the government through protracted guerrilla warfare. Jose Maria Sison, the chairman of the CPP's Central Committee and the NPA's founder, reportedly directs CPP and NPA activity from the Netherlands, where he lives in self-imposed exile. Luis Jalandoni, a fellow Central Committee member and director of the CPP's overt political wing, the National Democratic Front (NDF), also lives in the Netherlands and has become a Dutch citizen. Although primarily a rural-based guerrilla group, the NPA had an active urban infrastructure to support its terrorist activities and, at times, used city-based assassination squads.

Activities: The CPP/NPA primarily targeted Philippine security forces, government officials, local infrastructure, and businesses that refused to pay extortion, or "revolutionary taxes." The CPP/NPA charged politicians running for office in CPP/NPA-influenced areas for "campaign permits." Despite its focus on Philippine governmental targets, the CPP/NPA has a history of attacking U.S. interests in the Philippines. In 1987, the CPP/NPA conducted direct action against U.S. personnel and facilities when three American soldiers were killed in four separate attacks in Angeles City. In 1989, the CPP/NPA issued a press statement taking credit for the ambush and murder of Colonel James Nicholas Rowe, chief of the Ground Forces Division of the Joint U.S.-Military Advisory Group.

In 2010, the CPP/NPA's attacks continued unabated. Most notably, 40 CPP/NPA guerillas ambushed an army convoy escorting election officials on May 11 in the Compostela Valley, an attack that culminated in five deaths. On June 25, the Philippine government arrested Renelo Creita for allegedly masterminding the May 11 attack. On August 21, 40 CPP/NPA assailants launched a synchronized landmine improvised explosive device and light arms attack against a police vehicle that resulted in nine deaths in Cataman, Philippines.

Strength: The Philippines government estimated there are approximately 5,000 members.

Location/Area of Operations: The CPP/NPA operates in rural Luzon, Visayas, and parts of northern and eastern Mindanao. There are cells in Manila and other metropolitan centers.

External Aid: Unknown.

CONTINUITY IRISH REPUBLICAN ARMY

aka Continuity Army Council; Continuity IRA; Republican Sinn Fein

Description: The Continuity Irish Republican Army (CIRA) was designated as a Foreign Terrorist Organization on July 13, 2004. CIRA is a terrorist splinter group formed in 1994 as the clandestine armed wing of Republican Sinn Fein, which split from Sinn Fein in 1986. "Continuity" refers to the group's belief that it is carrying on the original Irish Republican Army's (IRA) goal of forcing the British out of Northern Ireland. CIRA cooperates with the larger Real IRA (RIRA).

Activities: CIRA has been active in Belfast and the border areas of Northern Ireland, where it has carried out bombings, assassinations, kidnappings, hijackings, extortion, and robberies. On occasion, it provided advance warning to police of its attacks. Targets have included the British military, Northern Ireland security forces, and Loyalist paramilitary groups. CIRA did not join the Provisional IRA in the September 2005 decommissioning and remained capable of effective, if sporadic, terrorist attacks. On April 3, 2010, authorities defused a vehicle-borne improvised explosive device in Crossmaglen, Northern Ireland for which CIRA claimed responsibility.

Strength: Membership is small, with possibly fewer than 50 hard-core activists. Police counterterrorist operations have reduced the group's strength.

Location/Area of Operation: Northern Ireland and the Irish Republic.

External Aid: CIRA supported its activities through criminal activities, including smuggling. CIRA may have acquired arms and materiel from the Balkans, in cooperation with the RIRA.

GAMA'A AL-ISLAMIYYA

aka al-Gama'at; Egyptian al-Gama'at al-Islamiyya; GI; Islamic Gama'at; IG; Islamic Group

Description: Gama'a al-Islamiyya (IG) was designated as a Foreign Terrorist Organization on October 8, 1997. IG, once Egypt's largest militant group, was active in the late 1970s, but is now a loosely organized network. The majority of its Egypt-based members have renounced terrorism, although some located overseas have begun to work with or have joined al-Qa'ida (AQ). In 2010, the external wing, composed of mainly exiled members in several countries, maintained that its primary goal was to replace the Egyptian government with an Islamic state. IG's spiritual leader, Sheik Umar Abd al-Rahman, is serving a life sentence in a U.S. prison for his involvement in the 1993 World Trade Center bombing. Supporters of Sheikh Abd al-Rahman still remain a possible threat to U.S. interests and have called for reprisal attacks in case of his death in prison.

Activities: In the 1990s, IG conducted armed attacks against Egyptian security and other government officials and Coptic Christians. IG claimed responsibility for the June 1995 assassination attempt on Egyptian President Hosni Mubarak in Addis Ababa, Ethiopia. The group also launched attacks on tourists in Egypt, most notably the 1997 Luxor attack. IG did not launch any attacks in 2010.

Strength: At its peak, IG probably commanded several thousand hardcore members and a similar number of supporters. Security crackdowns following the 1997 attack in Luxor and the 1999 cease-fire, along with post-September 11 security measures and defections to AQ have probably resulted in a substantial decrease in what is left of an organized group.

Location/Area of Operation: The IG maintained an external presence in Afghanistan, Yemen, Iran, the United Kingdom, Germany, and France. IG terrorist presence in Egypt was minimal due to the reconciliation efforts of former local members.

External Aid: IG may have obtained some funding through various Islamic non-governmental organizations.

HAMAS

aka the Islamic Resistance Movement; Harakat al-Muqawama al-Islamiya; Izz al-Din al Qassam Battalions; Izz al-Din al Qassam Brigades; Izz al-Din al Qassam Forces; Students of Ayyash; Student of the Engineer; Yahya Ayyash Units; Izz al-Din al-Qassim Brigades; Izz al-Din al-Qassim Forces; Izz al-Din al-Qassim Battalions

Description: Hamas was designated as a Foreign Terrorist Organization on October 8, 1997. Hamas possesses military and political wings, and was formed in late 1987 at the onset of the first Palestinian uprising, or Intifada, as an outgrowth of the Palestinian branch of the Muslim Brotherhood. The armed element, called the Izz al-Din al-Qassam Brigades, conducts anti-Israeli attacks, previously including suicide bombings against civilian targets inside Israel. Hamas also manages a broad, mostly Gaza-based network of "Dawa" or ministry activities that include charities, schools, clinics, youth camps, fund-raising, and political activities. A Shura Council based in Damascus, Syria, sets overall policy. After winning Palestinian Legislative Council elections in January 2006, Hamas seized control of significant Palestinian Authority (PA) ministries in Gaza, including the Ministry of Interior. Hamas subsequently formed an expanded militia called the Executive Force, subordinate to the Interior Ministry. This force and other Hamas cadres took control of Gaza in a military-style coup in June 2007, forcing Fatah forces to either leave Gaza or go underground.

Activities: Prior to 2005, Hamas conducted numerous anti-Israeli attacks, including suicide bombings, rocket launches, improvised explosive device attacks, and shootings. Hamas has not directly targeted U.S. interests, though the group has conducted attacks against Israeli targets frequented by foreigners. The group curtailed terrorist attacks in February 2005 after agreeing to a temporary period of calm brokered by the PA and ceased most violence after winning control of the PA legislature and cabinet in January 2006. After Hamas staged a June 2006 attack on Israeli Defense Forces soldiers near Kerem Shalom that resulted in two deaths and the abduction of Corporal Gilad Shalit, Israel took steps that severely limited the operation of the Rafah crossing. In June 2007, after Hamas took control of Gaza from the PA and Fatah, an international boycott was imposed along with the closure of Gaza borders. Hamas has since dedicated the majority of its activity in Gaza to solidifying its control, hardening its defenses, tightening security, and conducting limited operations against Israeli military forces.

Hamas fired rockets from Gaza into Israel in 2008 but focused more on mortar attacks targeting Israeli incursions. In June 2008, Hamas agreed to a six-month cease-fire with Israel and temporarily halted all rocket attacks emanating from Gaza by arresting Palestinian militants and violators of the agreement. Hamas claimed responsibility for killing nine civilians, wounding 12 children and 80 other civilians in an attack at the residence of Fatah's Gaza City Secretary in Gaza in August 2008. Hamas also claimed responsibility for driving a vehicle into a crowd in Jerusalem, wounding 19 soldiers and civilians in September 2008. Hamas fought a 23-day war with Israel from late December 2008 to January 2009, in an unsuccessful effort to break an international blockade on Gaza and force the openings of the international crossings. Since Israel's declaration of a unilateral ceasefire on January 18, 2009, Hamas has largely enforced the calm, focusing on rebuilding its weapons caches, smuggling tunnels, and other military infrastructure in Gaza. Hamas carried out multiple rocket attacks on Israel in 2009 but was relatively inactive in 2010. In September 2010, Hamas claimed responsibility for carrying out a series of drive-by shootings in the West Bank that killed four Israelis near Hebron.

Strength: Hamas is believed to have several thousand Gaza-based operatives with varying degrees of skills in its armed wing, the Izz al-Din al-Qassam Brigades, along with its reported 9,000-person Hamas-led paramilitary group known as the "Executive Force."

Location/Area of Operation: Hamas has a presence in every major city in the Palestinian territories. The group retains a cadre of leaders and facilitators that conduct diplomatic, fundraising, and arms-smuggling activities in Lebanon, Syria, and other states. Hamas also increased its presence in the Palestinian refugee camps in Lebanon, probably with the goal of eclipsing Fatah's long-time dominance of the camps.

External Aid: Hamas receives the majority of its funding, weapons, and training from Iran. In addition, the group raises funds in the Persian Gulf countries and receives donations from Palestinian expatriates around the world. Some fundraising and propaganda activity takes place in Western Europe and North America. Syria provides safe haven for its leadership.

HARAKAT-UL JIHAD ISLAMI

aka HUJI, Movement of Islamic Holy War, Harkat-ul-Jihad-al Islami, Harkat-al-Jihad-ul Islami, Harkat-ul-Jehad-al-Islami, Harakat ul Jihad-e-Islami, Harakat-ul Jihad Islami

Description: Harakat-ul Jihad Islami (HUJI) was designated as a Foreign Terrorist Organization on August 6, 2010. HUJI was founded in 1980 in Afghanistan to fight against the Soviet Union. Following the Soviet withdrawal from Afghanistan in 1989, the organization re-focused its efforts on India. HUJI seeks the annexation of Indian Kashmir and expulsion of Coalition Forces from Afghanistan. In addition, some factions of HUJI espouse a more global agenda and conduct attacks in Pakistan as well. HUJI is composed of militant Pakistanis and veterans of the Soviet-Afghan war. It has also supplied fighters for the Taliban in Afghanistan. HUJI has experienced a number of internal splits and a portion of the group has aligned with al-Qa'ida (AQ) in recent years, including training its members in AQ training camps.

Activities: HUJI has been involved in a number of terrorist attacks in recent years. On March 2, 2006, a HUJI leader was the mastermind behind the suicide bombing of the U.S. Consulate in Karachi, Pakistan, which killed four people, including U.S. diplomat David Foy, and injured 48 others. HUJI is also responsible for terrorist attacks in India including the May 2007 Hyderabad mosque attack, which killed 16 and injured 40, and the March 2007 Varanasi attack, which killed 25 and injured 100. In January 2009, a U.S. District Court indicted HUJI and AQ leader Mohammad Ilyas Kashmiri for conspiracy to murder and maim and for providing material support for terrorism in connection with an attack against the Jyllands-Posten newspaper in Denmark.

Strength: HUJI has an estimated strength of several hundred members located in Kashmir and Pakistan.

Location/Area of Operations: HUJI's area of operation extends throughout South Asia, with its terrorist operations focused primarily in India and Afghanistan. Some factions of HUJI conduct attacks within Pakistan.

External Aid: HUJI's access to resources is unknown.

HARAKAT UL-JIHAD-I-ISLAMI/BANGLADESH

aka HUJI-B, Harakat ul Jihad e Islami Bangladesh; Harkatul Jihad al Islam; Harkatul Jihad; Harakat ul Jihad al Islami; Harkat ul Jihad al Islami; Harkat-ul-Jehad-al-Islami; Harakat ul Jihad Islami Bangladesh; Islami Dawat-e-Kafela; IDEK

Description: Harakat ul-Jihad-i-Islami/Bangladesh (HUJI-B) was designated as a Foreign Terrorist Organization on March 5, 2008. HUJI-B was formed in April 1992 by a group of former Bangladeshi Afghan veterans to establish Islamic rule in Bangladesh. The group was banned by Bangladeshi authorities in October 2005. HUJI-B has connections to the Pakistani militant groups such as Lashkar e-Tayyiba (LT), which advocates similar objectives. The leaders of HUJI-B signed the February 1998 fatwa sponsored by Usama bin Ladin that declared American civilians legitimate targets for attack.

Activities: Three HUJI-B members were convicted in December 2008 for the May 2004 grenade attack that wounded the British High Commissioner in Sylhet, Bangladesh. Bangladeshi courts issued warrants in December 2008 for the arrest of eight HUJI-B members for the bombing at a festival in April 2001 that killed 10 and injured scores of people. In May 2008, Indian police arrested HUJI-B militant Mohammad Iqbal, a.k.a. Abdur Rehman, who was charged with plotting attacks in Delhi, India. In December 2010, five leaders of HUJI-B were arrested in a raid on a training camp in Bangladesh. The detained HUJI-B members admitted to running the training camp, and authorities seized explosives, grenades, and bomb-making manuals in the raid.

Strength: HUJI-B leaders claim that up to 400 of its members are Afghan war veterans, but its total membership is unknown.

Location/Area of Operation: The group operates primarily in Bangladesh and India. HUJI-B trains and has a network of madrassas in Bangladesh.

External Aid: HUJI-B funding comes from a variety of sources. Several international Islamic non-governmental organizations may have funneled money to HUJI-B and other Bangladeshi militant groups. HUJI-B also draws funding from local militant madrassa leaders and teachers.

HARAKAT UL-MUJAHIDEEN

aka HUM; Harakat ul-Ansar; HUA; Jamiat ul-Ansar; JUA; Al-Faran; Al-Hadid; Al-Hadith; Harakat ul-Mujahidin

Description: Harakat ul-Mujahideen (HUM) was designated as a Foreign Terrorist Organization on October 8, 1997. HUM seeks the annexation of Indian Kashmir and expulsion of Coalition Forces in Afghanistan. Reportedly, under pressure from the Government of Pakistan, HUM's long-time leader Fazlur Rehman Khalil stepped down and was replaced by Dr. Badr Munir as the head of HUM in

January 2005. Khalil has been linked to Usama bin Ladin, and his signature was found on bin Ladin's February 1998 fatwa calling for attacks on U.S. and Western interests. HUM operated terrorist training camps in eastern Afghanistan until Coalition air strikes destroyed them in 2001. Khalil was detained by Pakistani authorities in mid-2004 and subsequently released in late December of the same year. In 2003, HUM began using the name Jamiat ul-Ansar (JUA). Pakistan banned JUA in November 2003.

Activities: HUM has conducted a number of operations against Indian troops and civilian targets in Kashmir. It is linked to the Kashmiri militant group al-Faran, which kidnapped five Western tourists in Kashmir in July 1995; the five reportedly were killed later that year. HUM was responsible for the hijacking of an Indian airliner in December 1999 that resulted in the release of Masood Azhar, an important leader in the former Harakat ul-Ansar, who was imprisoned by India in 1994 and then founded Jaish-e-Mohammed (JEM) after his release. Another former member of Harakat ul-Ansar, Ahmed Omar Sheik was also released by India as a result of the hijackings and was later convicted of the abduction and murder in 2002 of U.S. journalist Daniel Pearl.

HUM is still actively planning and carrying out operations against Indian security and civilian targets in Kashmir. In 2005, such attacks resulted in the deaths of 15 people. In November 2007, two Indian soldiers were killed in Kashmir while engaged in a firefight with a group of HUM militants. Indian police and army forces have engaged with HUM militants in the Kashmir region, killing a number of the organization's leadership in April, October, and December 2008. In February 2009, Lalchand Kishen Advani, leader of the Indian opposition Bharatiya Janata Party, received a death threat that was attributed to HUM.

Strength: HUM has several hundred armed supporters located in Azad Kashmir, Pakistan; India's southern Kashmir and Doda regions; and in the Kashmir valley. Supporters are mostly Pakistanis and Kashmiris, but also include Afghans and Arab veterans of the Afghan war. HUM uses light and heavy machine guns, assault rifles, mortars, explosives, and rockets. After 2000, a significant portion of HUM's membership defected to JEM.

Location/Area of Operation: Based in Muzaffarabad, Rawalpindi, and several other cities in Pakistan, HUM conducts insurgent and terrorist operations primarily in Kashmir and Afghanistan. HUM trains its militants in Afghanistan and Pakistan.

External Aid: HUM collects donations from wealthy and grassroots donors in Pakistan, Kashmir, Saudi Arabia, and other Gulf states. HUM's financial collection methods include soliciting donations in magazine ads and pamphlets. The sources and amount of HUM's military funding are unknown. Its overt fundraising in Pakistan has been constrained since the government clampdown on extremist groups and the freezing of terrorist assets.

HIZBALLAH

aka the Party of God; Islamic Jihad; Islamic Jihad Organization; Revolutionary Justice Organization; Organization of the Oppressed on Earth; Islamic Jihad for the Liberation of Palestine; Organization of Right Against Wrong; Ansar Allah; Followers of the Prophet Muhammed

Description: Hizballah was designated as a Foreign Terrorist Organization on October 8, 1997. Formed in 1982, in response to the Israeli invasion of Lebanon, the Lebanese-based radical Shia group takes its ideological inspiration from the Iranian revolution and the teachings of the late Ayatollah Khomeini. The group generally follows the religious guidance of Khomeini's successor,

Iranian Supreme Leader Ali Khamenei. Hizballah is closely allied with Iran and often acts at its behest, though it also acts independently. Hizballah shares a close relationship with Syria, and like Iran, the group is helping advance its Syrian objectives in the region. It has strong influence in Lebanon, especially with the Shia community. The Lebanese government and the majority of the Arab world still recognize Hizballah as a legitimate "resistance group" and political party.

Hizballah provides support to several Palestinian terrorist organizations, as well as a number of local Christian and Muslim militias in Lebanon. This support includes the covert provision of weapons, explosives, training, funding, and guidance, as well as overt political support.

Activities: Hizballah's terrorist attacks have included the suicide truck bombings of the U.S. Embassy and U.S. Marine barracks in Beirut in 1983; the U.S. Embassy annex in Beirut in 1984; and the 1985 hijacking of TWA flight 847, during which a U.S. Navy diver was murdered. Elements of the group were responsible for the kidnapping, detention, and murder of Americans and other Westerners in Lebanon in the 1980s. Hizballah was also implicated in the attacks on the Israeli Embassy in Argentina in 1992 and on the Argentine-Israeli Mutual Association in Buenos Aires in 1994. In 2000, Hizballah operatives captured three Israeli soldiers in the Sheba'a Farms area and, separately, kidnapped an Israeli non-combatant in Dubai. Although the non-combatant survived, on November 1, 2001, Israeli army rabbi Israel Weiss pronounced the soldiers dead. The surviving non-combatant, as well as the bodies of the IDF soldiers, were returned to Israel in a prisoner exchange with Hizballah on January 29, 2004.

Since at least 2004, Hizballah has provided training to select Iraqi Shia militants, including om the construction and use of shaped charge improvised explosive devices (IEDs) that can penetrate heavily-armored vehicles. Senior Hizballah operative, Ali Mussa Daqduq, was captured in Iraq in 2007 while facilitating Hizballah training of Iraqi Shia militants attacking U.S. and coalition forces. When captured, Daqduq had detailed documents that discussed tactics to attack Iraqi and coalition forces. In July 2006, Hizballah attacked an Israeli Army patrol, kidnapping two soldiers and killing three, starting a conflict with Israel that lasted into August.

Senior Hizballah officials have repeatedly vowed retaliation for the February 2008 killing in Damascus of Imad Mughniyah, Hizballah's military and terrorism chief, who was suspected of involvement in many attacks. Rawi Sultani was arrested in 2009 for providing targeting information to Hizballah on the Israeli Defense Chief of Staff.

The group's willingness to engage in violence and its increasing stockpile of weapons continues to threaten stability in the region. In a two-week period in May 2008, Hizballah's armed takeover of West Beirut – which occurred after the Lebanese government announced its plan to remove Hizballah's telephone network – resulted in more than 60 deaths. Egyptian authorities in late 2008 disrupted a Hizballah cell that was charged with planning to attack Israeli interests including tourists in the Sinai Peninsula, and Israeli ships passing through the Suez Canal. The network was also engaged in smuggling weapons, supplies, and people through tunnels to Gaza. Twenty-six men belonging to this Hizballah cell were convicted in April 2010. In November 2009, the Israeli navy seized a ship carrying an estimated 400-500 tons of weapons originating in Iran and bound for Hizballah, via Syria.

Strength: Several thousands of supporters and members.

Location/Area of Operation: Operates in the southern suburbs of Beirut, the Bekaa Valley, and southern Lebanon.

External Aid: Hizballah receives training, weapons, and explosives, as well as political, diplomatic, monetary, and organizational aid from Iran; and training, weapons, diplomatic, and political support from Syria. Hizballah also receives funding from private donations and profits from legal and illegal businesses. Hizballah also receives financial support from Lebanese Shia communities in Europe, Africa, South America, North America, and Asia.

ISLAMIC JIHAD UNION

aka Islomiy Jihod Ittihodi; Islamic Jihad Group; al-Djihad al-Islami; Dzhamaat Modzhakhedov; Islamic Jihad Group of Uzbekistan; Jamiat al-Jihad al-Islami; Jamiyat; The Jamaat Mojahedin; The Kazakh Jama'at; The Libyan Society

Description: The Islamic Jihad Union (IJU) was designated as a Foreign Terrorist Organization on June 17, 2005. The IJU is a Sunni extremist organization that splintered from the Islamic Movement of Uzbekistan. The group opposes secular rule in Uzbekistan and seek to replace it with a government based on Islamic law.

The IJU primarily operated against Coalition forces in Afghanistan but continued to plan and carry out attacks in Central Asia. The group first conducted attacks in March and April 2004, targeting police at several roadway checkpoints and at a popular bazaar, killing approximately 47 people, including 33 IJU members, some of whom were suicide bombers. In July 2004, the group carried out near-simultaneous suicide bombings of the Uzbek Prosecutor General's office and the U.S. and Israeli Embassies in Tashkent. In September 2007, German authorities disrupted an IJU plot by detaining three IJU operatives, including two German citizens. The operatives had acquired over 1,500 pounds of hydrogen peroxide and an explosives precursor stockpiled in a garage in southern Germany. The materials were thought to have been used in multiple car bomb attacks in Western Europe including at Frankfurt International Airport and U.S. military installations such as Ramstein Air Base. The IJU subsequently claimed responsibility for the foiled attacks. The IJU claimed responsibility for attacks targeting Coalition forces in Afghanistan in 2008, including a March suicide attack against a U.S. military post. It also claimed responsibility for two May 2009 attacks in Uzbekistan. In 2010, the Government of Kazakhstan arrested dozens of suspected IJU members, who were plotting attacks against western interests in the country. There were also reports of IJU members arrested in Uzbekistan and Pakistan. The IJU remained active in Germany, where they have made inroads, are recruiting locals, and have been planning attacks within Europe.

Strength: Unknown.

Location/Area of Operation: IJU members are scattered throughout Central Asia, Europe Pakistan, and Afghanistan.

External Aid: Unknown.

ISLAMIC MOVEMENT OF UZBEKISTAN

aka IMU

Description: The Islamic Movement of Uzbekistan (IMU) was designated as a Foreign Terrorist Organization on September 25, 2000. The IMU is a coalition of Islamic extremists from Uzbekistan, other Central Asian states, and Europe, whose goal is to overthrow the Uzbek regime and to establish an Islamic state. For most of the past decade, however, the group has focused on fighting in Afghanistan and Pakistan. The IMU has a relationship with the Taliban and Tehrik-e Taliban Pakistan.

Activities: The IMU primarily targeted Uzbek interests before October 2001 and is believed to have been responsible for several explosions in Tashkent in February 1999. In August 1999, IMU militants took four Japanese geologists and eight Kyrgyz soldiers hostage. In May 2003, Kyrgyz security forces disrupted an IMU cell that was seeking to bomb the U.S. Embassy and a nearby hotel in Bishkek, Kyrgyzstan. In November 2004, the IMU was blamed for an explosion in the southern Kyrgyz city of Osh that killed one police officer and one terrorist.

Since the beginning of Operation Enduring Freedom, the IMU has been predominantly occupied with attacks on U.S. and Coalition soldiers in Afghanistan. In late 2009, NATO forces reported an increase in IMU-affiliated foreign fighters in Afghanistan. Government authorities in Russia arrested three suspected IMU-affiliated extremists in November 2009. In 2010, the IMU continued to fight in Afghanistan and the group claimed credit for the September 19 ambush that killed 25 Tajik troops in Tajikistan.

Strength: Several hundred members.

Location/Area of Operation: IMU militants are located in South Asia, Central Asia, and Iran.

External Aid: The IMU receives support from a large Uzbek diaspora, terrorist organizations, and donors from the Middle East, Central Asia, and South Asia.

JAISH-E-MOHAMMED

aka the Army of Mohammed; Mohammed's Army; Tehrik ul-Furqaan; Khuddam-ul-Islam; Khudamul Islam; Kuddam e Islami; Jaish-i-Mohammed

Description: Jaish-e-Mohammed (JEM) was designated as a Foreign Terrorist Organization on December 26, 2001. JEM is a terrorist group based in Pakistan that was founded in early 2000 by Masood Azhar, a former senior leader of Harakat ul-Ansar, upon his release from prison in India. The group's aim is to annex Indian Kashmir and expel Coalition Forces in Afghanistan, and it has openly declared war against the United States. Pakistan outlawed JEM in 2002. By 2003, JEM had splintered into Khuddam-ul-Islam (KUI), headed by Azhar, and Jamaat ul-Furqan (JUF), led by Abdul Jabbar, who was released from Pakistani custody in August 2004. Pakistan banned KUI and JUF in November 2003. In March 2010, five JEM members recruiting for operations in India were arrested in Bangladesh.

Activities: JEM continues to operate openly in parts of Pakistan despite the 2002 ban on its activities. Since Masood Azhar's 1999 release from Indian custody – in exchange for 155 hijacked Indian Airlines hostages – JEM has conducted many fatal terrorist attacks in the region.

JEM claimed responsibility for several suicide car bombings in Kashmir, including an October 2001 suicide attack on the Jammu and Kashmir legislative assembly building in Srinagar that killed more than 30 people. The Indian government has publicly implicated JEM, along with Lashkar e-Tayyiba, for the December 2001 attack on the Indian Parliament that killed nine and injured 18. In 2002, Pakistani authorities arrested and convicted a JEM member for the abduction and murder of U.S. journalist Daniel Pearl. Pakistani authorities suspect that JEM members may have been involved in the 2002 anti-Christian attacks in Islamabad, Murree, and Taxila that killed two Americans. In December 2003, Pakistan implicated JEM members in the two assassination attempts against President Musharraf. In 2006, JEM claimed responsibility for a number of attacks, including the killing of several Indian police officials in the Indian-administered Kashmir capital of Srinagar. Indian police and JEM extremists continued to engage in firefights throughout 2008 and 2009. In August 2009, JEM was believed to have fired upon three police officers in two separate incidents, killing one. In 2010, JEM used flooding in Pakistan as an excuse to illegally raise funds for terrorist activity.

Strength: JEM has at least several hundred armed supporters – including a large cadre of former HUM members – located in Pakistan, India's southern Kashmir and Doda regions and in the Kashmir Valley.

Location/Area of Operation: Pakistan, particularly southern Punjab; Afghanistan; Bangladesh; and Kashmir.

External Aid: In anticipation of asset seizures by the Pakistani government, JEM withdrew funds from bank accounts and invested in legal businesses, such as commodity trading, real estate, and production of consumer goods. In addition, JEM collects funds through donation requests in magazines and pamphlets.

JEMAAH ISLAMIYA

aka Jemaa Islamiyah; Jema'a Islamiyah; Jemaa Islamiyya; Jema'a Islamiyya; Jemaa Islamiyyah; Jema'a Islamiyyah; Jemaah Islamiah; Jemaah Islamiyah; Jema'ah Islamiyah; Jemaah Islamiyyah; Jema'ah Islamiyyah; JI

Description: Jemaah Islamiya (JI) was designated as a Foreign Terrorist Organization on October 23, 2002. Southeast Asia-based, JI is a terrorist group that seeks the establishment of an Islamic caliphate spanning Indonesia, Malaysia, southern Thailand, Singapore, Brunei, and the southern Philippines. More than 400 JI operatives, including operations chief and al-Qa'ida associate Hambali, have been captured since 2002. The death of top JI bomb maker Azahari bin Husin in 2005 and a series of high-profile arrests between 2005 and 2008, in combination with additional efforts by the Government of Indonesia, likely reduced JI's capabilities.

Since 2006, many high profile JI operatives have been either captured or killed. These include the 2006 arrests of several members connected to JI's 2005 suicide attack in Bali, the 2007 arrests of former acting JI emir Muhammad Naim (a.k.a. Zarkasih) and JI military commander Abu Dujana, the 2008 arrests of two senior JI operatives in Malaysia, the mid-2008 arrest of a JI-linked cell in Sumatra, and the September 2009 death of JI-splinter group leader Noordin Mohammad Top in a police raid. Progress against JI continued in 2010 when a crackdown on JI's base in Aceh, Indonesia resulted in the capture of over 60 militants and led authorities to JI leader Dulmatin, one of the masterminds of the 2002 Bali bombing. Dulmatin was killed in March outside of Jakarta. In June, wanted JI commander Abdullah Sunata was captured while planning to bomb the Danish Embassy in Jakarta. In August JI co-founder Abu Bakar Bashir was arrested while planning multiple attacks in Jakarta. In December, JI weapons expert Abu Tholut was also captured by Indonesian police.

Activities: In December 2000, JI coordinated bombings of numerous Christian churches in Indonesia and was involved in the bombings of several targets in Manila. In December 2001, Singaporean authorities uncovered a JI plot to attack the U.S., Israeli, British, and Australian diplomatic facilities in Singapore. Other significant JI attacks included the September 2004 bombing outside the Australian Embassy in Jakarta, the August 2003 bombing of the J. W. Marriott Hotel in Jakarta, and the October 2002 Bali bombing, which killed more than 200. JI's October 2005 suicide bombing in Bali left 26 dead, including the three suicide bombers.

A JI faction led by Noordin Mohammad Top conducted the group's most recent high-profile attack on July 17, 2009 at the J.W. Marriott and Ritz-Carlton hotels in Jakarta when two suicide bombers detonated explosive devices. The attack killed seven and injured more than 50, including seven Americans. In 2010, JI continued to threaten attacks in Southeast Asia and in March suspected JI operatives also killed three police officers and one civilian during a raid on a terrorist camp.

Strength: Estimates of total JI members vary from 500 to several thousand.

Location/Area of Operation: JI is based in Indonesia and is believed to have elements in Malaysia, and the Philippines.

External Aid: Investigations indicate that JI is fully capable of its own fundraising through membership donations and criminal and business activities, although it also has received financial, ideological, and logistical support from Middle Eastern contacts and non-governmental organizations.

JUNDALLAH

aka People's Resistance Movement of Iran (PMRI); Jonbesh-i Moqavemat-i-Mardom-i Iran; Popular Resistance Movement of Iran; Soldiers of God; Fedayeen-e-Islam; Former Jundallah of Iran; Jundullah; Jondullah; Jundollah; Jondollah; Jondallah; Army of God (God's Army); Baloch Peoples Resistance Movement (BPRM)

Description: Jundallah was designated as a Foreign Terrorist Organization on November 4, 2010. Since its inception in 2003, Jundallah, a violent extremist organization that operates primarily in the province of Sistan va Balochistan of Iran, has engaged in numerous attacks resulting in the death and maiming of scores of Iranian civilians and government officials. Jundallah's stated goals are to secure recognition of Balochi cultural, economic, and political rights from the government of Iran and to spread awareness of the plight of the Baloch situation through violent and nonviolent means. In October 2007, Amnesty International reported that Jundallah has by its own admission, carried out gross abuses such as hostage-taking, the killing of hostages, and attacks against non-military targets.

Activities: In March 2006, Jundallah attacked a motorcade in eastern Iran, which included the deputy head of the Iranian Red Crescent Security Department, who was taken hostage. More than 20 people were killed in the attack. The governor of Zahedan, his deputy, and five other officials were wounded, and seven others were kidnapped in the attack. In May 2006, Jundallah barricaded a road in Kerman province and killed 11 civilians and burned four vehicles. The assailants then killed another civilian and wounded a child by firing at a passing vehicle. In 2007, Jundallah killed 18 border guards on the Iranian-Afghan border. Jundallah seized 16 Iranian police officers near the border with Pakistan in 2008. When the Iranian government refused to release 200 Jundallah prisoners in exchange for the hostages, Jundallah killed them. In May 2009, Jundallah attacked the crowded Shiite Amir al-Mo'menin mosque in Zahedan, destroying the mosque and killing and wounding numerous worshipers. An October 2009 suicide bomb attack in a marketplace in the city of Pishin in the Sistan va Balochistan province, which killed more than 40 people, was reportedly the deadliest terrorist attack in Iran since the 1980s. In a statement on its website, Jundallah claimed responsibility for the December 15, 2010 suicide bomb attack inside the Iman Hussein Mosque in Chabahar, which killed an estimated 35 to 40 civilians with 60-100 wounded. In July 2010, Jundallah attacked the Grand Mosque in Zahedan, killing approximately 30 and injuring an estimated 300.

Strength: Reports of Jundallah membership vary widely from 500 to 2000.

Location/Area of Operation: Throughout Sistan va Balochistan province in southeastern Iran and the greater Balochistan area of Afghanistan and Pakistan.

External Aid: Unknown

KAHANE CHAI

aka American Friends of the United Yeshiva; American Friends of Yeshivat Rav Meir; Committee for the Safety of the Roads; Dikuy Bogdim; DOV; Forefront of the Idea; Friends of the Jewish Idea Yeshiva; Jewish Legion; Judea Police; Judean Congress; Kach; Kahane; Kahane Lives; Kahane Tzadak; Kahane.org; Kahanetzadak.com; Kfar Tapuah Fund; Koach; Meir's Youth; New Kach Movement; Newkach.org; No'ar Meir; Repression of Traitors; State of Judea; Sword of David; The Committee Against Racism and Discrimination (CARD); The Hatikva Jewish Identity Center; The International Kahane Movement; The Jewish Idea Yeshiva; The Judean Legion; The Judean Voice; The Qomemiyut Movement; The Rabbi Meir David Kahane Memorial Fund; The Voice of Judea; The Way of the Torah; The Yeshiva of the Jewish Idea; Yeshivat Harav Meir

Description: Kach – the precursor to Kahane Chai – was founded by radical Israeli-American Rabbi Meir Kahane with the goal of restoring Greater Israel, which is generally used to refer to Israel, the West Bank, and Gaza. Its offshoot, Kahane Chai, (translation: "Kahane Lives") was founded by Meir Kahane's son Binyamin following his father's 1990 assassination in the United States. Both organizations were designated as Foreign Terrorist Organizations on October 8, 1997 after they were declared terrorist organizations in 1994 by the Israeli Cabinet under its 1948 Terrorism Law. This designation followed the group's statements in support of Baruch Goldstein's February 1994 attack on the Ibrahimi Mosque in Hebron and its verbal attacks on the Israeli government. Palestinian gunmen killed Binyamin Kahane and his wife in a drive-by shooting in December 2000 in the West Bank. The group has attempted to gain seats in the Israeli Knesset over the past several decades but won only one seat in 1984.

Activities: Kahane Chai has harassed and threatened Arabs, Palestinians, and Israeli government officials, and has vowed revenge for the death of Binyamin Kahane and his wife. The group is suspected of involvement in a number of low-level attacks since the start of the First Palestinian Intifada in 2000. Since 2003, Kahane Chai activists have called for the execution of former Israeli Prime Minister Ariel Sharon and physically intimidated other Israeli and Palestinian government officials who favored the dismantlement of Israeli settlements.

Strength: Kahane Chai's core membership is believed to be fewer than 100. The group's membership and support networks are overwhelmingly composed of Israeli citizens, most of whom live in West Bank settlements.

Location/Area of Operation: Israel and West Bank settlements, particularly Qiryat Arba' in Hebron.

External Aid: Receives support from sympathizers in the United States and Europe.

KATA'IB HIZBALLAH

aka Hizballah Brigades; Hizballah Brigades In Iraq; Hizballah Brigades-Iraq; Kata'ib Hezbollah; Khata'ib Hezbollah; Khata'ib Hizballah; Khattab Hezballah; Hizballah Brigades-Iraq Of The Islamic Resistance In Iraq; Islamic Resistance In Iraq; Kata'ib Hizballah Fi Al-Iraq; Katibat Abu Fathel Al A'abas; Katibat Zayd Ebin Ali; Katibut Karbalah

Description: Kata'ib Hizballah (KH) was designated as a Foreign Terrorist Organization on July 2, 2009. Formed in 2006, KH is a radical Shia Islamist group with an anti-Western outlook and extremist ideology that has conducted attacks against Iraqi, U.S., and Coalition targets in Iraq. KH has threatened the lives of Iraqi politicians and civilians that support the legitimate political process in Iraq. The group is notable for its extensive use of media operations and propaganda by filming and releasing videos of attacks. KH has ideological ties to Lebanese Hizballah and may have received support from that group and that group's sponsor, Iran.

Activities: KH has been responsible for numerous violent terrorist attacks since 2007, including improvised explosive device bombings, rocket propelled grenade attacks, and sniper operations. KH gained notoriety in 2007 with attacks on U.S. and Coalition forces designed to undermine the establishment of a democratic, viable Iraqi state. KH was particularly active in summer 2008, recording and distributing video footage of its attacks against U.S. and Coalition soldiers. Using the alias "Hizballah Brigades in Iraq," KH filmed attacks on U.S. Stryker vehicles, Abrams tanks, and Bradley armored personnel carriers. In 2009, KH continued to record and distribute via the internet videos of attacks ranging in date from 2006 to 2008.

The group's activities continued into 2010. In February, a firefight between U.S. and Coalition forces and suspected KH militants resulted in 12 arrests. In July, U.S. Army General Ray Odierno cited KH as the reason behind increased security at some U.S. bases in Iraq. General Odierno also said that Iran continued to support KH with weapons and training.

Strength: Membership is estimated at approximately 400 individuals.

Location/Area of Operation: KH's operations are predominately Iraq-based. KH currently conducts the majority of its operations in Baghdad but has been active in other areas of Iraq, including Kurdish areas such as Mosul.

External Aid: KH receives support from Iran and Lebanese Hizballah.

KURDISTAN WORKERS' PARTY

aka the Kurdistan Freedom and Democracy Congress; the Freedom and Democracy Congress of Kurdistan; KADEK; Partiya Karkeran Kurdistan; the People's Defense Force; Halu Mesru Savunma Kuvveti; Kurdistan People's Congress; People's Congress of Kurdistan; KONGRA-GEL

Description: The Kurdistan Workers' Party (PKK) or Kongra-Gel (KGK) was designated as a Foreign Terrorist Organization on October 8, 1997. The PKK was founded by Abdullah Ocalan in 1978 as a Marxist-Leninist separatist organization. The group, composed primarily of Turkish Kurds, launched a campaign of violence in 1984. The PKK's original goal was to establish an independent Kurdish state in southeastern Turkey, but in recent years it has spoken more often about autonomy within a Turkish state that guarantees Kurdish cultural and linguistic rights.

In the early 1990s, the PKK moved beyond rural-based insurgent activities to include urban terrorism. In the 1990s, southeastern Anatolia was the scene of significant violence; some estimates place casualties at approximately 30,000 persons. Following his capture in 1999, Ocalan announced a "peace initiative," ordering members to refrain from violence and requesting dialogue with Ankara on Kurdish issues. Ocalan's death-sentence was commuted to life-imprisonment; he remains the symbolic leader of the group. The group foreswore violence until June 2004, when the group's hard-line militant wing took control and renounced the self-imposed cease-fire of the previous five years. Striking over the border from bases within Iraq, the PKK has engaged in terrorist attacks in eastern and western Turkey.

Activities: Primary targets have been Turkish government security forces, local Turkish officials, and villagers who oppose the organization in Turkey. In 2006, 2007, and 2008, PKK violence killed or injured hundreds of Turks.

In an attempt to damage Turkey's tourist industry, the PKK has bombed tourist sites and hotels and kidnapped foreign tourists. PKK activity was lower in 2009, but was still a constant throughout the year. The group either claimed responsibility for or was believed responsible for at least 21 attacks in 2010. In September, the PKK was believed responsible for detonating an explosive device near a bus that killed 10 civilians, including seven children, and wounded 14 others.

Strength: Approximately 4,000 to 5,000, of which 3,000 to 3,500 are located in northern Iraq.

Location/Area of Operation: Operated primarily in Turkey, Iraq, Europe, and the Middle East.

External Aid: In the past, the PKK received safe haven and modest aid from Syria, Iraq, and Iran. Syria ended support for the group in 1999 and since then has cooperated with Turkey against the PKK. Since 1999, Iran has also cooperated in a limited fashion with Turkey against the PKK. In 2008, Turkey and Iraq began cooperating to fight the PKK. The PKK continues to receive substantial financial support from the large Kurdish diaspora in Europe and from criminal activity there.

LASHKAR E-TAYYIBA

aka al Mansooreen; Al Mansoorian; Army of the Pure; Army of the Pure and Righteous; Army of the Righteous; Lashkar e-Toiba; Lashkar-i-Taiba; Paasban-e-Ahle-Hadis; Paasban-e-Kashmir; Paasban-i-Ahle-Hadith; Pasban-e-Ahle-Hadith; Pasban-e-Kashmir; Jamaat-ud-Dawa, JUD; Jama'at al-Dawa; Jamaat ud-Daawa; Jamaat ul-Dawah; Jamaat-ul-Dawa; Jama'at-i-Dawat; Jamaiat-ud-Dawa; Jama'at-ud-Da'awah; Jama'at-ud-Da'awa; Jamaati-ud-Dawa; Idara Khidmat-e-Khalq; Falah-i-Insaniat Foundation; FiF; Falah-e-Insaniat Foundation; Falah-e-Insaniyat; Falah-i-Insaniyat; Falah Insania; Welfare of Humanity; Humanitarian Welfare Foundation; Human Welfare Foundation

Description: Lashkar e-Tayyiba (LT) was designated as a Foreign Terrorist Organization (FTO) on December 26, 2001. LT is one of the largest and most proficient of the traditionally Kashmir-focused militant groups. It has the ability to severely disrupt already delicate regional relations. LT formed in the late 1980s as the militant wing of the Islamic extremist organization Markaz Dawa ul-Irshad, a Pakistan-based Islamic fundamentalist mission organization and charity founded to oppose the Soviet presence in Afghanistan. LT, which is not connected to any political party, is led by Hafiz Muhammad Saeed. Shortly after LT was designated as an FTO, Saeed changed the name to Jamaat-ud-Dawa (JUD) and began humanitarian projects to avoid restrictions. LT disseminates its message through JUD's media outlets. Elements of LT and Jaish-e-Muhammad (JEM) combined with other groups to mount attacks as "The Save Kashmir Movement." The Pakistani government banned LT in January 2002 and JUD in 2008 following the Mumbai attack. LT and Saeed continued to spread ideology advocating terrorism, as well as virulent rhetoric condemning the United States, India, Israel, and other perceived enemies.

Activities: LT has conducted a number of operations against Indian troops and civilian targets in Jammu and Kashmir since 1993, as well as several high profile attacks inside India. LT claimed responsibility for numerous attacks in 2001, including a January attack on Srinagar airport that killed five Indians. The Indian government publicly implicated LT, along with JEM, for the December 2001 attack on the Indian Parliament building. Indian governmental officials hold LT responsible for the July 2006 train attack in Mumbai, and multiple attacks in 2005 and 2006. Senior al-Qa'ida (AQ) lieutenant Abu Zubaydah was captured at an LT safe house in Faisalabad in March 2002, which suggested that some members were facilitating the movement of AQ members in Pakistan.

LT conducted the November 2008 attacks in Mumbai against luxury hotels, a Jewish center, a train station, and a popular café that killed at least 183, including 22 foreigners, and injured more than 300. India has charged 38 people in the case, including the lone surviving alleged attacker Mohammad Ajmal Amir Kasab, who was captured at the scene. While most of those charged are at large and thought to be in Pakistan, Kasab was sentenced to death for his involvement in the Mumbai massacre. His case is currently on appeal before the Bombay High Court. In March 2010, Pakistani-American businessman David Headley pleaded guilty in a U.S. court to crimes relating to his role in the November 2008 LT attacks in Mumbai as well as to crimes relating to a separate plot to bomb the Danish newspaper Jyllands-Posten.

In 2010, LT kept a relatively low profile and confined its operations largely to Afghanistan and the Kashmir region. LT was suspected of an attack that took place on February 26 in Kabul, when two suicide bombers detonated improvised explosive devices and other assailants fired small arms and detonated a vehicle-borne improvised explosive device targeting downtown hotels. The attack killed 14 civilians (nine Indian; four Afghan; one French), three police officers, two Indian soldiers, and one Italian diplomat; and wounded 32 Afghan and Indian civilians, six police officers, and five Indian soldiers.

LT has also played a prominent role in Afghanistan through its efforts to oppose the Najibullah regime. Following that regime's ouster, LT cultivated links with the Taliban and al-Qa'ida operatives in Afghanistan.

Strength: The actual size of LT is unknown, but it has several thousand members in Azad Kashmir and Punjab Pakistan and in the southern Jammu, Kashmir, and Doda regions. Most LT members are Pakistanis or Afghans and/or veterans of the Afghan wars. The group uses assault rifles, light and heavy machine guns, mortars, explosives, and rocket-propelled grenades.

Location/Area of Operation: LT maintains a number of facilities, including training camps, schools, and medical clinics in Pakistan. It has global connections and a strong operational network throughout South Asia.

External Aid: LT collects donations from the Pakistani expatriate communities in the Middle East and Europe, particularly the United Kingdom, Islamic non-governmental organizations, and Pakistani and other Kashmiri business people. LT coordinates its charitable activities through its front organizations JUD and, more recently, Falah-i-Insaniat Foundation (FIF), both of which have provided humanitarian relief to the victims of various natural disasters in Pakistan.

LASHKAR I JHANGVI

Description: Lashkar I Jhangvi (LJ) was designated as a Foreign Terrorist Organization on January 30, 2003. LJ is the militant offshoot of the Sunni Deobandi sectarian group Sipah-i-Sahaba Pakistan. LJ focuses primarily on anti-Shia attacks and other attacks in Pakistan as well as Afghanistan and was banned by Pakistan in August 2001 as part of an effort to rein in sectarian violence. Many of its members then sought refuge in Afghanistan with the Taliban, with whom they had existing ties. After the collapse of the Taliban as the ruling government in Afghanistan, LJ members became active in aiding other terrorists, providing safe houses, false identities, and protection in Pakistani cities, including Karachi, Peshawar, and Rawalpindi. LJ works closely with Tehrik-e-Taliban Pakistan (TTP).

Activities: LJ specializes in armed attacks and bombings and has admitted responsibility for numerous killings of Shia religious and community leaders in Pakistan. In January 1999, the group attempted to assassinate former Prime Minister Nawaz Sharif and his brother Shabaz Sharif, Chief Minister of Punjab Province. Media reports linked LJ to attacks on Christian targets in Pakistan, including a March 2002 grenade assault on the Protestant International Church in Islamabad that killed two U.S. citizens. Pakistani authorities believe LJ was responsible for the July 2003 bombing of a Shia mosque in Quetta, Pakistan. Authorities also implicated LJ in several sectarian incidents in 2004, including the May and June bombings of two Shia mosques in Karachi, which killed more than 40 people.

LJ's activities increased in 2010. LJ's most significant attack occurred in March when LJ and TTP claimed responsibility for two improvised explosive device (IED) attacks on the Pakistani army, which killed 48 civilians, nine soldiers, and wounded over 130. In April, the group claimed responsibility for an IED attack on a World Food Program relief distribution point in Pakistan's Khyber-Pakhtunkwa Province. The attack killed 43 Internally Displaced Persons, one journalist, and wounded 70 others. In September, LJ and TTP claimed a grenade and suicide bomber attack on a Shia Muslim procession in Lahore, Pakistan that killed 40 and wounded 270. Two days later, a suicide bomber attack in Balochistan, Pakistan killed 66 civilians and one media worker, and injured over 180. LJ and TTP both claimed responsibility for this attack. On December 7, a LJ suicide bomber attacked the chief minister of the southwestern province of Baluchistan, wounding 10 people. The same month, a LJ bomb killed 10 people in an attack at a hospital in northwest Pakistan. The target of the attack was Shia residents who ran the hospital and a nearby prayer house. The group conducts brutal attacks for al-Qa'ida in Pakistan and TTP. It has stepped up suicide attacks against government officials, anti-TTP tribes, and Shia Muslims, and has carried out three other suicide attacks since December 6, including one against a bus carrying Shia refugees attempting to return to their homes in the tribal agency of Orakzai. The attack killed 18 civilians.

Strength: Probably fewer than 100.

Location/Area of Operation: LJ is active primarily in Punjab, FATA, Karachi, and Baluchistan. Some members travel between Pakistan and Afghanistan.

External Aid: Funding comes from wealthy donors in Pakistan as well as the Middle East, particularly Saudi Arabia. The group also engages in criminal activity to fund its activities to include extortion and protection money.

LIBERATION TIGERS OF TAMIL EELAM

aka Ellalan Force; Tamil Tigers

Description: The Liberation Tigers of Tamil Eelam (LTTE) was designated as a Foreign Terrorist Organization on October 8, 1997. Founded in 1976, the LTTE became a powerful Tamil secessionist group in Sri Lanka. Despite its military defeat at the hands of the Sri Lankan government in 2009, the LTTE's international network of financial support persists. This network continued to collect contributions from the Tamil diaspora in North America, Europe, and Australia, where there were reports that some of these contributions were coerced by locally-based LTTE sympathizers. The LTTE also used Tamil charitable organizations as fronts for its fundraising.

Activities: Although LTTE has been largely inactive since its military defeat in Sri Lanka in 2009, in the past LTTE was responsible for an integrated a battlefield insurgent strategy that targeted key personnel in the countryside and senior Sri Lankan political and military leaders. It conducted a sustained campaign targeting rival Tamil groups, and assassinated Prime Minister Rajiv Gandhi of India in 1991 and President Ranasinghe Premadasa of Sri Lanka in 1993. Although most notorious for its cadre of suicide bombers, the Black Tigers, the organization included an amphibious force, the Sea Tigers, and a nascent air wing, the Air Tigers. Fighting between the LTTE and the Sri Lanka government escalated in 2006 and continued through 2008.

In early 2009, Sri Lankan forces recaptured the LTTE's key strongholds and killed LTTE's second in command. As a result, the Sri Lankan government declared military victory over LTTE in May 2009. In 2010, LTTE members reportedly fled Sri Lanka and have since attempted to reorganize in India. In June, assailants claiming LTTE membership may have been responsible for an attack against a railway in Tamil Nadu, India. No one was injured when the targeted train was able to stop in time to prevent derailment. Other LTTE members continued to procure weapons while the LTTE diaspora continued to support the organization financially. For example, in March, German police arrested six Tamil migrants living in Germany for using blackmail and extortion to raise funds for the LTTE.

Strength: Exact strength is unknown.

Location/Area of Operation: Sri Lanka and India.

External Aid: The LTTE has used its international contacts and the large Tamil diaspora in North America, Europe, and Asia to procure weapons, communications, funding, and other needed supplies. The group employed charities as fronts to collect and divert funds for their activities.

LIBYAN ISLAMIC FIGHTING GROUP

aka LIFG

Description: The Libyan Islamic Fighting Group (LIFG) was designated as a Foreign Terrorist Organization on December 17, 2004. In the early 1990s, the LIFG emerged from the group of Libyans who had fought Soviet forces in Afghanistan and pledged to overthrow Libyan leader Muammar al-Qadhafi. In the years following, some members maintained a strictly anti-Qadhafi focus and targeted Libyan government interests. Others, such as Abu al-Faraj al-Libi, who in 2005 was arrested in Pakistan, aligned with Usama bin Ladin, and are believed to be part of the al-Qa'ida (AQ) leadership structure or active in international terrorism. On November 3, 2007, AQ leader Ayman al-Zawahiri announced a formal merger between AQ and LIFG. However, on July 3, 2009, LIFG members in the United Kingdom released a statement formally disavowing any association with AQ. In September 2009, six imprisoned LIFG members issued a 417-page document that renounced violence and claimed to adhere to more sound Islamic theology than that of AQ. More than 100 LIFG members pledged to adhere to this revised doctrine and have been pardoned and released from prison in Libya since September 2009.

Activities: LIFG has been largely inactive operationally in Libya since the late 1990s when members fled predominately to Europe and the Middle East because of tightened Libyan security measures. To date, the November 3, 2007 merger with AQ, which many LIFG members in Europe and Libya did not recognize, has not resulted in a significant increase in LIFG activities within Libya. LIFG engaged Libyan security forces in armed clashes during the 1990s and attempted to assassinate Qadhafi four times. On July 3, 2009, the LIFG released a statement that the group would cease terrorist activities in Libya. In March 2010, the Libyan government released three top LIFG leaders and 200 LIFG members from prison, successfully concluding a three-year peace process that also produced an alliance against AQ.

Strength: Unknown.

Location/Area of Operation: Since the late 1990s, many members have fled to southwest Asia, and European countries, particularly the UK.

External Aid: Unknown.

MOROCCAN ISLAMIC COMBATANT GROUP

aka Groupe Islamique Combattant Marocain; GICM

Description: The Moroccan Islamic Combatant Group (GICM) was designated as a Foreign Terrorist Organization on October 11, 2005. GICM is a clandestine transnational terrorist group centered in the Moroccan diaspora communities of Western Europe. Its goals include establishing an Islamic state in Morocco. The group emerged in the 1990s and is composed of Moroccan recruits who trained in armed camps in Afghanistan, including some who fought in the Soviet war in Afghan. GICM members interact with other North African extremists, particularly in Europe.

Activities: GICM members are believed to be among those responsible for the 2004 Madrid train bombings, which killed 191 people. GICM members were also implicated in the recruitment network for Iraq, and at least one GICM member carried out a suicide attack against Coalition

Forces in Iraq. GICM individuals are believed to have been involved in the 2003 Casablanca attacks. However, the group has largely been inactive since these attacks, and has not been attributed to or claimed responsibility for any attacks since the Madrid train bombings.

Strength: Much of GICM's leadership in Morocco and Europe has been killed, imprisoned, or is awaiting trial. Alleged leader Mohamed al-Guerbouzi was convicted in absentia by the Moroccan government for his role in the Casablanca attacks but remains free in exile in London..

Location/Area of Operation: Morocco, Western Europe, and Afghanistan.

External Aid: GICM has been involved in narcotics trafficking in North Africa and Europe to fund its operations.

MUJAHADIN-E KHALQ ORGANIZATION

aka MEK; MKO; Mujahadin-e Khalq; Muslim Iranian Students' Society; National Council of Resistance; NCR; Organization of the People's Holy Warriors of Iran; the National Liberation Army of Iran; NLA; People's Mujahadin Organization of Iran; PMOI; National Council of Resistance of Iran; NCRI; Sazeman-e Mujahadin-e Khalq-e Iran

Description: The Mujahadin-E Khalq Organization (MEK) was originally designated as a Foreign Terrorist Organization on October 8, 1997. The MEK is a Marxist-Islamic Organization that seeks the overthrow of the Iranian regime through its military wing, the National Liberation Army (NLA), and its political front, the National Council of Resistance of Iran (NCRI).

The MEK was founded in 1963 by a group of college-educated Iranian Marxists who opposed the country's pro-western ruler, Shah Mohammad Reza Pahlavi. The group participated in the 1979 Islamic Revolution that replaced the Shah with a Shiite Islamist regime led by Ayatollah Khomeini. However, the MEK's ideology – a blend of Marxism, feminism, and Islamism – was at odds with the post-revolutionary government, and its original leadership was soon executed by the Khomeini regime. In 1981, the group was driven from its bases on the Iran-Iraq border and resettled in Paris, where it began supporting Iraq in its eight-year war against Khomeini's Iran. In 1986, after France recognized the Iranian regime, the MEK moved its headquarters to Iraq, which facilitated its terrorist activities in Iran. Since 2003, roughly 3,400 MEK members have been encamped at Camp Ashraf in Iraq.

Activities: The group's worldwide campaign against the Iranian government uses propaganda and terrorism to achieve its objectives. During the 1970s, the MEK staged terrorist attacks inside Iran and killed several U.S. military personnel and civilians working on defense projects in Tehran. In 1972, the MEK set off bombs in Tehran at the U.S. Information Service office (part of the U.S. Embassy), the Iran-American Society, and the offices of several U.S. companies to protest the visit of President Nixon to Iran. In 1973, the MEK assassinated the deputy chief of the U.S. Military Mission in Tehran and bombed several businesses, including Shell Oil. In 1974, the MEK set off bombs in Tehran at the offices of U.S. companies to protest the visit of then U.S. Secretary of State Kissinger. In 1975, the MEK assassinated two U.S. military officers who were members of the U.S. Military Assistance Advisory Group in Tehran. In 1976, the MEK assassinated two U.S. citizens who were employees of Rockwell International in Tehran. In 1979, the group claimed responsibility for the murder of an American Texaco executive. Though denied by the MEK, analysis based on eyewitness accounts and MEK documents demonstrates that MEK members participated in and supported the

1979 takeover of the U.S. Embassy in Tehran and that the MEK later argued against the early release the American hostages. The MEK also provided personnel to guard and defend the site of the U.S. Embassy in Tehran, following the takeover of the Embassy.

In 1981, MEK leadership attempted to overthrow the newly installed Islamic regime; Iranian security forces subsequently initiated a crackdown on the group. The MEK instigated a bombing campaign, including an attack against the head office of the Islamic Republic Party and the Prime Minister's office, which killed some 70 high-ranking Iranian officials, including Chief Justice Ayatollah Mohammad Beheshti, President Mohammad-Ali Rajaei, and Prime Minister Mohammad-Javad Bahonar. These attacks resulted in an expanded Iranian government crackdown that forced MEK leaders to flee to France. For five years, the MEK continued to wage its terrorist campaign from its Paris headquarters. Expelled by France in 1986, MEK leaders turned to Saddam Hussein's regime for basing, financial support, and training. Near the end of the 1980-1988 Iran-Iraq War, Baghdad armed the MEK with heavy military equipment and deployed thousands of MEK fighters in suicidal, mass wave attacks against Iranian forces.

The MEK's relationship with the former Iraqi regime continued through the 1990s. In 1991, the group reportedly assisted the Iraqi Republican Guard's bloody crackdown on Iraqi Shia and Kurds who rose up against Saddam Hussein's regime. In April 1992, the MEK conducted near-simultaneous attacks on Iranian embassies and consular missions in 13 countries, including against the Iranian mission to the United Nations in New York, demonstrating the group's ability to mount large-scale operations overseas. In June 1998, the MEK was implicated in a series of bombing and mortar attacks in Iran that killed at least 15 and injured several others. The MEK also assassinated the former Iranian Minister of Prisons in 1998. In April 1999, the MEK targeted key Iranian military officers and assassinated the deputy chief of the Iranian Armed Forces General Staff, Brigadier General Ali Sayyaad Shirazi.

In April 2000, the MEK attempted to assassinate the commander of the Nasr Headquarters, Tehran's interagency board responsible for coordinating policies on Iraq. The pace of anti-Iranian operations increased during "Operation Great Bahman" in February 2000, when the group launched a dozen attacks against Iran. One attack included a mortar attack against a major Iranian leadership complex in Tehran that housed the offices of the Supreme Leader and the President. The attack killed one person and injured six other individuals. In March 2000, the MEK launched mortars into a residential district in Tehran, injuring four people and damaging property. In 2000 and 2001, the MEK was involved in regular mortar attacks and hit-and-run raids against Iranian military and law enforcement personnel, as well as government buildings near the Iran-Iraq border. Following an initial Coalition bombardment of the MEK's facilities in Iraq at the outset of Operation Iraqi Freedom, MEK leadership negotiated a cease-fire with Coalition Forces and surrendered their heavy-arms to Coalition control. Since 2003, roughly 3,400 MEK members have been encamped at Ashraf in Iraq.

In 2003, French authorities arrested 160 MEK members at operational bases they believed the MEK was using to coordinate financing and planning for terrorist attacks. Upon the arrest of MEK leader Maryam Rajavi, MEK members took to Paris' streets and engaged in self-immolation. French authorities eventually released Rajavi.

Strength: Estimates place MEK's worldwide membership at between 5,000 and 10,000 members, with large pockets in Paris and other major European capitals. In Iraq, roughly 3,400 MEK members are gathered at Camp Ashraf, the MEK's main compound north of Baghdad. As a condition of the 2003 cease-fire agreement, the MEK relinquished more than 2,000 tanks, armored personnel carriers, and heavy artillery.

Location/Area of Operation: The MEK's global support structure remains in place, with associates and supporters scattered throughout Europe and North America. Operations have targeted Iranian government elements across the globe, including in Europe and Iran. The MEK's political arm, the National Council of Resistance of Iran, has a global support network with active lobbying and propaganda efforts in major Western capitals. NCRI also has a well-developed media communications strategy.

External Aid: Before Operation Iraqi Freedom began in 2003, the MEK received all of its military assistance and most of its financial support from Saddam Hussein. The fall of Saddam Hussein's regime has led the MEK increasingly to rely on front organizations to solicit contributions from expatriate Iranian communities.

NATIONAL LIBERATION ARMY

aka ELN, Ejercito de Liberacion Nacional

Description: The National Liberation Army (ELN) was designated as a Foreign Terrorist Organization on October 8, 1997. The ELN is a Colombian Marxist-Leninist group formed in 1964 by intellectuals inspired by Fidel Castro and Che Guevara. It is primarily rural-based, although it also has several urban units. Peace talks between the ELN and the Colombian government began in Cuba in December 2005 and continued through August 2007. To date, Colombia and the ELN have yet to agree on a formal framework for peace negotiations and talks stalled in early 2008, although sporadic efforts have been made to revive them. The ELN remains focused on attacking economic infrastructure, in particular oil pipelines and electricity pylons, and extorting foreign and local companies.

Activities: The ELN engages in kidnappings, hijackings, bombings, drug trafficking, and extortion activities. Historically, the ELN has been one of the biggest users of anti-personnel mines in Colombia. In recent years, the ELN has launched joint attacks with the Revolutionary Armed Forces of Colombia (FARC), Colombia's largest terrorist organization. Authorities believe that the ELN was involved in at least 23 attacks in 2010, some of which were carried out jointly with the FARC. Authorities hold the ELN responsible for a June 20 attack in Norte de Santander, which killed seven police officers and damaged one police truck. In early July, the ELN claimed responsibility for kidnapping three humanitarian workers and an official from the Colombian Office of the Vice President. The hostages were released on July 22. In September, in a joint attack with the FARC, the ELN killed three police officers and injured 12 others, including civilians in an attack in Narino.

Strength: Approximately 2,000 armed combatants and an unknown number of active supporters.

Location/Area of Operation: Mostly in rural and mountainous areas of northern, northeastern, and southwestern Colombia, as well as the border regions with Venezuela.

External Aid: The ELN has no known external aid.

PALESTINE LIBERATION FRONT - ABU ABBAS FACTION

aka PLF; PLF-Abu Abbas; Palestine Liberation Front

Description: The Palestinian Liberation Front – Abu Abbas Faction (PLF) was designated as a Foreign Terrorist Organization on October 8, 1997. In the late 1970s, the Palestine Liberation Front (PLF) splintered from the Popular Front for the Liberation of Palestine-General Command (PFLP-GC), and then later split into pro-PLO, pro-Syrian, and pro-Libyan factions. The pro-PLO faction was led by Muhammad Zaydan (a.k.a. Abu Abbas) and was based in Baghdad prior to Operation Iraqi Freedom.

Activities: Abbas's group was responsible for the 1985 attack on the Italian cruise ship Achille Lauro and the murder of U.S. citizen Leon Klinghoffer. In 1993, the PLF officially renounced terrorism when it acknowledged the Oslo accords, although it was suspected of supporting terrorism against Israel by other Palestinian groups into the 1990s. In April 2004, Abu Abbas died of natural causes while in U.S. custody in Iraq. The PLF took part in the 2006 Palestinian parliamentarian elections but did not win a seat. In 2008, as part of a prisoner exchange between Israel and Hizballah, Samir Kantar, a PLF member, and purportedly the longest serving Arab prisoner in Israeli custody, was released from an Israeli prison. After going approximately 16 years without claiming responsibility for an attack, PLF claimed responsibility for two attacks against Israeli targets on March 14, 2008, according to media reports. One attack was against an Israeli military bus in Huwarah, Israel, and the other involved a PLF "brigade" firing at an Israeli settler south of the Hebron Mountain, seriously wounding him. On March 28, 2008, shortly after the attacks, a PLF Central Committee member reaffirmed PLF's commitment to using "all possible means to restore" its previous glory and to adhering to its role in the Palestinian "struggle" and "resistance," through its military.

Strength: Estimates have placed membership between 50 and 500.

Location/Area of Operation: Based in Iraq from 1990 until 2003. Current PLF leadership and membership are based in Lebanon and the Palestinian territories.

External Aid: Unknown.

PALESTINE ISLAMIC JIHAD - SHAQAQI FACTION

aka PIJ; Palestine Islamic Jihad; PIJ-Shaqaqi Faction; PIJ-Shallah Faction; Islamic Jihad of Palestine; Islamic Jihad in Palestine; Abu Ghunaym Squad of the Hizballah Bayt Al-Maqdis; Al-Quds Squads; Al-Quds Brigades; Saraya Al-Quds; Al-Awdah Brigades

Description: Palestine Islamic Jihad (PIJ) was designated as a Foreign Terrorist Organization on October 8, 1997. Formed by militant Palestinians in Gaza during the 1970s, PIJ is committed to both the destruction of Israel through attacks against Israeli military and civilian targets and the creation of an Islamic state in all of historic Palestine, including present day Israel.

Activities: PIJ terrorists have conducted numerous attacks, including large-scale suicide bombings against Israeli civilian and military targets. PIJ continued to plan and direct attacks against Israelis both inside Israel and in the Palestinian territories. Although U.S. citizens have died in PIJ attacks, the group has not directly targeted U.S. interests. PIJ attacks in 2008 and 2009 were primarily rocket attacks aimed at southern Israeli cities, and have also included attacking Israeli targets with explosive devices. PIJ continued operations into 2010, most recently claiming responsibility for rockets and mortars fired from Gaza into Israel's Negev Desert on December 7.

Strength: PIJ currently has fewer than 1,000 members.

Location/Area of Operation: Primarily Gaza with minimal operational presence in the West Bank and Israel. The group's senior leadership resides in Syria. Other leadership elements reside in Lebanon and official representatives are scattered throughout the Middle East.

External Aid: Receives financial assistance and training primarily from Iran. Syria provides the group with safe haven.

POPULAR FRONT FOR THE LIBERATION OF PALESTINE

aka PFLP; Halhul Gang; Halhul Squad; Palestinian Popular Resistance Forces; PPRF; Red Eagle Gang; Red Eagle Group; Red Eagles; Martyr Abu-Ali Mustafa Battalion

Description: The Popular Front for the Liberation of Palestine (PFLP) was designated as a Foreign Terrorist Organization on October 8, 1997. The PFLP, a Marxist-Leninist group founded by George Habash, broke away from the Arab Nationalist Movement in 1967. The PFLP views the Palestinian struggle as a broader non-religious revolution against Western imperialism. The group earned a reputation for spectacular international attacks in the 1960s and 1970s, including airline hijackings that killed at least 20 U.S. citizens. A leading faction within the PLO, the PFLP has long accepted the concept of a two-state solution but has opposed specific provisions of various peace initiatives.

Activities: The PFLP stepped up its operational activity during the Second Intifada. This was high-lighted by at least two suicide bombings since 2003, multiple joint operations with other Palestinian terrorist groups, and the assassination of Israeli Tourism Minister Rehavam Ze'evi in 2001 to avenge Israel's killing of the PFLP Secretary General earlier that year. The PFLP was involved in several rocket attacks, launched primarily from Gaza, against Israel in 2008 and 2009; and also claimed responsibility for numerous attacks on Israeli forces in Gaza, including a December 2009 ambush of Israeli soldiers in central Gaza. The group remained active in 2010, claiming responsibility for numerous mortar and rocket attacks fired from Gaza into Israel as well as an February attack on a group of Israeli citizens.

Strength: Unknown.

Location/Area of Operation: Syria, Lebanon, Israel, the West Bank, and Gaza.

External Aid: Receives safe haven from Syria.

POPULAR FRONT FOR THE LIBERATION OF PALESTINE--GENERAL COMMAND

aka PFLP-GC

Description: The Popular Front for the Liberation of Palestine - General Command (PFLP-GC) was designated as a Foreign Terrorist Organization on October 8, 1997. The PFLP-GC split from the PFLP in 1968, claiming it wanted to focus more on resistance and less on politics. Originally, the group was violently opposed to the Arafat-led PLO. Ahmad Jibril, a former captain in the Syrian Army, has led the PFLP-GC since its founding. The PFLP-GC is closely tied to both Syria and Iran.

Activities: The PFLP-GC carried out dozens of attacks in Europe and the Middle East during the 1970s and 1980s. The organization was known for cross-border terrorist attacks into Israel using unusual means, such as hot-air balloons and motorized hang gliders. The group's primary recent focus was supporting Hizballah's attacks against Israel, training members of other Palestinian terrorist groups, and smuggling weapons. The PFLP-GC maintained an armed presence in several Palestinian refugee camps and at its own military bases in Lebanon and along the Lebanon-Syria border. The PFLP-GC was implicated by Lebanese security officials in several rocket attacks against Israel in 2008. In May 2008, the PFLP-GC claimed responsibility for a rocket attack on a shopping center in Ashkelon that wounded at least 10 people. The PFLP-GC remained active into 2010. On the nights of March 20 and 21 in the Negev desert, assailants fired two rockets at an Israeli military base, causing no injuries or damage. The PFLP-GC's Jihad Jibril Brigades claimed responsibility.

Strength: Several hundred to several thousand.

Location/Area of Operation: Headquartered in Damascus, with bases in southern Lebanon and a presence in the Palestinian refugee camps in Lebanon and Syria. The group also maintains a small presence in Gaza.

External Aid: Receives safe haven, as well as logistical and military support from Syria and financial support from Iran.

REAL IRA

aka RIRA; Real Irish Republican Army; 32 County Sovereignty Committee; 32 County Sovereignty Movement; Irish Republican Prisoners Welfare Association; Real Oglaigh Na hEireann

Description: The Real IRA (RIRA) was designated as a Foreign Terrorist Organization on May 16, 2001. The RIRA was formed in 1997 as the clandestine armed wing of the 32 County Sovereignty Movement, a "political pressure group" dedicated to removing British forces from Northern Ireland and unifying Ireland. The RIRA has historically sought to disrupt the Northern Ireland peace process and did not participate in the September 2005 weapons decommissioning. The 32 County Sovereignty Movement opposed Sinn Fein's adoption in September 1997 of the Mitchell principles of democracy and non-violence. Despite internal rifts and calls by some jailed members, including the group's founder Michael "Mickey" McKevitt, for a cease-fire and disbandment, the RIRA has pledged additional violence and continued to conduct attacks.

Activities: Many RIRA members are former Provisional Irish Republican Army members who left the organization after that group renewed its cease-fire in 1997. These members brought a wealth of experience in terrorist tactics and bomb-making to the RIRA. Targets have included civilians (most notoriously in the Omagh bombing in August 1998), British security forces, and police in Northern Ireland. The Independent Monitoring Commission, which was established to oversee the peace process, assessed that RIRA members were likely responsible for the majority of the shootings and assaults that occurred in Northern Ireland in 2008. In November 2008, Lithuanian authorities arrested a RIRA member for attempting to arrange a shipment of weapons to Northern Ireland. In March 2009, the group claimed responsibility for an attack that killed two British soldiers outside a British Army barracks in County Antrim, Northern Ireland. In 2010, there were 12 attacks attributed to RIRA in Northern Ireland. One of these resulted in a fatality. A total of eight civilians were wounded in the other attacks.

Strength: According to the Irish government, the RIRA has approximately 100 active members. The organization may receive limited support from IRA hardliners and Republican sympathizers who are dissatisfied with the IRA's continuing cease-fire and with Sinn Fein's involvement in the peace process. Approximately 40 RIRA members are in Irish jails.

Location/Area of Operation: Northern Ireland, Great Britain, and the Irish Republic.

External Aid: The RIRA is suspected of receiving funds from sympathizers in the United States and of attempting to buy weapons from U.S. gun dealers. The RIRA was also reported to have purchased sophisticated weapons from the Balkans and to have occasionally collaborated with the Continuity Irish Republican Army.

REVOLUTIONARY ARMED FORCES OF COLOMBIA

aka FARC; Fuerzas Armadas Revolucionarias de Colombia

Description: The Revolutionary Armed Forces of Colombia (FARC) was designated as a Foreign Terrorist Organization on October 8, 1997. The FARC is Latin America's oldest, largest, most capable, and best-equipped terrorist organization. It has been degraded by a continuing Colombian military offensive targeting key FARC units and leaders that has, by most estimates, halved the FARC's numbers and succeeded in capturing or killing a number of FARC senior and mid-level commanders. The FARC began in the early 1960s as an outgrowth of the Liberal Party-based peasant self-defense leagues, but took on Marxist ideology. Today, it only nominally fights in support of Marxist goals. The FARC is responsible for large numbers of ransom kidnappings in Colombia and in past years has held more than 700 hostages.

Activities: The FARC has carried out bombings, murder, mortar attacks, kidnapping, extortion, and hijacking, as well as guerrilla and conventional military action against Colombian political, military, and economic targets. The FARC has also used landmines extensively. The group considers U.S. persons legitimate targets and other foreign citizens are often targets of abductions carried out to obtain ransom and political leverage. The FARC has well-documented ties to the full range of narcotics trafficking activities, including taxation, cultivation, and distribution. Over the years, the FARC has perpetrated a large number of high profile terrorist acts, including the 1999 murder of three U.S. missionaries working in Colombia, and multiple kidnappings and assassinations of Columbian government officials and civilians. In July 2008, the Colombian military made a dramatic rescue of 15 high-value FARC hostages including three U.S. Department of Defense contractors Marc Gonsalves, Keith Stansell and Thomas Howe, who were held in captivity for more than five years along with former Colombian presidential candidate Ingrid Betancourt.

In 2010, the FARC was held responsible for an estimated 134 deaths. The group claimed responsibility for an attack on February 24 in Carchi, Ecuador that killed 10 civilians. Authorities held the FARC responsible for a car bomb attack on March 24 in Valle del Cauca, which left nine dead and 51 wounded, and for an August 12 car bomb that wounded nine people in Bogota and damaged hundreds of buildings. The FARC also claimed responsibility for killing eight police officers and wounding five in a small arms and mortar attack in Putumayo in September.

Strength: Approximately 8,000 to 9,000 combatants, with several thousand more supporters.

Location/Area of Operation: Primarily in Colombia with activities including extortion, kidnapping, weapons sourcing, and logistics in neighboring countries.

External Aid: Cuba provided some medical care, safe haven, and political consultation. The FARC often used the Colombia/Venezuela, Colombia/Panama, and Colombia/Ecuador border areas for incursions into Colombia and also used Venezuelan and Ecuadorian territory for safe haven, although the degree of government acquiescence is not always clear.

REVOLUTIONARY ORGANIZATION 17 NOVEMBER

aka Epanastatiki Organosi 17 Noemvri; 17 November

Description: The Revolutionary Organization 17 November (17N) was designated as a Foreign Terrorist Organization on October 8, 1997. 17N is a radical leftist group established in 1975 and named for the student uprising in Greece in November 1973 that protested the ruling military junta. 17N is opposed to the Greek government, the United States, Turkey, and NATO and seeks the end of the U.S. military presence in Greece, the removal of Turkish military forces from Cyprus, and the severing of Greece's ties to NATO and the EU.

Activities: Initial attacks consisted of assassinations of senior U.S. officials and Greek public figures. Five U.S. Embassy employees have been murdered since 17N began its terrorist activities in 1975. The group began using bombings in the 1980s. In 1990, 17N expanded its targets to include Turkish diplomats, EU facilities, and foreign firms investing in Greece. 17N's most recent attack was a bombing attempt in June 2002 at the port of Piraeus in Athens. After the attempted attack, Greek authorities arrested 19 17N members, including a key leader of the organization. The convictions of 13 of these members have been upheld by Greek courts.

Strength: Unknown.

Location/Area of Operation: Athens, Greece.

External Aid: Unknown.

REVOLUTIONARY PEOPLE'S LIBERATION PARTY/FRONT

aka DHKP/C; Dev Sol; Dev Sol Armed Revolutionary Units; Dev Sol Silahli Devrimci Birlikleri; Dev Sol SDB; Devrimci Halk Kurtulus Partisi-Cephesi; Devrimci Sol; Revolutionary Left

Description: The Revolutionary People's Liberation Party/Front (DHKP/C) was designated as a Foreign Terrorist Organization on October 8, 1997. The DHKP/C originally formed in 1978 as Devrimci Sol, or Dev Sol, a splinter faction of Dev Genc (Revolutionary Youth). It was renamed in 1994 after factional infighting. "Party" refers to the group's political activities, while "Front" is a reference to the group's militant operations. The group espouses a Marxist-Leninist ideology and vehemently opposes the United States, NATO, and Turkish establishments. Its goals are the establishment of a socialist state and the abolition of harsh Turkish prisons. DHKP/C finances its activities chiefly through donations and extortion.

Activities: Since the late 1980s, the group has primarily targeted current and retired Turkish security and military officials. It began a new campaign against foreign interests in 1990, which included attacks against U.S. military and diplomatic personnel and facilities. Dev Sol assassinated two U.S. military contractors, wounded an Air Force officer, and bombed more than 20 U.S. and NATO military, commercial, and cultural facilities. In its first significant terrorist act as DHKP/C in 1996, the group assassinated a prominent Turkish businessman and two others. DHKP/C added suicide bombings to its repertoire in 2001, with successful attacks against Turkish police in January and September. Since the end of 2001, DHKP/C has typically used improvised explosive devices against official Turkish targets and U.S. targets of opportunity.

Operations and arrests against the group have weakened its capabilities. In late June 2004, the group was suspected of a bus bombing at Istanbul University, which killed four civilians and wounded 21. In July 2005, in Ankara, police intercepted and killed a DHKP/C suicide bomber who attempted to attack the Ministry of Justice. In June 2006, the group killed a police officer in Istanbul; four members of the group were arrested the next month for the attack.

The DHKP/C was dealt a major ideological blow when Dursun Karatas, leader of the group, died in August 2008 in the Netherlands. After the loss of their leader, the DHKP/C reorganized in 2009 and was reportedly competing with the Kurdistan Workers Party for influence in Turkey and Turkish diaspora Europe. In April 2009, a female DHKP/C member conducted an unsuccessful suicide bomb attack against former Justice Minister Hikmet Turk during a visit to Bilkent University when the device failed to detonate. The assailant then fired a gun at him but was blocked by Turk's bodyguards. The Government of Turkey has made significant progress against the DHKP/C, including disrupting a bomb plot in May 2010, which resulted in numerous arrests of DHKP/C operatives and supporters.

Strength: Probably several dozen members inside Turkey, with a limited support network throughout Europe.

Location/Area of Operation: Turkey, primarily in Istanbul, Ankara, Izmir, and Adana.

External Aid: DHKP/C raises funds in Europe. The group also raises funds through extortion.

REVOLUTIONARY STRUGGLE

aka RS; Epanastatikos Aghonas; EA

Description: Revolutionary Struggle (RS) was designated as a Foreign Terrorist Organization on May 18, 2009. RS is a radical leftist group with a Marxist ideology that has conducted attacks against both Greek and U.S. targets in Greece. RS emerged in 2003 following the arrests of members of the Greek leftist groups 17 November and Revolutionary People's Struggle.

Activities: RS first gained notoriety when it claimed responsibility for the September 5, 2003, bombings at the Athens Courthouse during the trials of 17 November members. From 2004 to 2006, RS claimed responsibility for a number of improvised explosive device (IED) attacks, including a March 2004 attack outside of a Citibank office in Athens. RS claimed responsibility for the January 12, 2007 rocket propelled grenade (RPG) attack on the U.S. Embassy in Athens, which resulted in damage to the building. In 2009, RS increased the number and sophistication of its attacks on police, financial institutions, and other targets. RS successfully bombed a Citibank branch in Athens in March 2009, but failed in its vehicle-borne IED attack in February 2009 against the Citibank headquarters building in Athens. In September 2009, RS claimed responsibility for a car bomb attack on the Athens Stock Exchange, which caused widespread damage and injured a passerby.

In 2010, the Greek Government made significant strides in curtailing RS's terrorist activities. On March 9, Greek police engaged in a shootout with two suspected RS members who were attempting to steal a car, which resulted in the death of one the suspects. At the scene, important information was acquired that led to the arrest of other suspected RS members. On April 10, Greek police arrested six suspected RS members, including purported leadership figure Nikos Maziotis. In addition to the arrests, the Greek raid resulted in the seizure of a RPG launcher, possibly the one used against the U.S. Embassy in Athens in January 2007. The six suspected RS members arrested – five men and one woman – face charges for arms offenses, causing explosions, and multiple counts of attempted homicide. If found guilty, each of the six face up to 25 years in prison.

Strength: Unknown but numbers presumed to be small.

Location/Area of Operation: Athens, Greece.

External Aid: Unknown.

SHINING PATH

aka SL; Sendero Luminoso; Ejercito Guerrillero Popular (People's Guerrilla Army); EGP; Ejercito Popular de Liberacion (People's Liberation Army); EPL; Partido Comunista del Peru (Communist Party of Peru); PCP; Partido Comunista del Peru en el Sendero Luminoso de Jose Carlos Mariategui (Communist Party of Peru on the Shining Path of Jose Carlos Mariategui); Socorro Popular del Peru (People's Aid of Peru); SPP

Description: Shining Path (SL) was designated as a Foreign Terrorist Organization on October 8, 1997. Former university professor Abimael Guzman formed SL in Peru in the late 1960s. Guzman's teachings created the foundation of SL's militant Maoist doctrine. SL's stated goal is to destroy existing Peruvian institutions and replace them with a communist peasant revolutionary regime. It also opposes any influence by foreign governments. In the 1980s, SL was one of the most ruthless terrorist groups in the Western Hemisphere. The Peruvian government made dramatic gains against SL during the 1990s, capturing Guzman in 1992 and killing a large number of militants. More recently, SL members have attempted to influence the local populace through indoctrination. SL responded to the government's stepped up counterterrorism efforts with a series of bloody counterattacks in late 2008 and throughout 2009.

Activities: In the past, SL has conducted indiscriminate bombing campaigns, ambushes, and selective assassinations. However, in the last five years, SL activities have included intimidation of U.S.-sponsored non-governmental organizations involved in counternarcotics efforts, the ambushing of counternarcotics helicopters, and attacks against Peruvian police perpetrated in conjunction with narcotics traffickers.

In 2008, SL conducted over 64 attacks and killed at least 34 people in remote coca growing areas. In one of its most devastating attacks, on October 10, 2008, Peru's military command said a bomb killed 12 soldiers and seven civilians in the country's southeastern mountains. Activities in 2009 included attacks against Peruvian helicopters. In January 2010, 15 suspected SL fighters were arrested after a confrontation with the military, which left one officer dead and another wounded in the Apurimac and Ene River Valleys. Authorities believed SL killed a civilian in Huanuco in March and a police officer in April near Ayacucho. Authorities held SL responsible for an April 27 attack on a coca eradication team in Huanuco that left two field workers and one police officer dead and wounded another police officer. A series of Peruvian National Police counterterrorism operations from May to October 2010 killed or captured five SL commanders in the Huallaga valley region and more than 50 other SL members.

Strength: Unknown but estimated to be between 300 and 500 armed militants.

Location/Area of Operation: Peru, with most activity in rural areas, specifically the Huallaga Valley, the Ene River, and the Apurimac Valley of central Peru.

External Aid: None known.

TEHRIK-E TALIBAN PAKISTAN

aka Pakistani Taliban, Tehreek-e-Taliban, Tehrik-e-Taliban, Tehrik-e Taliban Pakistan, Tehrik-i-Taliban Pakistan, TTP

Description: Tehrik-e Taliban Pakistan (TTP) is a Pakistan-based terrorist organization and was designated on September 1, 2010. TTP formed in 2007 in opposition to Pakistani military efforts in the Federally Administered Tribal Areas. Previously disparate militant tribes agreed to cooperate and eventually coalesced into TTP under the leadership of now deceased leader Baitullah Mehsud. The group officially presented itself as a discrete entity in 2007. TTP is now led by Hakimullah Mehsud, who has been the group's emir since August 2009. Other senior leaders include Wali Ur Rehman, the TTP emir in South Waziristan, Pakistan. TTP's goals include usurping the Government of Pakistan by waging a campaign of terror against the civilian leader of Pakistan, its military, and against NATO forces in Afghanistan. TTP uses the tribal belt along the Afghan-Pakistani border to train and deploy its operatives, and the group has a symbiotic relationship with AQ.

Activities: TTP has carried out and claimed responsibility for numerous terrorist acts against Pakistani and U.S. interests; including a December 2009 suicide attack on a U.S. military base in Khowst, Afghanistan, which killed seven U.S. citizens, and an April 2010 suicide bombing against the U.S. Consulate in Peshawar, Pakistan, which killed six Pakistani citizens.

TTP is suspected of being involved in the 2007 assassination of former Pakistani Prime Minister Benazir Bhutto. Most recently, TTP claimed to have supported the failed attempt by Faisal Shahzad to detonate an explosive device in New York City's Times Square on May 1, 2010. TTP's claim has been validated by investigations that revealed that TTP directed and facilitated the plot.

Strength: Several thousand, precise number is unknown.

Location: Federally Administered Tribal Areas (FATA), Pakistan

External aid: TTP and AQ have a symbiotic relationship. TTP draws ideological guidance from AQ, while AQ relies on TTP for safe haven in the Pashtun areas along the Afghan-Pakistani border. This arrangement gives TTP access to both AQ's global terrorist network and the operational experience of its members. Given the proximity of the two groups and the nature of their relationship, TTP is a force multiplier for AQ.

UNITED SELF-DEFENSE FORCES OF COLOMBIA

aka AUC; Autodefensas Unidas de Colombia

Description: The United Self-Defense Forces of Colombia (AUC) was designated as a Foreign Terrorist Organization on September 10, 2001. The AUC, commonly referred to as the paramilitaries, was formed in April 1997. AUC was designed to serve as an umbrella group for loosely affiliated, illegal paramilitary groups retaliating against leftist guerillas, which in turn were fighting the Colombian government and the landed establishment. However, as the Colombian government increasingly confronted terrorist organizations, including the AUC, the group's counter-guerilla activities decreased. After a large-scale demobilization process that began in 2010, most of the AUC's centralized military structure has been dismantled, and all of the top paramilitary chiefs have stepped down. Despite AUC's overall demobilization, the group's armed wing Cacique Pipinta Front refused to demobilize.

Activities: The AUC has carried out political killings and kidnappings of, among others, human rights workers, journalists, teachers, and trade unionists. As much as 70 percent of the AUC's paramilitary operational costs were financed with drug-related earnings. Some former members of the AUC never demobilized or are recidivists, and these elements have continued to engage heavily in criminal activities.

Strength: Unknown.

Location/Areas of Operation: Paramilitary forces were strongest in northwest Colombia, with affiliate groups in Valle del Cauca, on the West coast, and Meta Department, in Central Columbia.

External Aid: None.

CHAPTER 7.
LEGISLATIVE REQUIREMENTS AND KEY TERMS

Country Reports on Terrorism 2010 is submitted in compliance with Title 22 of the United States Code, Section 2656f (the "Act"), which requires the Department of State to provide Congress a full and complete annual report on terrorism for those countries and groups meeting the criteria of the Act. Statutory excerpts relating to the terms used in this report and a discussion of the interpretation and application of those terms in this report are included below.

Excerpts and Summary of Key Statutory Terms:

Section 2656f(a) of Title 22 of the United States Code states as follows:

(a) ... The Secretary of State shall transmit to the Speaker of the House of Representatives and the Committee on Foreign Relations of the Senate, by April 30 of each year, a full and complete report providing -

(1) (A) detailed assessments with respect to each foreign country -

(i) in which acts of international terrorism occurred which were, in the opinion of the Secretary, of major significance;

(ii) about which the Congress was notified during the preceding five years pursuant to Section 2405(j) of the Export Administration Act of 1979; and

(iii) which the Secretary determines should be the subject of such report; and

(B) detailed assessments with respect to each foreign country whose territory is being used as a sanctuary for terrorist organizations;

(2) all relevant information about the activities during the preceding year of any terrorist group, and any umbrella group under which such terrorist group falls, known to be responsible for the kidnapping or death of an American citizen during the preceding five years, any terrorist group known to have obtained or developed, or to have attempted to obtain or develop, weapons of mass destruction, any terrorist group known to be financed by countries about which Congress was notified during the preceding year pursuant to section 2405(j) of the Export Administration Act of 1979, any group designated by the Secretary as a foreign terrorist organization under section 219 of the Immigration and Nationality Act (8 U.S.C. 1189), and any other known international terrorist group which the Secretary determines should be the subject of such report;

(3) with respect to each foreign country from which the United States Government has sought cooperation during the previous five years in the investigation or prosecution of an act of international terrorism against United States citizens or interests, information on -

(A) the extent to which the government of the foreign country is cooperating with the United States Government in apprehending, convicting, and punishing the individual or individuals responsible for the act; and

(B) the extent to which the government of the foreign country is cooperating in preventing further acts of terrorism against United States citizens in the foreign country; and

(4) with respect to each foreign country from which the United States Government has sought cooperation during the previous five years in the prevention of an act of international terrorism against such citizens or interests, the information described in paragraph (3)(B).

Section 2656f(d) of Title 22 of the United States Code defines certain key terms used in Section 2656f(a) as follows:

(1) the term "international terrorism" means terrorism involving citizens or the territory of more than one country;

(2) the term "terrorism" means premeditated, politically motivated violence perpetrated against non-combatant targets by subnational groups or clandestine agents; and

(3) the term "terrorist group" means any group practicing, or which has significant subgroups which practice, international terrorism.

Interpretation and Application of Key Terms. For purposes of this report, the terms "international terrorism," "terrorism," and "terrorist group" have the definitions assigned to them in 22 USC 2656f(d) (see above). The term "non-combatant," which is referred to but not defined in 22 USC. 2656f(d)(2), is interpreted to mean, in addition to civilians, military personnel (whether or not armed or on duty) who are not deployed in a war zone or a war-like setting.

It should be noted that 22 USC 2656f(d) is one of many U.S. statutes and international legal instruments that concern terrorism and acts of violence, many of which use definitions for terrorism and related terms that are different from those used in this report. The interpretation and application of defined and related terms concerning terrorism in this report is therefore specific to the statutory and other requirements of the report, and is not intended to express the views of the U.S. government on how these terms should be interpreted or applied for any other purpose. Accordingly, there is not necessarily any correlation between the interpretation of terms such as "non-combatant" for purposes of this report and the meanings ascribed to similar terms pursuant to the law of war (which encapsulates the obligations of states and individuals with respect to their activities in situations of armed conflict).

Statistical Information. Pursuant to 22 USC § 2656f(b), this report must contain "to the extent practicable, complete statistical information on the number of individuals, including United States citizens and dual nationals, killed, injured, or kidnapped by each terrorist group during the preceding calendar year." This requirement is satisfied through the inclusion of a statistical annex to the report that sets out statistical information provided by the National Counterterrorism Center (NCTC). The statistical annex includes a discussion of the methodology employed by NCTC in compiling the relevant data. This report does not contain statistical information specifically concerning combatants. The focus of the terrorism report, as is clear from the definition of terrorism, is on violence against noncombatant targets. Further, it would not be practicable to provide such statistics, as the government does not maintain - and would have great difficulty maintaining - statistics that distinguish between incidents against combatants by terrorist groups and by others, including insurgents, in Iraq and Afghanistan.

Contextual Reporting. Adverse mention in this report of individual members of any political, social, ethnic, religious, or national population is not meant to imply that all members of that population are terrorists. Indeed, terrorists rarely represent anything other than a tiny fraction of such larger populations. It is terrorist groups—and their actions—that are the focus of this report.

Furthermore, terrorist acts are part of a larger phenomenon of violence inspired by a cause, and at times, the line between the two can become difficult to draw. This report includes some discretionary information in an effort to relate terrorist events to the larger context in which they occur, and to give a feel for the conflicts that spawn violence.

Thus, this report will discuss terrorist acts as well as other violent incidents that are not necessarily "international terrorism" and therefore are not subject to the statutory reporting requirement.

National Counterterrorism Center

Annex of Statistical Information

Information cut off date: 23 MAR 2011

DEVELOPING STATISTICAL INFORMATION

Consistent with its statutory mission to serve as the United States government's knowledge bank on international terrorism, the National Counterterrorism Center (NCTC) is providing the Department of State with required statistical information to assist in the satisfaction of its reporting requirements under Section 2656f of title 22 of the US Code (USC).

This statute requires the State Department to include in its annual report on terrorism "to the extent practicable, complete statistical information on the number of individuals, including United States citizens and dual nationals, killed, injured, or kidnapped by each terrorist group during the preceding calendar year." While NCTC keeps statistics on the annual number of incidents of "terrorism," its ability to track the specific groups responsible for each incident involving killings, kidnappings, and injuries is significantly limited by the availability of reliable open source information, particularly for events involving small numbers of casualties. Moreover, specific details about victims, damage, perpetrators, and other incident elements are frequently not fully reported in open source information.

- The statistical material in this report, therefore, is drawn from the incidents of "terrorism" that occurred in 2010 as reported in open source information. This material is the most comprehensive body of information available to NCTC for compiling data that it can provide to satisfy the above-referenced statistical requirements.

This Annex is provided for statistical purposes only. The statistical information contained in the Annex is based on factual reports from a variety of open sources that may be of varying credibility. Any assessments regarding the nature of the incidents or the factual circumstances thereof are offered only as part of the analytic work product of the National Counterterrorism Center and may not reflect the assessments of other departments and agencies of the United States Government. Nothing in this report should be construed as a determination that individuals associated with the underlying incidents are guilty of terrorism or any other criminal offense. As with all entries in the Worldwide Incident Tracking System, the statistical information will be modified, as necessary and appropriate, when and if the underlying incidents are finally adjudicated.

In deriving its figures for incidents of terrorism, NCTC in 2005 adopted the definition of "terrorism" that appears in the 22 USC § 2656f(d)(2), i.e., "premeditated, politically motivated violence perpetrated against noncombatant targets by subnational groups or clandestine agents."

NCTC posts information in the repository for the US government's database on terror attacks, the Worldwide Incidents Tracking System (WITS). WITS is accessible on the NCTC Web site <www.nctc.gov> for the public to have an open and transparent view of the NCTC data. A detailed description of the methodology and counting rules is also available on the Web site, as is a geospatial tool to allow mapping of the data. NCTC will ensure that the data posted to the Web site is updated as often as necessary by regularly posting information about new or prior attacks.

Tracking and analyzing terrorist incidents can help to understand important characteristics about terrorism, including the geographic distribution of attacks and information about the perpetrators, their victims, and other details. Year-to-year changes in the gross number of attacks across the globe, however, may tell little about the international community's effectiveness either for preventing these incidents or for reducing the capacity of terrorists to advance their agenda through violence against the innocent.

INCIDENTS OF TERRORISM WORLDWIDE*					
	2006	2007	2008	2009	2010
Attacks worldwide	14,371	14,414	11,662	10,969	11,604
Attacks resulting in at least 1 death, injury, or kidnapping	11,258	11,085	8,358	7,874	8,249
Attacks resulting in the death of at least 10 individuals	295	353	234	236	192
Attacks resulting in the death of at least 1 individual	7,393	7,229	5,040	4,761	4,702
Attacks resulting in the death of only 1 individual	4,117	3,982	2,870	2,695	2,690
Attacks resulting in the death of 0 individuals	6,978	7,185	6,622	6,208	6,902
Attacks resulting in the injury of at least 1 individual	5,771	6,230	4,829	4,530	4,715
Attacks resulting in the kidnapping of at least 1 individual	1,343	1,156	946	882	1,116
People killed, injured or kidnapped as a result of terrorism, worldwide	74,695	71,795	54,263	58,711	49,901
People killed as a result of terrorism, worldwide	20,487	22,719	15,708	15,310	13,186
People injured as a result of terrorism, worldwide	38,413	44,095	33,885	32,651	30,665
People kidnapped as a result of terrorism, worldwide	15,795	4,981	4,670	10,750	6,050

INCIDENTS OF TERRORISM IN IRAQ AND AFGHANISTAN*					
	2006	**2007**	**2008**	**2009**	**2010**
Attacks in Iraq resulting in at least 1 death, injury, or kidnapping	6,010	5,575	2,900	2,179	2,359
People killed, injured, or kidnapped as a result of terrorism in Iraq	38,817	44,014	19,077	16,869	15,109
Attacks in Afghanistan	964	1,122	1,221	2,125	3,307
Attacks in Afghanistan resulting in at least 1 death, injury, or kidnapping	691	889	950	1,451	2,053
People killed, injured, or kidnapped as a result of terrorism in Afghanistan	3,534	4,647	5,479	7,582	9,016

Attacks are limited to attacks against noncombatant targets. Numbers represented in table for 2006 through 2009 are updated since the 2009 publication and based on data in the Worldwide Incidents Tracking Systems www.nctc.gov.

NCTC OBSERVATIONS RELATED TO TERRORIST INCIDENTS STATISTICAL MATERIAL

Over 11,500 terrorist attacks occurred in 72 countries in 2010, resulting in approximately 50,000 victims, including almost 13,200 deaths. Although the number of attacks rose by almost 5 percent over the previous year, the number of deaths declined for a third consecutive year, dropping 12 percent from 2009. This decline reflected a combination of two factors: a decrease in the number of attacks causing more than five deaths along with an increase in attacks causing no deaths. For the second year in a row, the largest number of reported attacks occurred in South Asia, which also had the largest number of victims for the third consecutive year. More than 75 percent of the world's terrorist attacks and deaths took place in South Asia and the Near East.

- The Near East and South Asia in 2010 suffered a combined total of 8,960 attacks that caused 9,960 deaths.

- Attacks in Afghanistan and Iraq rose in 2010. Almost a quarter of worldwide attacks occurred in Iraq, a slight increase from 2009, although deaths fell for the fourth consecutive year.

- The number of deaths in Africa fell by more than 30 percent, from 3,239 in 2009 to 2,131 in 2010, although attacks rose slightly, from 853 in 2009 to 878 in 2010. The number of Lord's Resistance Army attacks in the Democratic Republic of Congo declined sharply, but in June Algeria saw its first suicide vehicle-borne improvised explosive device (VBIED) since September 2008.

- The number of attacks and deaths in Europe and Eurasia declined slightly in 2010, with the vast majority again occurring in Russia. Attacks fell from 737 in 2009 to 706 in 2010, and deaths fell from 367 in 2009 to 355 in 2010.

- The fewest incidents in 2010 were reported in the Western Hemisphere, where both attacks and deaths declined by roughly 25 percent. Western Hemisphere attacks fell from 444 in 2009 to 340 in 2010, and deaths fell from 377 in 2009 to 279 in 2010.

- Terrorist attacks in East Asia declined in 2010, most significantly in Thailand and the Philippines.

PERPETRATORS

Sunni extremists committed almost 60 percent of all worldwide terrorist attacks. These attacks caused approximately 70 percent of terrorism-related deaths, a significant increase from the almost 62 percent in 2009. The following noteworthy attacks are cataloged in WITS.

Largest Sunni Extremist Attacks:

- On 4 April 2010, in the Mansur and Al Karkh districts of Baghdad, Iraq, three suicide bombers detonated VBIEDs near the Egyptian, German, and Iranian Embassies, killing a combined 42 people and wounding approximately 250 individuals. Police officers safely defused a fourth VBIED in the Karradah district. Islamic State of Iraq (ISI) claimed responsibility for all the attacks. ICN 201007393

- On 7 July 2010, in the northern 'Azamiyah district of Baghdad, Iraq, a suicide bomber detonated an improvised explosive device (IED) near a group of Shia pilgrims making their way to the Imam Musa al-Kadhim shrine, killing between 29 and 48 pilgrims and several Sunni civilians and wounding between 133 and 315 pilgrims and several Sunni civilians. No group claimed responsibility, although the Islamic State of Iraq ISI was believed to be responsible. ICN 201012531

Other Notable Sunni Extremist Attacks:

- On 1 January 2010, in a village in North-West Frontier Province, Pakistan, a suicide bomber detonated a VBIED at a volleyball game, killing 97 civilians, six soldiers, and two police officers. Another 100 civilians, three soldiers, and several children were wounded in the attack. No group claimed responsibility, although the Taliban was widely believed to be responsible. ICN 201000049

- On 11 July 2010, al-Shabaab conducted and claimed responsibility for its largest and most complex attack to date in Kampala, Uganda, killing 76 and wounding 114 civilians. ICN 201010950

- On 1 September 2010, assailants threw a grenade and two suicide bombers detonated IEDs targeting a Shia Muslim procession in Lahore, Pakistan, killing 40 and wounding 272. The Tehrik-i-Taliban Pakistan and Lashkar i Jhangvi both claimed responsibility. ICN 201014275

TYPES OF ATTACKS

Armed attacks in 2010 continued to be the most prevalent form of attack, accounting for more than a third of the total. Bombings, including suicide attacks, were far more lethal, causing almost 70 percent of all deaths. In particular, suicide bombings continued to be the most lethal type of terrorist attack, resulting in nearly 13.5 percent of all terrorism-related deaths. Sunni extremists conducted 93 percent of all suicide attacks in 2010.

- Suicide attacks declined for a second consecutive year, from 299 in 2009 to 263 in 2010, just under 2 percent of all terrorist attacks last year.

- On the Indian subcontinent in 2010, armed attacks increased but bombings decreased.

- Kidnapping events declined worldwide, although they jumped in the Gaza Strip from 767 in 2009 to 1,057 during 2010 as HAMAS targeted Fatah leaders and members.

VICTIMS AND TARGETS OF ATTACKS

Muslims continued to bear the brunt of terrorism based on the fact that most terrorist attacks occurred in predominantly Muslim countries. Somalia hosted the largest number of attacks with 10 or more deaths followed by Pakistan. Although Iraq and Pakistan had the same number of attacks with 10 or more deaths, those in Iraq produced more fatalities.

- Iraq had the largest overall number of terrorism victims with 12,087, of whom 2,704 died.

- Afghanistan had the second largest number of terrorism victims at 7,039; 2,475 died. Pakistan had 5,555 victims; 1,680 died.

- Analysis of WITS data indicates that more than half of those killed by terrorist attacks worldwide in 2010 were civilians; more than 600 were children.

- Police and other paramilitary or private security officers accounted for more than 2,000 victims. The percentage of police victims in 2010 rose nearly 2 percent over 2009.

TERRORISM DEATHS, INJURIES, KIDNAPPINGS OF PRIVATE U.S. CITIZENS, 2010

Provided by the Bureau of Consular Affairs, U.S. Department of State

The term "Private U.S. Citizen" refers to any U.S. citizen not acting in an official capacity on behalf of the U.S. Government; therefore these figures do not include, for example, U.S. military personnel killed or injured in a terrorism-related incident while on active duty or employees of the Department of State and other federal agencies. Members of U.S. government employees' households are considered private U.S. citizens.

Although every effort was made to include all terrorism-related deaths and injuries involving private U.S. citizens, the figures below reflect only those cases reported to, or known by, the U.S. Department of State, and may not reflect actual numbers of injured, which may not always be reported depending on their severity. As NCTC also notes, in the cases of Iraq and Afghanistan, it is particularly difficult to gather comprehensive information about all incidents and to distinguish terrorism from the numerous other forms of violence.

U.S. citizens worldwide killed as a result of incidents of terrorism:	5
U.S. citizens worldwide injured as a result of incidents of terrorism:	9
U.S. citizens worldwide kidnapped as a result of incidents of terrorism:	0

TERRORISM DEATHS OF PRIVATE U.S. CITIZENS IN 2010 (BY COUNTRY)

COUNTRY	DATE OF DEATH	NUMBER	LOCATION
AFGHANISTAN	July 10, 20010	1	Kandahar, Afghanistan
	July 29, 2010	1	Sheberghan, Afghanistan
	August 5, 2010	6	Faizabad, Badakhshan, Afghanistan
	September 6, 2010	2	Kandahar, Afghanistan
	September 6, 2010	2	Kabul, Afghanistan
	September 7, 2010	1	Kandahar, Afghanistan
IRAQ	July 23, 2010	1	FOB Kasul, Iraq
UGANDA	July 11, 2010	1	Kampala, Uganda

TERRORISM INJURIES OF PRIVATE U.S. CITIZENS IN 2010 (BY COUNTRY)

COUNTRY	DATE OF INJURY	NUMBER	LOCATION
UGANDA	July 11, 2010	7	Kampala
PHILIPPINES	August 5, 2010	1	Manila
GERMANY	March 12, 2010	1	Berlin
SOMALIA	September 17, 2009	1	Mogadishu, Somalia

www.ingramcontent.com/pod-product-compliance
Lightning Source LLC
Chambersburg PA
CBHW080402270326
41927CB00015B/3324